THE
RANDALL HOUSE
BIBLE
COMMENTARY

THE
RANDALL HOUSE
BIBLE
COMMENTARY

THE
GOSPEL OF
JOHN

by
Jack Wilson Stallings

FIRST EDITION

RANDALL HOUSE PUBLICATIONS
NASHVILLE, TENNESSEE 37217

RANDALL HOUSE BIBLE COMMENTARY, THE GOSPEL OF JOHN
© Copyright 1989
RANDALL HOUSE PUBLICATIONS
NASHVILLE, TN 37217
ISBN 0-89265-137-7 (THE GOSPEL OF JOHN)
ISBN 0-89265-115-6 (SET)
LIBRARY OF CONGRESS CATALOG CARD NUMBER: 89-060532

General Editor:
ROBERT E. PICIRILLI
Academic Dean, Free Will Baptist Bible College
Nashville, Tennessee

Associate Editor:
Harrold D. Harrison
Editor-in-Chief, Randall House Publications
Nashville, Tennessee

ACKNOWLEDGEMENTS

The author expresses thanks to these publishers for permission to quote from the following works:

Bruce, F. F., *The Gospel of John* (Eerdmans, 1983). Used by permission.
Morris, Leon, *The New International Commentary on the New Testament: The Gospel According to John* (Eerdmans, 1971). Used by permission.
Robinson, John A. T., *Redating the New Testament* (Westminster, 1976). Used by permission.
Schnackenburg, Rudolf, *The Gospel According To St. John,* Volume I, translated by Kevin Smyth. Copyright 1968 by Herder KG. Reprinted by permission of The Crossroad Publishing Company. Used by permission.

PREFACE

This commentary on the Gospel of John is the fourth volume of the *Randall House Bible Commentary* to appear. The volumes already published are *Romans* (1987), *1, 2 Corinthians* (1987), and *Galatians through Colossians* (1988).

I refer the reader to the General Editor's Preface to the volume on Romans. There I have indicated, in greater detail, the doctrinal stance of the publishers and writers of this series. It is a "nuanced" Arminianism, holding to Reformation theology as Arminius held to it. This Arminianism emphasizes salvation by grace through faith alone, insists on the satisfaction view of the atonement, believes in total depravity, and readily acknowledges that God is Sovereign and knew from eternity all things as certain, including the free (and sinful) acts of men.

It is not the purpose of these commentaries, of course, to set forth a systematic theology. Instead, they are intended to provide reverent and thorough exegesis of the Biblical text, but as the "popular" level. We have set a course midway between the highly technical and the merely devotional. We want the reader to know what the text says and what it means.

Technical comments about Greek words or syntax are usually put in parenthesis, so that the reader who is not interested in that or does not understand it may read around the parenthetic insertions with no loss of meaning. Notes about sources are also indicated in parenthesis, using our own variation of the method suggested by the Modern Language Association. The bibliography at the end of the commentary gives full information on all sources cited.

Textual problems are not dealt with in detail, nor are the writers encouraged to try to solve manuscript differences.

Just enough reference will be made to these to enable the reader to understand why some versions may have differences of wording. This by no means implies that dealing with manuscript differences is unimportant or that the writer is ignorant or unconcerned about them. It only indicates that the scope of this series is not intended to be that broad.

We also intend that these commentaries be practical. Commentary on each passage ends with both a summary and a section entitled "Application: Teaching and Preaching the Passage." The Bible is meant not only to be understood but also to be lived.

In this volume on John, Jack Stallings reveals both his expertise in handling the Scripture and his pastor's heart. He has given us a commentary on John that makes the teachings and events in Christ's ministry come alive. We always feel that we are right there, aware of the intentions and attidues of our Lord, His disciples, and His antagonists. Stallings lays open the method of the Fourth Evangelist, including his "open secrets" and his overriding purpose. The Gospel becomes a work with an obvious unity, moving purposefully through the material, providing us with a thrust very different from that of the Synoptics, and yet without contradiction.

There are a few places in the Gospel where the texts have theological implications that speak specifically to issues involved in the "Arminian" theology referred to above. Pastor Stallings preferred that I develop such comments. Consequently, at certain locations I have inserted extended comments on these theological issues. These will be found in connection with the comments on John 3:16-18; 5:24; 6:44; 10:27-29; 12:32; 13:1-17; 15:2, 6.　　Robert E. Picirilli

Nashville, Tennessee 1989

CONTENTS

COMMENTARY ON JOHN

INTRODUCTION

The Gospel of John is at once both profound and simple, "a pool in which a child may wade or an elephant may swim" (Morris 7). This commentary will attempt to explore the shallows around the edge where children wade, venturing out only from time to time into the depths where the elephants swim.

Authorship

The internal evidence relating to the authorship of the Gospel of John is of two types: direct and indirect. The direct evidence consists of three passages within the book which, when properly understood, clearly imply that the author is John the son of Zebedee. (1) In 1:14 the writer speaks of himself in the first person plural as an eyewitness to the glory of the incarnation. (2) In 19:35 he speaks of himself in the third person as an eyewitness of the crucifixion. (3) In 21:24 the writer identifies himself as the Beloved Disciple and states directly that he is the author of the Gospel. (See commentary on each reference.)

There is also a great deal of indirect evidence within the Gospel that John is the author. This evidence has been presented by Bishop Westcott in his commentary (I:x-lii) as follows.

The author of the Gospel was a Jew. He is familiar with Jewish opinions and customs. His thought is grounded in the Old Testament. The style and form of his writing are those of a Jew. The Dead Sea Scrolls confirm this beyond all doubt (see Morris 13,14).

The author was a Jew of Palestine.

He is familiar with the details of the topography of Palestine. He is at home in the city of Jerusalem as it was before the destruction of A.D. 70. His teaching concerning the Word in the prologue, far from revealing a Hellenistic or Gnostic background, is now seen to be entirely Hebraic, growing out of the O.T. concept of the Word as the revealer of God to man.

The author was an eyewitness to that which he describes. His narrative is marked by minute details of person, time, number, place, and manner which must be the evidence either of an eyewitness or a deliberate deceiver. It is highly unlikely that all these details were gratuitously inserted into the narrative after the fact to give it the appearance of authenticity. Modern archaeology has confirmed far too many of the merely incidental details for that to be the case. It should be added that there was no archaeology in the second century that would have enabled a fraud to be aware of such details.

The author was an apostle. He was an intimate acquaintance of the band of twelve. He knew their thoughts and feelings. He was familiar with their haunts. He was aware of false impressions which were made upon them. He reveals a very close personal relationship to Christ. He is aware of His feelings. He knows the reasons for His actions. He speaks as though he knows the whole mind of the Lord.

The author was the Apostle John. This conclusion is obviously the most significant. Therefore, the evidence for it will be presented in more detail.

The internal evidence that the author of the Fourth Gospel was the Apostle John centers around the personage referred to in the Gospel as the "beloved disciple." There are two aspects to the evidence: (1) that the beloved disciple was the author and (2) that the beloved disciple was the Apostle John.

That the Gospel was written by the beloved disciple is inescapable if one accepts its own statement at face value. In its context, 21:24 clearly attributes authorship to the beloved disciple. Some critical scholars would limit this verse to saying that the beloved disciple was merely the authority behind the Gospel who "caused it to be written," rather than the actual writer of it (see Barrett 100,101). This is a forced interpretation shaped by the assumption that the beloved disciple simply could not have written the Gospel (see Guthrie, *Introduction* 219).

The identification of the beloved disciple as the Apostle John, if not absolutely obvious, is logically certain. The following is an overview of the evidence for that identification. There are three types of references to anonymous disciples in the Gospel (see Brown I:xciii,xciv). (1) There is a disciple who, as a companion of Andrew, follows Jesus on the day after His baptism (1:35ff.). (2) There are references to "another disciple" (18:15) and "that/the other disciple" (18:16; 20:3,4,8). (3) There are references to "that/the disciple whom Jesus loved" (13:23; 19:26; 20:2; 21:7,20, and by inference 21:24). All conclusions as to the identity of the beloved disciple must be drawn from the evidence provided in these verses.

Several suggestions as to this identification have been made over the years—suggestions which seem but desperate efforts to avoid the obvious. They include the identification of the beloved disciple with John Mark or Lazarus of Bethany. There is also the idea that the beloved disciple was not a real personage at all, but a symbolical representation of the ideal Christian. None of these ideas is credible.

The evidence seems to indicate clearly that the beloved disciple is the Apostle John. Several facts are to be inferred from the Scriptural evidence.

1. The beloved disciple is one of the innermost circle of Christ's disciples. He is pictured as being present at the Last Supper and leaning upon Jesus' breast (21:20; 13:23). He is present at the crucifixion, where Jesus commends to him the care of Mary, His mother (19:26). He, with Peter, goes to the tomb on Easter morning and sees that it is empty (20:2-8). On this occasion a special reference is made to his internal subjective experience. He is present with a small group of disciples in Galilee when the risen Christ appears to them (21:7).

2. The beloved disciple is clearly differentiated from Peter, yet bears a very close relationship to him (13:23,24; 20:2; 21:7,20,21).

3. The beloved disciple must be the Apostle John. The Synoptics (the first three Gospels) mention three disciples as standing in a particularly close relationship to Christ. These were Peter and the two sons of Zebedee, James and John. These would seem to constitute the inner circle, of which the beloved disciple has been shown to be a part. Therefore, the beloved disciple must be either Peter, James, or John. Peter is obviously excluded, since he is repeatedly differentiated from the beloved disciple. James must also be eliminated, since he died so early (Acts 12:2) that he cannot realistically be supposed to have authored the Fourth Gospel. This leaves only John.

The Synoptics and the early chapters of Acts picture John as a very close associate of Peter. This satisfies yet another of the requirements for the beloved disciple as pictured in the Gospel. Finally, the beloved disciple must be among the group mentioned in 21:2. Only three of this group meet the qualification of being a part of the inner circle: Peter and "the sons of Zebedee." Peter and James are to be excluded on the grounds already given. This leaves only the Apostle John. It seems evident that the Apostle John was the beloved disciple.

There are two additional reasons for believing that John was the beloved disciple and the author of the Fourth Gospel. First, in this Gospel, John the Baptist is simply called "John." There is no attempt to differentiate between him and the Apostle John. It seems reasonable that the only person who could refer to John the Baptist in this fashion without any fear that such a reference would be confused with the Apostle John would be the Apostle John himself. The author usually differentiates clearly between people with the same or similar names (e.g. 14:22). This rather singular exception is explicable if the apostle himself is the writer.

The second reason is that neither James nor John is mentioned by name in the Fourth Gospel. It is very difficult to explain why these two major characters should be so completely ignored. Surely they were not simply forgotten, but were purposely excluded from direct mention. This makes sense if John himself is the author, especially if one accepts that he does refer to himself obliquely. It hardly makes sense if the author is someone other than John. Some would say that the mention of the sons of Zebedee (21:2) destroys this logic. I do not believe this to be the case. Rather, this verse should be seen as the author's cryptic clue to his riddle, his device of indirect and oblique reference to himself throughout his Gospel.

There are many objections that have been raised against the view that John was the beloved disciple and the author of the Fourth Gospel. Some, while allowing the identification of the beloved disciple as the Apostle John, hold that this identification argues against his authorship of the Gospel. They emphasize that the apostle would not designate himself as the beloved disciple, since to do so would show a singular lack of humility. It would also be contrary to the supposed purpose of the usage— anonymity. This line of reasoning leads either to the conclusion that John was not the author at all or that the references to the beloved disciple are all editorial additions by some hand other than John's.

This view is inherently weak, in that it superimposes upon an ancient oriental individual a modern western concept of modesty and propriety. Such concepts vary widely from culture to culture and era to era. Furthermore, since this designation has an obviously cryptic flavor, it is unfair to evaluate it with absolute and pedantic literalness. Indeed, by the time the Gospel was written, it might have become common to refer to John as the beloved disciple. At any rate, an "elder statesman," writing to a group comprised of his own followers, is not compelled to manifest undue modesty. John's status of unchallenged preeminence within the church at the time the Gospel was written would certainly have placed him beyond any suspicion of self-aggrandizement. Patriarchs sometimes act patriarchally.

Another objection to the Johannine authorship of the Gospel centers upon the idea that a simple Galilean fisherman could not have produced such a sophisticated and theologically advanced work. Reference is made to the designation of Peter and John by the Jewish authorities (Acts 4:13) as "unlearned and ignorant men." The answer to this is quite simple. A simple Galilean fisherman did not write the Gospel. A man who had *formerly* been a simple Galilean fisherman wrote the Gospel. This man had undergone an intensive program of instruction with the Master Teacher Himself. He had, in fact, been one of the star pupils. Certainly, intimate and prolonged association with such an overarching genius could have produced a great amount of learning and sophistication in the mind of a naturally bright young man. In fact, that seems to be the case. The authorities were impressed that such a profound defense could come from men who had no formal training. To suppose that their comment proves Peter and John to be dull-witted provincials is to miss the point entirely.

Some have observed that there are differences in style between John and the Synoptics (see Morris 19-21), suggesting that John the son of Zebedee could not possibly have written so differently from the Synoptics. This is a rather weak argument based on modern men's opinions of what "could not have happened" in ancient times. It is unreasonable to suppose that all of the apostles had to see everything exactly the same way and write in the same style. According to Morris, "It is more convincing to put (this) objection in the form that if Jesus was as He is depicted in the Synoptics, He could not be as John depicts Him" (19).

Such an argument fails to take into account all the realities of the situation. Jesus was obviously the most complex and inspiring person ever to live on the planet. To suppose that He must have been perceived in one way only with no variations of perspective or dimension is unreasonable. There were obviously many and varied facets of His personality which could have made very different impressions on various people. Surely there is room for more than one stereotyped perspective on such a personality as Jesus. The difference between the Synoptists and John can further be ex-

plained by the assumption that the Synoptists emphasize the public teaching of Christ while John gives an insight into the private and informal teaching which Jesus directed at the inner circle of His followers. This hypothesis, while unproven, conforms to the known facts and offers a helpful explanation, demonstrating that the portraits of Christ presented in John and the Synoptics, respectively, are not necessarily mutually exclusive.

It has sometimes been asserted, in opposition to Johannine authorship, that there are certain events omitted from the Gospel that one would expect to be included if the son of Zebedee were, in fact, the author (Brown I:xcvii, Morris 18,19). The events often mentioned in this connection are the transfiguration and the agony in Gethsemane. Some say that John would not have omitted two such important events, especially since he was very prominent in both.

In answer to this argument one should understand that John chose his materials for reasons other than mere chronology. He chose particular events as illustrative of theological principles which he sought to convey. It is obvious that he left out many things which the Synoptists included. It is also obvious that his reason for inclusion was not his awareness of, or his involvement in, a particular episode. It can never be established that the author should have included any particular event. He obviously left out the institution of the Lord's Supper at which he was certainly present—indeed, prominent.

Another objection to Johannine authorship is that since John was a Galilean, he would have centered his narrative on Galilee rather than Jerusalem (see Brown I:xcviii). The answer to this objection is that it was John's theological purpose which focused upon Jerusalem, where the drama of the incarnation was played out. Here the Jewish authorities rejected and crucified the Messiah. The

Gospel was written after the fact; looking back upon the life of Christ, its focus was clearly Jerusalem.

Still another objection to the belief that the Apostle John wrote the Fourth Gospel is the assertion that he was martyred very early with his brother, James. The evidence for this assertion is very weak, very late, and very suspect (see Bernard I:xxxvii-xlv). Galatians 2:9 clearly demonstrates that John was alive and well long after the death of James. The tradition of John's long life and residence at Ephesus, when coupled with the indisputable fact of his exile on Patmos (Rev. 1:9), more than counteract this weak and doubtful tradition.

The final objection to be considered is one made by certain scholars to the effect that very early the author of the Gospel came to be confused with the Apostle John (see Bernard I:lxx). There are various theories as to the identity of that author and the reasons for his coming to be confused with the apostle. Some have suggested that the author was John Mark. This is an exceedingly improbable suggestion. It has been almost universally accepted that John Mark is to be associated with the Gospel of Mark, not the Gospel of John (see Brown I:xcvi).

The most widely credited suggestion as to the identity of this author who came to be confused with the Apostle John is a rather shadowy figure known as John the Elder. His very existence is established by only the most tenuous reasoning. Eusebius (3:39) quotes, from a no longer extant work of Papias, a paragraph which may be interpreted to imply that there were two Johns at Ephesus during the latter part of the first century—the Apostle John and John the Elder. It should be noted, however, that many scholars believe that there is only one John to be found in this passage—the Apostle (see Tenney 8). Furthermore, the mere existence of

John the Elder does not, in itself, indicate that he was the author of the Fourth Gospel. Not even Eusebius thought that; he believed the Apostle John to be the author (see below).

The idea that John the Elder was the author is a modern theory. It exists only because critical scholars came to believe, on the basis of their presuppositions, that there should be someone who could be identified as the real author who had come to be confused with the Apostle John. When John the Elder turned up, he was immediately taken to be the most likely candidate. There is no sound evidence to confirm any of this theory. Even critical scholars admit as much. "The hypothesis of [John the Elder's] having been confused at an early date with the Apostle John, and of his being the author of the Gospel, is much more fragile than is sometimes admitted, and it would be better to drop it" (Schnackenburg I:91).

The external evidence for the Johannine authorship of the Gospel consists of quotations from various church fathers which indicate the opinion and understanding of the early church on the subject. It is interesting to note that there is little real controversy on this issue. Even critical scholars agree that the evidence shows that the early church believed the Apostle John to be the author of the Fourth Gospel. "Thus, it is fair to say that the only ancient tradition about the authorship of the Fourth Gospel for which any considerable body of evidence can be adduced is that it is the work of John the son of Zebedee" (Brown I:xcii). The following is but a brief overview of the patristic evidence.

Irenaeus (c. 170) expresses his clear opinion, "After that, John, the disciple of the Lord, he who had leaned on his breast, also published a Gospel, while living at Ephesus in Asia" (*Against Heresies* 3:1:1). Theophilus of Antioch (c.

180) clearly attributes the Gospel to John, "And hence the holy writings teach us, and all the spirit-bearing [inspired] men, one of whom, John, says, 'In the beginning was the Word...'" (*To Autolycus* II:22). Clement of Alexandria (c. 190), in a quotation preserved by Eusebius from a lost work, indicated his belief that John wrote the Fourth Gospel, "Last of all, aware that the physical facts had been recorded in the Gospels, encouraged by his pupils and irresistibly moved by the Spirit, John wrote a spiritual Gospel" (*Eusebius* 6:14). The Muratorian Canon (c. 160-170) gives its assent to Johannine authorship by saying, "The author of the fourth among the Gospels is John, one of the disciples" (Godet 168). The Old Latin Prologues (c. 150-200), while they contain much that is of uncertain value, add their voice to the chorus advocating Johannine authorship, "The Gospel of John was revealed and given to the churches by John while still in the body..." (Barrett 96). Eusebius (c. 339), in spite of his belief that John the Elder wrote the Revelation, clearly believed that the Gospel was written by the Apostle John (*Eusebius* 3:24:5-15).

True, there were some who denied that the Apostle John wrote the Fourth Gospel. However, these were small, isolated groups who were regarded by the church as heretics. There was no significant doubt of Johannine authorship in the early church (see Brown I:xcii).

Place of Origin

There is no clear indication within the Gospel as to the place of its origin. There is, however, a good deal of evidence to support the tradition that it was written at Ephesus in Asia Minor. Irenaeus is the primary source of this tradition. He has already been quoted as saying that John wrote the Gospel "while living at Ephesus in Asia"

(*Against Heresies* 3:1:1). He states that John lived in Ephesus until the time of Trajan (2:22:5). He refers to John's encountering Cerinthus at the baths in Ephesus and mentions again that John remained "permanently" there until the time of Trajan (3:3:4). In addition, Polycrates (c. 190) says that John is buried at Ephesus (*Eusebius* 3:31:3). Clement of Alexandria says that John came to Ephesus from the Isle of Patmos after the death of Domitian (*Who Is the Rich Man* 42). This would seem to tie in with John's being on Patmos when he wrote the Revelation. Of course, Patmos is not far from Ephesus and would be a logical place to exile a resident of Ephesus.

It can be confidently said that the Scriptural evidence coincides with a Johannine residence at Ephesus in his later life. While John was still in Jerusalem when Paul made the visit mentioned in Gal. 2:9, neither he nor Peter seems to be present when Paul comes to Jerusalem after the third missionary journey (Acts 21:8). It seems very possible that John had, in the interim, begun a missionary enterprise of his own. In fact, Robinson believes that in Gal. 2:9 is to be seen the occasion for John's leaving Jerusalem. He sees in this verse an agreement that Paul would go to the Gentiles and that Peter and John would go to the Jews *of the dispersion* (see *Redating* 303-305). While it is not absolutely certain that the Gospel was written at Ephesus, that seems the most logical assumption.

Date

The question of the date of the composition of the Gospel is closely tied to the question of authorship. If one believes the author to be the Apostle John, then the Gospel must have been written within his lifetime. Tradition indicates that John lived to be very old, perhaps over one hundred. Since it has already been shown that John was the author, the Gospel must have been written sometime prior to A.D. 110. If John was only the source of the material and not the actual author, then it could have been written later.

Another reason for dating the Gospel prior to A.D. 100 is the discovery of certain papyrus texts of John. The Rylands Papyrus (P 52) dates from about A.D. 125-135. It contains portions of the Gospel of John. The text of this papyrus indicates that it had already been copied several times. In order to allow time for this process of textual development, the date for the original publication would have to be pushed back earlier. Evidence from other papyri, while less dramatic, confirms the indication of an early date (see Brown I:lxxxii-lxxxiii).

It has been shown that the latest possible date for the publication is approximately A.D. 100. What, then, is the earliest possible date? It has been traditional to date the publication of the Gospel at approximately A.D. 95 (see Westcott I:lxxxii). Robinson rejects this idea. He argues (*Redating* 257) that, while the traditional evidence indicates that John lived to a great age and that he was the last of the Evangelists to write, this does not necessarily indicate that he wrote as a very old man. He could have written at age 65 or so and still have been the last to write and still have held the position of a patriarch within the church. If one questions the dependence of John upon the Synoptics, as many scholars do (see Morris 31), the necessity for a late dating is significantly reduced.

A strong indication of an early date for the Gospel is the lack of any awareness of the destruction of Jerusalem in A.D. 70. Arguments from silence are always tenuous, yet this does seem a remarkable omission. That this catastrophic event which forever changed Judaism, Christianity, and their relationship to each other could have simply been overlooked in a work such as John is hard to conceive.

Some have suggested that the Gospel was written so late that the event was no longer in people's minds. This seems most unlikely. It is hard to imagine that John would not have recalled it in connection with 2:18-22, where he gives an after-the-fact interpretation of Jesus' words. Added to this argument from silence is the apparently incidental remark (5:2) that there is in Jerusalem a certain pool. The writer speaks of the pool in the present tense as if it still exists. Of course, this could be an historical present, but the context indicates otherwise. It seems entirely probable that the city of Jerusalem was still standing when John wrote these words.

The last factor to be considered in establishing the date of publication is the death of Peter. Some have held (see Zahn 241-243) that the death of Peter was the immediate occasion of the Epilogue (21:18,19). At any rate, it seems that Peter's death is presupposed. If this is the case, then the publication of the Gospel (or at least the Epilogue) would come after A.D. 64, the approximate date of Peter's execution. If the Gospel was published after Peter's death but prior to the destruction of Jerusalem, then the date would be between A.D. 64 and A.D. 69. This seems to be a reasonable dating and is finding acceptance among both critical and evangelical scholars.

Destination and Purpose

Destination and purpose will be considered together since John's purpose in writing is clearly controlled by his consciousness of his readers and their situation. John himself states his purpose for writing (20:31). He writes that his readers may know the glorious facts of Christ's life; that they may be led by those facts to believe that Jesus really is the Christ, the Son of God; and that, by believing, they may have eternal life. John wants people to believe in Christ and go to Heaven. In one sense, therefore, the purpose is obvious. Yet even this apparently obvious statement is subject to different interpretations, and there are other data which bear upon the question.

First of all, there is a textual variation in 20:31. In a few of the best texts (Sinaiticus and Vaticanus) the word for "believe" is in the Greek present tense, while in the great majority of texts it is an aorist. The present tense would indicate that the Gospel is written to enable Christians to continue believing, while the aorist would indicate that it was written to enable unbelievers to believe for the first time.

So the first question to be answered comes into focus: "Is the Gospel written to evangelize unbelievers or to strengthen and encourage Christians?" Zahn believes strongly that it is written to Christians: "The entire character of the book being against the assumption that it is intended as a written sermon for the conversion of persons not yet believers" (see 300). Morris, on the other hand, believes 20:31 establishes beyond all doubt that the purpose of the Gospel is evangelism (39,40). That these two scholars could disagree so completely indicates that there is strong evidence on both sides. Perhaps the answer is that the Gospel actually contains both elements, that it is intended both to evangelize unbelievers and to strengthen the faith of believers. These elements need not be mutually exclusive.

Another question to be addressed is whether the Gospel was written primarily for Jews or Gentiles. It has been customary among critical scholars to view the Gospel as a work intended for Gentiles only. The late date usually assigned to it puts it after the break between the church and the synagogue was complete, when a Christian writer would hardly direct such a work at Jews. The Logos (Greek for "Word" in 1:1) doctrine and the explanations given for Jewish customs were also seen as indications that the Gospel was intended for Gentile readers.

The present trend is in the other direction. The Dead Sea Scrolls have revealed that the Gospel is obviously grounded in first century Palestinian Judaism. The Logos doctrine is actually based on the O.T. rather than Hellenistic Gnosticism. Robinson (*Twelve* 107-125) believes that the Gospel is directed to the Jews of the western Diaspora. Again, there is evidence on both sides. One is inclined toward a synthesis, toward the belief that John addressed both Gentiles and Jews (Brown I:lxxvii).

The proper concept of the purpose of the Fourth Gospel seems to be that it was directed at the Johannine church (Smalley 145-148). John was instructing and exhorting his own followers (actual or potential). These would have included both Jews and Gentiles, with no need to focus exclusively on either group. Since there is no good reason to reject the tradition that places John's later ministry in Ephesus and Asia Minor, it seems logical to assume that the Gospel is directed toward the Johannine church in Asia Minor.

There are many other views as to the purpose of John's Gospel (see Smalley 122-149 and Morris 35-39). The oldest theory is that John wrote to supplement the Synoptic Gospels. This idea comes from Clement of Alexandria and his remark quoted above. Clement implies that John was in possession of the Synoptics and wrote to supply a "spiritual" interpretation of the "physical facts" which they contained (see *Eusebius* 6:14).

While Clement must have had some basis for his statement, there are difficul-

JOHN

ties connected with it. It obviously pre-supposes a significantly later date for John than for the Synoptics. An early dating for John would preclude this possibility. Clement's view also presupposes some degree of literary dependence of John upon the Synoptics. Such dependence is no longer accepted by many scholars (see Morris 35). They believe that John embodies an independent and authentic perspective. If John was written without any knowledge of or reference to the Synoptics, it could not have as its primary purpose to supplement them. That it was actually John's purpose to write a supplemental Gospel is unlikely, but that the Gospel came to serve such a function is apparent. Perhaps this observation occasioned Clement's remark.

Another theory is that the Gospel was a polemic against Gnosticism or Docetism. This is not possible if the Gospel was written by the Apostle John, for both these heresies were second century phenomena and would have been unknown to him. However, elements of Docetism did manifest themselves quite early. Therefore, it seems reasonable to believe that, while he was not dealing with the full-blown heresy which developed a century later, John may well have been dealing with an error of an essentially Docetic nature (see Morris 36). While John's Gospel is not primarily a polemic against incipient heresy, there certainly is a polemical element in it.

C. K. Barrett offers an interesting suggestion. He says, in essence, that the apostle had no specific purpose nor any specific people in mind at all. He wrote simply because he had some things he wanted to say. It was important to him that he say them, but it was a matter of indifference whether anybody actually read them (115). While this sounds rather bizarre, there is an element of truth in it. John felt an overwhelming compul-

sion to speak those things which he had seen and heard (Acts 4:20). Yet, it was not merely the glory and wonder of his knowledge that moved him to write, but his awareness of the glorious potential his knowledge portended for his readers. This knowledge, accepted and believed, meant Heaven. It had to be shared.

Unity and Authority

The authority and value of the Gospel of John are determined by one's view of its essential nature. Some have held that the Gospel is an allegory. According to this view, "Its truth depends not on the actual accuracy of the symbolizing appearances, but on the truth of the ideas and experiences thus symbolized" (Bernard I:lxxxii). Bernard, a critical scholar, convincingly refutes this view (I:lxxxii-xc). While once very popular, this view no longer commands many adherents.

The more common theories among critical scholars center around the belief that the Gospel in its present form cannot possibly be the work of John the son of Zebedee. These scholars feel that there are difficulties which force them to reject the possibility that the Gospel was composed by one man from memory. Those difficulties are: (1) differences in style in various sections of the Gospel, (2) breaks and inconsistencies in the sequence, and (3) repetitions in the discourses and sections of discourses which do not belong in their contexts (Brown I:xxiv-xxv).

The theories which scholars have proposed to deal with these difficulties are of three basic types: (1) theories of dislocation, (2) theories of multiple sources, and (3) theories of multiple editions. Each of these will be examined briefly.

Bernard is the chief advocate of the theory that there are dislocations in the text. He believes that pages from a cor-

9

JOHN

rect copy of the Gospel in codex form were either by accident or design rearranged. He believes that he can demonstrate a correspondence between the units of material that have been rearranged and pages or multiples of pages from such a codex. This would account for what seems to be a confused and illogical sequence in the Gospel (see I:xvi-xxx). This view has been rejected by most modern scholars (Brown I:xxvi-xxviii, Morris 53-56, Guthrie *Introduction* I:287-291). It is quite arbitrary, it requires too many secondary assumptions, and it rejects the order as it now stands on the basis of insufficient evidence.

Another theory is that the author used various sources in composing his Gospel. While there is not complete unanimity as to the sources used, those most often mentioned are: the Synoptics, a "signs" source, a "sayings" or "discourses" source, and perhaps some original material from the son of Zebedee. This theory is thought to explain the various asymmetries and inconsistencies that are supposedly observed in the Gospel. Rudolf Bultmann is the foremost exponent of this view. Again, this view is rejected by many scholars as being without real merit. Robinson says that the unity of style throughout the Gospel "has rendered unconvincing all attempts to analyze out written sources" (*Redating* 297). He also quotes favorably another writer as saying, "It looks as though, if the author of the Fourth Gospel used documentary sources, he wrote them all himself." He goes on to say that detailed analysis "has told heavily in favor of a unity of style throughout the Gospel, including the last, additional chapter" (*Twelve* 97). In other words, the problems which the theory of multiple sources supposedly explains do not exist.

The third theory is that the Gospel is not the product of any one man, but the work of at least three different individuals working over a period of time. Brown adopts such a view (I:xxxiv-xxxix and xcix-ci). He posits five separate stages in the composition of the Gospel. Stage 1: A body of material concerning the life of Christ was composed through a process of preaching over a period of years by an eyewitness who was most likely John the son of Zebedee. Stage 2: This material was "sifted, selected, thought over and molded" into the stories and discourses which were later to become the Gospel of John by the disciples of John, but especially one principle disciple. That principle disciple was an individual of "dramatic genius and profound theological insight" who is actually to be thought of as the author of the Gospel (the Evangelist). While his identity is not certain, he may very well have been John the Elder. Stage 3: The material was shaped into a chronological story which actually became the first edition of the Gospel. Stage 4: The material was edited and re-edited through a lifetime of preaching and teaching. Stages 2-4 are all attributed to one person—the Evangelist. Stage 5: The material underwent a final editing by someone other than the Evangelist. This was probably done by one of his disciples shortly after the Evangelist's death. Barrett and Schnackenburg hold similar views (see Barrett 113,114; Schnackenburg I:100-104).

Robinson (*Redating* 270-272) rejects the main contentions of Brown's argument. He states that the process which Brown postulates may very well have taken place over a relatively short period in the mind of the original eyewitness author. The Apostle John, in his preaching and teaching ministry, could have shaped the material into the form it has in the Fourth Gospel.

I believe that this is essentially what happened. The N.T. makes plain that the early ministry of the apostles was an oral one (1 Cor. 11:2,23; 15:3-5; 1 Th.

JOHN

2:13; 2 Th. 2:15 and 3:6) and that their oral testimony, confirmed by miracles, was the voice of authority within the church. It was this apostolic authority which became the basis and test for the authority and canonicity of the N.T. books as they were written. Thus the Gospel represents the eyewitness testimony of the Apostle John to the life and teaching of Christ as it was shaped and organized by several decades of his own apostolic preaching and careful reflection.

Literary Structure

The Gospel of John makes no pretense at being a complete biography of Jesus of Nazareth. Rather, it is a stylized narrative which more nearly approximates the literary form of a drama than a history. The author selects and arranges his materials primarily for their dramatic impact. He presents the identity, personality, and significance of Jesus Christ in the most forceful manner possible. This does not mean that the account is inaccurate in either fact or chronology; it only means that John's purpose far transcends mere accuracy of detail.

There have been various suggestions as to the unifying theme of the Gospel. As with any great literary work, there are many themes which interact and sustain one another. Scholars have not been able to agree as to which of these many themes is the theme of the Gospel. One theme is the geographical dichotomy between Galilee and Jerusalem. Another is related to the chronological progression of Jesus' ministry, indicated by the feasts which He attended in Jerusalem. Yet another theme is thought to center on the extremely vivid characters whom Christ encounters and His discussions with them. Westcott (I:lxxxix) believed the theme to be the development of three

paired sets of ideas: witness and truth, glory and light, and judgment and life. Many think they see the unifying plan of the Gospel in a format of successive cycles of symbolic signs followed by revelatory discourses.

It is my belief that, while all of these themes are present within the Gospel and are helpful in understanding it, the primary theme of the Gospel is belief and its corollary, witness. The Gospel is a witness to the truth to guide men to belief (see Bernard I: xc-xcii). The drama of the Gospel is a controversy between belief and unbelief, between acceptance of truth and its rejection (1:11,12). This drama is reenacted for the reader. Witnesses, so to speak, are called forth from the memory of the author into the courtroom of reason and compelled to give their testimony once again.

Repeatedly John places himself on the witness stand and assures his readers of the veracity of his account. He is quite aware that his own credibility is a crucial issue, for all the other witnesses speak only through him (1:14; 19:35; 21:24).

John calls, as his first witness, John the Baptist. This greatest of all mortals save one speaks with an official solemnity, "And I saw, and bare record that this is the Son of God" (1:34). The Samaritan woman is the next to testify, "Come, see a man, which told me all things that ever I did: is not this the Christ?" (4:29). Her Samaritan compatriots insist on testifying for themselves, "Now we believe, not because of thy saying: for we have heard *him* ourselves, and know that this is indeed the Christ, the Saviour of the world" (4:42). The man born blind answers the taunt of the Pharisees, "Whether he be a sinner *or no*, I know not: one thing I know, that, whereas I was blind, now I see" (9:25). Finally, the skeptical Thomas reiterates his reluctant testimony, given only in the face of overwhelming evidence: "My Lord and my

11

God" (20:28). This time, however, by John's design, he speaks to readers quite remote from the original setting to establish, so to speak, their faith from afar.

John's star witness, however, is none other than Jesus Himself. Over and over John allows Him to take the witness stand for Himself. He repeatedly asserts His own Messiahship and Godhood (4:26; 5:17,18; 6:38a,41; 9:35-37; 13:13,14; 14:7,9). Jesus personally speaks to every reader, imploring him to accept His testimony and believe Him: "Though I bear record of myself, *yet* my record is true: for I know whence I came, and whither I go" (8:14). "Believe me that I *am* in the Father, and the Father in me" (14:11a). John rests his case with this appeal from the Saviour's own lips. Christ's witness to Himself is the strongest evidence John can conceive of. He has given his witness to the truth; the verdict rests with his reader (20:31).

The New Look on John

Currently, the scholarly study of the Gospel of John is dominated by what is called "the new look." This new look rejects much of the conventional wisdom of the past century of critical scholarship and has a great deal in common with the traditional views that are still held by conservative scholars. Even so this phenomenon is not a return to pre-critical orthodoxy or a rejection of higher critical methodology. It is, rather, a rejection of the extreme skepticism that had come to characterize Johannine studies in favor of a view that finds much that is authentic, accurate and valuable in the Fourth Gospel. In a way, the critical scholars have, by their own methods, arrived back very near the point which those methods originally forced them to abandon. The impact of the new look is that it has challenged many of the critical assumptions concerning the Gospel and has aroused a new interest in its study. (For further comments on "the new look," see Robinson, *Twelve* 94-106 and Smalley 11-13.)

12

JOHN

OUTLINE OF THE GOSPEL OF JOHN

I. Prologue: The Word Among Men (1:1-18)
   A. His Essential Nature (1:1-5)
   B. His Incarnation (1:6-13)
   C. His Transcendent Glory (1:14-18)
II. The Book of Signs: Christ Revealed in His Life (1:19—12:50)
   A. The Testimony of John the Baptist (1:19-34)
      1. As given to the deputation from Jerusalem (1:19-28)
      2. As given publicly the next day (1:29-34)
   B. The Testimony of the First Disciples (1:35-51)
   C. The First Sign: Water to Wine (2:1-12)
   D. The Challenge in the Temple (2:13-25)
   E. The First Discourse: The New Birth (3:1-21)
   F. The Baptist's Final Testimony (3:22-36)
   G. The Second Discourse: The Water of Life (4:1-42)
   H. The Second Sign: The Nobleman's Son Healed (4:43-54)
   I. The Third Sign: The Lame Man Healed (5:1-16)
   J. The Third Discourse: "Equal With God" (5:17-47)
   K. The Fourth Sign: Feeding the Multitude (6:1-15)
   L. The Fifth Sign: Walking on Water (6:16-21)
   M. The Fourth Discourse: The Bread of Life (6:22-71)
   N. Confrontation with Unbelief (7:1-36)
   O. The Fifth Discourse: The Water of Life (7:37-52)
   P. The Woman Taken in Adultery (7:53—8:11)
   Q. The Sixth Discourse: The Light of the World (8:12-59)
   R. The Sixth Sign: Healing the Man Born Blind (9:1-41)
   S. The Seventh Discourse: The Good Shepherd (10:1-18)
   T. Controversy Concerning Christ (10:19-42)
   U. The Seventh Sign: The Raising of Lazarus (11:1-57)
   V. The Climax of the Public Ministry (12:1-50)
III. The Book of Glory: Christ Revealed in His Death and Resurrection
    (13:1—20:31)
   A. The Last Supper (13:1-30)
      1. The footwashing (13:1-17)
      2. Prediction of Judas' betrayal (13:18-30)
   B. The Farewell Discourses (13:31—17:26)
      1. The new commandment (13:31-38)
      2. The Way, the Truth, and the Life (14:1-14)
      3. "I will not leave you comfortless" (14:15-31)
      4. The vine and the branches (15:1-11)
      5. "My friends" (15:12-17)
      6. Warning of the world's mindless hatred (15:18-27)
      7. Preparation for persecution (16:1-4)
      8. The Comforter (16:5-15)
      9. The resurrection predicted (16:16-22)
      10. Special encouragement for the disciples (16:23-33)
      11. Christ's great high priestly prayer (17:1-26)
   C. The Passion Narrative (18:1—19:42)

JOHN

I. PROLOGUE—THE WORD AMONG MEN (1:1-18)

The prologue is an integral part of the Gospel. While some view it as an originally separate hymn that has merely been adapted to the Gospel, it seems obviously to have been a part of it as John wrote it. The vocabulary and style do not indicate otherwise. Furthermore, the prologue does not appear to have been intended to stand alone. Its cryptic statements are intelligible only in light of the complete account which follows in the main body of the Gospel. Its purpose is to introduce and anticipate that account. It sets forth the theme of the Gospel: that the glory of God is perfectly and uniquely revealed in Jesus Christ.

A. His Essential Nature (1:1-5)

1 In the beginning was the Word, and the Word was with God, and the Word was God.

The Gospel begins with the opening words of the Book of Genesis: "In the beginning." John wishes to relate Christ to the timeless eternity which God alone inhabited before there was anything but Himself. Even in that primeval era, Christ already "was." The tense of this verb (Greek imperfect) indicates that Christ was even then what He has uninterruptedly continued to be. There is an absolute continuity in His existence from eternity past to eternity future (cf. Heb. 13:8; Rev. 1:8; Jn. 8:58).

John refers to Jesus as "the Word" (Greek *logos*). To a Hebrew this term would refer to the spoken word, that by which thought is communicated. Jesus, therefore, is that by which God reveals His thought to man, the revelation of all that God inherently is. Another aspect of the Hebrew understanding of this term is that of creative power and action. It was by His word that God cre-

ated the heavens and earth. The designation of Jesus as "the Word" associates Him with the act of creation. To a Greek, on the other hand, the term would refer to the principle of order and reason which governs the universe. Jesus is the ultimate expression of this principle. John draws primarily upon the Hebrew concept, but he probably also intends the Greek concept to be attributed to Christ by a sort of *ad hoc* logic. Certainly the old idea that John uses the term in some Gnostic sense may be safely rejected.

While the first clause emphasizes Christ's eternity, the second emphasizes His equality and intimate association with, yet distinction from, the Father. He was (has always been) with the Father. "With" (Greek *pros*) means, literally, "face to face with." To be "face to face with" implies equal standing yet clearly necessitates distinction. One cannot be face to face with himself.

The final clause emphasizes Christ's essential deity. Much has been made of the fact that the word "God" (Greek *theos*) lacks the article. This has been thought by some to indicate that John is saying that Christ is *a* god. (See, e.g., the *New World Translation* published by the Jehovah's Witnesses.) Jesus would be god only in some generic sense and not fully equal with the Father. There are two basic objections to this view. (1) It does not fit the context. John has been ascribing to Christ attributes appropriate to God only— eternality and equality with the Father. It is illogical that the climax toward which he is headed should be simply that Jesus is divine in some generic sense only, yet quite distinct from and inferior to God the Father. (2) It misconstrues the significance of the absence of the article, which simply indicates that *God* is the predicate nominative rather than the subject of the clause. This distinction is necessary because John, for the sake of emphasis, has placed *God* first. The order of the words is, "And God was the word." John places *God* first because he wants to emphasize that "God" was what the Word actually was. This is the natural climax of his three-fold statement.

It should also be noted that the significance of the absence of the article would not be that the Word was *a* god even if it were not necessary as an indication that "God" is a predicate nominative. The absence of the article in Greek grammar does not indicate any lack of definitude, rather it indicates a stress upon the qualitative aspect of the noun in contrast to its mere identity (see Dana and Mantey, *A Manual Grammar of the Greek New Testament*, 149). The same word is used without the article again in v. 18, where it clearly refers to the God of Heaven.

The last of the three clauses is actually a climax. Not only is it true that Christ was eternal and equal with the Father, but He was also qualitatively, in His own essential being, God.

2 The same was in the beginning with God.

While this verse is often thought to be but emphatic repetition, it does seem to add something new. It synthesizes the assertions of v. 1 into a summary statement and then personalizes that statement. "The same" (Greek *houtos*) may be better understood as "this one." It is a person about whom John speaks. This person, Jesus, was actually with (see comments on "with," v. 1) the Father, sharing His existence from the very beginning (see Jn. 8:58; 17:5).

3 All things were made by him; and without him was not any thing made that was made.

As the subject changes from Christ

to the creation, the verb changes from a form of "to be" (Greek *eimi*) to a form of "to become" (Greek *ginomai*). A basic distinction is thus established between the creation which "came to be" or "became" and Christ who simply "was." One is reminded of God's designation of Himself to Moses as "I am" (Ex. 3:14). There is also a change from the Greek imperfect to the aorist tense. The "became" (aorist) indicates that, in contrast to "the Word" which from all eternity has constantly been all that He presently is, there was a specific point in time at which the creation came into existence and from which it has continued into the present. It should be noted that the tense of the last verb, "was made" (Greek perfect *gegonen*), indicates an emphasis upon the existing result of the creative act.

"All things" refers to each of the created things severally. Every single thing was made by Him. "By Him" (Greek *dia*) has the sense of "through Him," indicating agency. While the Father was the ultimate cause of creation, Christ was the proximate cause or mediate agent most immediately involved in its actual execution (see 1 Cor. 8:6; Col. 1:16b; Heb. 1:2). Nothing was made "without" (Greek *choris*) Him or apart from His involvement. There is not one single thing that presently exists which He did not personally bring to be as it is.

4 In him was life; and the life was the light of men.

Some scholars, on the basis of the textual evidence, place the division between vv. 3 and 4 before "that was made" (Greek *ho gegonen*; see Westcott I:59-63). This would make v. 4 read, "That which had come to be in Him was life..." (Brown I:3). All in all, it is best to reject this division and retain the one in the text, which seems to make more sense (see Barrett). John is saying that life itself inheres in Jesus, not that that which He has made is alive. The focus continues to be on Christ. It does not shift to the creation.

Not only is Christ the source of the universe but also of that animating force which energizes it—life. In Christ is embodied the absolute and self-existent life of the Creator as opposed to the contingent and derivative life of the creature. Inherent in the possession of such life is the power to impart it to others (Gen. 2:7). Life, then, is "in" Christ in the sense that through Him it is available to men (5:26; 11:25; 14:6). There are at least three senses in which "life" inheres in Christ: (1) physical life, (2) abundant life (10:10), and (3) eternal life (11:25).

In the second part of the verse "the life" should be understood as a personification of Christ. Thus Christ, who essentially is life, is also the light of men. Light is used symbolically of truth and knowledge as opposed to the darkness of error and ignorance. Through "the Word" God reveals Himself, and "the Word" communicates the truth to men. Christ is the light, the truth for mankind (8:12; 9:5; 12:46; 14:6).

Notice that "the Word" is the light "of men." To one special category of creation Jesus is most truly "the light," that category being human beings. Human beings are clearly differentiated from the rest of creation. Jesus comes to men and becomes part of their race. Among them He will dwell. They will behold His glory (1:14). However, there is an obvious lack of any further differentiation. *All* within the category of mankind are included. He comes to be the light of them all, both Jew and Gentile (Isa. 9:2; 42:6).

5 And the light shineth in darkness; and the darkness comprehended it not.

There is a clear parallel between this verse and Gen. 1:2,3. As God commanded the light to shine forth into the primordial darkness, so "the light of men," "the Word," shines forth in the darkness of error and ignorance.

The second part of the verse presents a small problem. The KJV translates the Greek verb (*katalambano*) "comprehend." While it is clear that the word can have this meaning, there is another meaning which seems to fit the context better. That meaning is "overcome." This meaning is the one John uses for this verb in 12:35. Thus, the second clause would read, "and the darkness did not overcome it." This fits the parallel with Genesis 1 better. Just as the darkness could not overwhelm the physical light which God commanded to shine, so the spiritual darkness of this world cannot extinguish the light of God's truth that shines through Jesus Christ.

The present tense of the verb "shineth" (Greek *phainei*) indicates continuous, ongoing action while the past tense of the verb "overcame" (Greek aorist *katelaben*) indicates an action at a certain point in time. The significance seems to be that the light is still shining, Satan's one great attempt to extinguish it at Calvary having failed.

**Summary
(1:1-5)**

John uses "the Word" to describe the essential nature of Jesus Christ as the communication to man of all that God is. Christ is shown to be eternal, equal with the Father, and, in the fullest sense, divine. He is spoken of as having shared the Father's mode of existence with Him from all eternity. He is personally responsible for bringing into existence everything that now is. He embodies in His own person the creative impulse of life and the unchanging beacon of truth. As He shines forth into the darkness

around Him, His light cannot be re-
sisted. The darkness must give way before Him.

Application: Teaching and Preaching the Passage

Particular note should be taken of the
third clause in v. 1. The Jehovah's Witnesses and others use the misleading
translation, "the Word was a god." They
attempt to cash in on the English idiom
to demonstrate that Christ was not truly
God in the fullest sense. The Greek idiom, however, does not in any way substantiate their contention. Quite the opposite.

One might approach this section using the question, "Who is Jesus?" He is
first of all the eternal God (vv.1,2). Second, He is the Creator of all that is (v.
3). One could truthfully modify the familiar hymn to sing, "This is my Savior's
world." Every single flower came to be
as it is by Christ's design. Third, He is
the Giver of life, the one from whom the
very quality and power of life emanate
(v. 4a). Fourth, He is the Light of the
world (vv.4b,5) from whom the darkness
of this evil world must flee away (c.f.
Rev. 1:16b).

The full implication of "the Word," in
both its Hebrew and Greek contexts,
can be very profitably explored. Christ is
the communication of all that God is,
that which reveals God to men. Christ is
the focal point, the dynamic expression
of God's creative power. Christ is the
ordering principle, the eminent manifestation and personal agent of God's providential control of the universe. It is literally true that "He rules the world with
truth and grace."

B. His Incarnation (1:6-13)

6 There was a man sent from God, whose name *was* John.

The first word, "there came to be,
appeared, arose" (Greek *egeneto*)
stands alone as a complete verb in itself.
It is not simply to be read as a helping
verb with "sent" (not a "periphrastic
construction" in Greek, combined with
apestalmenos). It has a force of its own:
"There appeared a man." Notice again
the contrast between this "was" (Greek
ginomai) and the "was" in v. 1 (Greek
eimi). Christ always "was." John, like
the universe, "came to be." Notice also
that John is designated simply as "man"
(Greek *anthropos*), while Christ is actually "God" (Greek *theos*).

This man has "been sent" (Greek
perfect passive participle of *apostello*)
"from beside of" (Greek *para*) God. His
ministry has its ultimate source in the
mind of God. While John is not God (as
Christ is), he holds a very special and
unique place in God's plan (Mal. 3:1).
This idea must not be pressed to imply
pre-existence for John.

This personage is identified simply as
"John." He is not called "the Baptist."
Such an additional designation is unnecessary upon the theory adopted in the
introduction. The apostle may also wish
to call attention to the symbolic meaning
of the name John ("Jehovah has been
gracious"). This name was specifically
chosen by God (Lk. 1:13); it is therefore
not unreasonable to suppose that it
bears a special significance in regard to
God's purpose for him. His designation
simply as "John" also seems to indicate
a playing down of his role as "baptizer"
in view of the stress that this Gospel
places upon his role as "witness."

7 The same came for a witness, to bear witness of the Light, that all *men* through him might believe.

This person has come "as a witness"
(Greek *eis marturian*) "in order that he
might bear witness" (Greek *hina martu-
rese*). This repetition, as well as the

tense of "bear witness" (Greek aorist, stressing the unitary and completed nature of his witness), emphasizes the centrality of·John's role as witness in this Gospel (cf. 1:15, 29,32,34; 3:27ff.; 5:33-36). "The light" refers back to vv. 4,5 and is an obvious reference to Christ.

The two purpose clauses establish an interesting parallelism. John came as a witness "in order to" (Greek *hina*) give witness. But, by the same token, he came as a witness "in order that" (same Greek word) through him (that is, through His witness) all may believe. Witness and belief are thus paired logically together. This verse not only gives a true assessment of John's significance and impact; it also introduces the two major themes of the gospel, witness and belief (20:30,31).

8 He was not that Light, but *was sent* to bear witness of that Light.

John is not, himself, the Christ. Rather, he has been sent to bear witness "concerning" (Greek *peri*) the Christ. The specific negation of the idea that John is the Christ has led some to believe that the writer intends to counteract a false belief that John, rather than Jesus, is the Christ. This seems untenable. Such a basic misconception would require more than a mild, indirect correction. People who believe such would have missed the whole point of the Gospel, the central tenet of Christianity. They would be denounced as absolute heretics. The writer is merely clarifying and emphasizing John's role, not correcting a cult of "John-worshippers." Verse 8 bears the same relation to v. 7 that v. 2 does to v. 1. The writer mentions John the Baptist so prominently because he himself was originally John's disciple. He wishes to explain fully John's role and importance.

9 *That* was the true Light, which lighteth every man that cometh into the world.

This verse can be translated in several ways. The NIV is very good: "The true light that gives light to every man was coming into the world." Translating it this way, the first verb "was" (Greek *en*) is linked directly to the participle "coming" (Greek *erchomenon*) as one verb (a Greek periphrastic imperfect; see Godet, Bernard, Barrett, and especially Brown). John uses such constructions frequently. In such a construction there is a certain independence granted to the main verb, the idea then being that "there was a real light and it was coming into the world" (Brown I:9). This interpretation, of necessity, rules out the idea that "coming into the world" modifies "every man." However, the universality of "every man" is not thereby diminished.

The term "true" (Greek *alethinos*) should be taken in the sense of "real" or "genuine." The meaning is not that Jesus is the true light and that all others are false, but that Jesus is the quintessential light which renders all lesser lights secondary and inferior. Christ, by coming into the world, brings light into a world where there has previously been only darkness. The light that He brings is available to, and has some impact on, every human being even if many reject the light and remain in darkness (3:19).

10 He was in the world, and the world was made by him, and the world knew him not.

There is a play upon the word "world" (Greek *kosmos*). The verse consists of three clauses, each using the word. In the first instance "world" refers to the physical world. In the third it refers to the world of human society and culture. The second instance may be understood, like the first, as referring to the physical world, but it very likely includes both ideas, retaining the connotation of the first usage and anticipating that of the third, thus involving a subtle change from one to the other. Jesus was in the (physical) world, the world (both physical and societal) was made by Him, and the (societal) world knew Him not.

Some have supposed the first clause to refer to Christ's preincarnate existence, the "was" being understood in the same sense as in v.1. It seems more likely that "was" (as a Greek progressive imperfect of duration rather than of description) calls attention to the fact that there was a period of time (now concluded) in which Jesus was in the world. The context favors this interpretation since v. 9 has been shown to place Jesus upon the earthly scene, and any reference to a prior state of immanence would seem to be out of sequence.

Some liberal scholars see this supposed break in context (Jesus on earth in v. 9 and pre-incarnate in v. 10) as an indication of a transition from an inserted section back to the original *Logos* hymn. Verses 6-9, in their view, constitute the addition, with v. 10 marking the return to the original hymn (see Brown). It is much better to leave the context intact and use it to interpret the text than to interpret the text and then adjust the context.

The second clause reiterates the foundational truth of v. 3, but its impact is to focus that truth as a part of an ironic sequence. The sequence moves from a primary assumption (He was in the world) to a secondary assumption (the world was made by Him) to an absolutely ludicrous conclusion (the world knew Him not). The logical conclusion would have been, "And so the world recognized and welcomed Him." That is precisely what the world did *not* do. It did not "know" (Greek *ginosko*) Him. It did not recognize or greet Him. It did

not comprehend who He was.

11 He came unto his own, and his own received him not.

Again, in this verse, there is a play on words and irony. The word played upon is "his own" (Greek *idios*). "Unto His own (Greek neuter plural) He came, and His own (masculine plural) did not receive Him." "His own," in the first clause, refers to the world in general and summarizes the truth of v. 10. The world into which Jesus came is truly His own. It belongs to Him in the most ultimate sense imaginable: He has created it from nothing. His ownership was demonstrated constantly while He was present in it, perhaps never more dramatically than when He hushed the storm on Galilee (e.g. Mk. 4:39). The same "His own" is used in Jn. 19:27 to refer to John's own home. Certainly, the term implies ownership in a most absolute and personal sense.

In the second clause, "His own" retains its connection with "His own" in the first. The connection must exist in order for the contrast and irony to be expressed. However, the term is modified and redirected by the change of gender and number. Now the focus is upon Christ's own people, the Jews. His own people did not receive Him. He was not welcomed and greeted with joy and thanksgiving (as would seem reasonable). His own people, the nation brought into existence for the express purpose of providing Him to the world (Gen. 12:2,3), His fellow-citizens of Nazareth, His own half brothers, did not receive Him with open arms and clasp Him to their bosoms. Rather, they rejected, spurned, and killed Him. Jesus apparently pictured this rejection in the Parable of the Wicked Husbandman (Mt.21:33-46). The prophet Isaiah (53:3) expressed it poignantly, "He is despised and rejected of men; a man of sorrows, and acquainted with grief: and we hid as it were *our* faces from him; he was despised, and we esteemed him not."

12 But as many as received him, to them gave he power to become the sons of God, *even* to them that believe on his name.

While the Jewish nation as a whole rejected Jesus, an indefinite number of individuals do receive Him. The contrast between reception and rejection is a major theme of the Fourth Gospel. The first twelve chapters focus upon Christ's rejection by the Jewish nation while the remainder from 13:1 onward focuses upon His reception by a relatively small group of disciples.

To those who do receive Jesus, God gives the power to become His children. God simply "gives" this blessing of His own free grace. It cannot be earned or merited. Receiving Jesus is an occasion for God's grace, not a meritorious claim upon His justice. Yet He gives to those who receive Him an "authority" (Greek *exousia*, translated "power" in KJV), a right, an authorization, a warrant to become His children. That He *gives* them a *right* seems a paradox. By this warrant they "become" (Greek aorist tense) God's own children. There is a point in time at which their status is supernaturally changed and they are placed (born) into the family of God. Their status is that of "children of God" (Greek *tekna theou*) which involves a familial connection and bond and a likeness of nature.

The last part of the verse equates "receiving" Jesus with "believing on His name." This provides an insight into the meaning of "belief," the most basic condition of salvation. To "believe" on Jesus is to "receive" Him—to appropriate Him to one's self—as the Word, the Life, the Light, as Creator, and as God. To believe on His name means to believe in all that He is. In ancient times one's name

was not a mere appellation, but a reference to his most basic and essential qualities. Thus to believe on Jesus' name means to accept His essential identity as the Son of God. It is not certain whether the particular name in view here is "Jesus" or "the Word." Either one would involve a comprehension of Christ's true identity.

13 Which were born, not of blood, nor of the will of the flesh, nor of the will of man, but of God.

The structure of this phrase is an essential element of its meaning. Resolution is suspended until the very end by withholding the verb until the last word. This structure obviously functions to place an emphasis on the verb. Literally the verse reads, "Who, not of bloods, nor of the will of the flesh, nor of the will of a man, but of God, were begotten (or born)."

The central idea is that those who receive and believe on Christ are supernaturally "begotten" (Greek *gennao*) of God. This word can mean either "begotten" or "born," depending on the context. The interpretation is not essentially different whichever is chosen here. The idea is clearly that such people have their status radically altered by a supernatural action of God.

This supernatural work is contrasted with three aspects of the natural process of reproduction. "Not of blood," means not by the natural combination of sex cells euphemistically referred to as "bloods" (the Greek plural apparently indicating the male and female). It may be noted that one still refers to his children as "his own flesh and blood" even today. "Nor of the will of the flesh" is to be equated with the normal sexual desire or attraction. Such desire is considered perfectly normal and healthy and is not in any way deprecated here. "Nor of the will of a 'man' or 'husband'" (Greek *andros*) apparently refers to the normal masculine impulse. The word focuses upon one's male identity and role as husband rather than his membership in the human race. It is not by these natural processes that those who receive Jesus become the children of God, but by a definite supernatural action of God.

Summary
(1:6-13)

There came upon the earthly scene a man called John. This man's essential function was to "witness" to the identity and significance of Christ. His role was not focused upon himself but upon Christ, the true light, life, hope, and glory of the world. Christ actually came into the world which belonged to Him by right of creation and, unbelievably, was not recognized or received even by His own people, the Jews. Yet, while the Jews as a nation rejected Him, certain individuals (primarily from among the Jews) did receive Him and believe on His name. To these individuals God graciously accorded the authorization to become His own children. This status was not conferred upon them by any natural human means but by a supernatural action of God.

Application: Teaching and
Preaching the Passage

In vv. 6-9 attention is focused upon John the Baptist. He is presented as a man of great significance, yet absolutely inferior to Christ. While he was, in Jesus' words, "a burning and a shining light" (Jn. 5:35), he was as darkness in the presence of the "true light." John was like a mighty searchlight which pierces the night darkness, yet is entirely invisible in the brightness of noonday. The rising of the sun renders all lesser lights superfluous. The writer uses the acknowledged greatness of John as a pedestal upon which to display the incomparable glory of Christ. The whole reason for God's raising John to a position of influence and honor was for him to use that position to bear testimony to Christ. John, when all is said and done, was a witness, a great and influential witness, but a witness. Every Christian should have as his goal in life to shine as brightly as possible. He should strive to make the very most of himself and achieve the greatest stature and influence he can. Yet he should understand that his only real function in life is to bear witness to Christ. All that he is or can be is meaningful only to the degree that it glorifies Christ and points men to Him. Greatness inheres in mirroring Christ, in reflecting His glory, in bearing witness to Him.

In vv. 10-13 John is entirely eclipsed. Attention is focused exclusively upon the Christ. The underlying tenor of these verses is irony. How ironic that the Creator could be present in His world unrecognized! How ironic that He could come into the world unwelcomed even by His own peculiar people, the Jews! Yet how ironic also, that in the midst of this rejection some few should receive Him into their hearts by faith and thereby become so much the object of God's grace as to be, by a miraculous action, translated into the very family of God, actually made God's own children! Paul describes this status very beautifully in Rom. 8:16-21.

In these verses are revealed the utter blindness and depravity of mankind. The King of Heaven was in their midst, and they did not recognize or receive Him. Christians ought not, therefore, to feel undue sadness or rejection when they are scorned and slighted. They may have been rejected by men, but they have been accepted through Christ Jesus into the family of God. Their status as God's children is assured by God's own warrant. It depends upon no action of any human being but on God alone.

C. His Transcendent Glory (1:14-18)

14 And the Word was made flesh, and dwelt among us, (and we beheld his glory, the glory as of the only begotten of the Father,) full of grace and truth.

"And" (Greek *kai*) should be understood as adversative rather than merely continuative and thus translated "and yet." While the believer's new nature is wonderfully "non-fleshly," Christ Himself must assume the form of flesh. How ironic that He must assume the very finitude from which He is to deliver those who believe in Him.

"Was made" (Greek *ginomai*, "became") is contrasted with v. 1 which represents Christ as having always been what He continues to be. This verb was used in v. 3 to refer to the creation coming into existence. In v. 6 it referred to John the Baptist's appearing on the scene. Now it is used of Christ Himself. The Christ who always was now comes to be what He has not been previously. The tense of the verb (Greek aorist) indicates that at a given point in time there occurred a fundamental change of status: the Word became flesh. "It expresses the unmistakable paradox that the Logos who dwelt with God, clothed in the full majesty of the divinity and possessing the fullness of the divine life, entered the sphere of the earthly and human, the material and perishable, by becoming flesh" (Schnackenburg I:266).

He did not just "assume" humanity as something which can be laid aside. He "became" truly and completely human, yet in such a way that He never ceases to be God. He became the God-man and shall remain such throughout eternity (see Westcott). There is no room for any Docetic idea that Christ is merely a spirit or apparition without any physical substance. John insists upon the true humanity of Christ (1 Jn. 4:2; 2 Jn. 7).

The Incarnate Word also "dwelled" (Greek *skenao*) among us. This verb literally means "to dwell in a tent." The idea that it emphasizes the temporary character of Christ's dwelling among men is incorrect. This idea grows from the modern conception of a tent as a temporary shelter (Yeager) rather than from N.T. usage (Bernard). The word should be understood as referring to the Tent or Tabernacle of the Congregation so that now God has come to dwell among men in a Tabernacle of Flesh. This imagery would have been quite obvious to a Jew.

The word "us," along with "we" in the next clause, focuses attention upon the writer. Just whom does he intend to designate by his use of the first person plural pronoun? There are two possibilities. He could be referring to a group of actual eyewitnesses of which he himself is a part, or he could be making a generic reference to Christians as an aggregate including both himself and his readers. It seems clear that he uses "we" in the second sense in v. 16. Yet, on the assumption that John is also the author of the First Epistle of John, his parallel usage there (1:1-4) seems to indicate that he is speaking literally of what he and others actually saw and heard. Therefore, it appears that John is referring here to his own function as an eyewitness to the glory of Christ's person.

There is another interesting parallel between this passage and that in 1 John, for there also John uses "we" in subsequent verses to refer to himself and his readers (all Christians generically). Perhaps John means to include both meanings and to symbolically include his readers with himself (and the other eyewitnesses) in what he actually saw and heard. This would fit very well with his stated purpose for writing the Gospel

(20:31).

In the next clause, "We beheld" (Greek *theaomai*) "...is never used in the N.T. of spiritual vision, while it is used 22 times of seeing with the bodily eyes....Neither here nor at I Jn. 1:1 is there any question of a supersensuous, mystical perception of spiritual facts, in both passages the claim being that the author has 'seen' with his eyes (the aorist points to a definite moment in the historic past) the manifested glory of the Incarnate Word" (Bernard I:21).

"His glory" (Greek *doxa*) must be understood in terms of the previous reference to the Tabernacle. Just as the Shekinah glory of God was present within the Tabernacle, so there is a "glory" about Jesus. It is not a visible manifestation but an obvious majesty of character and spirit that is apparent to all who come to know Him. It is, in fact, such a majestic glory as to be entirely compatible with one who sustains an absolutely unique connection with the Father. Though Jesus lives in very humble circumstances, John gives his readers to understand that there is an inherent splendor about Him that is entirely consistent with the idea that He is the Word Incarnate, the Son of God. Apparently there is here also an echo of the Transfiguration where John will see Christ's heavenly glory.

(The incidental similarity between the Greek *skenao*, "to dwell," and the Hebrew *shekinah*, "that which dwells," would serve to reenforce the analogy between Christ and the Tabernacle in the mind of a bilingual Jew of the first century.)

The word translated "only begotten" (Greek *monogenes*) is a compound of the noun meaning "kind" or "genus" (Greek *genos*) rather than the verb "born" (Greek *gennao*). It therefore literally means "of a single kind" rather than "only begotten." Verse 13 has already referred to others who are begotten/born by God. Here John means to emphasize the deity of Christ, God's Son in a *unique* sense. *He* is God's Son in a way that no one else is God's Son.

"Although *genos* is distantly related to *gennan*, 'to beget,' there is little Greek justification for the translation of *monogenes* as 'only begotten.' The Old Latin correctly translated it as *unicus*, 'only,' and so did Jerome where it was not applied to Jesus. But to answer the Arian claim that Jesus was not begotten but made, Jerome translated it as *unigenitus*, 'only begotten' in passages like this one (also 1:18; 3:16,18). The influence of the Vulgate on the KJ made 'only begotten' the standard English rendition....*Monogenes* describes a quality of Jesus, his uniqueness, not what is called in Trinitarian theology his 'procession.' It reflects the Hebrew *yahid* 'only, precious,' which is used in Gen. 22:2,12,16 of Abraham's son Isaac, as *monogenes* is used of Isaac in Heb. 11:17. Isaac was Abraham's uniquely precious son, but not his only begotten" (Brown I:13,14).

Jesus is "of a single kind" with the Father. He is uniquely like the Father. He bears a unique relationship to the Father. His glory is entirely appropriate to this unique status and position. This phrase conveys the same basic truth as 10:30 where Jesus says, "I and *my* Father are one."

The last phrase, "full of grace and truth," refers to Jesus. It appears that these particular qualities are mentioned at this point because of another O.T. analogy. In Ex. 34:5,6 these qualities are mentioned as characteristic of God in connection with an appearance of His glory to Moses. Also in Ps. 85:9,10 mercy and truth are mentioned in close proximity with God's glory. So, as the glory of Jesus is revealed, these qualities are mentioned as being characteristic of Him. It is as "the life" that Christ is full of grace and as "the light" that He is full of truth. He is the only source of both life and light, grace and truth for mankind. He is "the way, the truth and the life" (14:6); no man may come to God but through Him.

15 John bare witness of him, and cried, saying, This was he of whom I spake, He that cometh after me is preferred before me: for he was before me.

"Bare witness" (Greek present tense *marturei*) and "cried" (Greek *kekragen*, a perfect tense with the force of a present) are not to be taken simply as historic presents (i.e. merely using the present tense to refer to the past) but as referring to the Baptist's action as still going on at the time of writing. To John, the Baptist is still speaking, still giving his witness, even though long dead (see Morris).

In quoting the Baptist, John uses the past tense (Greek imperfect) "was" when it would have been natural to expect another present. This serves to heighten the impact of the present tenses in the first part of the verse, and it also seems purposely to emphasize the past nature of the Baptist's words. Apparently John is here revealing his intimate knowledge of the thoughts of the Baptist who had first spoken these words before he knew the identity of the Messiah. Here the Baptist explains (and John preserves) the nature of his relationship to Christ in its earliest form (see Westcott, Bernard).

In the last part of the verse there is another of those subtle shifts of meaning. This time it involves a shift in the meanings of the prepositions, "after" (Greek *opiso*), "before" (Greek *emprosthen*), and "before" (Greek *protos*). The

Baptist says that the one coming "behind" him or "after" him in point of time is actually "before" him in terms of rank or importance. The irony is that the one "behind" is really the one "before." Yet there is an even greater irony. The one "behind" (in point of time) is "before" (in terms of importance) because He actually is "before" (in point of time). Jesus actually predates the Baptist. He is the Word who has been from all eternity.

Some have supposed that the Baptist could not know the truth of Christ's preincarnate existence and that John himself formulates this statement and places it into the Baptist's mouth (Bernard, Brown). This is a rather arbitrary assumption grounded in the liberal theory of a gradual development of Christian doctrine. There is no inherent reason for believing the Baptist to be ignorant of Christ's true identity and nature. Surely Elisabeth told him something of the circumstances of his own birth and that of her cousin Mary's son as well (Lk. 1). Since the form of this verse is so uniquely Johannine, it seems reasonable to attribute its final form to the apostle. But the thought it conveys is clearly that of the Baptist.

16 And of his fulness have all we received, and grace for grace.

In the best manuscripts (those most highly regarded by the textual specialists) the first word is a conjunction (Greek *hoti*) which means "for" or "because" rather than simply "and" (Greek *kai*). Thus, this verse helps to explain how it can be known that Jesus is the eternal "Word." Not only does the testimony of the eyewitnesses (v. 14) and John the Baptist (v. 15) reveal this to be true, but so also does the experience of the church. "We" here refers to John and his readers, thus, the church (see comments v. 14).

"Fulness" (Greek *pleroma*) refers

back to "full" (Greek *pleres*) in v. 14. The fullness of v. 14 was of "grace and truth." These two qualities are still implicit in "fulness" here. "Grace" is in focus in this verse, both "grace" and "truth" in v. 17 and "truth" in v. 18. It also seems likely that John means to include the Pauline idea of "fulness" (Col.1:19; 2:9) as the plenitude and full measure of all the divine powers and graces which are concentrated absolutely in Christ, the Incarnate Word (see Westcott).

Every Christian has "received" (Greek culminative aorist indicating a completed process) "out of" (Greek *ek*) Christ's inexhaustible abundance of divine virtue, an absolutely sufficient provision for his every need. The first aspect of this provision is "grace" (Greek *charis*), the quality of unrestrained magnanimity of spirit to which, in its purest form, only God can aspire. There is an obvious emphasis upon this quality that is indicated by the rather difficult phrase, "grace for (Greek *anti*) grace." This phrase can be understood in the sense of grace after grace or grace upon grace, the implication being that each blessing appropriated becomes the basis for greater blessing (see Westcott). Godet believes that John anticipates here his reference to the law in v. 17 and wishes to exclude it absolutely from the process of grace.

17 For the law was given by Moses, *but* grace and truth came by Jesus Christ.

"For" (Greek *hoti*) again indicates that what follows is intended to explain what has gone before. Christians receive God's fullness and grace (v. 16) because, while the law which condemns men was given long before by God through Moses, grace and truth, which redeem them, were not available until they "came into existence" (Greek *ginomai*)

"through" (Greek *dia* for agency; see v. 3) Jesus Christ. Truth is paired with grace because the full truth of God's character was not revealed until the quality of grace came to be manifested in Christ. While grace and truth did exist before Christ came, they actually did so only in anticipation of Him. Jesus Christ is as exclusively the ground and channel of grace and truth as He is the agent of creation (v. 3), the only true light (v. 9), or the only one uniquely like the Father (v. 14).

Jesus Christ is actually named here for the first time. It becomes absolutely certain that the "Word" is Jesus Christ. The majestic figure whom John has described so beautifully is the God-man, John's closest friend, Jesus Christ.

18 No man hath seen God at any time; the only begotten Son, which is in the bosom of the Father, he hath declared *him*.

In the Greek, "God" (*theos*) is placed first for emphasis, as in the last clause of v. 1. Also as in that clause it has no article, thus stressing the quality of God's nature rather than His person. Attention is focused upon "the Deity": The Deity—that is something no one has ever seen. "Nobody" (Greek *oudeis*)—by inference not even Moses (v. 17)—has "ever" (Greek *popote*) really seen the Deity. Moses (Ex. 33:18-23) and others (e.g. Is. 6:1,5) saw certain manifestations of His glory, but not His essential nature. It remains for some being other than a mere man to convey the true essence of the Deity to mankind. The climax of the prologue consists of the revelation that the "Word," Jesus Christ, is precisely such a person accomplishing precisely this function.

For "only begotten" as meaning unique, the only one of a kind, see the comments on v. 14. Here, many important manuscripts read "the unique God"

(Greek *monogenes theos*) rather than "the unique Son" (Greek *monogenes huios*). If this is correct (and the textual evidence is very strong), Jesus is thereby ideally suited to the role of revealing God to men. He is absolutely unique. He is, although a man, actually God. "For man to have any direct knowledge of God as God, [he must] ...come to know Him only through One who shares both the human and divine natures, and who is in vital fellowship with both God and man" (Westcott I:27). This reading is also supported by the fact that in referring to Jesus as God, it is reaffirming the very pivotal assertion of the third clause of v. 1. It would be fitting for John to incorporate the climactic truth of his initial statement into the final climax of the prologue.

Not only is Jesus Himself uniquely God, He enjoys an especially close relationship to the Father. He is "in the bosom of the Father." This expression conveys the idea of a place of special favor such as John occupied at the last supper (13:23). It expresses a relationship of intimacy and love between Christ and the Father. Constant reference is made to Christ's awareness of such a relationship between the Father and Himself (e.g. 5:17; 10:30; 17:1ff.).

This unique person, Jesus Christ, has "declared" (Greek *exegeomai*, from which the English word "exegesis") the nature of God. The object of the verb is not given and must be logically supplied. This word originally meant "to tell or narrate" but came to mean "expound or fully explain." Jesus, since He is Himself God, is able to explain to men the ultimate truth—the essential nature and being of their Creator. He communicates all that there is to know of God through His own personality. As He says to Philip, "He that hath seen me hath seen the Father" (14:9).

This marks the climax of the prologue. John has brought his readers to the point from which he wants to launch his narrative. He has established the context in which he wishes the events of the life of Christ to be understood. Every event in the record to follow will illustrate and explain the seminal themes of this prologue.

Summary
(1:14-18)

Christ, who always simply was, now becomes something new: flesh. He becomes completely human yet never ceases to be God. As the O.T. Jehovah dwelled in a hand-made tabernacle, so He dwells among men in a tabernacle of flesh, revealing to all who will see the glory and fullness of God which He possesses by virtue of His unique likeness with the Father. His unique status is affirmed as John the Baptist acknowledges His absolute superiority. It is confirmed by the church's experience of His grace. It is further demonstrated by His inherent superiority to Moses. Moses was used by God to give the law, but grace and truth come to be only in Christ. Finally, it is revealed in the fact that, unlike mere humans who know God hardly at all, He, because of His intimate relationship with Him, is able to communicate to men all that God is.

Application: Teaching and Preaching the Passage

The central focus of this passage, the revelation of the God of Heaven in the person of Jesus Christ, can provide the answer to a very basic question, "What is God like?" God is like Jesus. Jesus is the ultimate object lesson, the ultimate anthropomorphic expression of the character of God. Jesus is God on a human plane, in human terms. Charles Wesley expressed this truth beautifully:

Veiled in flesh the Godhead see,
Hail the incarnate Deity.

Pleased as man with men to dwell,
   Jesus, our Immanuel.

It is most instructive to observe the relationship of the two basic aspects of Christ's revelation of God to men—grace and truth. Grace is the object and purpose of the revelation, in that man is to be redeemed from sin and restored to fellowship with God. Truth is the means by which this grace is to be communicated. The ultimate reality is God, and the ultimate truth is the knowledge and understanding of Him. Grace comes only by truth and Jesus is the truth. Therefore, both grace and truth come by Jesus Christ.

II. THE BOOK OF SIGNS—CHRIST REVEALED IN HIS LIFE (1:19—12:50)

A. The Testimony of John the Baptist (1:19-34)

In the context of the Gospel being presented as a courtroom trial, the prologue may be thought of as the opening statement. Now the Evangelist begins the formal presentation of his evidence; he calls, as his first witness, John the Baptist. He has already alluded to John's testimony in his opening statement; now it is actually going to be presented for the jury's (reader's) scrutiny.

1. As Given to the Deputation From Jerusalem (vv. 19-28)

**19 And this is the record of John, when the Jews sent priests and Levites from Jerusalem to ask him, Who art thou?
20 And he confessed, and denied not; but confessed, I am not the Christ.**

John the Baptist is not actually present, but the writer introduces, as it were, a deposition of his testimony, the accu-

racy of which he himself can certify, having been present to hear it given. Thus he assures his readers, "This is the testimony of John." He remembers the details very clearly. It was given when the Jews sent from Jerusalem an official delegation of priests and Levites to inquire of John as to his identity.

They put the question to him directly, "Who are you?" John understands that they are asking this in the context of the widespread speculation that the Messiah will soon come (cf. Lk. 2:38; Jn. 4:25; 7:26,31,40-42) and the great ministry that he is presently enjoying, so he replies, "I am not the Christ." The emphasis upon "I" is indicated by the use of the pronoun (Greek *ego*) in addition to the verb form "I am" (Greek *eimi*). It is also placed first in the clause. This emphasis indicates that while John is not the Messiah, the Messiah is near at hand.

The rather odd form of the phrase "answered, and denied not, but answered," indicates extreme solemnity. Brown (I:42) translates: "declared without any qualification, avowing." This conveys the sense very well.

The word "Christ" derives from the Greek (*christos*, the anointed one) and corresponds to "Messiah," which derives from the Hebrew (*mashiach*, the anointed one). The terms are doctrinally interchangeable. In the O.T., anointing was the rite of consecration for kings and priests. The Messiah was to be the anointed one, the great king and priest, the great personage who would establish God's kingdom perfectly upon earth.

21 And they asked him, What then? Art thou Elias? And he saith, I am not. Art thou that prophet? And he answered, No.

When John replies that he is not the Messiah, the delegation responds with another question, "Who, then, are you? Are you Elijah?" They move to eliminate other Messianic possibilities for John. If he is not actually the Messiah, then perhaps he is one of the other personages commonly expected to be revealed in connection with the Messiah. The first of these to come to mind is Elijah; on the basis of Mal. 4:5, it was believed that Elijah would return to earth in connection with Messiah's advent (Mt. 16:14; 17:10).

John's reply that he was not Elijah creates something of a problem for us, in light of Jesus' statements that he was (Mt. 17:11-13). There is a sense in which John was Elijah and a sense in which he was not. He was not Elijah in the sense that he was not that individual returned to earth. John's denial should be understood in this light. He was Elijah in the sense that he came "in the spirit and power of Elijah" and performed the role of Messiah's herald that Malachi predicted. There is an element of the paradoxical and esoteric involved in this identification; all are not intended to comprehend it. Certainly there is not any contradiction between John and the Synoptists or between Christ and the Baptist at this point (see Morris 135, note 18).

This answer provokes yet another question, "Are you the prophet?" There is clearly a note of antagonism in this. They do not really believe John to be either the Messiah or any of the Messianic personages. Rather, they are saying in effect, "By what right do you conduct your ministry? Are you the Messiah, Elijah, or the Prophet? If not, then why are you conducting yourself as though you were?" The Jews believed that others of the prophets in addition to Elijah would appear to herald the Messiah (Mt. 16:14; also 2 Esdras 2:17). "But more specific than this expectation of the return of one of the older prophets was the expectation of one who was preeminently 'the prophet,' whose coming was looked for on the basis of Deut. 18:15" (Bernard

I:37; see also 6:14; 7:40).

Again there is a paradoxical and esoteric tone in John's reply."No, I am not the prophet." He does not add that they are mistaken in differentiating between "the prophet" and the Messiah. He does not add that while he is not the prophet, the prophet is on the scene. Their question and his answer here underlie the whole conversation from v. 23 to v. 28.

22 Then said they unto him, Who art thou? that we may give an answer to them that sent us. What sayest thou of thyself?

The denials by John that he is either the Messiah, Elijah, or the Prophet prompt the delegation to inquire of him directly, "Then who are you?" His conduct and preaching, in themselves, constitute a claim to Messianic or eschatological significance. The delegation must have some sort of positive statement from him as to his identity so they press him, "Come now, we must have some answer to give to the authorities in Jerusalem. What do you say concerning yourself? If you are not any of the great Messianic personages, then what is the justification for your Messianic pretensions?" The underlying antagonism is obvious.

23 He said, I am the voice of one crying in the wilderness, Make straight the way of the Lord, as said the prophet Esaias.

John answers in effect, "If you wish to find me foretold among the oracles of the prophets (among the Messianic personages) you may identify me with the voice which calls for the preparation of a way for the Lord in the desert" (Bruce 48). The Synoptists (Mt. 3:3; Mk. 1:3; Lk. 3:4) all apply these words from Is. 40:3 to John. Here he applies them to himself. "The point of the quotation is that it gives no prominence to the preacher whatever. He is not an important person, like a prophet or the Messiah. He is no more than a voice...with but one thing to say...'Make straight the way of the Lord'" (Morris 137). "The Baptist's one desire is to be the 'voice of one calling...in the desert'" (Schnackenburg I:291). This agrees entirely with the Johannine presentation of the Baptist as essentially a "witness." That is precisely how the Baptist understood himself.

24 And they which were sent were of the Pharisees.

There is a minor textual question in this verse in that several manuscripts do not have an article with "having been sent," as would be expected. With the article the verse reads, "And the ones who had been sent were of the Pharisees." Without the article the meaning may be either "and they had been sent from/by the Pharisees," or "And (some) who had been sent were of the Pharisees." This last seems to be the best rendering on both textual evidence and logic. The entire delegation is not composed of Pharisees, neither is there a second delegation of Pharisees, but the one delegation is composed partially of Pharisees (see Bruce, Morris, Schnackenburg).

25 And they asked him, and said unto him, Why baptizest thou then, if thou be not that Christ, nor Elias, neither that prophet?

The Pharisees here give evidence of their preoccupation with ceremonial religious activities. They want to know about John's baptizing. Why, by what authority, does he baptize? Baptism was the regular rite of admitting converts from other religions to Judaism, representing the removal of the pollution of the Gentile culture. It was not difficult

for the Pharisees to understand why it should be applied to Gentile proselytes, but it seemed strange that it should be applied to Jews. Gentiles were obviously defiled and in need of cleansing, but not Jews (see Morris).

The only justification that the Pharisees could think of for baptizing Jews was as an eschatological sign of the Messiah's advent. They believed, on the basis of Is. 52:15; Ezek. 36:25; and Zech. 13:1, that Messiah and his heralds would baptize. However, by his own admission, John was not the Messiah, Elijah, or the Prophet. By what authority, then, did he baptize Jews? Note that John clearly attaches an eschatological significance to his baptism (Mt. 3:5-12).

26 John answered them, saying, I baptize with water: but there standeth one among you, whom ye know not.

As usual, John directs attention away from himself to Christ. His reply, however, is quite awesome in its implication. "You are right about my baptism," he says. "Even though I am not the Messiah, I baptize because the Messianic advent is upon us, because the Messiah himself now stands in your midst." Some believe that Jesus was actually standing in the crowd as John spoke (see Godet, Bernard). John's baptism is presented in the limited context of a witness to Christ's coming although its meaning as a sign of repentance (Mt. 3:11; Mk. 1:4; Lk. 3:3) is clearly presupposed.

There is an implied contrast between John's knowledge of the Messiah and the Pharisees' total ignorance on the point. The emphatic use of "I" and "you" (Greek ego and humeis) point up this contrast. "I baptize because I know that Messiah is present. You, on the other hand, do not know Him even though He stands at this moment among you." His words "are heavy with foreboding: the divine revelation is not given them, and they also lack readiness to receive it. They are not just ignorant for the moment. They are profoundly estranged" (Schnackenburg I:294).

27 He it is, who coming after me is preferred before me, whose shoe's latchet I am not worthy to unloose.

John again makes a veiled reference to Christ as "the one coming after me" (1:15). He emphasizes the rank of this mysterious personage by means of a comparison. He says that he, John, is not worthy to loosen the strap of the Great One's sandal. There was a saying current among the Jews that a disciple should be willing to perform every service for his teacher that a slave would for his master except the loosing of his sandal thong (see Morris). Even if this particular saying is not in John's mind, it is an indication of the extremely menial nature of the task in the mentality of the time.

While the language is very similar to that attributed to him in the synoptics (Mt. 3:11; Mk. 1:7; Lk. 3:16), John's words here have an ominous ring not sensed there. It is as though John is warning the Pharisees that the Personage he heralds is of such rank and importance that failure to recognize and acknowledge Him is a very serious offense. On this rather negative and confrontational note, the interview is terminated. There is no indication of any meeting of the minds between John and the Pharisees.

28 These things were done in Bethabara beyond Jordan, where John was baptizing.

The section closes with a geographical note. This certainly supports the idea

that the writer considers himself to be giving literal, historical information. In addition, "The concluding remark makes John's testimony read almost like an affidavit" (Schnackenburg I:295). This conforms to the analogy of the courtroom presentation of evidence mentioned above.

There is uncertainty about the location identified in this verse. The majority of the Greek manuscripts have "Bethany beyond the Jordan" rather than "Bethabara beyond the Jordan." If Bethany is correct, the qualification "beyond the Jordan" serves to distinguish this from the well-known Bethany near Jerusalem. (It is interesting that John qualifies his references to that other Bethany as well: 11:1,18; 12:1.) Whether "Bethany" or "Bethabara," the site cannot be identified for sure.

Summary
(1:19-28)

The writer opens his narrative with the testimony of John the Baptist. He tells of an official delegation sent from Jerusalem to get from the Baptist's own mouth a statement as to his identity. John states without hesitation that he is not the Messiah, Elijah, or the Prophet. When pressed to identify himself, he admits only to being a voice crying, "Prepare in the desert the highway of the Lord." He agrees only that he is a witness, a herald of the Messiah. When asked by the Pharisees why he baptizes, he replies, in essence, that he baptizes as a testimony to the imminent advent of the Messiah, that his baptizing is primarily an aspect of his essential function of witness. He draws attention to the extreme majesty of the Messiah by means of a comparison with himself and leaves his hearers the ominous implication that failure to respond to Him properly will have frightening consequences. The writer closes the section with a geographical specification, as if to certify the validity of the testimony that has been given.

Application: Teaching and Preaching the Passage

John the Baptist's essential function of witness is the underlying theme of this section. He utilized an inquiry about himself as an occasion for bearing witness to Christ. He gave his witness to an essentially hostile and skeptical delegation of Jewish officials. One might treat this passage under the following headings: (1) Who John wasn't (vv. 19-21). (2) What John was (vv. 22,23). (3) Why John baptized (vv. 24-27). He was not the Christ, Elijah, or the Prophet. He was but one thing: a voice, a witness to the advent of Messiah. He baptized not only to symbolize repentance and cleansing but as a testimony to Israel of its own sinfulness and to the imminence of the Messianic age. Even his baptizing was an aspect of his function as a witness to the identity and excellence of Jesus Christ.

2. As Given Publicly the Next Day (vv. 29-34)

29 The next day John seeth Jesus coming unto him, and saith, Behold the Lamb of God, which taketh away the sin of the world.

On "the next day" after the confrontation with the deputation from Jerusalem, John sees Jesus coming toward him. Jesus has been baptized earlier by John (vv. 32-34), has gone into the wilderness to be tempted (Mt. 4:1; Mk.1:12; Lk. 4:1), and has now returned to the Jordan where John is baptizing, apparently for the purpose of receiving just such an endorsement from John as is forthcoming.

John has previously spoken only of the greatness and imminence of the Messiah; now he identifies Him as a particular individual. He does so by means of a solemn and mysterious pronouncement, "Behold the Lamb of God." There is disagreement as to the exact significance of the term "Lamb" (Greek *amnos*) which John intends. Several possibilities exist: (1) The apocalyptic lamb who will judge the world and destroy evil. Such an interpretation would fit in well with aspects of John's message (Mt. 3:7-12). Such a lamb is referred to in the Revelation (e.g. 6:16,17; 14:10; 17:14); however, the word translated "lamb" there is different (Greek *arnion* rather than *amnos*). (2) The pascal lamb of the Passover. (3) The lamb of Is. 53 where the Suffering Servant is referred to as "a lamb [brought] to the slaughter." (4) As the substitutionary lamb that God was to provide for Abraham (Gen. 22:8).

Morris (147,148) seems to have the correct view when he says that none of these views totally explains John's usage: "He is making a general allusion to sacrifice. The lamb figure may well be intended to be composite, evoking memories of several, perhaps all [of these ideas]." The article "the" before lamb may have the same force as with "the Prophet." If so, it would indicate that "the lamb" was a specialized term then in use among the Jews and would be understood by them as referring to a specific apocalyptic figure.

Some would hold that the Baptist only intended to convey the apocalyptic idea and that it is the Evangelist who intends to convey the idea of a substitutionary sacrifice. They would say that the Baptist could not possibly anticipate Christ's substitutionary death for sinners. This view cannot be correct if the words "which taketh away the sin of the world" were actually spoken by the Baptist. It is very possible that he had been given such an understanding of the One of whom he was the herald. Certainly he is portrayed as having specialized knowledge of the "one coming after (him)."

The phrase "of God" (Greek genitive) suggests both possession and origin. The lamb belongs to and is provided by God. Notice that it is "sin" in its totality rather than "sins" severally that the lamb takes away or removes (Greek *airo*), the sin not just of John's converts or the Jews alone, but of the "world." The universal note struck here is heard often in this Gospel (3:16f.; 4:42; 6:51; see Bruce).

30 This is he of whom I said, After me cometh a man which is preferred before me: for he was before me.

The Baptist, having designated Jesus as the Lamb of God, now proceeds to identify Him with the great personage whom he has been sent to herald and upon whom his message has been focused from the very beginning. He says, in effect, "This is the one I have been talking about." There is some debate as to exactly which of his own past statements John means. The best explanation seems to be that John has said *many* times that one is coming after him who is greater than he and who was actually prior to him in point of time. The teaching is stated in its fullest summary form here and in the prologue (1:15). In 1:27 and in the synoptics (e.g. Mt. 3:11), the reference is only to "the one coming after" with nothing said about the fact that He was prior in point of time. This should be understood as a synecdoche, a figure of speech in which a part is taken for the whole. As to the possibility that John comprehended Christ's pre-existence, see comments 1:15.

31 And I knew him not: but that he should be made manifest to Israel, therefore am I come baptizing with water.

John explains to his hearers, "Even I did not know Him (at first)." By this John does not mean that he had no acquaintance with Christ at all, but that he did not recognize Him as the Messiah. (Luke presents John as Jesus' distant cousin.) By the same token, John's reluctance to baptize Jesus (Mt. 3:14) does not of necessity imply that he knew Jesus to be the Messiah at that point, only that he recognized in Him a person superior to himself.

It is not really surprising that John was ignorant of the Messiah's identity early on. It was precisely that ignorance which his baptizing ministry was intended by God to remedy. He had come baptizing for the express purpose of revealing Messiah. It is interesting that the apocalyptic act which symbolically revealed the Messiah to Israel, revealed Him literally to John himself. As he baptized, he revealed Messiah to Israel and to himself as well. In the subsequent verses John will relate that particular baptism which is to be the quintessential revelation of Messiah.

32 And John bare record, saying, I saw the Spirit descending from heaven like a dove, and it abode upon him.

The entire ministry of John the Baptist as witness to the Messiah (see comments 1:7) reaches its climax in this verse and the two that follow (see Godet). One should again note the solemnity and the courtroom format. This is the most critical point of the Baptist's testimony. The reader (juror) should listen very carefully. The testimony begins.

John states that he, himself, actually "saw" (Greek *theaomai*) with the physical eyes the (Holy) Spirit descend and remain upon Jesus. This sentence is thought by the Evangelist to prove incontrovertibly that Jesus is the Messiah. The coming of the Holy Spirit upon Him is a clear-cut indication of this (Is. 11:1; 42:1; 66:1). Put together with the fact that no one less than John the Baptist has seen it and so interpreted it, this constitutes in the Evangelist's (and the Baptist's) view an air-tight case. The Baptist testifies categorically that he has no doubt whatever that Jesus is the Messiah.

The tense of the verb "remained" (Greek aorist *meno*) may very well have both a constative and an ingressive quality. In the constative sense it calls attention to the fact that "the Spirit came to the prophets only from time to time, but with Jesus it remains unchangeably" (Westcott I:44). In the ingressive sense it emphasizes that the Spirit first came upon Jesus at this time and remained upon Him for the rest of His ministry (Morris).

33 And I knew him not: but he that sent me to baptize with water, the same said unto me, Upon whom thou shalt see the Spirit descending, and remaining on him, the same is he which baptizeth with the Holy Ghost.

John again states that he has not always known the Messiah's identity. He has explained in v. 32 the event which revealed that identity to him. Now he explains that he had been given a supernatural revelation from God which enabled him to make his identification. God had revealed to him that the one upon whom he would see the Spirit descending and remaining was the Messiah. This revelation may have come as John reflected upon such passages as Is. 11:1; 42:1; and 66:1. When John saw "the Spirit descending as a dove," he realized that this was the sign he had

been told to expect.

Everything became very plain. The one upon whom the Spirit descended and remained would, in turn, be the one who would baptize with the Spirit. The Spirit was upon Him that He might impart the Spirit to others. Here may be seen the primary contrast between the ministry of the Baptist and that of Jesus. The first was in water, the second is in the Holy Spirit. John's baptism in water was only a figure of the true baptism of the Spirit (see Bernard). John's "baptism in water [has] essentially a negative significance. It [is] a cleansing from. But [Christ's] baptism with the Spirit is positive. It is a bestowal of new life in God" (Morris 153).

34 And I saw, and bare record that this is the Son of God.

The Baptist concludes his testimony with a solemn affirmation: "And I saw and have given testimony that this one (this man Jesus) is the Son of God." One would expect "Messiah" here but instead encounters a new phrase (see comments 1:18), "the Son of God." This term was used of the Messiah in the O.T. (Ps. 2:7,12; 89:27) and was apparently used in this way by the Jews (1:49; 11:22), but it is also a clear reference to the actual deity of Christ (5:18). So the climax of the Baptist's testimony is that Jesus is the Son of God. This conforms to the writer's purpose for his Gospel as stated in 20:31. He wants his readers to believe that Jesus is the Christ, the Son of God.

Summary
(1:29-34)

The narrative continues by relating another occasion when John the Baptist witnessed to Christ. On this occasion John specifically identified the man Jesus as the Messiah. He referred to Jesus as the Lamb of God, thus emphasizing both His apocalyptical identity and His substitutionary sacrifice for sin. He assured his hearers that this man Jesus is in fact the great Messiah. He admitted that even he did not realize His identity at first, but that God had revealed it to him by means of a precisely defined sign. On the basis of this sign, he was prepared to state unequivocally that Jesus is the Messiah, the Son of God.

Application: Teaching and Preaching the Passage

John's statement in v. 29 summarizes this entire section and could very well be the basis for a textual message on Christ. One could emphasize His essential identity and function as the Lamb, His heavenly origin as the Lamb of God and His practical impact in taking away the sin of the world.

One could also deal with the whole passage using the following headings: I. An incomplete revelation (v. 31). While John knew that the Messiah was at hand, he did not know His actual identity. II. An unusual sign (v. 33). John was informed by God of a unique means by which this knowledge would be communicated to him. III. An unmistakable event (vv. 32,34a). John actually saw this sign literally fufilled. IV. An unequivocal witness (vv. 29,34b). John had no hesitation whatever in proclaiming that Jesus was the heavenly personage that he had been sent to herald.

It is interesting that John came to understand the truth fully only as he obediently complied with the truth that he did understand. As he obeyed the command to baptize, his uncertainties were dispelled.

B. The Testimony of the First Disciples (1:35-51)

**35 Again the next day after John stood, and two of his disciples;
36 And looking upon Jesus as he walked, he saith, Behold the Lamb of God!
37 And the two disciples heard him speak, and they followed Jesus.**

One day later in the time sequence, that is, the second day after the confrontation between the Baptist and the Jerusalem delegation, John stands with two of his disciples (perhaps discussing the events of the previous two days). As he observes Jesus walking around (Greek *peripateo*), he says to the two, "Behold the Lamb of God." This is not mere repetition. John means to imply much more than his words might indicate. He is saying, "He (not I) is the Lamb of God. He is the Great One whom God has sent into the world. It is He who takes away sin. It is He that you must follow." That John was so understood is apparent in the action of the two disciples: they followed (Greek *akoloutheo*) Jesus. The tense of this verb seems to indicate that they begin to follow Christ from this moment on (Greek ingressive aorist).

At the beginning of v. 35 John is standing with two of his disciples. At the end of v. 37 Jesus is being followed by two of His disciples. This is John's ministry in microcosm, pointing men away from himself to Christ.

This episode is not incompatible with the synoptic account of the call of the apostles (Mt. 4:18-22; Mk. 1:16-20; Lk. 5:1-11) which seems to presuppose earlier contact between them and Jesus, while this account does not preclude some more absolute commitment at a later time (see Schnackenburg). John "tells of a call to be disciples; the Synoptists of a call to be Apostles" (Morris 155).

38 Then Jesus turned, and saw

them following, and saith unto them, What seek ye? They said unto him, Rabbi, (which is to say, being interpreted, Master,) where dwellest thou?
39 He saith unto them, Come and see. They came and saw where he dwelt, and abode with him that day: for it was about the tenth hour.

Jesus does not allow the two disciples to follow unnoticed (see Westcott). He turns about and as He looks upon them (Greek *theaomai*; a circumstantial rather than a temporal participle) says, "What are you looking for?" His question, intended rather to encourage than confront, elicits the rather awkward yet utterly sincere response, "Rabbi, where are you abiding?" Their use of "Rabbi" seems to indicate their awareness that they are no longer the disciples of John, but of this Great One, this stranger to whom their former master has directed them. They do not know exactly what they want. They only know that whatever it is, it is to be found in Him. In effect they are saying, "Sir, we have been sent to follow you, but we do not fully understand why. We don't know exactly what to say." Jesus does not leave them hanging. He answers with an utter graciousness that completely allays their apprehensions: "Come and see."

Very likely, one of these two disciples is the Apostle John. This fits his pattern of indirect reference to himself (see Introduction; also Westcott, Brown, and Bernard). If this is the case, John is giving his own first-hand account of his first encounter with Jesus. He remembers it perfectly. They went with Jesus. It was about the tenth hour, i.e. the tenth hour of the day or 4 p.m. (see also v. 40 and 19:14). They saw His "lodgings." Perhaps there is a note of nostalgia, tenderness, even humor in this recollection of His "lodgings." In light of Mt. 8:20 they

were quite likely very meager, perhaps only a cave and a campfire. Yet what a wonderful afternoon and evening it must have been as the disciples sat talking with Jesus.

It should be noted that here and in vv. 41,42 the apostle translates the original Aramaic into Greek for the benefit of his Gentile readers. He is writing in Greek but he remembers in Aramaic.

40 One of the two which heard John *speak*, and followed him, was Andrew, Simon Peter's brother.
41 He first findeth his own brother Simon, and saith unto him, We have found the Messias, which is, being interpreted, the Christ.

The other of the two disciples who have followed Christ at the Baptist's instruction is Andrew, Simon Peter's brother. While he is to be an apostle in his own right, he is always to be remembered as "Simon's brother." Sometime during the evening, Andrew is so impressed with what he hears that he wants Simon to hear it also. So he goes and finds him. The supposed problem with all these events transpiring after 4 p.m. can be eliminated either by inserting an extra day into the time before v. 43 or by making "the tenth hour" of v. 39 mean 10 a.m. (see Plummer on this verse and 19:14). Either way, there is no real problem with 4 p.m. (see Bruce on v. 43).

Andrew's words to Simon are absolutely momentous, "We have found the Messiah." While Andrew may not fully understand all of the implications of Jesus' identity, he clearly does not intend to convey something merely mundane or conventional. By "Messiah" he means the expected "King of Israel" and "Great One." The mood of Messianic awareness and expectation among the Jews generally, as well as the specialized insight provided by the Baptist, explain how Andrew could use the term "Messiah" knowingly.

42 And he brought him to Jesus. And when Jesus beheld him, he said, Thou art Simon the son of Jona: thou shalt be called Cephas, which is by interpretation, A stone.

Andrew brings Peter to Jesus. Mere words about Him are insufficient. Jesus must be encountered to be comprehended. Jesus looks fixedly and knowingly (Greek *emblepo*) upon Peter (see Brown, Godet) and gives a penetrating analysis of his personality both as it is and as it will later be. He is now Simon, the namesake of the Patriarch Simeon who had rashly and ruthlessly avenged the violation of his sister, Dinah. This is an accurate characterization of Peter's volatile and impulsive personality. He will later become by God's grace a great rock of steadfastness upon which the church will be founded (see Tenney).

Jesus' insight regarding Peter should be understood as essentially supernatural rather than merely intuitive. His action, like that involving Nathanael in subsequent verses, clearly involves supernatural insight. Jesus' supernatural being and powers as the Messiah are clearly in focus here (see Schnackenburg).

43 The day following Jesus would go forth into Galilee, and findeth Philip, and saith unto him, Follow me.
44 Now Philip was of Bethsaida, the city of Andrew and Peter.

On the next day, the third (or fourth: see the comment on vv. 40,41) day after the confrontation between John and the Jerusalem delegation, Jesus decides to leave the area where John is baptizing and return to His home area, Galilee. This decision is apparently occasioned by the fact that Jesus' immediate purpose in Judea (to receive John's endorsement and to recruit His first disciples from among those of John) is now accomplished. It is altogether natural for Him to return to Galilee. This action is rendered all the more feasible by the fact that the new disciples are also Galileans.

On that same day, under unspecified circumstances, Jesus finds another disciple, Philip. The verb (Greek *heurisko*) is the same one used for Andrew's finding Simon and Philip's finding Nathanael. It seems to indicate a purposeful search on Christ's part rather than an accidental encounter. Perhaps His three new disciples have told Jesus of Philip and have asked Him to find him before leaving the area. At any rate, Jesus finds Philip and issues the simple command, "Follow me." Philip, like many after him, finds this challenge utterly compelling. He is overwhelmed by the sheer force of Jesus' personality. That Philip complies is not stated but assumed; the next statement is simply that the newest disciple's hometown was Bethsaida ("Fishertown") in Galilee.

Subsequent references to Philip (6:7; 12:21f.; 14:8f.; the synoptics only list him among the apostles) do not indicate that he was among the greatest of the apostles. Morris says that he always appears to be somewhat out of his depth and of very limited ability. Yet Jesus "went out of His way to find this perfectly ordinary Philip and to enlist him in the apostolic band" (Morris 162).

45 Philip findeth Nathanael, and saith unto him, We have found him, of whom Moses in the law, and the prophets, did write, Jesus of Nazareth, the son of Joseph.

Just as Andrew must share his discovery of Christ with his brother Simon, so Philip must share Him with his friend Nathanael. There is disagreement as to the identity of Nathanael. Some identify him with Matthew, some with Simon the Cananaean, while others believe him to be a disciple who is not one of the twelve. (Still others, without warrant, believe him to be merely a symbolic representation of Israel and not a real person at all.) An interesting possibility is that he

...is to be identified with Bartholomew, an apostle who is never mentioned in John, just as Nathanael is never mentioned in the Synoptists. Bartholomew is coupled with Philip in all three Synoptists (Mt. 10:3; Mark 3:18; Luke 6:14), while another link is that he is mentioned immediately after Thomas in Acts 1:13 and Nathanael is in the same position in John 21:2. Moreover Bartholomew is not really a personal name, but a patronymic meaning 'son of Tolmai' (cf. Barjona = 'son of Jona'). The man who bore it almost certainly had another name (Morris 164).

Since all the rest of these early disciples later became apostles, even "ordinary Philip," it is reasonable to suppose that Nathanael did so as well and that he is to be identified with Bartholomew.

Philip's use of the pronoun "we" indicates that he already considers himself to be one of Christ's disciples. Philip says, "We have found him of whom Moses in the Law and the prophets wrote." This evidently refers to Dt. 18:15 and is equivalent to calling Jesus the Messiah. Philip assumes Nathanael's awareness of the Messianic implications of the O.T. and expectation of Messiah's appearance (see Schnackenburg).

Philip refers to the one he has found as "Jesus the son of Joseph, from Nazareth."

This must not be taken as a denial of the Virgin Birth. Joseph was the legal father of Jesus, and the Lord would accordingly be known as Joseph's son. In any case it is unlikely that the Virgin Birth would have been already communicated to such a new disciple as Philip. This is a good example of 'the irony of St. John.' Again and again he allows his characters to state, without refutation, ideas which Christian people would know to be false (Morris 165).

46 And Nathanael said unto him, Can there any good thing come out of Nazareth? Philip saith unto him, Come and see.

There are two ways to take Nathanael's reply, "Can anything good come from Nazareth?" The usual view has been to suppose that he speaks with incredulity and sarcasm, much like some other Jews in 7:41 and 51, that he is expressing the conventional wisdom of the time that Christ could not possibly come from anywhere but Bethlehem. To this may be added a note of provincial prejudice and jealousy toward a rival village, it being stated in 21:2 that Nathanael was from the village of Cana which is only a few miles from Nazareth. Another possibility is that Nathanael, being so familiar with Nazareth, is asking himself the question, "Could it actually be that the Messiah will come from Nazareth, so near my own home? Is that possible?"

Philip does not attempt to convince him by argumentation. He knows that once Nathanael meets Jesus any doubts will be dispelled. The reply is very simple, "Come and see."

47 Jesus saw Nathanael coming to him, and saith of him, Behold an Israelite indeed, in whom is no

guile!

Again as in v.42, "Jesus shows that he is possessed of supernatural knowledge" (Schnackenburg I:316). He is the searcher of hearts (Plummer). Nathanael is a true Israelite in whom there is none of the spirit of Jacob (the deceiver, the one full of guile). The contrast is not between two stages of Nathanael's life (as it was with Simon), but between the two stages of the patriarch Jacob's life and his two names. This is the only use of the term "Israelite" in the Gospel of John, and one must suppose that it is used purposely. Nathanael is a true Israelite in that he is without pretense or hypocrisy.

48 Nathanael saith unto him, Whence knowest thou me? Jesus answered and said unto him, Before that Philip called thee, when thou wast under the fig tree, I saw thee.

Some believe that Nathanael was convinced by Jesus' answer that He was the Messiah, that Jesus' specialized knowledge of his personality convinced him. This is unlikely, however. Jesus' remarks were of a very general nature and do not necessarily indicate supernatural insight. Furthermore, such an assumption is psychologically unlikely in a person like Nathanael. He would not be likely to think, "This man must be the Messiah since he has so accurately described my superior qualities." Nathanael replies very soberly and carefully to Jesus' compliment, "How do you know me, how are you able to make such statements about a person's inner being, assuming that I am such a wonderful person as you say?" He is, at this point, intrigued but not convinced. His objective, restrained skepticism is still intact.

It is Jesus' next answer that clearly indicates His supernatural insight and overwhelms Nathanael's skepticism (this is made explicitly clear in v. 50). He says to Nathanael, "Before Philip called you, while you were under the fig tree, I saw you." The precise nature of the experience to which Christ refers is not clear. Perhaps Nathanael recently had some particularly meaningful religious experience or spiritual insight while studying the Scripture. Whatever, it is very clear to Philip. It convinces him instantaneously and overwhelmingly of Christ's supernatural identity.

49 Nathanael answered and saith unto him, Rabbi, thou art the Son of God; thou art the King of Israel.

Nathanael now addresses Jesus as Rabbi whereas previously he has not. However, his use of this term of respect is rendered almost irrelevant by the much more glorious titles which he proceeds to confer upon Him, "Rabbi, you are the Son of God, you are the King of Israel." These titles apparently come from Ps. 2:6,7. For the significance of "Son of God" see v. 34. While Nathanael does not fully comprehend at this early point all that is involved in the term, he clearly means by it to ascribe a supernatural and Messianic identity to Jesus.

"King of Israel" is an unusual expression. In the New Testament it is used, apart from this passage, three times only. In Mt. 27:42 Jesus is saluted as "King of Israel" and invited to come down from the cross (so that Nathanael uses sincerely at the beginning of Jesus' ministry a title which is to recur in mockery at the very end!). In Mk. 15:32 "the Christ" and "the King of Israel" are almost synonyms. Finally in Jn. 12:13 at the triumphal entry Jesus is hailed in these words by the multitude. In the O.T. God is the King of His people, and it is clear that in the intervening period the Messiah came to be thought of as exercising the divine prerogative of rule. Nathanael is speaking in the highest terms open to him.... Nor should we overlook the fact that Nathanael has just been called "an Israelite." In calling Jesus "the King of Israel" he is acknowledging Jesus to be his own King (Morris 168).

While Nathanael is an "Israelite indeed," Jesus is "King of the Israelites."

50 Jesus answered and said unto him, Because I said unto thee, I saw thee under the fig tree, believest thou? thou shalt see greater things than these.

Jesus indicates here that it was His statement about the fig tree rather than His designation of Nathanael as "an Israelite indeed" that caused him to believe. He tells him that he is going to see in the future much more convincing evidence than this. He is setting the stage for the miracle that is soon to occur in Nathanael's hometown of Cana and, indeed, for all the miracles that He will perform throughout this "Book of Signs."

51 And he saith unto him, Verily, verily, I say unto you, Hereafter ye shall see heaven open, and the angels of God ascending and descending upon the Son of man.

The formula with which Jesus begins this statement, "Verily, verily," (Greek *amen, amen*) marks what follows as especially solemn and significant, as uttered before God. The change from singular to plural, "thee" to "you," indicates that Jesus intends for this statement to apply to the rest of those present as well as Nathanael.

The promise itself is to be understood in light of Jacob's vision at Bethel (Gen. 28:12,13). Just as the original Israel saw the heavens opened, so would this archtypical Israelite, Nathanael. Jesus may also have in mind the Baptist's vision of Him (vv. 32,33). Exactly which event fulfills this prediction is not clear. Probably the reference is to the whole life of Christ among the disciples (v. 14) and especially His death, resurrection, and ascension.

Jesus uses the title "Son of Man" as a characteristic designation for Himself (3:13,14; 5:27; 6:27,53,62; 8:28; 12:2,34; 13:31). It apparently is derived from Dan. 7:13,14 where the "Son of Man" (a man-like figure in contrast to the beast-like figures which preceded him) assumes royal authority over the world. By this designation Jesus asserts His claim to dominion, yet in such a way as not to be readily understood by all who hear Him. He would designate Himself by this term as He stood before Caiaphas (Mt. 26:64), obviously with the context of Daniel 7 in mind. So here Jesus is referring to Himself as an eschatological-apocalyptic personage, as the ultimate King, not only of Israel, but of the universe.

Summary
(1:35-51)

The Baptist's mission is to point men to Christ. In this section he points some of his own disciples to Jesus in such a way that they actually forsake the Baptist to follow Him. John points out to them that Jesus, not he, is the Messiah. He virtually orders them to follow Jesus. At Jesus' invitation these two disciples spend the evening with Him. As He talks with them they become convinced that He is the Messiah. So excited does one of them (Andrew) become that he excuses himself and goes to find his brother to share the wonderful discovery with him. He brings Simon to Jesus, who speaks to him in such a way that he also believes.

The day after this, Jesus finds Philip, apparently another of the Baptist's disciples, who responds to His almost irresistible challenge, "Follow me." Philip, in turn, brings his friend Nathanael to Jesus with the assurance, "We have found the one of whom Moses and the prophets did write." Nathanael's initial skepticism is overcome as Jesus reveals a supernatural knowledge of his personal affairs, and he recognizes Jesus as the Son of God, the King of Israel. Jesus assures him that he is going to see far greater miracles than this in the future.

Application: Teaching and Preaching the Passage.

This passage presents a picture of the primary function of the church and every individual Christian: bringing men to Jesus. This function is presented as a perfectly normal response to discovering Christ for one's self. To experience Him is to want to share Him with others. This function is also presented as having every likelihood of success. Jesus is always equal to the expectations of those who are brought to Him. No one ever needs to fear that those he brings will be disappointed in Jesus or that He will fail to live up to the introduction that He has been given. The encounter with Jesus will render even the most enthusiastic introduction totally inadequate.

C. The First Sign: Water to Wine (2:1-11)

This first sign serves both as a climax to the previous section, which presented the Messiah as acclaimed but not fully understood by His earliest disciples, and as a starting-point for the following section, where He will fully reveal Himself through many sign miracles. It is the first

installment of many to follow in fufilling His promise to Nathanael that he would "see greater things than these" (see Schnackenburg).

1 And the third day there was a marriage in Cana of Galilee; and the mother of Jesus was there:
2 And both Jesus was called, and his disciples, to the marriage.

The "third day" is used inclusively and thus refers to the second day after the day of 1:43. The remainder of the day when Philip and Nathanael were called and the following day (day 2 of the sequence) were spent in the journey from Bethabara to Galilee. Now, on the third day, Jesus and His disciples find themselves at the wedding in Cana, a small village traditionally located about five miles northeast of Nazareth. The contrast between their old master and their new one must be quite obvious to the disciples at this point. The ascetic John would never have taken them to a wedding feast, but that is the very first place Jesus takes them (see Lk. 7:31-34).

It seems safe to conclude that the bridal couple are among either the family or very close friends of Jesus. Mary, whom John always calls "the mother of Jesus" (2:12; 6:42; 19:25, a usage quite consistent with the relationship he later will bear to her, 19:26, 27), is present. Jesus "was bidden" (Greek *eklethe*, aorist rather than the perfect, had been bidden) after His return from Judea (see Westcott). His disciples were included because of their relationship to Him rather than because of an independent relationship to the bridal couple. Thus the tie seems to be one shared by Jesus and Mary, but not the disciples.

3 And when they wanted wine, the mother of Jesus saith unto him, They have no wine.

41

John abruptly confronts his readers with the problem: the wine has failed. That wine was an essential part of such occasions and that a shortage of it would be of great concern are simply assumed. Apparently such an occurrence would reflect poorly upon the hospitality of those in charge. At any rate, Mary takes it upon herself to bring this problem to Jesus.

Her action may indicate nothing other than a generalized trust in Jesus' resourcefulness. Certainly Jesus was the type of son His mother would be accustomed to rely on in times of difficulty. On the other hand, she was aware of her son's true identity. The fact that He had now, for the first time, gathered disciples around Him may have led her to think that He was ready to embark upon His ministry. She might be urging Him, in her own quiet way, to take action that would show all that He was the Messiah (see Bernard, Morris).

4 Jesus saith unto her, Woman, what have I to do with thee? mine hour is not yet come.

Jesus' address of His mother as "woman" (Greek *gune*) does not sound so harsh in the Greek as in the English. He uses this word to address her in 19:26 where He obviously means to speak with great tenderness. It is significant, however, that He calls her "woman" rather than "mother." He apparently means to make it clear that He has entered a new stage of His ministry and that His identity as her son has been eclipsed by His identity as Messiah. His question, "What is there between me and you?" should be seen as confronting Mary with the new relationship that must exist between the two of them from this moment onward.

Jesus' statement, "My hour is not yet come," does not mean that He is unwilling to perform a miracle at this time and

thereby reveal His Messiahship. Rather it is addressed to Mary in her current state of mind. She wishes Jesus to reveal Himself as Messiah, but she does not understand all that this revelation is to mean. She does not realize that the ultimate revelation will come only when her son is lifted up in death. Jesus is making a veiled reference to "His hour" of ultimate glorification when His mother will finally and fully comprehend His Messiahship. He will, on that future occasion, address her again as "woman" but in such a way as to assure her that He does indeed acknowledge her as His mother. It is as though, from this moment until His mission is finally completed on the cross, even this closest of all earthly ties must be suspended. When His Messianic task is finally completed He will be able to acknowledge Mary as His mother once again, even if but from the cross and for a moment. All of this has a very personal significance for John, and he shares it with his readers as a very tender memory. All through this Gospel, Jesus refers to His coming crucifixion, resurrection, and exaltation in a veiled way as His "hour" (Greek *hora*; see 7:30; 8:20; 12:23, 27; 13:1; 17:1) and His "time" (Greek *kairos*; 7:6,8). He will also use the terms "lifted up" and "glorified" in approximately the same way.

5 His mother saith unto the servants, Whatsoever he saith unto you, do it.

Mary does not interpret Jesus' reply as a rebuke. She is not unaccustomed to statements of His which she only partially comprehends. She has shared the problem with Him, and she feels certain that He will do what is best. She leaves the matter with Him. Her words to the servants reflect her complete trust in, and submission to, her son.

6 And there were set there six waterpots of stone, after the manner of the purifying of the Jews, containing two or three firkins apiece.

John interrupts his narrative to inform his readers of the presence of six stone waterpots; each holds approximately 20 gallons. One firkin (Greek *metretes*) equals eight or nine gallons. Such a large amount of water must be kept on hand because of the requirement that the Jews repetitively wash their hands and utensils in order to be ceremonially pure (see e.g. Mk. 7:1-5).

7 Jesus saith unto them, Fill the waterpots with water. And they filled them up to the brim.
8 And he saith unto them, Draw out now, and bear unto the governor of the feast. And they bare *it*.

Jesus instructs the servants to fill the waterpots. The obvious significance of this action is to enlarge the scope of the ensuing miracle. When this is done Jesus says, "Now draw out and bear unto the governor of the feast" (Greek *architriklinos*). This term was usually used of a head waiter or chief servant. Here it refers to one of the guests who had been designated as "master of ceremonies" for the festivities. This is indicated by his summoning the bridegroom, an action that a mere servant would not take.

The term "draw" (Greek *antleo*) usually means to draw from a well. Some (Bruce, Westcott) believe that this word indicates that more water is drawn from the well after the waterpots are filled and that the water drawn from the well rather than that in the pots is turned into wine. This view seems forced in light of the fact that the Greek verb can mean to draw from some source other than a well and that it renders the action of filling the pots meaningless (but see

Bruce).

9 When the ruler of the feast had tasted the water that was made wine, and knew not whence it was: (but the servants which drew the water knew;) the governor of the feast called the bridegroom,
10 And saith unto him, Every man at the beginning doth set forth good wine; and when men have well drunk, then that which is worse: *but* thou hast kept the good wine until now.

John does not specifically say how, when, or in what quantity the water becomes wine. The miracle is referred to as having already taken place when the ruler of the feast tastes the wine (Greek perfect passive participle of *ginomai*, the water that had been made wine). One may infer that it has been turned to wine before the servants carry it to him, for it is obviously carried to him as wine to be drunk rather than as water with which to wash his hands, and the servants are portrayed as being aware of the miracle. It does not seem probable that only the water actually born to the ruler became wine. Such an assumption is not consistent with mention of the precise number and size of the pots. Furthermore, it is unlikely that the servants would dip their wine pitchers into vessels filled with what they thought to be water to obtain wine to carry in to the feast. They must have believed the waterpots to be filled with wine at the time they filled their wine pitchers.

The ruler of the feast is so surprised at the excellence of this wine that he calls the bridegroom and comments on it. He says that it is the normal custom to serve the best wine first and save the worst till last, whereas his host has obviously done just the opposite. The ruler does not intend his remarks to verify a miracle, but that is precisely their effect.

The wine that he now tastes is superior to that which he has tasted previously and is obviously not more of the old supply that has been found. It is of a different type altogether.

The word translated "well drunk" (Greek *methusko*) means literally to be intoxicated or drunken. "Of course the man does not mean that the guests are intoxicated; it is a jocular statement of his own experience at feasts" (Plummer 92).

The word "wine" (Greek *oinos*) normally refers to fermented wine, there being another word (Greek *trux*) for unfermented grape juice or must. The question of whether the wine served at the feast and the wine made from water by Jesus were fermented cannot be determined exegetically from this passage. One must decide on the basis of the normative passages whether he believes that the word (*oinos*) can refer to a nonfermented wine and then interpret this passage accordingly.

11 This beginning of miracles did Jesus in Cana of Galilee, and manifested forth his glory; and his disciples believed on him.

That this event transpires in Cana of Galilee is mentioned again apparently to emphasize that it is factual. John refers to this event as the beginning of miracles (Greek *semeion*). This word means "signs" or "sign miracles," not just supernatural events as such. There is always a meaning or a message to these miracles. "They are all signs of some underlying reality" (Bruce 72).

The question is, "What is the underlying reality of which this miracle is a sign?" The most natural answer is that it is a sign of the identity, glory, and lordship of Christ. This certainly seems to be what the author goes on to say. The miracle "manifests forth His glory" with the result that "His disciples believe on

Him": they become completely convinced that Jesus is the Messiah.

Some believe that the underlying reality of this miracle is that the "water" of O.T. Judaism must be transformed into the "wine" of Christianity. Donald Guthrie clarifies this point. It is possible therefore that the passage suggests Christ's power to transform the weakness of Pharisaism into something much stronger. Jesus clearly does not choose to emphasize this significance, nor does the Evangelist call attention to it (see Guthrie, *Jesus* 53). In this same tone Schnackenburg says, "What are the thoughts behind the narrative of the evangelist? The most important for the evangelist is the revelation of Jesus' glory and any interpretation which departs from this Christological perspective loses sight of the central issue" (I:337).

Summary
(2:1-11)

After the call of Philip and Nathanael, Jesus returns with His new disciples to Galilee. The first of the "greater things" He promised the disciples that they would see occurs at a wedding in the village of Cana at which Jesus, His mother, and the disciples are all present. When the wine supply is exhausted, Jesus' mother brings the problem to Jesus. She apparently wishes Him not only to solve the problem of the lack of wine but to reveal His Messianic identity as well. After a brief warning that such a revelation involves far more than she realizes, Jesus accedes to her request and solves the problem in such a way that His identity is clearly revealed. He miraculously changes water into wine. The exact manner of the miracle is not spelled out, but the fact that it occurs is plain. The new disciples are absolutely convinced by it that Jesus is the Messiah and they "believe on Him" even more completely than previously.

Application: Teaching and Preaching the Passage

John's purpose in relating this episode is to convince his readers that Jesus actually is the Messiah. He recreates the episode that was so convincing to the first disciples in the hope that it will have the same effect upon his readers.

One may approach the passage using the theme "the first sign" or "Christ's first miracle" and the following headings: (1) The occasion of the miracle (vv. 1-5): Jesus was at a wedding. He involved Himself in the mundane affairs of life and placed His seal of approval upon marriage. A problem emerged which, while it was not of any cosmic significance, was very important to those in charge of the wedding. Jesus' mother brought the problem to Jesus. While she did not fully understand the implications of what she asked, Jesus took her concern seriously and resolved to help her. (2) The essence of the miracle: transformation (vv. 6-10). Water was transformed into wine. Jesus' whole mission can be thought of as transformation. He came to transform the cold orthodoxy of Judaism into the glorious salvation of Christianity. He did not come to destroy Judaism and the Law but to fulfill, complete, and transform them into something better. He came to transform men from sinners to saints, from death to life, and from misery to blessedness. He completely transforms every sinner who comes to Him by faith. Personal identity is retained, yet the transformation is so radical that one becomes "a new creation" in Christ. (3) The impact of the miracle (v. 11): The disciples came to know for certain that Jesus was the Messiah and to focus their personal faith more clearly and exclusively upon Him.

D. The Challenge in the Temple (2:12-25)

12 After this he went down to Capernaum, he, and his mother, and his brethren, and his disciples: and they continued there not many days.

This verse provides a transition from the miracle in Cana to the cleansing of the Temple in Jerusalem. Historical accuracy is apparently John's only purpose for mentioning this brief sojourn in Capernaum, for he attaches no significance to it. Jesus is accompanied there by His disciples, His mother, and His brothers. These brothers must be His half brothers, the sons of Joseph and Mary. There is no real reason to believe them to be His cousins. One may only speculate about why Jesus went to Capernaum at this point or what transpired there.

This verse also helps us understand Lk. 4:23. Some have felt that the reference there to Jesus' works in Capernaum is erroneous since He had not yet been to Capernaum. This verse shows that Jesus did go to Capernaum before making it His headquarters (Mt. 4:13) and may in fact have performed miracles there.

13 And the Jews' passover was at hand, and Jesus went up to Jerusalem.

The Passover (Greek *pascha*) of the Jews (so designated for Gentile readers) is near. This is the first of three Passovers mentioned in the fourth Gospel (6:4 and 11:55); these provide a chronological framework for the ministry of Christ. The Passover celebrated annually the deliverance of Israel from Egyptian bondage. For its origin see Ex. 12; as indicated there (v. 18) it was observed on the fourteenth day of the first month of the Jewish calendar (14 Nisan, the March-April full moon).

Godet interprets Mal. 3:1-3 to mean

that Jesus must open His ministry in Jerusalem in the Temple. If this is correct then it explains why Jesus went up to Jerusalem at this time. Certainly Jesus' action fulfills Malachi's prophecy.

14 And found in the temple those that sold oxen and sheep and doves, and the changers of money sitting.

The key to understanding this verse and the reason for Jesus' anger is the phrase "in the temple" (Greek *en to hiero*). Jesus is not so much angry that animals are being sold and money being changed, but that these activities are being carried on within the Temple precincts (probably in the court of the Gentiles, an area surrounding the Temple proper into which the uncircumcised could come). The underlying reason for such practices was for the convenience of the worshippers. It would be difficult to bring a sacrificial animal from home and only natural that worshippers should want to purchase one after they reached Jerusalem. Often worshippers would not have the approved currency required for the various offerings and therefore needed to exchange their money. The problem arose when these activities came to be conducted within the Temple. Convenience became a higher priority than reverence for God's house. The exact nature of the required currency is not certain. Perhaps it could not bear the image of Caesar or must be of a specified type known for its consistently high quality (see Morris).

15 And when he had made a scourge of small cords, he drove them all out of the temple, and the sheep, and the oxen; and poured out the changers' money, and overthrew the tables;
16 And said unto them that sold doves, Take these things hence; make not my Father's house an
house of merchandise.

Jesus does not simply ignore this violation of the sanctity of the Temple. He takes forceful action against it. He makes a whip and drives out the animals, those selling them, and the money-changers. He says to them, "Get all of these things out of here; do not make my Father's house into a store."

While the irreverence that Jesus condemns is so extreme that it might reasonably be condemned by anyone, it is obvious from His use of the phrase "my Father's house" that John is presenting Him as acting in His Messianic capacity from the perspective of one possessing absolute moral authority. John's whole point in relating this episode is to convince his readers that Jesus' conduct on this occasion demonstrates Him to be the Messiah.

17 And his disciples remembered that it was written, The zeal of thine house hath eaten me up.

Clearly the effect of Christ's action upon His new disciples is to convince them even more completely that He is the Messiah. His action calls to their minds Ps. 69:9a, "The zeal of thine house hath eaten me up." In effect they are saying, "Yes, this is an appropriate action for the Messiah to take. One would expect the Messiah to be in conformity with the spirit of the Psalms and for His actions to fulfill them, for Him to be entirely taken up with the idea of preserving the sanctity of the Temple, and so He is."

18 Then answered the Jews and said unto him, What sign shewest thou unto us, seeing that thou doest these things?

The impact of Jesus' action upon the Jews is certainly not in doubt. They interpret it as a claim to great authority, as a Messianic action. Therefore, they demand from Jesus a Messianic sign. If He is going to exercise Messianic prerogatives, then He must demonstrate Messianic powers. The Jews are not so much questioning Christ's action of driving out the money-changers as they are questioning His authority to do such a thing, His claim to be the Messiah.

19 Jesus answered and said unto them, Destroy this temple, and in three days I will raise it up.

Jesus responds to the demand for a sign with an enigmatic prediction of His own death and resurrection. He makes reference to the "temple" (Greek *naos*), but by that term He actually refers to His body which is God's dwelling place in a sense that the Temple in Jerusalem never could be. He continues to speak as if of a building, "Tear down (Greek *luo*) this temple, and within three days I will raise it up or rebuild it (Greek *egeiro*)." Again, He speaks enigmatically. He is not talking about rebuilding the Temple after it has been torn down, but about rising from the dead after He has been crucified. However, His true meaning is hidden behind what is taken by the Jews to be some sort of threat against the Temple. Although he did not fully comprehend it at the time, John would later understand Christ's first prediction of His own resurrection to be the climax of this episode.

That Jesus did in fact make this statement is indicated by several subsequent references to it (Mt. 26:61; 27:40; Mk. 14:57-59; 15:29; Acts 6:14). The charge that Jesus made such a statement was so persistent that there must be some basis for it.

20 Then said the Jews, Forty and six years was this temple in building, and wilt thou rear it up in three days?

21 But he spake of the temple of his body.

The Jews' reply shows that they totally miss Jesus' veiled reference to His own resurrection. They understand Jesus to be speaking literally of the Temple, and therefore they consider His answer to be absurd. Obviously He cannot rebuild in three days this great edifice which had been 46 years in the building. Jesus was often misunderstood like this and forced to explain Himself (e.g. 3:3ff.; 4:10ff.;32ff.; 6:41ff.; 51ff.; 11:11ff.; 14:7ff.; see Morris). At this point John states clearly for his readers that Jesus is not speaking of the Temple at all, but of His own body and resurrection. (The exact meaning of the Jews' statement is difficult to ascertain. According to Josephus, Herod the Great began construction of the Temple in approximately 20 B.C. If this is correct, 46 years would bring one to about A.D. 26 at which time, apparently, some major phase of the construction was completed. For a more complete discussion of this point see Morris 200, note 81.)

22 When therefore he was risen from the dead, his disciples remembered that he had said this unto them; and they believed the scripture, and the word which Jesus had said.

After the resurrection, with the clear vision of hindsight, the disciples, reflecting upon His words, were able to see what Jesus meant. This insight enabled them to believe (and understand) the O.T. passages (e.g. Ps. 16:10) which taught the resurrection (see Lk. 24:27) and to believe in an even stronger way Jesus' own teaching about Himself. Here, as on other occasions, John makes reference to the disciples' or an individual's "believing," as if for the first time (e.g. v. 11; 20:8), when what he obviously means is that their faith was strengthened or deepened in some meaningful way.

Both John and the Synoptists mention a cleansing of the Temple. The problem is that John places this event at the opening of Christ's ministry while the Synoptists place it during His last week. There are two possible solutions to this problem. The first is that John and the Synoptists refer to the same event and that one of them (most would say John) does not place it in the proper chronological order. The second is that there are two separate cleansings, one at the beginning and one at the close of Jesus' ministry. The second solution is rejected by many scholars on the assumption that it is inherently improbable. Brown, for instance, dismisses the possibility of two separate cleansings as follows: "That we cannot harmonize John and the Synoptic by positing two cleansings of the temple precincts seems obvious. Not only do the two traditions describe basically the same actions, but also it is not likely that such a serious public affront to the Temple would be permitted twice" (I:117). Brown's "obvious" case rests on two points: that the two accounts are so similar that they must describe the same incident and that such an affront to the Temple would not be permitted to happen twice.

In answer to the argument that the accounts are so similar that they must refer to the same event, it should be noted that there are "major differences in wording and in setting, as well as in time.... The words in common are very few, 'sellers,' 'tables,' 'doves,' 'money-changers,' and without them it would be practically impossible to tell a story of temple-cleansing" (Morris 190).

The second argument is really very weak. It deals with likelihood rather than fact. Of course it is "unlikely" that the authorities would allow such an event to occur even once, yet they obviously did. If it can be shown that on both occa-sions the circumstances were such that the authorities could not prevent Christ's action, the whole argument falls to the ground.

On the first occasion Christ clearly caught the authorities unprepared. They did not know anything was going on until it was already over. All they could do would be to punish Christ after the fact. But they might have been reluctant to do so because of the popularity of Christ's action with the people. The people themselves might have been opposed to the practices of the money-changers. Certainly it would not be beyond the scope of Christ's intelligence to perceive all of this before acting.

On the second occasion, Christ was at the height of His popularity. Since the authorities had already decided to arrest Christ but were unable to do so for fear of the multitude (Mt. 21:46; Mk. 12:12; Lk.20:19), it does not appear that they could stop Him from cleansing the Temple at that time regardless how many times He had done it previously (see Tenney, v.14).

Some believe that there was just one cleansing and "that John takes it out of its chronological sequence and places it, with programmatic intent, in the forefront of his record of Jesus' Jerusalem ministry. If his readers understand the significance of this incident, they will know what the ministry was all about" (Bruce 77). Against this view are the differences of style mentioned above, the apparent sequential continuity of John's account (vv. 12-14), and that vv. 23-25 seem to ground this incident firmly within the context of a Passover visit to Jerusalem early in Jesus' ministry.

23 Now when he was in Jerusalem at the passover, in the feast *day*, many believed in his name, when they saw the miracles which he did.

24 But Jesus did not commit

himself unto them, because he knew all *men*,
25 And needed not that any should testify of man: for he knew what was in man.

These three verses serve as a transition from the Temple cleansing to the interview with Nicodemus. They are clearly tied to the context of Jesus' Passover visit to Jerusalem. They describe the context of Nicodemus' talk with Jesus.

That many "believed" in Jesus' name does not mean that they became believers in the sense of "an unreserved personal commitment (or a) practical acknowledgement of Him as Lord" (Bruce 78). The meaning of "believe" is understandable only in terms of a play on the Greek word (*pisteuo*) that is not apparent in the English. John says that while the people did "believe" (*pisteuo*) on Christ, Christ did not "reveal" (*pisteuo*) Himself to them. Christ realized that their belief was merely superficial so He did not recognize them as His disciples. They believed only because they were seeing His miracles (Greek *theorountes* is a causal rather than a temporal participle). Jesus was constantly plagued with these sign-seekers.

John's statement that Jesus knew men's thoughts reflects his mature understanding. He did not realize this when these events first occurred. But as he reflects upon them this realization enables him to fully understand them. This realization also prepares the reader to understand the encounters with Nicodemus and the woman of Samaria which follow.

Summary (2:12-25)

After the miracle at Cana, Jesus goes down to Capernaum for a short time. He then goes up to Jerusalem for the Passover. Upon entering the Temple,

He finds people selling sacrificial animals and exchanging money within the Temple precincts. Angered by this profaning of His Father's house, He makes a whip and drives them out. His action reminds His disciples of the zeal for the Temple described in Ps. 69:9.

The Jewish leaders demand that Jesus demonstrate by a sign His right to assume such authority. Jesus' enigmatic reference to His resurrection from the dead is totally misconstrued by them to be a threat against the Temple. Only after His resurrection did the disciples fully understand Jesus' words.

While Jesus is at Jerusalem, many people are impressed by His miracles and outwardly acknowledge Him as the Messiah. Jesus, however, supernaturally perceiving that their commitment is only superficial, does not recognize them as true disciples.

Application: Teaching and Preaching the Passage

In the miracle at Cana Jesus has privately demonstrated His Messiahship to His disciples. In His action of cleansing the Temple, He is making a public claim to Messianic authority. This action is presented by John as the official beginning of His Messianic mission.

Verses 13-17 may be developed under the theme of irreverence. The causes of irreverence are carelessness and convenience. These men have forgotten the holy nature of the Temple. Familiarity has bred contempt. They thoughtlessly desecrate God's sanctuary for no other reason than their own convenience. Christ's reaction is rage and rebuke. He does not simply tolerate or rationalize their actions. He does not simply look the other way. He speaks out. He lashes out. The underlying reason for Christ's action is His zeal for righteousness. Christ's action must not be perceived as negative but positive.

True love for God involves a hatred for sin and irreverence.

Verses 18-22 present a challenge to Christ's authority. Christ's answer to this challenge is restrained. He could call down fire upon His interrogators. His response is also confident. He speaks from an awareness of His own absolute superiority and power. He speaks quietly of a stupendous miracle which He knows to be within His own power. He speaks with the confidence of the inherently strong. He speaks as no other man could speak, with absolute confidence in His own omnipotence. Finally His answer is vindicated. He will do what He says He will do even though it seems impossible. He will rise on the third day from the dead. Christ stakes all on the resurrection. The resurrection is the ultimate proof of His authority.

E. The First Discourse: The New Birth (3:1-21)

John's pattern of alternating signs and discourses becomes observable at this point. The first discourse grows out of the general reaction described in 2:23-25 to various unspecified miracles performed in Jerusalem.

1 There was a man of the Pharisees, named Nicodemus, a ruler of the Jews.

Nicodemus is described as "a man" (Greek *anthropos*) of the Pharisees. "The use of *anthropos* is probably meant to link the opening words of this chapter with the closing words of the preceding, and so bring out Jesus' knowledge of man" (Morris 209, note 2). As a Pharisee, Nicodemus is representative of the most orthodox and conservative element of Judaism. He is also called a ruler of the Jews, which indicates that he was a member of the Sanhedrin, or "Council of Seventy,"

which the Romans allowed to exercise authority over the religious and minor political aspects of Jewish life. This would designate him as a member of the upper class, the aristocracy. He is intended to be representative of contemporary Judaism at its "best."

2 The same came to Jesus by night, and said unto him, Rabbi, we know that thou art a teacher come from God: for no man can do these miracles that thou doest, except God be with him.

The fact that Nicodemus comes to Jesus by night is generally thought to indicate a reluctance to be openly identified with Him. This attitude is apparently shared by other would-be disciples of his class such as Joseph of Arimathea (19:38a) and not entirely overcome until after the crucifixion (19:38b,39).

Nicodemus, addressing Christ by the title "Rabbi" (i.e. "Master," a title of respect), refers to Him as a "teacher come from God." He does not perceive Christ's true identity, but he does attribute to Him a certain transcendence. The basis for this exalted opinion is very simple—the miracles (Greek *semeia*; see comments on 2:11). These miracles must have been literal events to have had such an impact on Nicodemus.

3 Jesus answered and said unto him, Verily, verily, I say unto thee, Except a man be born again, he cannot see the kingdom of God.

While John does not give every word of this conversation, Jesus' reply is nevertheless abrupt and to the point. With solemnity and emphasis ("verily, verily," Greek *amen, amen*) He says, "You must be born from above (Greek *anothen*)." This word can be translated either "again" or "from above." The context seems to indicate "from above."

There is a logical symmetry in being born from above so as to enter the kingdom of Heaven. Being born from above logically includes the idea of being born again, as the natural birth is presupposed. Some of the rich implication Christ intends is lost by the translation "again." In order to enter the heavenly kingdom one must be born into it by a heavenly (from above) birth.

To "see" (Greek *horao*) the kingdom of God is to experience it, to participate in it as in Lk. 9:27. The concept of "the kingdom of God" is derived from such O.T. passages as Dan. 7:14 and refers primarily to the final and universally accepted manifestation of God's reign over the world. To participate in this future phase of God's reign necessarily involves future life (Job 19:25-27); therefore, "the kingdom of God" is synonymous with "the kingdom of heaven" or "eternal life" (see Mk. 9:43,45, and 47 where "life" and "the kingdom of God" are used interchangeably). There is a sense in which the kingdom of God is already present (as if by way of anticipation) in the hearts of believers. It was inaugurated by Christ at His first coming (Mt. 4:17; 10:7; 12:28) and will be consummated at His second coming (Mt. 6:10).

4 Nicodemus saith unto him, How can a man be born when he is old? can he enter the second time into his mother's womb, and be born?

Nicodemus apparently understands what Christ means by "the kingdom of God," but he is totally confused about being "born (again) from above." His reply seems to indicate that he understands Christ's figurative words in a literal sense. While his question about entering the womb a second time is constructed (in the Greek) so as to expect a negative reply, it seems only to reflect Nicodemus' utter perplexity and lack of comprehension of Christ's meaning.

Indeed, his reply is so simplistic that many commentators have suggested that he is, himself, using figurative language to answer Jesus, that he is referring to the difficulty of changing one's outlook when he is old or to the fact that only Gentiles need be "newly born." "Yet this is not the objection which Nicodemus is represented as urging. The words [attributed to him] rather suggest that he [takes] the metaphor of a new birth to mean literally a physical rebirth.... This would [be] a stupid misunderstanding of what Jesus [has] said, yet it is to this misunderstanding that the reply of Jesus is directed. It is not a fleshly rebirth that is in question, but a spiritual rebirth, which is a different thing" (Bernard I:103).

Notice that Nicodemus uses "a second time" (Greek *deuteros*) instead of "from above/again" (Greek *anothen*). He obviously interprets *anothen* to mean "again" rather than "from above." However, his understanding of Jesus' words is so clearly flawed that it should not be the basis for interpreting them.

5 Jesus answered, Verily, verily, I say unto thee, Except a man be born of water and *of* the Spirit, he cannot enter into the kingdom of God.

Jesus' reply is again accompanied by the "verily, verily" formula to indicate great solemnity. He is explaining what it means to be "born (again) from above." It means to be born of the Holy Spirit, to be inwardly, drastically, and supernaturally changed, to be miraculously infused by the Holy Spirit with a new quality of life, a new nature. Jesus is not presenting an entirely new teaching. He is building upon the O.T. teaching that the Spirit of God would be poured out in a special way during the "last days" (Is. 44:3; Ezek. 11:19, 20; 36:26-28; Jl. 2:28,29).

There is disagreement as to the meaning of "of water" (Greek *ex hudatos*). Some believe it to be a symbol of the Holy Spirit, actually synonymous with Him. Others believe it to refer to baptism. Another view is that it reflects physical birth. The last view seems best. Jesus is saying that just as one must have a physical birth, so also must he have a spiritual birth. Without such a spiritual birth a man is inadequate, incomplete, and shall not "enter into" the kingdom of God. (See comment below on v. 6.) "Enter into" means essentially the same thing as "see" in v. 3.

**6 That which is born of the flesh is flesh; and that which is born of the Spirit is spirit.
7 Marvel not that I said unto thee, Ye must be born again.**

The two births, the two natures, are entirely and absolutely distinct. That which has been born (Greek perfect tense) of the flesh is and continues to be (Greek present tense) flesh and that which has been born (Greek perfect tense) of the Spirit is (Greek present tense) Spirit. Sir Edwyn Hoskins has expressed the truth of this verse very succinctly, "There is no evolution from flesh to Spirit" (quoted in Morris 219). A radical, supernatural transformation wrought by God from Heaven is all that can provide an entrance into Heaven. When all of this is understood one is not at all surprised that Jesus should say,"Ye must be born (again) from above."

There is a parallelism between v. 6 and v. 5 that helps in understanding v. 5. In v. 6, being born of the flesh is contrasted with being born of the Spirit, obviously contrasting physical birth with spiritual birth. It is reasonable to sup

pose that the same contrast was in Jesus' mind in v. 5 and that "born of water," therefore, refers to physical birth.

8 The wind bloweth where it listeth, and thou hearest the sound thereof, but canst not tell whence it cometh, and whither it goeth: so is every one that is born of the Spirit.

There is a play upon the two meanings of the word translated "wind" (Greek *pneuma*) which can mean both "wind" and "spirit." The"wind" is used to illustrate the "Spirit." Men know the wind to be very real as they hear it blowing, even though they do not understand either its source or its destination. In just the same way, the presence and work of the Spirit in men's hearts are very real even though men do not fully understand them. The supernatural act of salvation is real even though it is not outwardly observable to men. Jesus is exhorting Nicodemus to put aside his intellectual misgivings and believe.

**9 Nicodemus answered and said unto him, How can these things be?
10 Jesus answered and said unto him, Art thou a master of Israel, and knowest not these things?**

Nicodemus' doubts are not so easily to be cast aside, however. His mind is focused on the "how" (Greek *pos*) of the matter. "How" is all of this going to be accomplished? Jesus rebukes Nicodemus at this point for his unbelief. He says that it is not reasonable that "a teacher in Israel" should be unable to understand what He is teaching, especially in light of the fact that it has been taught in the Old Testament.

11 Verily, verily, I say unto thee, We speak that we do know, and

testify that we have seen; and ye receive not our witness.

Again using the solemn "verily, verily" formula, Jesus proceeds to rebuke Nicodemus for his apparently willful failure to understand. Jesus designates Himself as the absolute and exclusive revealer of heavenly truth. He contrasts His own experientially derived and certain knowledge with the defective knowledge of Scripture possessed by Nicodemus, "the master of Israel" (see Schnackenburg). It seems also that Jesus makes a direct appeal to Nicodemus to believe Him, similar to the appeal He will make to Philip in 14:9-11. He assures Nicodemus that He is telling him what He knows from His own actual experience to be the truth.

Christ's use of "we" and "our" rather than "I" and "my" has been thought by some to indicate that John is anachronistically placing the words of the later Church into Jesus' mouth. A far better explanation is that of Brown, who says that Jesus picks up on Nicodemus' use of "we know" in v. 2 and turns it against him (Jesus has done the same thing with "teacher/master" in v. 10). Thus, the use of "we" is a subtle, sarcastic rebuke of Nicodemus' rather pompous and skeptical attitude.

12 If I have told you earthly things, and ye believe not, how shall ye believe, if I tell you *of* heavenly things?

Jesus reverts to "I" as He continues. Evidently He uses the term "earthly things" (Greek *epigeios*) to refer to what He has just said to Nicodemus about being born from above. The question is, "What are the "heavenly things?" (Greek *epouranios*). Godet (388) says that they are those things about which Nicodemus has come to ask Jesus: who He is, what He has come to do, how He

proposes to go about it. He paraphrases Jesus' reply, "If when I have declared to you the things whose reality you can, by consulting your own consciousness, discover, and you have not believed, how will you believe when I shall reveal to you the secrets of heaven, which must be received solely on the foundation of a word?" If Nicodemus cannot believe Christ on those matters which Scripture, conscience, and common sense confirm, how can he believe Him about things which depended entirely on Jesus' word, His special experiential knowledge as the one who has "come down from heaven" (v. 13), and the one who bears true witness of Himself (8:14)?

13 And no man hath ascended up to heaven, but he that came down from heaven, *even* the Son of man which is in heaven.

No one can speak knowledgeably or authoritatively about Heaven except Jesus. He has come down (Greek *katabaino*) from Heaven and, therefore, knows about it firsthand. No one else has ever ascended (Greek *anabaino*) to Heaven so as to have knowledge of it to share. Jesus has a monopoly on the experiential knowledge of Heaven. Godet, again, paraphrases Christ's words, "Indeed, without faith in my testimony, there is no access for you to those heavenly things which ye desire to know" (388). This is Jesus' first reference to His awareness of His own pre-existence.

While some believe that the last words "which/who is in heaven" are not spoken by Christ but are an explanatory comment by John analogous with 1:18b (these words are not in some of the best manuscripts), it seems more likely that Jesus is referring to a certain duality of existence that He experiences during His earthly life whereby He maintains a heavenly dimension and presence even while here upon earth.

14 And as Moses lifted up the serpent in the wilderness, even so must the Son of man be lifted up.

Jesus has appeared to be leading up to saying to Nicodemus that, since he cannot comprehend the "earthly," basic things, there is no point in carrying the discussion any further. Yet Jesus does go further. He proceeds to present the essence of saving faith by means of an object lesson. Just as the brazen (that is, *bronze*) serpent was lifted up as a provision of salvation by Moses in the wilderness (Num. 21:9), so Jesus is to be lifted up for the salvation of the whole world.

The term "lifted up" (Greek *huphoo*) seems to have a double meaning, referring both to Christ's being lifted up to die on the cross and His being lifted up in exaltation. It is used the same way in 8:28 and 12:32. Jesus is predicting the manner of His death (by crucifixion) but, more important, the redemptive significance of His death as the basis for human salvation.

Again, some believe that vv. 14 and 15 represent John's explanation rather than Jesus' words. However, the reference to Jesus as the "Son of man" seems to preclude this possibility. John never refers to Jesus by this title. It was Jesus' own (rather enigmatic) designation of Himself. Certainly Jesus was supernaturally aware of the manner of His own death at this time.

Those who believe that vv. 14 and 15 represent the explanatory comments of John rather than the words of Christ feel that their case is strengthened by the double meaning of "lifted up." They view the irony, double meaning, and play on words found in the Fourth Gospel as being manifestations of John's literary style. Therefore, they tend to credit the occurrences of such to John rather than Jesus. True, there are many instances of this usage when John himself is speaking and not quoting Christ. This would tend to confirm that this characteristic is John's rather than Christ's. However, it seems likely to me that John picked up on this ironic and enigmatic use of words from Christ. It would then be characteristic of both John and Christ and would no longer be a basis for ascribing every such instance to John rather than Christ.

15 That whosoever believeth in him should not perish, but have eternal life.

Jesus will be "lifted up" for a purpose—in order that (Greek *hina*) He may be the provision, the cure for sin to all who believe in Him. Just as those who looked on the brazen serpent did not die from the poisonous bite, so those who look in faith to Christ will not perish for their sins but be forgiven. Not only that, they will have eternal (Greek *aionios*) life. They will be a part of the age to come. Like the thief on the cross they will have part with Christ in His eternal kingdom. They will exist forever in a state of blessedness with Him.

16 For God so loved the world, that he gave his only begotten Son, that whosoever believeth in him should not perish, but have everlasting life.

There is disagreement as to whether vv. 16-21 should be viewed as a continuation of Jesus' statement to Nicodemus or John's comment and explanation of His words. The meaning is not affected either way.

There appears at this point a concept that is one of the great themes of this gospel: love. God's love is what makes salvation possible, directed at the whole world, not just the Jews. His love is not just theoretical or remote, but real and active. It is expressed in an act of overwhelming generosity and grace: God gives His absolutely "unique, one of a kind" Son (see 1:14) so that absolutely anyone who "believes" (see 1:12) on Him may have "everlasting" (Greek *aionios*; same as "eternal" in v. 15) life.

Almost unnoticed in this beautiful verse on love is an absolutely terrifying word: "perish" (Greek *apollumi*). It means (in the Greek middle voice, used here) "to perish, perish forever, die (especially eternal death), to be utterly ruined." God has given His Son that men may escape the utter ruin that would have been their fate apart from His gift. The reality behind this word "perish" is so utterly dreadful as to be beyond human understanding. Yet it alone enables one to comprehend the value of God's gift of His Son.

17 For God sent not his Son into the world to condemn the world; but that the world through him might be saved.

Christ's coming into the world, of necessity, involves and implies judgment (9:39; also v. 19 below), but this is not the purpose of His coming. The world would have been judged (in a sense, was already judged) without His coming. Christ's coming does not cause men to become lost. They are already lost. The purpose of His coming is salvation. He comes to bring salvation to those who are already condemned. He comes to bring the light of life into a dark world of death. He comes that men may have life and have it more abundantly (10:10).

18 He that believeth on him is not condemned: but he that believeth not is condemned already, because he hath not believed in the name of the only begotten Son of God.

John demonstrates the great importance of faith in Christ. The word "believe" (Greek *pisteuo*) is repeated three times in this verse for emphasis. Though Christ will die to provide salvation for everyone, it becomes operative only for those who believe. Failure to believe does not cause one to "become" condemned (he was condemned already); it only causes him to "remain" condemned. It is, however, a great tragedy for one to refuse to believe in Christ and therefore needlessly remain under condemnation.

Editor's Note: Doctrine in Jn. 3:16-18

This crucial passage has bearing on several points of doctrine. Only brief attention can be given to these here.

Most important is the doctrine of universal or unlimited atonement, long a source of disagreement between Calvinists and Arminians. Commentator Stallings notes, in his comments on v. 18, that Christ died to provide salvation for everyone, but that the provision becomes operative only for those who believe. This, in summary, is the position of Arminians, and it appears to be grounded solidly on the teaching of this passage, along with others in the N.T. (Consider 1 Jn. 2:2 and 1 Tim. 2:1-6 as outstanding examples.)

The key is the way John uses "the world." Those who believe that Christ died only for the elect suggest that he means the elect in all the world, a chosen people not limited by ethnic or racial boundary. But a careful following of John's usage of the word throughout the Gospel and his three letters will not confirm that limited meaning. In the passage before us, "the world" (vv. 16,17; cf. v. 19) clearly includes those who believe and are saved, as well as those who do not and are condemned. And the declaration of v. 16 that God loved the world, and gave His only-one-of-a-kind Son (in His atoning death) to manifest that love, is a clear statement of unlimited atonement.

Closely related to this, the passage makes faith and unbelief the decisive point of difference between the saved and the condemned. That difference, therefore, does not rest on election, except as election itself is election of *believers*. The responsibility of men is thus upheld. That some are finally condemned is not the result of Divine reprobation, or of lack of provision for them, but of their own persistence in unbelief. That the passage "blames" them, not just for their sins but for their rejection of Jesus Christ, strongly supports the argument that the work of Christ has provided them with genuine opportunity to be saved. If His atonement made no provision for them, if faith is not therefore possible, they can hardly be held accountable for unbelief.

We should also note the tense-action of the key verbs in the passage, especially in vv. 16,18. In each instance, negative and positive, the verbs express on-going action (the Greek present participles and subjunctive). Everyone who *is believing* (vs. 16) *is having* eternal life (as also in v. 15). The one who *is believing* (v. 18) is not being (perhaps, "is not going to be") condemned, while the one who *is not believing* rests under a condemnation already established. Throughout, then, the continuing of a given state is co-extensive with the continuing of faith or unbelief. (See also the comments on v. 36, below.)

Surely this indicates the Scriptural approach to the doctrine of the security of the believer. Clear, on the one hand, is the fact that faith, and faith alone, is the condition of salvation. Justification, first and finally, is not by works. But equally clear is the fact that continuing faith is the condition of final salvation (cf. 1 Pet. 1:5; Col. 1:23). Perseverance in salvation, like salvation itself, has faith for its condition.

19 And this is the condemnation, that light is come into the world, and men loved darkness rather than light, because their deeds were evil.

There is, indeed, a condemnation that comes upon men as Jesus comes into the world. But man's reaction is the cause, not His coming as such. What causes the condemnation is that when Jesus comes He is so completely holy and good that sinful men turn from Him and reject Him. Their love of darkness makes them turn from the light, the very light which alone can enlighten them. This is the consumate irony.

20 For every one that doeth evil hateth the light, neither cometh to the light, lest his deeds should be reproved.

Those who make a practice of doing evil "hate" (Greek *miseo*) the light. To come to the light is to have oneself revealed for what he is. In the presence of the "light" man's conscience (his moral nature as created in the image of God) rises up to condemn him (Is. 6:5). This is a very unpleasant process which sinners do their best to avoid. In fact, their aversion to it is so great as to be called "hatred." Sinful men actually "hate" righteousness.

21 But he that doeth truth cometh to the light, that his deeds may be made manifest, that they are wrought in God.

To "do" (Greek *poieo*) the "truth" (Greek *aletheia*) is to behave in keeping with the truth, to value and practice that which has real moral worth. A person who "does the truth" does not need to avoid the light; rather, he is anxious to come to it, for in its illumination his actions are revealed as having been motivated by true love and obedience to God.

Of course, there is no one who naturally does this. This verse should be understood as being either a description of the person who has been "born from above" or merely the hypothetical statement that such a person (if he existed) would react so, roughly equivalent to the statement, "An innocent man is anxious for the truth to be known."

Summary
(3:1-21)

One of those impressed by Jesus' miracles is Nicodemus, a Pharisee and ruler of the Jews, who comes by night to ascertain their meaning. Jesus gets right to the point and tells Nicodemus that unless one is born from above, he cannot be a part of the kingdom of God. Nicodemus takes Christ's answer literally and asks how one can be born a second time after he is old. Jesus explains that He is speaking of a spiritual birth, that to be born from above is to be miraculously infused by the Holy Spirit with a new nature. This new, spiritual nature is totally distinct from the fleshly nature. Such a radical transformation by God is all that can provide an entrance into Heaven. Just as men know that the wind is real even though they do not fully understand it, so they can know the reality of the heavenly birth without fully comprehending it.

Nicodemus is not satisfied with this answer. He wants to know "how" all of this is to be accomplished. Jesus becomes impatient with Nicodemus at this point because of his apparently willful unbelief. He says that a "teacher in Israel" should understand what He is saying. He is speaking what He Himself has experienced and knows to be true; if

Nicodemus cannot understand when he is told obvious and logical things, how can he hope to understand heavenly mysteries were Jesus to speak of such? Jesus goes on to say that, since He alone has an experiential knowledge of Heaven, only He can speak of it knowledgeably.

Jesus presents the truth to Nicodemus through an object lesson. Just as the serpent was lifted up as a provision of salvation by Moses, so Jesus is to be lifted up as the redemptive sacrifice for the whole world. Whoever will look to Christ in faith will be forgiven of his sins and have eternal life. God is providing this means of salvation because He deeply loves men and is not willing that they should perish. Christ comes to bring salvation, not condemnation. Men were already condemned without His coming. However, men will remain under condemnation if they do not exercise faith in Christ. Condemnation comes upon men, not because Jesus has come, but because of their rejection of Him since He has come. They reject Him because they are evil, and they know He will reveal them for what they are. If they were not evil, they would come to Him gladly.

Application: Teaching and
Preaching the Passage

The central teaching of this passage (stated in vv. 3 and 5) is that man, in his natural state, is unworthy and unable to enter Heaven and that, before he can enter, he must be radically and supernaturally "born from above" by believing in Christ.

Verses 1-5 present man in need of a heavenly birth. All men, even Pharisees like Nicodemus, are unacceptable to God as they are. They are incomplete, entirely unsuited for heavenly existence. They can never enter Heaven as they are naturally constituted but must be totally and drastically reconstituted. Their essential identity must be conformed to the heavenly pattern. They must be "born from above." Heaven must touch and radically alter their lives.

Verses 6-8 present the nature of the heavenly birth. The heavenly life (wrought by the Spirit) is of an entirely different order than the natural life. One can never achieve it by natural means. Its only entrance is the heavenly birth, a supernaturally wrought work of God which, while it cannot be fully understood, is absolutely real and completely efficacious.

Verses 9-21 present Jesus Christ as the basis of the new birth. First, vv. 9-13 present Jesus as the only contact with Heaven, the only source of heavenly truth. He is the only one who has a first-hand knowledge of Heaven, who actually has come from there. He is the only one who can explain with certainty how to get there. He is the only one who can give men God's heavenly truth.

Second, vv. 14,15 present Christ as the means by which the heavenly birth is provided. He is to be lifted up (in crucifixion) as the source of the miraculous regenerating power which will come to all who look to Him in faith.

Third, vv. 16,17 give an explanation of God's motive and purpose in sending His Son into the world. His motive is love. Nothing else is involved. There is no other explanation for His action. Nothing else could move Him to give His unique Son. His purpose is salvation. Judgment and condemnation are not in His mind at all. His only purpose is that men should have everlasting life rather than perish. I once heard the following poem and, although I cannot give proper credit for it, feel that it expresses this thought beautifully.

For God.........the Lord of earth
    and heaven,
So loved..........and longed to see
    forgiven,

The world............in sin and darkness mad,
That He gave........the greatest gift
He had,
His only begotten Son.

Finally, vv. 18-21 explain how Jesus' coming has caused men to bring condemnation upon themselves. Men are so inherently wicked that they are repulsed by Christ's absolute righteousness. Their action has succeeded in making Christ's coming the very opposite of what it was intended by God to be. Refusal to believe transforms God's gift of salvation into the basis of condemnation.

F. The Baptist's Final Testimony (3:22-36)

John the Baptist was presented in the first chapter as being a "witness" to Jesus. Now that Jesus has been presented as demanding a radical rebirth which comes about only by belief in Himself, the writer once again calls the Baptist to testify that, even in light of all this, he believes Jesus to be the Messiah (see Morris). Verses 22-24 form the historical setting for John's final testimony.

22 After these things came Jesus and his disciples into the land of Judaea; and there he tarried with them, and baptized.

"After these things" (apparently all that had happened in Jerusalem, 2:13—3:21), Jesus comes with His disciples "into the land of Judea." He apparently goes out of Jerusalem into the Judean countryside near Jericho on the west bank of the Jordan and "tarries" (Greek *diatribo*) there for an indefinite period (the Greek imperfect tense of both "tarried" and "baptized" indicates an extended period).

The fact that Jesus baptized is mentioned only by John. In 4:2 he indicates that Jesus' disciples did the actual baptizing. There is no contradiction here: "The moral act belonged to Jesus; the material operation was wrought by the disciples" (Godet 404). This is apparently a continuation of John's baptism of repentance. Jesus continued to preach John's message of repentance (Mt. 4:17; Mk.1:15) so it seems reasonable that He should continue the baptism of repentance as well.

23 And John also was baptizing in Aenon near to Salim, because there was much water there: and they came, and were baptized.

The statement that John is "also" baptizing seems to indicate that the baptisms are essentially similar (i.e. for repentance). This is the last time that John and Jesus will be in any sense "together," sharing the same task. From this point on their paths will diverge drastically. This is the last time that Jesus will closely associate His ministry with that of John. It is an appropriate time for John to express the truth of v. 30.

"Also" is important for a question of geography. Is John "also baptizing" (his location being Aenon) or "also baptizing at Aenon"? If the second option is taken, then Jesus and John are in very close proximity. At any rate, the whole point of this episode seems lost if they are separated by a great distance. The exact location of Aenon and Salim cannot be fixed with certainty.

The verbs "came" and "were baptized" indicate progressive duration (Greek imperfect tense) and should be understood as "they were coming (over a period of time) and being baptized."

24 For John was not yet cast into prison.

The Fourth Gospel does not actually tell of John's imprisonment but presupposes the reader's knowledge of it. The impact of this verse is that these events transpired before Jesus opened His Galilean ministry, which would not begin until "after John was put in prison" (Mk. 1:14). All that transpires in the Johannine account (up until the end of chapter 4) describes an early ministry of Jesus concurrent with the last phase of John's ministry, which the Synoptists do not mention.

25 Then there arose a question between *some* of John's disciples and the Jews about purifying.
26 And they came unto John, and said unto him, Rabbi, he that was with thee beyond Jordan, to whom thou barest witness, behold, the same baptizeth, and all *men* come to him.

A controversy arises between the disciples of John and some Jews over the question of purification (ceremonial cleansing in general, baptism in particular). The nature of this controversy can be deduced from the statement of John's disciples' to their master. They are confused as to the respective merits of John's and Jesus' baptisms. Whose baptism is valid? Jesus' popularity is growing while John's is waning. They are upset that their master's influence is being superseded by that of Jesus. They are both perplexed and hurt. They come to John for an explanation. They know that John has identified himself with Jesus, has born witness that He is the Messiah, and has even surbordinated himself to Him, but they cannot accept that Jesus is to totally eclipse their master, especially in their master's unique function of baptism.

27 John answered and said, A man can receive nothing, except it be given him from heaven.

John's answer demonstrates his spirit

of humility and total submission to Christ and stands in marked contrast to the jealous narrow-mindedness of his disciples. He says that everyone has his own particular function to fulfil in God's plan and that one can only try his best to fulfil the responsibility that God has given him. John has his mission; Jesus has His. Jesus is doing what God intends Him to do. His role is distinct from and superior to John's, but that in no way detracts from the validity and importance of what John is doing.

28 Ye yourselves bear me witness, that I said, I am not the Christ, but that I am sent before him.

John reminds his disciples that he has already made it very clear that he is not the Messiah (1:20), but that he is merely "a voice crying in the wilderness, 'Prepare ye the way of the Lord.'" Obviously Jesus is eclipsing him. Can it be any other way? Must not the Messiah be greater than His herald?

29 He that hath the bride is the bridegroom: but the friend of the bridegroom, which standeth and heareth him, rejoiceth greatly because of the bridegroom's voice: this my joy therefore is fulfilled.

John uses the figure of the groom and best man at a wedding to illustrate his relationship to Christ. At a wedding, the central male figure is the groom and the greatest happiness is his, but his is not the only joy. The best man, while he is not the groom, has a very real pleasure and honor in sharing with his friend the happiest day of his life. John is not the Messiah (groom), but he is His herald (best man), and that is cause enough to rejoice. To see the Messiah acclaimed by men as a result of his "witness" is for John the ultimate joy.

The figure of the wedding should not be pressed to identify the bride with Israel or the Church. The focus of the passage is on the groom and best man, not the bride. The emphasis is on the relationship between Jesus and John, not the relationship between Jesus and Israel or the Church (see Tenney).

30 He must increase, but I _must_ decrease.

This verse apparently marks the end of the Baptist's remarks, with vv. 31-36 a commentary upon his words by the Evangelist (see v.31). Upon this assumption, these are the last words of the Baptist to be recorded in this Gospel. At any rate, they provide a fitting climax to his ministry, expressing with terse simplicity the commitment of his heart and the impact of his life. They also mark a turning point in history. John's ministry is almost concluded, and Jesus' ministry is just beginning. The old era is about to give way to the new. John, like Moses, has led others to the brink of this new era, but now his function ceases. A new "Joshua" (Jesus) must lead men into the promised land. The new era belongs to Jesus. John has no part in it (see Mt. 11:11).

31 He that cometh from above is above all: he that is of the earth is earthly, and speaketh of the earth: he that cometh from heaven is above all.

The first question to be settled in connection with vv. 31-36 is the identity of the speaker. There are three possibilities. The first is that these verses are a continuation of John the Baptist's discourse. The second is that they are the writer's commentary on the Baptist's words. The third is that they are a discourse of Jesus spoken in reaction to John. The second view, that they are the writer's commentary, is accepted by most evangelical scholars (e.g. Morris, Bruce, Tenney, Westcott) and seems most satisfactory. However, the meaning and impact of the section is not affected whichever view is adopted.

The one "who comes from above" is obviously Jesus. He is utterly superior to all that is earthly. He is of an entirely different order. He comes from Heaven, knows Heaven, speaks of Heaven. He is, in His very essence, heavenly.

While some think that "the one who is of the earth" refers to all men generically, the better view is that it refers to John the Baptist and contrasts him with Jesus. John, knowing only this earth, can speak only from an earthly perspective. Jesus, since He comes from Heaven, speaks with both heavenly perspective and authority. His message is infinitely superior to John's.

32 And what he hath seen and heard, that he testifieth; and no man receiveth his testimony.

Jesus is giving facts, what He Himself knows from His own experience to be true (cf. v. 11). He constantly refers, in the Fourth Gospel, to His special heavenly knowledge (6:46; 8:26,38,40; 12:49; 15:15). In spite of this, men (on the whole) do not receive (Greek *lambano*; the same basic word as 1:11,12) His testimony. They do not believe Him. It is dreadfully ironic that men refuse to believe the only legitimate source of heavenly truth when they hear Him. His words do not convince them (5:19,43). They just cannot bring themselves to believe Him.

33 He that hath received his testimony hath set to his seal that God is true.

"Received" (a Greek aorist participle) refers to the decisive action when one

man decides to trust in Jesus and believe His witness. By doing so he "sets his seal to" (certifies, adds his endorsement to) the proposition that Jesus has come from Heaven and speaks officially for God. The word "God" should be emphasized. When a man accepts Christ he is not merely entering into a relationship with one of his fellow men; he is accepting what *God* has said. He is attesting that Jesus speaks for God (see Morris).

34 For he whom God hath sent speaketh the words of God: for God giveth not the Spirit by measure *unto him*.

When one believes Jesus, he is believing God. This is so because Jesus is the one whom God (the Father) has sent to speak for Him. Jesus is God's heavenly envoy. When He speaks, He speaks officially for God (12:44,45,49).

While God gave the O.T. prophets only limited, incremental insights into His truth (progressive revelation), there is no such restraint with Christ. Absolutely everything has been revealed to Him. The Holy Spirit has come and remains upon Christ (1:32,33; Is. 61:1,2) in all of His enlightening and revelatory fullness. This complete fullness guarantees the truth and authority of Christ's words. This verse expresses essentially the same truth as 1:18.

35 The Father loveth the Son, and hath given all things into his hand.

The reason for the bestowal of the Spirit upon Christ in full measure is the great love of the Father for Him. The Father has spoken of this love at Christ's baptism (Mt. 3:17) as will Jesus Himself in His high priestly prayer (17:23, 24, 26). The Father's love for the Son is so great that it will withhold nothing from Him. This seems parallel to Jesus' statement that all things have been delivered to Him by His Father (Mt. 11:27; Lk. 10:22). In both contexts Christ is referring to His special knowledge, as He has been in this passage. For this reason "all things" here apparently looks back to the unreserved outpouring of the Spirit upon Christ. Godet (413) thinks that "all things" here is an advance upon v. 34 and that it means "not only the Spirit, but all things," that Christ exercises a universal sovereignty over every aspect of reality (see Eph. 1:22).

36 He that believeth on the Son hath everlasting life: and he that believeth not the Son shall not see life; but the wrath of God abideth on him.

The person who "believes" (Greek present tense) on "the Son" (Jesus) already "has" (Greek present tense) "eternal life" (the life of the age to come) as his present possession. It is not just to be his someday; it is his already. As soon as one is reborn from above, he enters into an eternal life. His full experience of that life is yet future, but the decisive event that makes it his has already happened. On the other hand, the person who does not believe (Greek *apeitheo*— present tense—disobeys; literally, is not convinced or persuaded) shall not see (Greek future tense) life.

There is a future aspect of the consequence of refusing to believe. Such a person shall not be allowed to see or to enter into the final manifestation of the eternal kingdom of God. There is also a present result of unbelief: the wrath of God abides or remains upon such a person. This "wrath" (Greek *orge*) is not just God's judicial application of the moral law, but His strong personal anger against sin, His determination to punish it. This wrath is not just a future poten-

tial, but a present reality. The one who refuses to believe is not going to come under God's wrath at some future point (e.g. at death); he is under it already. God's righteous, indignant anger is already focused upon him. It is the constant abiding reality of his existence.

Summary
(3:22-36)

Soon after His conversation with Nicodemus, Jesus goes out with His disciples into the Judean countryside to a place near the Jordan. There, for an indefinite period, He carries on a baptismal ministry quite similar to that of the Baptist. Christ's proximity to John occasions a comparison of their ministries and significance.

This comparison is relatively unfavorable to John, and some of his disciples come to him for an explanation of why Jesus is becoming so much more popular than he. John uses the occasion of this inquiry to deliver his most profound "witness" to Christ. He points out that, in the plan of God, Christ and he have utterly diverse roles. He has always made it plain that he is not the Messiah, but the Messiah's herald. His whole ministry is but an aspect of the greater ministry of Christ. His entire significance is to introduce men to Christ. He has no other function or role. That done, his ministry is complete and he is satisfied. It is enough for him to know that he has performed his role, that Jesus is on the scene, and that His glorious career is about to begin. He can say with total sincerity and satisfaction, "He must increase, but I must decrease."

The Evangelist goes on to explain that John, who is of the earth, can speak only of earthly things, whereas Jesus, who actually comes from Heaven and possesses all the authority of Heaven, can speak from His own personal knowledge and with absolute certainty of heavenly things. How tragically ironic, therefore, that, by and large, men will refuse to believe what He tells them.

However, the person who does believe Him, does, by his action, set his own personal seal of approval upon the proposition that Jesus speaks the truth of God. Jesus, as the official heavenly envoy, speaks the truth of God in its entirety, for absolutely no knowledge or wisdom has been withheld from Him. The fullness of God's Spirit has been poured out upon Him. The radical nature of the love which the Father has for the Son makes it inappropriate, even impossible, for Him to withhold from Him any knowledge, authority, or glory whatever. The one who believes on this wonderful, heavenly Son of God thereby comes to have eternal life as his immediate possession. On the other hand, anyone so foolish as to reject Him not only will never possess eternal life, but is presently the object of God's righteous wrath.

Application: Teaching and Preaching the Passage

The major thought of this passage is expressed in v. 30, "He must increase, but I must decrease." It expresses perfectly John's understanding of his relationship to Christ. It is both appropriate and inevitable that Christ must increase and John decrease. There are several aspects to this truth. First, John's ministry is coming to a close and Christ's is just beginning (vv. 22-24). John will soon be cast into prison, which will mark both the end of his ministry and the beginning of Christ's. Second, Jesus is inherently so much greater than John that He will inevitably take precedence over him (vv. 25-28). Jesus is the Messiah, the Son of God. John is but His (entirely human) herald. Third, John has no desire other than to be a subordinate part of Christ's ministry (vv. 29,30). John's greatest joy

comes from functioning as Christ's "best man." Fourth, Jesus' heavenly origin and authority ensure that He will totally eclipse John, who is entirely of this earth (vv. 31-35). Finally, Jesus alone embodies the promise of eternal life (v. 36). He is the one in whom men must believe in order to be saved. What causes men to remain under God's wrath is rejection of Him. For all these reasons, Jesus must indeed increase while John (with all other men) decreases. Here, if but for a moment, a man completely loses himself in a cause and knows the exquisite joy of utter subordination of self to God.

G. The Second Discourse: The Water of Life (4:1-42)

The end of chapter 3 marks the end of the early Judean phase of Jesus' ministry. Verses 1-3 form a transition to the next major event, Christ's interview with the woman of Samaria.

1 When therefore the Lord knew how the Pharisees had heard that Jesus made and baptized more disciples than John,
2 (Though Jesus himself baptized not, but his disciples,)
3 He left Judaea, and departed again into Galilee.

The fact that Jesus is referred to as "the Lord" (Greek *kurios*), is thought by some to indicate that these words are supplied by an editor rather than the original writer, since it is not the usual practice to refer to Jesus as "Lord" at such an early point in His ministry. It must be remembered that John writes after the fact and could, himself, speak anachronistically of Jesus as "the Lord." He may do so on this occasion to avoid an awkward repetition of the name "Jesus" (see Godet).

One could wish that more specific information were given here. At some point in time, Jesus comes to know that the Pharisees are aware (have heard) of Him and cognizant of many of the details of His ministry (e.g. the number of His converts relative to John's). Aware of the Pharisees' interest, He leaves (Greek *aphiemi*, leave behind, abandon, or forsake) Judea again (1:43) for (Greek *eis*, unto) Galilee. Bruce believes that Jesus leaves Judea because he thinks the Pharisees are going to try to exploit the dissension between His disciples and those of John to destroy both ministries. The more common view is that He is trying to avoid any premature confrontation with the Pharisaical establishment in Jerusalem. It is important to note that Jesus already considers the Pharisees to be dangerous enemies of whom He must beware. (For explanation of v. 2 see comments on 3:22.)

4 And he must needs go through Samaria.

The writer's statement that Jesus "must of necessity" (Greek *dei*) go through Samaria can easily be misunderstood. This is not a geographical necessity, for Jesus is somewhere in the Jordan valley near Jericho and could easily follow the preferred route up the Jordan valley and into Galilee via Bethshan, thus avoiding Samaria completely. The "necessity" is that there is a special purpose of God for Him in Samaria (see 3:14; 9:4; 10:16; 12:34; 20:9). There is someone there with whom God intends Him to speak (see Brown).

Samaria was the region between Judea on the south and Galilee on the north. It was inhabited by the descendants of people brought in by the kings of Assyria to populate the area after the Northern Kingdom of Israel was carried away captive and the few Israelites left behind who had intermarried with them. These people combined the worship of their heathen gods with that of Jehovah;

the result was a strange mishmash of truth and error. The Jews of the Southern Kingdom, upon their return from Babylon, refused to acknowledge the Samaritans as true worshipers of God, and therefore the Samaritans established their own system of worship around their temple on Mt. Gerizim. This confirmed their apostasy in the minds of the Jews. A terrible spirit of mutual antagonism prevailed between the Jews and the Samaritans at the time of Christ. (See further comment on vv. 19, 20.)

5 Then cometh he to a city of Samaria, which is called Sychar, near to the parcel of ground that Jacob gave to his son Joseph.

The small village of Sychar was near the ancient city of Shechem. There is some controversy as to its precise location, but its general proximity to Shechem and Jacob's well is certain. John locates it for his readers in terms of a certain "parcel of ground that Jacob gave to his son Joseph." This apparently refers to Gen. 48:22 where Jacob bequeathed to Joseph an extra "portion" (Hebrew *shechem*) above his brothers. Jacob apparently was making a play on words. Joseph's special *shechem* was to be the city of Shechem. This interpretation is borne out by the fact that in Jos. 24:32, Joseph's bones were buried in Shechem, which then became the inheritance of his descendants (see Godet).

6 Now Jacob's well was there. Jesus therefore, being wearied with *his* journey, sat thus on the well: *and* it was about the sixth hour.

Jacob's well is one of the best attested sites in Palestine. John's mention of it provides a precise geographical reference point for this episode. Near the well there is a fork in the road from

Judea, with one road leading between Mt. Gerizim and Mt. Ebal through the city of Samaria into central Galilee and the other branching off toward Bethshan and the southern shore of the Sea of Galilee.

Jesus waits, sitting on the edge of the well, while His disciples go into the village to get some food (see v. 8). He is very tired after His journey. The sixth hour, in keeping with John's usage, should probably be understood as 12 noon, although it may refer to 6 p.m. (see comments on 1:39; 19:14).

7 There cometh a woman of Samaria to draw water: Jesus saith unto her, Give me to drink.

As Jesus sits on the edge of the well, a Samaritan woman comes to draw some water. Since there were other wells nearer to the village, she may have come out to this one to avoid contact with other women who would be indignant at her immoral life style.

Jesus enters into conversation with the woman by making a very simple request for a drink of water, yet these few words begin the process of breaking down the long-standing wall of separation between the Samaritans and the Jews.

8 (For his disciples were gone away unto the city to buy meat.)

The point of this parenthetic statement is that the disciples have taken their vessel(s) with them so that Jesus has no way to draw water for Himself. His request of the woman is therefore sincere and not just a device to draw her into conversation. He really is thirsty. The presence of such mundane detail is certainly an indication of the authenticity of the account.

9 Then saith the woman of Sama-ria unto him, How is it that thou, being a Jew, askest drink of me, which am a woman of Samaria? for the Jews have no dealings with Samaritans.

The Samaritan woman is amazed that a Jewish man (which Jesus plainly is) would even speak to her, let alone make such a request. The Jews considered the Samaritans, especially women, to be unclean. A Jew would be defiled by eating or drinking from a vessel belonging to one of them. Some believe that there is an element of sarcasm and resentment in her reply. They suppose her to be saying, in effect, "Haven't you forgotten something? I'm one of those no-good Samaritan women. An upright, pious Jew like you wouldn't want to drink any water out of my unclean vessel. You might be defiled." Others believe that her attitude is simply surprise and amazement.

The last phrase, "for the Jews have no dealings with the Samaritans," is probably an explanatory note from the writer rather than part of the woman's answer. "Have no dealings" (Greek *sugchraomai*) literally means "to use together" and refers to the shared use of cooking and eating utensils and thus, in a derived sense, to any intimate social contact. Christ's requesting to drink from this woman's vessel was totally out of keeping with the usual Jewish scruple.

10 Jesus answered and said unto her, If thou knewest the gift of God, and who it is that saith to thee, Give me to drink; thou wouldest have asked of him, and he would have given thee living water.

Jesus' reply ignores the woman's reference to the estrangement between Samaritans and Jews and focuses, rather, upon the two of them as individuals. In effect He says, "Let us forget momentarily our respective racial identities. Let us speak on a personal level. If you really understood who I am you would forget this Jew-Samaritan business and deal with me on a personal basis. You would ask of me the spiritual blessings which I alone can provide. It is a great mistake for you to think of me as just another Jew. I am far more than that."

If the woman understood the free gift of God to men (Jesus Himself, 3:16), if she understood Jesus' identity, their roles would be reversed. Instead of Jesus asking her for a drink of water from the well, she would ask Him for the "living water" which He would freely give to her. "Living water" refers to running water, the water from a stream or spring as opposed to the water collected in a cistern. Jesus uses the term figuratively to refer to salvation and the indwelling presence of the Holy Spirit.

11 The woman saith unto him, Sir, thou hast nothing to draw with, and the well is deep: from whence then hast thou that living water?

Just as Nicodemus misunderstood Christ's reference to being "born from above," so the Samaritan woman misunderstands His reference to "living water." She takes His words literally and thinks He is referring to physical water. Accordingly, she draws His attention to the impracticality of His statement. The well is deep (over 100 feet) and He has no vessel to draw water with. How, then, will He come by the water which He proposes to give her?

12 Art thou greater than our father Jacob, which gave us the well, and drank thereof himself, and his children, and his cattle?

There is clearly a note of sarcasm in

her next question, "You are not greater than our father Jacob, are you?" The fact that her question begins with the Greek negative (*me*) indicates that it is a rhetorical question expecting the answer, "No." Here is another example of the irony of this Gospel. The woman, while she thinks her words preposterous, is actually stating the truth. Jesus is far greater than Jacob, and the water from Jacob's well is completely inferior to the "living water" which Jesus offers.

There is apparently a note of pride in her words as she calls Jacob "our father." She is pointing out that she and Jesus have at least one thing in common: they are both descended from Jacob. Jesus does not challenge her claim to equality. He does not point out the polluted genealogy of the Samaritans. Later on (v. 22), He will reject a somewhat similar claim to equality because it involves a doctrinal error, but on this occasion He leaves her harmless, if pathetic, pride intact.

13 Jesus answered and said unto her, Whosoever drinketh of this water shall thirst again:
14 But whosoever drinketh of the water that I shall give him shall never thirst; but the water that I shall give him shall be in him a well of water springing up into everlasting life.

Jesus answers the woman's sarcastic rhetorical question seriously. He says in effect, "Yes, I am greater than Jacob and here is why. The water from this well that Jacob dug will quench one's thirst temporarily, but he will soon get thirsty again. On the other hand, the person who drinks the water that I give will never be thirsty again. The water that I give is the ultimate 'living water' in that it does not just flow from a spring; it actually, itself, becomes a spring which perpetually pours forth an inexhaustible internal supply of spiritual water within one's soul. It is the 'living water' in yet another sense; it is the water of life, the water which produces life, the water which is life, eternal life."

15 The woman saith unto him, Sir, give me this water, that I thirst not, neither come hither to draw.

Again displaying a woodenly literal understanding, the woman says to Jesus, "Give me some of this (amazing) water you speak of. Let me drink some of it so that I need not ever have to go to all the trouble of coming to this well (or some other one) and drawing water to drink." Is she serious? Is she being facetious? Either way, she has completely missed Jesus' point.

16 Jesus saith unto her, Go, call thy husband, and come hither.

This line of reasoning is not getting anywhere so Jesus abruptly changes His approach and asks the woman to go and get her husband. Jesus' purpose in doing this must be understood in terms of His supernatural knowledge, as is clear from vv.18 and 19. Therefore, His purpose is not so much to include her husband in the conversation as to force upon her a sense of her own sinfulness and need. He has to break through her veneer of smug complacency. He can help her only if He deals with reality.

17 The woman answered and said, I have no husband. Jesus said unto her, Thou hast well said, I have no husband:
18 For thou hast had five husbands; and he whom thou now hast is not thy husband: in that saidst thou truly.

Jesus has clearly hit a nerve. For the first time, she has no rejoinder. She can but curtly reply, "I have no husband." She is not at all eager to discuss this subject. Jesus, however, is not about to let her off the hook. He presses His attack with devastating force. "You are right in saying that you have no husband. That is true, but not in the sense that you imply—that you are a widow or have never been married. Actually, you have been married five times and are now living with a man to whom you are not married. This is the sense in which it is accurate to say that you have no husband."

19 The woman saith unto him, Sir, I perceive that thou art a prophet.
20 Our fathers worshipped in this mountain; and ye say, that in Jerusalem is the place where men ought to worship.

Jesus has cut this poor woman's pretensions to shreds. He has revealed her for what she is, yet she cannot abandon her attempt to divert His attack. Whereas, previously, she has been entirely oblivious to the religious implications of Jesus' statements, now she is suddenly eager to discuss religion. Jesus is obviously a prophet, a man of religion. Very well, she will guide the conversation into the area of His special interest. Anything to change the subject. What better than the old question that has divided the Jews and the Samaritans for so long: Where is the correct place to worship God, on Mt. Gerizim or at Jerusalem? Better this than the seventh commandment.

On the origin of the Samaritan people, see the comments on v. 4, above. Rejected by the Jews who returned from Babylonian captivity to rebuild the Temple in Jerusalem (Ez. 4:1-3), they ultimately built their own rival temple on Mt. Gerizim and used only their version of the first five books of Moses ("the Samaritan Pentateuch") as their Bible. Although that temple had been destroyed by Jewish zealots during the time of the Maccabean kings, in 128 B.C., the Samaritans continued to worship on Mt. Gerizim. (A small remnant does so until this day.)

21 Jesus saith unto her, Woman, believe me, the hour cometh, when ye shall neither in this mountain, nor yet at Jerusalem, worship the Father.
22 Ye worship ye know not what: we know what we worship: for salvation is of the Jews.
23 But the hour cometh, and now is, when the true worshippers shall worship the Father in spirit and in truth: for the Father seeketh such to worship him.

Jesus replies with solemnity ("Woman, believe me") to the woman's insincere and evasive statement: "That issue really is not relevant. The full truth about the worship of God is not to be found in either of those positions, and both of them are about to be set aside. Insofar as there is a distinction between the Samaritan and the Jewish positions, the Jewish is the correct one. The Samaritan religion is so confused that it has obscured the very person of God. It is by the Jewish teaching that men may truly come to know God. However, the important quality of worship is not geographical, but spiritual. In order to worship God, men must realize that He is a Spirit and that He must be worshipped in spirit and in truth. The hour is soon coming when such a spiritual worship of God will be instituted. That spiritual worship will completely eclipse all the worship of the past and render all questions about its particulars completely irrelevant."

The new worship Jesus speaks about

is to be "in spirit and in truth." "Spirit" does not refer here to the Holy Spirit but to the highest aspect of man's being, that essence of the image of God in man which distinguishes him from the rest of the physical creation, that capacity which enables him to commune with God. One must worship God with his whole being, in total sincerity. This requirement is directed at the hypocrisy and pretense of the Jews. That the worship of God is to be "in truth" indicates that it is to be based upon reality and in accordance with correct doctrine. Sincerity alone will not suffice. This is obviously directed at the confused worship of the Samaritans. It seems as though Jesus is saying that the new worship of God will be free from the characteristic weaknesses of both Judaism and Samaritanism.

24 God *is* a Spirit: and they that worship him must worship *him* in spirit and in truth.

There is no article before "Spirit." This clause is similar to the last clause of 1:1. The absence of the article emphasizes the qualitative aspect of the noun rather than its mere identity. Jesus is saying, "Spirit is what God, in essence, is. Therefore, those who wish to worship Him must do so in a manner compatible with His essential nature. They must utilize that highest aspect of their own being, their spirit. That is the only aspect of their being that is capable of interacting with or worshipping God."

25 The woman saith unto him, I know that Messias cometh, which is called Christ: when he is come, he will tell us all things.

Once more, the woman tries to evade Christ's point (which is becoming increasingly clear). While she does not deny the truth of what Jesus says, she seeks to avoid seriously considering it or taking action on it. She says, in effect, "Yes, this is all very interesting, but it is rather beyond me. The Messiah is coming soon and this is just the sort of question that He will settle. Perhaps we had better just wait and let Him deal with this issue." This is clearly the high point of her evasive maneuvering. She has found the perfect rejoinder, "We must defer on this issue to the Messiah." The woman is probably pretty pleased with herself at this point. She has backed Jesus into a corner. Only the Messiah is competent to expound on these matters. It is only to Him that she will listen.

26 Jesus saith unto her, I that speak unto thee am *he*.

There is only one reply which can parry the thrust of her argument and strike straight at her heart with the truth: "I that speak unto thee am he." These words perfectly embody the restrained majesty so characteristic of Jesus. How masterfully has He guided the conversation to this point, yet His *coup de grace* is delivered quietly, even tenderly, "I am the Messiah." How these quiet, yet awesome words must thunder through the woman's mind. This one with whom she talks, this Jew who has all the answers, who knows the secrets of her life, is actually the great Messiah. What does this mean?

27 And upon this came his disciples, and marvelled that he talked with the woman: yet no man said, What seekest thou? or, Why talkest thou with her?

At this precise point in the conversation (literally, "upon this"), the disciples return from the village. The implication is that they remain at a discreet distance until the conversation is completed. They are surprised that Jesus is talking with a woman (the Greek has no "the" with "woman"). They are amazed that He would talk with a *Samaritan*; that He would talk with a Samaritan *woman* is beyond belief. Yet they do not ask the woman what she wants, nor do they ask Jesus why He is talking with her. One can only speculate as to the reason for their reticence. Perhaps they sense something of the drama of the occasion.

28 The woman then left her waterpot, and went her way into the city, and saith to the men.

Apparently, there are some final words between Jesus and the woman which are not recorded. This follows from the fact that the disciples arrive just as Jesus is speaking the words of v. 26 and that the conversation does not terminate at that point (see v. 27). After these final words, the woman leaves her waterpot behind. The mention of this detail seems to indicate an excitement and complete preoccupation on her part, the availability of the "living water" completely superseding any further concern for natural water. She goes into the village for the purpose of delivering the challenge of v. 29. One might reasonably suppose that her action is a response to Christ's final words to her and, therefore, an indication of what they may be.

29 Come, see a man, which told me all things that ever I did: is not this the Christ?
30 Then they went out of the city, and came unto him.

With childlike candor the woman calls upon her fellow townsmen to share in her wonderful experience: "Come see a man who told me all that I have ever done." Her statement calls attention to her great sinfulness and is an indication of an attitude of true confession and repentance on her part. It also has a great impact upon her hearers. They cannot help but be interested in a person who has had such a radical effect upon this unsavory character. Anyone who could get such a person as this talking about religion must have something going for him. Her very wickedness is her greatest claim to their attention.

The woman's words, "Is not this the Christ?" should not be seen as an indication of any uncertainty on her part, but as a cautious suggestion that such is, in fact, the case, a leading question designed to place the idea into their minds. She does not, herself, try to convince them of the truth. She is simply trying to stir up enough curiosity in their minds to get them to go out and meet Jesus for themselves. Her words have the desired effect, for they do exactly as she hopes. They go out of the village and come to Jesus.

31 In the mean while his disciples prayed him, saying, Master, eat.

"In the mean while" means during the time between the woman's leaving and the Samaritans' arrival. The disciples have kept trying to persuade a strangely reluctant (from their point of view) Jesus to eat some of the food they have brought from the village. John preserves their very words, "Rabbi, eat." They are naturally concerned for His physical condition.

32 But he said unto them, I have meat to eat that ye know not of.

Jesus uses the disciples' urging that He eat something as an occasion to impart a spiritual lesson. Both "I" (Greek *ego*) and "ye" (Greek *humeis*) are emphatic and point up the contrast between Christ and the disciples. He has food to eat which they are not aware of. There is a source of fulfillment and satisfaction available to Him which they

know nothing about. This satisfaction is, of course, spiritual in nature.

33 Therefore said the disciples one to another, Hath any man brought him *ought* to eat?

As usual, the disciples miss the point, taking Jesus' figurative language literally. They begin to inquire of one another (literally), "No one brought Him anything to eat, did he?" Their obtuseness is almost comical. Will they ever catch on? Certainly the humor of the situation has not been lost on John as he remembers this scene.

34 Jesus saith unto them, My meat is to do the will of him that sent me, and to finish his work.

Jesus patiently (He apparently never lost His patience) explains to them that He is not speaking of normal physical food, but that His food (i.e. what really satisfies and fulfills Him) is doing the will of the One who has sent Him (God). To do God's will and to finish the work which He has sent Him into the world to do were Christ's greatest satisfaction and joy.

35 Say not ye, There are yet four months, and *then* cometh harvest? behold, I say unto you, Lift up your eyes, and look on the fields; for they are white already to harvest.

As Jesus thinks of the great harvest of souls that He is about to reap (perhaps, even at this moment, He sees the crowd of Samaritans on their way out to Him), He wants to impress upon His disciples the significance of what is happening. He therefore makes reference to a saying common among the people of the time, "Say not ye ("ye" is emphatic), there are yet four months, and then cometh the harvest." The usage here is similar to that in Mt. 5, where Jesus quotes a common proverb which expresses the conventional wisdom of the time and then contrasts it with the real truth by the repeated formula, "But I say" (vv. 22, 28, 32, etc.). So, here, He goes on to say, "Behold, I say unto you, Lift up your eyes, and look on the fields; for they are white already unto harvest."

Jesus is saying, in effect, "Look, I have just sown the seed and the grain is already ripe for harvest. It took but a few minutes. There does not have to be a long delay between spiritual sowing and reaping. Remember this later on in your own ministries. Do not be satisfied merely to sow and rationalize within yourselves that someone else will take care of the harvest, later. Always be thinking in terms of harvesting, and you will find many more opportunities than you suppose."

36 And he that reapeth receiveth wages, and gathereth fruit unto life eternal: that both he that soweth and he that reapeth may rejoice together.
37 And herein is that saying true, One soweth, and another reapeth.

The one who reaps (in this instance, the disciples) receives a wonderful reward (the Greek *misthos* may be so translated). His harvest is a harvest of souls whom he garners unto eternal life. In so doing he comes to share with the sower (in this instance, Jesus) the wonderful joy of the harvest in which they each have had a part. Jesus is about to let the disciples share with Him in the joy of reaping the harvest which He, alone, has sown. He wants them to understand from this a principle: one may sow and another may reap, but their work is one. He who reaps is enjoying the results of the sower's effort. On the other hand, the sower has a very real

part in the harvest even though he may not, himself, reap. So it has been on this occasion. Jesus has sown the seed and now the disciples are going to share with Him the joy of the harvest.

38 I sent you to reap that whereon ye bestowed no labour: other men laboured, and ye are entered into their labours.

Jesus now draws from this particular episode a general principle that applies, in a much broader sense, to the future ministry of the disciples. The past tense of the verb "sent" (Greek aorist) must be taken seriously (Schnackenburg). Jesus apparently places Himself into the future and looks back upon their ministry and evaluates it from that perspective. Their ministry is to be built upon the efforts of others (e.g. the O.T. prophets, John the Baptist, Jesus Himself). These past efforts will be an essential part of their success. Jesus wants the disciples to be aware of the transcendent unity of God's servants of every era (past, present, future).

39 And many of the Samaritans of that city believed on him for the saying of the woman, which testified, He told me all that ever I did.

The interlude of vv. 31-38 completed, the narrative is resumed. The Samaritan woman's simple testimony apparently has a profound effect upon her fellow townsmen and plays a significant role in their faith. It is, in fact, the decisive factor for some of them. At the very least, it is the stimulus that brings them into Christ's presence.

40 So when the Samaritans were come unto him, they besought him that he would tarry with them: and he abode there two days.

41 And many more believed because of his own word.

The Samaritans are so impressed with Jesus that they desire Him to remain with them, and He does so for two days. During this time many more Samaritans believe on Jesus because of the impact of His personality and teaching upon them.

42 And said unto the woman, Now we believe, not because of thy saying: for we have heard *him* ourselves, and know that this is indeed the Christ, the Saviour of the world.

This statement of the Samaritans should be seen as a comparative negative. It is not intended to belittle the woman so much as to honor Christ. They are, in effect, saying to the woman, "While your words may have had a part in causing us to believe, the truly decisive thing was our encounter with Christ Himself. That encounter has completely convinced us that He is indeed the Messiah, the Savior of the world."

Summary
(4:1-42)

Being concerned over the Pharisees' heightened interest in Him, Jesus decides to leave Judea and return to Galilee. He purposely goes by way of Samaria. At about noon, He and the disciples arrive at Jacob's well near the village of Sychar. The disciples go into the village to purchase some food while Jesus, who is very weary, waits beside the well.

As He is sitting there, a Samaritan woman comes to the well to draw water. Jesus asks her to give Him a drink. She is surprised that a Jew would make such a request of a Samaritan. Jesus replies to her that if she knew who He really was, she would be the one who would make a request of Him and He would give her "living water." The woman mistakenly supposes Jesus to be speaking of literal water and asks Him how He is going to give her any water since He has nothing with which to draw it from the well. She asks sarcastically if Jesus considers Himself to be greater than the patriarch Jacob. Jesus replies that if one drinks from Jacob's well, he will get thirsty again; whereas if he drinks of the water which He provides, he will never again be thirsty because that water will become a perpetual spring of water within him. It will be living water indeed, the water of eternal life.

The woman again takes Jesus literally and asks Him to give her some of His magic (as she saw it) water. At this point, Jesus changes the subject abruptly and requests that the woman go and get her husband. The woman answers that she has no husband. Jesus responds that she is certainly right about that, since she has been married five times and is now living with a man to whom she is not married. She tries to divert the conversation from her own guilt by saying that, since Jesus is apparently a prophet, it might be nice for them to discuss a religious question. The best she can think of is the old question of whether the Samaritan or the Jewish system of worship is correct.

Jesus explains to her that, while the Jewish system is, by far, the better of the two, actually both of them are about to be rendered obsolete by something far better. The hour is upon them when men will begin to worship God "in spirit and in truth." Men will worship God with their whole being and in accordance with true doctrine.

The woman tries, one last time, to evade Jesus by saying that, since the Messiah is coming, and since He will settle all such questions, it would be best to leave this kind of thing to Him. Jesus answers that He is the Messiah.

At this point, the disciples return from the village. They are shocked to see Jesus conversing with a Samaritan woman, but they do not dare say anything. After the conversation is completed, the woman leaves her waterpot and goes into the village where she tells the townspeople how Jesus has told her all about herself, suggesting to them that He might very well be the Messiah. Her statements persuade the villagers to go and see Jesus for themselves.

While all of this is going on in the village, the disciples try to get Jesus to eat something. He replies that He has food to eat that they do not know about. They are puzzled by His words and begin to say to themselves, "Nobody gave Him anything to eat, did he?" Jesus then explains that He is not speaking literally, but that His food is to do God's will and complete His work. He then gives them some principles of the harvest (of souls). First, there does not always have to be a long delay between sowing and harvest, the present instance being a case in point. Therefore, they should always be thinking in terms of harvesting. Second, sowing and harvesting are but two phases of the same operation. Sowers and harvesters are partners. The harvester must not overlook the role of the sower and claim all the credit for himself.

Back in the village, the woman has been having quite an impact: many have believed on Jesus. Being asked to remain among them, He does so for two days, during which time many more believe. The Samaritans' encounter with Jesus totally convinces them that He is indeed the Messiah and the Savior of the world.

Application: Teaching and Preaching the Passage

The Evangelist's primary purpose in this passage is to reveal certain truths about Jesus and the plan of salvation. To achieve his purpose, he relates Jesus' conversation with the Samaritan woman wherein He explains these things to her. As an added bonus, so to speak, this passage also gives a valuable insight into Jesus' method of dealing with people. There are, therefore, two parallel themes to be followed in this passage: (1) the truths Jesus reveals about Himself and the plan of salvation and (2) the manner in which He goes about revealing them.

His revelation of Himself and the plan of salvation is given in incremental steps as follows: (1) He is someone out of the ordinary who is able to grant a particularly desirable blessing which He refers to as "living water" (v. 10). (2) He is, by implication, greater than the patriarch Jacob in that the "living water" which He offers perpetually replenishes itself and, in some way, has the potential of eternal life (vv. 13,14). (3) He has a supernatural knowledge of the most intimate details of the woman's affairs (vv. 17,18), implying that He is, at the very least, a prophet. It is revealed later that this has a much more profound effect on the woman than she at first admits (vv. 29, 39). (4) God is, in essence, spirit and this must be taken into account by those who would know and worship Him. The only way to worship God is in spirit and in truth (vv. 21-24). Neither mere formality nor erroneous sincerity will suffice. One must be very particular how he approaches God. (5) Jesus actually is the Messiah from whom she may correctly learn "all things," and in whom she may trust for eternal life (v. 26).

Jesus' method of presenting the truth about Himself and the plan of salvation is also very instructive. (1) His policy is to be constantly searching for souls. In v. 4, He must needs go through Samaria for the express purpose of encountering just such people as the Samaritan woman. (2) He approaches this woman directly with a simple request for a drink (v. 7) and moves naturally from point to point. (3) He ignores the barriers of prejudice and pride that exist in His time and speaks with a person from outside his own race and culture (v. 9). (4) He speaks so as to arouse the woman's curiosity and interest (v. 10). (5) He confronts her sin directly (vv. 16-18). (6) He refuses to be sidetracked by her diversions and actually works her efforts into His presentation (vv. 21-24). (7) He skillfully brings the conversation to the point where He can present the woman with a direct challenge (v. 26). (8) He uses one convert as a means to reach others (vv. 28,29,41).

H. The Second Sign: The Nobleman's Son Healed (4:43-54)

The next major event which John relates is the healing of the nobleman's son. In his discourses with Nicodemus and the Samaritan woman, Jesus has claimed to be able to grant eternal life. This second great sign miracle is an "object lesson" which illustrates, in an earthly way, that Christ does indeed have the power to grant life; Christ's words are, "Your son lives" (v. 50). Another important aspect of this event is that it involves healing at a distance. The first three verses provide a transition from Samaria to Galilee where the episode will transpire.

43 Now after two days he departed thence, and went into Galilee. 44 For Jesus himself testified, that a prophet hath no honour in his own country.

After two days (Greek: "*the* two days") with the Samaritans (v. 40), Jesus continues on His journey to Galilee (v. 3). The reason for His action (i.e. the trip from Judea to Galilee considered in its entirety) is that "a prophet has no

honor in his own country." The logical assumption is that one would take a journey for such a reason because the unhappy condition described exists in the place he is leaving rather than the one to which he is going. This would seem to indicate that "his own country" was, in this instance, Judea. However, essentially the same statement is made in the Synoptics (Mt. 13:57; Mk. 6:4; Lk. 4:24) with reference to Galilee (Nazareth), and some argue that Galilee is in mind here also. Some others think it refers to this world as opposed to Heaven, the only place where Jesus is properly honored. However, it is hard to see how this would provide a motive for Jesus to leave Judea and go to Galilee. This is a very difficult question, and there is no certain answer.

45 Then when he was come into Galilee, the Galilaeans received him, having seen all the things that he did at Jerusalem at the feast: for they also went unto the feast.

When Jesus arrives in Galilee, the Galileans welcome Him. Many of them were in Jerusalem at the "feast" (the Passover, 2:13,23) and had seen the miracles which Jesus had performed there (2:23). Their positive reception is based on a carnal reaction to Christ's miracles rather than a deep understanding and acceptance of His identity and mission. Their devotion to Jesus will later prove itself to be superficial and transitory.

46 So Jesus came again into Cana of Galilee, where he made the water wine. And there was a certain nobleman, whose son was sick at Capernaum.

Jesus returns (apparently by way of Nazareth: Lk. 4:16; Mt. 4:13) to the village of Cana where He turned the water into wine (2:1,11). John's casual reference to the former episode is a sure indicator of its historicity.

There is a "royal officer" (Greek *basilikos*), a high official of Herod Antipas, whose son is very sick. This man apparently lives at Capernaum. (At any rate, that is where his son is.)

47 When he heard that Jesus was come out of Judaea into Galilee, he went unto him, and besought him that he would come down, and heal his son: for he was at the point of death.

Apparently, there is a great deal of publicity concerning Jesus' reappearance in Galilee (v. 45; Lk. 4:14,15). When the news comes to this man, he goes to meet Jesus at Cana and begins to beseech (Greek inceptive imperfect of *erotao*) Him to come down to Capernaum and heal his son. The man is desperate, for his son is at the point of death. Obviously, he assumes that Jesus must be physically present in order to heal the lad, a basic misunderstanding of Christ's identity and power. He views Him as merely another Rabbi whose prayer might have some influence with God. He fails to comprehend that, because Christ has the very power of life within Him, He can simply grant life on His own authority. Physical proximity is not necessary. He can grant life from a distance as well as from near at hand.

48 Then said Jesus unto him, Except ye see signs and wonders, ye will not believe.

While Jesus' reply seems rather harsh, it is actually directed at the whole crowd of Galileans as the plural "ye" indicates. Jesus is not just answering the man. He is, rather, describing the attitude which is prevalent among the Galileans (see v. 45). His words may also be intended as a kind of rhetorical statement, a test of the man's faith, a challenge to believe (e.g. Mk. 7:27). He wants the man to comprehend His identity and power.

49 The nobleman saith unto him, Sir, come down ere my child die.

The man is desperate for Jesus to do something, and he refuses to be put off by Christ's rather negative reply. He repeats his request with great sincerity and emotion, "Sir, come down before 'my little son' (Greek *paidion*, a word different from that used in vv. 46 and 47, a term of endearment and tenderness) dies."

50 Jesus saith unto him, Go thy way; thy son liveth. And the man believed the word that Jesus had spoken unto him, and he went his way.

While the reply is undoubtedly a complete surprise to everyone else, including the man, it is the reply toward which Jesus' previous statement was leading. He is not going to perform an outward sign miracle such as those which so impressed the crowds previously. The man is not to have such an aid to his faith. He is being called upon to believe the bare word of Jesus without any confirmatory sign.

The man's faith is equal to the occasion. He "believes" Jesus' words, "Your son lives." This apparently means "is going to live" (interpreting the Greek present tense as futuristic). He accepts Jesus' statement as fact. He acts upon the assumption that things are indeed as Jesus says they are. He accepts that Jesus' authority is so great that He can perform the miracle at a distance. He goes home to see his son.

51 And as he was now going

**down, his servants met him, and told *him* , saying, Thy son liveth.
52 Then enquired he of them the hour when he began to amend. And they said unto him, Yesterday at the seventh hour the fever left him.**

As the man is going down to Capernaum, he encounters some of his slaves (Greek *doulos*) coming to meet him. Their thrilling words are direct: "Your son lives." Even in the midst of his rejoicing, he cannot restrain himself from asking them just what time it was when the boy started to get better. Without fully comprehending the purpose of his question, they replied, "Yesterday at about 1 p.m. the fever left him" (see 1:39; 4:6). The fever's breaking is considered to be the crucial moment of his recovery.

53 So the father knew that *it was* at the same hour, in the which Jesus said unto him, Thy son liveth: and himself believed, and his whole house.

The man is thrilled! That is the very time when Jesus spoke to him those momentous words, "Your son lives!" There can no longer be any doubt. The man has already "believed" Jesus' word (v. 50); now he "believes" in the fullest sense of the word. He becomes a believer. He is born from above. He reaches the same conclusion as the Samaritans (v. 42), "This is indeed the Christ, the Saviour of the world." The impact of this episode is so great that all the man's family and slaves (his whole house) believe in Christ also.

54 This *is* again the second miracle *that* Jesus did, when he was come out of Judaea into Galilee.

This somewhat difficult verse obviously does not mean that this is only the second miracle which Jesus had performed (see 2:23). There are several ways it can be understood without creating any real problem or contradiction. The important points are: (1) that this is the second of the seven great *sign* miracles around which John has woven his Gospel, (2) that it, like the first (2:11), takes place in Galilee, and (3) that it happens shortly after Jesus has returned from Judea to Galilee.

Some have held that this episode is a variant of the story of the healing of the centurion's slave (Mt. 8:5-13; Lk. 7:2-10). But about the only things in common are some interesting verbal parallels, and the healing at a distance. There it is a centurion (probably a heathen), here an officer of Herod (probably a Jew); there a slave, here a son. There Jesus speaks His word of power in Capernaum, here in Cana; there the centurion's faith evokes Jesus' praise, here the father's faith is weak; there the centurion asks Jesus not to come to his home, here the father begs Him to come. There the illness is paralysis, here a fever. There the elders plead for the man, here he pleads in person. This story takes place just after Jesus' return from Judea, that is evidently much later. Despite the verbal parallels the two stories are distinct (Morris 288).

Summary
(4:43-54)

After spending two days with the Samaritans, Jesus continues on to Galilee. Apparently, the reason for His going to Galilee is that He is not accepted as the Messiah by the people of Judea. The Galileans welcome Him because they are impressed by the miracles He has performed at Jerusalem.

Jesus returns to the scene of His first great miracle, Cana. A certain official whose son is deathly ill comes to Him there and pleads with Him to come down to his home in Capernaum and heal his son. Jesus responds enigmatically, perhaps to test the man's faith. However, the man simply repeats his plea with added desperation. Jesus then gives the man a promise: "Your son lives." There is no visible sign, only the promise; yet the man believes Jesus and trusts in His power.

On his way home he meets his servants who tell him that his son is going to live. He specifically asks them the time when he started to improve and determines that it was at the same time that Jesus spoke to him. As a result of this manifestation of Christ's great power (the power to heal at a distance) the man, with his whole household, trusts in Christ for salvation. This is the second great sign miracle.

Application: Teaching and Preaching the Passage

In order to understand this section, one must think in terms of the Evangelist's overall purpose for the Gospel, which is to persuade his readers to believe that Jesus is the Son of God so that they might thereby have eternal life (20:31). This passage illustrates the principle that Christ taught both Nicodemus and the woman of Samaria, that He has the power to grant eternal life to those who believe and trust in Him.

The passage has three major themes: (1) the fact of Christ's lifegiving power, (2) the nature of that power, and (3) the terms upon which that power is communicated. The fact of Christ's life-giving power is clearly established by the nature of the miracle, His giving life to one obviously at the point of death. The nature of that power is revealed to be absolute and autonomous by the fact that

He restores life from a distance by His mere word, not needing to be physically present. This power is communicated upon the terms of faith alone, faith in Christ's word and power apart from any physical sign or confirmation (see 20:29).

I. THE THIRD SIGN: THE LAME MAN HEALED (5:1-16)

Chapter 5 marks the beginning of a period of conflict between Christ and the religious authorities at Jerusalem. His statements in defense of the Sabbath healing arouse within those authorities an antagonism which will lead ultimately to the crucifixion.

1 After this there was a feast of the Jews; and Jesus went up to Jerusalem.

"After these things" (Greek plural) indicates that there is no direct connection between this event and those which have preceded it (Westcott) and that there has been a rather extended interval since they occurred (Godet). Just how long that interval has been is uncertain, as is the identity of the particular feast referred to. Although several suggestions have been put forward, none of them can be substantiated, and it is probably still best to refer to it as "the unknown feast." Brown, in fact, suggests that John purposely fails to identify the feast since such an identity might detract from his emphasis that the episode transpires on the Sabbath. If the particular identity of the feast were of importance in understanding the meaning of the episode, it would be given.

John's primary purpose for mentioning the fact that there is a feast is to explain why Jesus goes up to Jerusalem. The statement that Jesus goes up to Jerusalem is like a stage direction. Jesus is now back to stage center, Jerusalem. The drama proceeds.

Some have reversed the order of chapters 5 and 6, thus identifying the feast of chapter 5 with the "Passover" of chapter 6 (v. 4). The sheer improbability of such a reversal, coupled with the fact that there is no manuscript evidence for it, justifies its complete rejection.

Jesus apparently comes to Jerusalem alone, there being no mention of the disciples. During this early part of His ministry, Jesus apparently acts alone most of the time, His disciples having returned to their normal affairs. They will become full-time apostles only upon His return to Galilee after this episode.

2 Now there is at Jerusalem by the sheep _market_ a pool, which is called in the Hebrew tongue Bethesda, having five porches.

John's statement that there _is_ (present tense) at Jerusalem such a pool may very well indicate that the city of Jerusalem still stands as he writes and, therefore, that he writes before the fall of Jerusalem (see introduction). At any rate, such a pool did exist at the time of Christ.

There is no noun with the adjective "sheep." John supposes the place will be understood by his readers. He probably refers to the sheep _gate_. There was such a gate in the north wall of the city (Neh. 3:1, 32; 12:39). The name of the pool is Bethesda. Archaeology has identified this with a pool mentioned in the Dead Sea Scrolls called Betheshdathain (the equivalent of Bethesda except that it is dual, in the Hebrew, rather than singular). Apparently there were two pools beside each other. Just such a site has been found to the north of the Temple complex in Jerusalem: the remains of two pools surrounded by five porticos, just as John describes.

3 In these lay a great multitude of impotent folk, of blind, halt, with-ered, waiting for the moving of the water.
4 For an angel went down at a certain season into the pool, and troubled the water: whosoever then first after the troubling of the water stepped in was made whole of whatsoever disease he had.

Around the pool lay a great number of unfortunate people with various afflictions. The last part of v. 3 and all of v. 4 are not found in the oldest manuscripts of the Gospel, raising the question whether they were original (see Morris, Bruce, Brown, Bernard, and especially Godet). Regardless, the explanation does accurately reflect the superstition of the people and provides a proper understanding of the context for Christ's miracle.

The people were under the impression that from time to time an angel came and stirred up the water and that whoever first entered the water after this would be healed. The question may be asked as to how this (obviously incorrect) belief could be maintained over any extended period of time. The answer is that since many ailments are psychosomatic in nature, they can be "healed" if the victim believes strongly enough in the cure. This type of thing is quite common among primitive or otherwise superstitious peoples.

5 And a certain man was there, which had an infirmity thirty and eight years.

Among the great multitude of impotent folk is one particular man whose case is especially tragic and to whom Christ's attention is drawn. John does not state that this man remained constantly by the pool, only that he was there beside it on this occasion. Perhaps he thought it more likely that the angel would "stir the water" on the occasion of the feast than on just an ordinary day. Perhaps it was only during the feasts that the pool was so crowded. Speaking after the fact, John informs his readers that the man had been in his pathetic condition for 38 years. He mentions this to emphasize the severity and longevity of the man's affliction and, thus, the greatness of Christ's miracle. This is no mere psychosomatic or imaginary ailment. Thirty-eight years of wishful thinking have not helped one iota. There is no symbolical significance in the number of years that the man has been sick. It is simply a detail of fact.

6 When Jesus saw him lie, and knew that he had been now a long time *in that case,* he saith unto him, Wilt thou be made whole?

The occasion for Jesus' question to the impotent man is expressed in two Greek aorist participles, "saw" and "knew." When He perceived the man's misery and despair (as only He can) and when He became aware (this is the proper sense of "knew") that he had been in this pitiable condition for so long, His heart went out to the poor man.

He asks him with tenderness and solemnity, "Would you like to be well?" The question is not a request for information, but a challenge designed to focus the man's thoughts upon his plight and his need for deliverance. Such words would be cruel apart from Jesus' intention to heal.

7 The impotent man answered him, Sir, I have no man, when the water is troubled, to put me into the pool: but while I am coming, another steppeth down before me.

The impotent man answers from the perspective of the prevailing superstition. He says, by implication, "Of course I would, but the reason that I cannot is that I do not have anyone to assist me into the water when it is troubled. It takes me so long to drag myself to the water that someone else always gets there before me."

What a sad picture of loneliness, disappointment, and despair these words convey. How many times this scene had been reenacted one can only guess. The clear implication of his words is that if Jesus were really concerned about him, then He could assist him into the pool the next time it was stirred. He obviously had no idea who Christ was or what He intended to do. He saw no possibility of help for himself apart from the pool.

**8 Jesus saith unto him, Rise, take up thy bed, and walk.
9 And immediately the man was made whole, and took up his bed, and walked: and on the same day was the sabbath.**

One cannot help noticing the abruptness of Jesus' next words. He ignores the man's misguided comment about the healing powers of the pool. He offers no explanation of His own identity or power. He simply issues a challenge, a command which demands instantaneous obedience, "Arise, take up your bed and walk." (The bed was a straw mat and could be easily rolled up for carrying.)

Something in Christ's words, perhaps His tone of voice or His demeanor, must make a powerful impression upon the man, for he instantaneously obeys and his obedience brings instantaneous healing. Indeed, the act of obedience presupposes the healing, since it would be impossible had the healing not already occurred. Standing makes him whole, yet he can stand only because he is whole. Having experienced this much of the miracle, he picks up his pallet and begins to walk around. While the exact nature of the man's affliction is not known, it is reasonable to assume that it involved his legs and an inability either to stand or to walk.

At the end of the verse John adds what may seem but an afterthought but what he knows to be an important and ominous fact which is actually the whole point of the episode: "This transpired on a Sabbath Day." Apparently Jesus purposely chose to perform this miracle on the Sabbath. He wished to challenge the empty legalism of the Jewish leaders and, more important, to declare His own identity and authority as the Messiah. Previously he assumed authority over the Temple (2:18-21); now He assumes authority over the Sabbath. In both instances He exercised (and was understood by the Jews to be exercising) the prerogatives of God.

10 The Jews therefore said unto him that was cured, It is the sabbath day: it is not lawful for thee to carry _thy_ bed.

Therefore (i.e. since it is the Sabbath), the Jewish authorities in Jerusalem say to the man whom Jesus has healed, "It is the Sabbath; it is not lawful for you to carry your bed (today)." They may be motivated by the knowledge that the whole institution of the Sabbath could be jeopardized by the cumulative effect of piecemeal violations and, therefore, feel compelled to deal more harshly with individual instances of noncompliance than would seem reasonable if each case were viewed in isolation. If this is so, it demonstrates how one may fall into error even as he attempts to implement a sound policy. Regardless of the basis for the Pharisaic attitude, it had by the time of Jesus hardened into a harsh and pedantic legalism which had lost all sense of both the spirit and the purpose of the law and was totally insen-

sitive to human suffering. Their attempt to preserve the Sabbath by strict observance had actually perverted its true meaning.

11 He answered them, He that made me whole, the same said unto me, Take up thy bed, and walk.

The man's reply is not simply an attempt to shift responsibility for breaking the Sabbath from himself to Jesus. It is a subtle, sarcastic defense of himself and Jesus. It is as if he says, "The one who demonstrated the power to heal me of my infirmity of 38 years told me to take up my bed and walk. I assumed that one who had such authority was one whom I could safely obey. I didn't even think about it. I obeyed instinctively. You'll have to excuse me. This was rather an unusual situation. One just isn't himself on days when he is healed!"

12 Then asked they him, What man is that which said unto thee, Take up thy bed, and walk?
13 And he that was healed wist not who it was: for Jesus had conveyed himself away, a multitude being in _that_ place.

The authorities pick up immediately on the significance of his reference to a mysterious, miracle-working (and obviously heterodox) person. They want to know who this person is. They may even guess that it is Jesus. Regardless, such a person is very likely to cause them problems. Still, they are disappointed, because the man has no idea who his benefactor is. In the excitement, Jesus has disappeared into the crowd without a word. There has been no further conversation after the command of v. 8.

14 Afterward Jesus findeth him

in the temple, and said unto him, Behold, thou art made whole: sin no more, lest a worse thing come unto thee.

If Jesus' purpose were only to heal the impotent man physically, the episode would end with v. 13. The fact that Jesus later seeks out the man in the Temple shows that His purpose is not yet completely accomplished.

He still wants to help the man spiritually. He assures him that he has, indeed, been completely cured and that his cure is permanent. (The perfect tense of the Greek *ginomai* places emphasis upon the existing result of the verb and is a strong way of saying that a thing now is.) He also warns him to stop sinning (the Greek present imperative indicates the continuing nature of his sin). While there may not be any direct connection between the man's sin and his infirmity, Jesus wants him to understand that continuing in his sin is not the appropriate response to God's grace in healing him. He warns him, further, that if he does not stop sinning, something worse is going to happen to him. (This episode seems to indicate that salvation was not always simultaneous with healing.)

It also seems inescapable that Jesus wants to supply the information as to His identity which the man has previously lacked so that he can inform the Jewish leaders. It seems that Jesus does not wish to avoid a confrontation with them, that He is actually wanting to challenge them on their Sabbath traditions. Apparently, part of His purpose in performing this miracle has been to provoke such a confrontation.

15 The man departed, and told the Jews that it was Jesus, which had made him whole.

As soon as the man knows Jesus' identity, he goes straight to the authorities with the information. John makes no attempt to judge his motives at this point. Perhaps we can infer that his motives are positive on the assumption that specific attention would be called to the fact if they were negative.

16 And therefore did the Jews persecute Jesus, and sought to slay him, because he had done these things on the sabbath day.

The authorities now know for certain that Jesus was the one who healed the man, told him to carry his bed, and thereby (in their opinion) desecrated the Sabbath. Their anger is especially intense because they see it as being much worse to induce another to break the Sabbath than to break it oneself, and because they perceive this action as being part of a pattern of Sabbath desecration. Jesus "was doing" (Greek iterative imperfect tense) these things repeatedly. While the violation of the man who was healed was unintentional, even understandable, Jesus had acted knowingly. He was obviously involved in a campaign to destroy the sanctity of the Sabbath as they understood it.

The Jewish authorities did not take this matter lightly but mounted a campaign of persecution against Jesus that would eventually culminate in His crucifixion. They would seek, from this moment on, an opportunity to eliminate Him.

Summary
(5:1-16)

At some point after the healing of the nobleman's son, Jesus goes up alone to Jerusalem for the celebration of an unspecified feast. While there He comes to a pool called Bethesda near the Sheep Gate where a great many physically afflicted people are congregated. They believe that they may be healed there by

81

the magical action of the water after it is, supposedly, stirred by an angel from time to time.

Jesus is particularly drawn to one of these afflicted people, who has been in his sad condition for 38 years. There is apparently something especially pathetic about his case. Jesus asks him if he would like to be healed, and he replies that he surely would but that it is impossible since he has no one to help him into the pool after it is stirred by the angel. Ignoring this reply, Jesus commands him to rise, take up his bed, and walk. Spontaneously, instinctively, the man obeys. He rises, picks up his pallet, and begins to walk around. This would be a perfectly wonderful scene but for one thing: it is the Sabbath.

The Jewish authorities are not long in pointing out the impropriety of this man's carrying his bed on the Sabbath. They are quite expert in these matters and adept at such admonitions. The man who has been healed replies that the one who has healed him has told him to rise, take up his bed, and walk, and that he has done so without thinking. In the midst of being healed, he has forgotten that it is the Sabbath. The authorities want to know who it is that has healed him and encouraged him to violate the Sabbath. The man replies that he does not know his identity, that it has all happened so fast that he did not even get his name.

Later on, Jesus finds the man in the Temple and tells him that his healing is permanent, but He warns him to abandon his sin lest a worse fate befall him. Jesus obviously identifies Himself, because the man goes immediately and tells the authorities that it is Jesus who has healed him. When the authorities know this, they begin to plan how they can eliminate Jesus. They put in motion a program of opposition that will eventually lead to His crucifixion.

Application: Teaching and Preaching the Passage

There are three basic characters in this passage: the impotent man, Jesus, and the Pharisees. In the impotent man one sees a picture of humanity in its natural, sinful state. Men are utterly miserable in their sin and depravity. They are completely unable to remedy their own situation. They are totally confused as to the means of salvation. They are seeking for salvation where none is to be found. Many today are waiting for angels to come and trouble the waters—angels that will never come, angels that do not exist. These "angels" of superstition and religiosity will never come to save them, though they lie by their pools forever.

In Jesus may be seen the Savior sent from Heaven to earth, from God to men, to provide salvation for all who will receive it. He is sensitive to man's miserable condition. He empathizes with the suffering, the hopelessness, the despair. He wants to help. He is able to help. All that one must do to experience the sufficiency of His power is to trust Him and to obey Him. Obedience brings instant deliverance.

Finally, in the Jewish authorities one may see the ugly face of false religion. They are concerned only for their perverted legalistic traditions. The letter is all; the spirit is nothing. People do not count. Rules and ceremonies are everything. Love and concern are utterly foreign to their thinking. Instead of being the means of bringing men and God together, they serve to keep them apart.

J. The Third Discourse: "Equal With God" (5:17-47)

In this third discourse Jesus offers an explanation of His own identity and role. He reveals His unity and equal authority with the Father. He offers confirming evidence (witnesses) that His statements are true.

17 But Jesus answered them, My Father worketh hitherto, and I work.

Jesus "answers" the authorities in the sense that He makes a formal and public defense of Himself in response to their continuing accusations and harassment. His defense does not center on the humanitarian argument that it is obviously permissible to use the Sabbath for doing good (Mk. 3:4; Lk. 6:9; 13:15; Mt. 12:11). Rather, He develops a principle which He has laid down on another occasion, that He is actually superior to the Sabbath (Mk. 2:28; Mt. 12:8; Lk. 6:5). He claims the same immunity from Sabbath restrictions as God.

Just as God obviously continues His providential management of the universe on the Sabbath, so Jesus exercises the divine prerogative to do whatever He thinks appropriate on the Sabbath. Sabbath restrictions are designed to facilitate the worship of God by men, not to restrict the sovereign prerogatives of God. Jesus is obviously claiming to be God. He reenforces this claim by saying that God is His "Father." This implies that He considers Himself to be intimately related to God in a unique way which other men do not share. It implies that He is on a par with and of the same essential nature as God. That He is thus understood by the Jews is apparent from their reply in v. 18.

18 Therefore the Jews sought the more to kill him, because he not only had broken the sabbath, but said also that God was his Father, making himself equal with God.

The implication of this argument is not lost upon the Jewish leaders. They grasp immediately that Jesus is claiming to be "equal with God." When they understand this, they are more determined than ever to kill Him. It is bad enough that He has broken the Sabbath, but to claim that God is "His own father" (Greek *pater idios*), and thereby to make Himself equal with God, is utter blasphemy.

This verse makes it clear that the Jews at the time of Christ understood the term "Son of God" to mean equality, likeness, and identity with God (see also 10:30,33). It was not just a generic reference to the fact that Jesus, like all other men, was created in God's image. It was for claiming to be the Son of God (that God was His father) that Jesus would be crucified (19:7; Mt. 26:63,64; Mk. 14:61,62).

19 Then answered Jesus and said unto them, Verily, verily, I say unto you, The Son can do nothing of himself, but what he seeth the Father do: for what things soever he doeth, these also doeth the Son likewise.

With this verse Jesus begins a detailed defense of Himself against the charge of defiling the Sabbath. He will expand His pithy statement of v. 17 into a full-blown presentation of His own identity. The formula "verily, verily" (Greek *amen, amen*) indicates that what is to follow is especially solemn and significant (see 1:51).

Jesus first states the same truth negatively, then positively. Negatively, the relationship between the Father and the Son is so intimate that it is morally inconceivable that the Son should ever act independently of the Father. The emphasis is not so much the submission of the Son to the Father as the complete unanimity of perspective and purpose that exists between them.

Positively, the Son, though upon earth, shares totally the heavenly perspective and will of the Father. He is continuously aware of (sees) and acquiesces in everything that the Father is doing on the heavenly plane. His actions in the earthly sphere are entirely compatible with those of the Father in the heavenly sphere. The Son is merely adapting the heavenly program of the Father to the earthly plane.

20 For the Father loveth the Son, and sheweth him all things that himself doeth: and he will shew him greater works than these, that ye may marvel.

The reason the Son knows so intimately and perfectly the Father's most intimate thoughts and purposes is that the Father reveals them to Him; and the reason the Father reveals them to Him is that He dearly and personally loves Him. The word used here for "love" (Greek *phileo*), emphasizes the personal nature of this love. Such a love withholds nothing of itself from its object.

In the same way that Christ has sensed the will of God and acted upon it in regard to healing the lame man on the Sabbath, He is going to act in regard to matters of far greater importance. He is going to exercise divine prerogatives in ways that will completely astound His interrogators. This is the point of v. 20b. The immediate reference is to the works of resurrection and judgment which are mentioned in the verses immediately following, but subsequent miracles such as the raising of Lazarus may also be in view.

21 For as the Father raiseth up the dead, and quickeneth *them*; even so the Son quickeneth whom he will.

The first example of the Son's sharing the divine perspective and prerogatives of His Father is the power of resurrection. Just as the Father exercises the divine prerogative to raise the dead, so also does the Son. He has within Himself the authority to restore to life whomever He will. He is not a mere instrument of the Father's will; He is an independent source of autonomous, life-giving authority in His own right.

22 For the Father judgeth no man, but hath committed all judgment unto the Son.

Another way the Son exercises the divine perspective and prerogatives of His Father is in judgment. In fact, though judgment is obviously a prerogative reserved to God alone (Dt. 1:17; 32:35; Ps. 95:1), the Father has opted not to become actively involved in this function personally, but to place it solely within the jurisdiction of the Son.

23 That all *men* should honour the Son, even as they honour the Father. He that honoureth not the Son honoureth not the Father which hath sent him.

The divine prerogative of judgment has been committed exclusively to the Son so that men will ultimately be forced to honor the Son just as they honor the Father (Phil. 2:9-11). The same honor that is due to the Father is due also to the Son.

Men often tend to honor the first person of the Trinity more than the other two. God wants the very same honor that is accorded to the "Father in heaven" to be extended to the incarnate Son upon earth. The Son is "Immanuel"— God with us—and as such the representative of the Godhead upon earth. It is important that the same honor be extended to God come near us in tangible form as to the transcendent King of Heaven. Failure to honor the incarnate Son is failure to honor the Father in Heaven as well. Again, Christ makes a clear-cut claim to unity with the Father.

24 Verily, verily, I say unto you, He that heareth my word, and believeth on him that sent me, hath everlasting life, and shall not come into condemnation; but is passed from death unto life.

Again the words "verily, verily" indicate that Christ considers the statement to follow especially solemn and significant (see 1:51). There are actually two truths set forth. First, He continues to emphasize His unity with the Father by saying that to hear (hear with appreciation, take heed to) His word (His whole teaching) is to believe the Father who sent Him. He is so intimately identified with the Father that to hear Him is to hear the Father, and to believe Him is to believe the Father just as to see Him is to see the Father (see 10:30; 14:9).

Second, the person who believes on Christ (and thereby on the Father) has (presently possesses) eternal life and will not ever come under the condemnation of God's righteous wrath. He has already passed from death unto life. Eternal life, the life of the age to come, the life of the heavenly sphere, is already his present possession. He is already living on the heavenly plane.

EDITOR'S NOTE ON JOHN 5:24: DO PROMISES TO BELIEVERS GUARANTEE THEIR SECURITY?

Those who teach the unconditional security of a person once regenerated often use, as an argument for their position, the strong *promises* that the Bible makes to Christians. Many of these are contained in the Gospel of John, and John 5:24 is one of the outstanding examples: He that...believeth...hath everlasting life, and *shall not come into condemnation*; but is passed from death unto life.

There are two important things about such a promise. First, and most important, if it is interpreted as a guarantee that the believer's saving relationship to God can never change, then it proves too much! The problem is that the very same kind of promises are made to *unbelievers*! And if a promise of condemnation to unbelievers does not mean that an unbeliever cannot change his state and become a believer, then a promise of no condemnation to a believer also does not mean he can never change his state and become an unbeliever.

Consider John 3:36, for example, and put the two side by side:

"He that believeth not *shall not see life*" (3:36). "He that believeth *shall not come into condemnation*" (5:24).

The grammar of the two is identical; they must be interpreted in the same way. No one would say that 3:36 means one who is presently an unbeliever is forever doomed to that promised destiny. He can become a believer. All 3:36 means, then, is that the person who remains in the camp of unbelievers will inevitably share the destiny promised to unbelievers. Just so, all 5:24 means is that the person who remains in the camp of believers will inevitably share the destiny promised to believers.

Second, the tense-action in the verb *believe* sustains this understanding of the meaning. In this verse "believing" (a present tense participle) is in linear action—just as it usually is in the Gospel of John. The faith that saves is an ongoing faith, a continuing belief. We could appropriately render the verse thus: "The one who *is believing* has eternal life and shall not come into condemnation." Certainly, the person who maintains faith will share the destiny promised believers. And the very same thing applies to 3:36 about unbelief. "He that believeth not" (another present tense participle) is also linear action. The one who persists in unbelief will share the destiny promised those who do not believe.

25 Verily, verily, I say unto you, The hour is coming, and now is, when the dead shall hear the voice of the Son of God: and they that hear shall live.

Again the formula "verily, verily" indicates great solemnity and significance (see 1:51). The hour is coming when Jesus is going to speak the word of power and all the dead will hear His voice and come to life (6:40; 1 Th. 4:16; Rev. 20:5,12). Furthermore, in a sense, that hour is already present because those who are spiritually dead in trespasses and sins may pass from death unto life even now if they will hear and believe in the Son of God. This is one of only three times in this Gospel where Jesus refers to Himself directly as the Son of God (see 10:36; 11:4). Of course, that He is such is often presupposed, as just above in vv. 17-23.

26 For as the Father hath life in himself; so hath he given to the Son to have life in himself.

The basis for Jesus' ability to grant life (v. 21) is that He is, Himself, an independent and autonomous source of life. Just as the Father has life "in Himself" (Greek *en heauto*), so the Son has life "in Himself." That is to say that as the Father possesses life by His essential inherent nature, so also does the Son. As the Father is able to impart life to others (Gen. 2:7), so also is the Son (v. 21; cf.10:17,18). He is able to grant life on His own authority (6:44; 11:25, 26).

This independent and autonomous life was "given" to the Son by the Father in the sense that He was endowed with it when He was sent as Immanuel into the world. Christ's eternal self-existence is an attribute of His deity rather than a gift conferred upon Him by the Father. This phrase does not refer to Christ's eternal status vis-a-vis the Father or the doctrine of the eternal generation of the Son (see Plummer, Bernard).

27 And hath given him authority to execute judgment also, because he is the Son of man.

In addition to the power of life (v. 23; v. 26), the Father has also given to Christ the power of judgment (v. 22). This verse advances that idea by stating that Jesus has been given the authority to execute judgment because He is "(the) Son of Man." Some interpret this to mean simply that since He is Himself a man that He is uniquely qualified to judge men. This seems to be out of keeping with the theme of the section, which is the likeness of the Son with the Father.

The more likely interpretation is that this term refers back to the apocalyptic personage of Dan. 7:13, "the Son of Man." This personage was to be given dominion, glory, and a kingdom. He was to rule forever over all peoples, nations, and languages. Jesus, therefore, has been given the authority to execute judgment because He is this great apocalyptic figure.

The absence of the Greek article with the phrase "Son of Man" does not indicate that it should be understood as "a son of man." Rather, it means that "Son of Man" has become an established phrase or official title. Such titles have a tendency to be used without an article (see Bernard, Schnackenburg). Another reason for the absence of the article is that there is no article in the LXX (Greek O.T.) of Dan. 7:13 (see Brown).

28 Marvel not at this: for the hour is coming, in the which all that are in the graves shall hear his voice,

29 And shall come forth; they that have done good, unto the resurrection of life; and they that have done evil, unto the resurrection of damnation.

The fact of Jesus' equality with the Father, as evidenced by His exercise of two exclusively divine prerogatives, resurrection and judgment, ought not to be the cause of amazement or unbelief. On the great day of the Lord, His exercise of these prerogatives will be obvious to everyone. Then Jesus will not only raise all the dead to life but judge them as well. The dead shall awaken at His voice (Dan. 12:2a), and come forth to be judged (Rev. 20:12). Those who have done righteously shall awaken to eternal life (Dan. 12:2b) and those who have done wickedly to eternal punishment (Dan. 12:2c).

30 I can of mine own self do nothing: as I hear, I judge: and my judgment is just; because I seek not mine own will, but the will of the Father which hath sent me.

Jesus reiterates and expands what He said in v. 19, relating the truth expressed there especially to His role as judge. His unity with the Father is so complete that it is morally inconceivable that He should ever judge differently from the Father. Just as Jesus does upon earth what He "sees" the Father doing in Heaven, so He judges upon earth exactly as He "hears" the Father giving judgment in Heaven. This being the case, Christ's judgments upon earth must be truly just and must conform completely to the will of the Father. His verdicts can in no way be prejudiced, for He has no other purpose than to fulfil the perfect will of the Father.

There is a subtle emphasis hidden in these words. In effect Jesus is saying, "How could one who is to judge all mankind, one who shares intimately and completely the absolute justice of the Father, speak anything but the truth? Cannot such a one as this bear witness to Himself and be believed?"

31 If I bear witness of myself, my witness is not true.

These words express the general principle that a man's own testimony is not sufficient to establish beyond all doubt the truth of what he says. However, there is a note of irony that the word of the one who will someday judge the world should not be taken as utterly conclusive.

32 There is another that beareth witness of me; and I know that the witness which he witnesseth of me is true.

Jesus hastens to add that there is one who is bearing witness (Greek present tense, indicating ongoing action) to the truth of all that He has said. Jesus knows that this one's testimony is absolutely reliable.

Who is this unnamed witness? Some have supposed that Jesus means John the Baptist, but that is highly unlikely. John the Baptist was in prison at this time and his active witness to Christ had ceased, whereas the witness referred to here was still going on as Jesus spoke. The witness of John the Baptist was fully developed in the early part of the Gospel. Now the focus has shifted from John's witness to the Father's witness.

Christ is referring here to the Father as the chief source of confirming testimony concerning His identity and mission. Christ knows that this witness can verify His claims. There is no apprehension that the witness will not be convincing. With the Father Himself ready and willing to speak in His defense, Jesus has no fear of being discredited.

33 Ye sent unto John, and he bare witness unto the truth.

The Baptist is mentioned only for the purpose of a negative comparison (v. 36). When the Jews sent the delegation to him (1:19), John gave clear witness to the fact that he was not the Messiah and later made clear that Jesus was the Messiah.

34 But I receive not testimony from man: but these things I say, that ye might be saved.

Jesus does not wish to rest His case on the testimony of mere human beings. Still, He is willing to refer to the testimony of the Baptist because He realizes that it carries weight with some of His hearers, and He does not wish to withhold from them any evidence that might convince them to believe on Him and be saved. Jesus' rejection of merely human witness to His identity clearly implies the existence and availability of the Father as a *divine* witness.

35 He was a burning and a shining light: and ye were willing for a season to rejoice in his light.

The imperfect tense of "was" indicates that John is no longer active. He is apparently either in prison or dead as Jesus speaks. John has been a burning and shining lamp (Greek *luchnos*). He has spoken forth the message of God; he has called men to repentance; he has been the Messiah's herald. For a while the Jews have accepted him as a prophet and honored him as such, but they have never really understood or obeyed him, and before long they will have completely forgotten him.

36 But I have greater witness than *that* of John: for the works which the Father hath given me

to finish, the same works that I do, bear witness of me, that the Father hath sent me.

After digressing to explain that the source of testimony which He has referred to (v. 32) is not John the Baptist, Jesus goes on to explain that the confirming witness to his identity and authority is, of course, the Father. The first aspect of the Father's confirmation is the miracles which He empowered Christ to perform. These miracles speak for themselves. They clearly demonstrate a supernatural dimension in Christ (3:2). They show Him to possess a divine origin and sanction. At the very least, they present a prima facie basis for accepting His claims. This argument is especially strong in its context, coming so soon after the miraculous healing of the impotent man.

37 And the Father himself, which hath sent me, hath borne witness of me. Ye have neither heard his voice at any time, nor seen his shape.
38 And ye have not his word abiding in you: for whom he hath sent, him ye believe not.

Not only by empowering Him to perform miracles does the Father bear witness to the Son. He speaks even more directly to the hearts of those who are sensitive to His voice, confirming to their inner consciousness that Jesus is indeed His Son. These verses must be understood in terms of 1 Jn. 5:9,10, which clearly state that the witness of the Father to His Son is given within the believer's heart.

Jesus indicates that this method is not effective with the Jewish leaders because they are totally insensitive to God's voice. They are not on His wave length. They are not permeated with the knowledge of His Word. There is no

Spirit-wrought sensitivity to or appreciation for the truth within them. They hear Immanuel speak, but nothing registers. His words strike no harmonious or responsive chord within them.

39 Search the scriptures; for in them ye think ye have eternal life: and they are they which testify of me.
40 And ye will not come to me, that ye might have life.

Jesus challenges His accusers to search the (O.T.) Scriptures which they wrongly suppose to substantiate their own legalistic viewpoint and to offer them eternal life on their own terms. Actually, if correctly interpreted, the Scriptures bear their own witness to Jesus. He is the theme of every page. Ironically, these people, because of their misguided hope of obtaining eternal life through their legalistic and perverted use of the Scriptures, actually reject the one of whom the Scriptures speak and who is the only source of the eternal life which they seek. Their rejection is both knowing and willful.

41 I receive not honour from men.
42 But I know you, that ye have not the love of God in you.

As in v. 34 Jesus did not need the testimony of mere men, so here He has no need for the honor which they could give Him if they would receive Him. Yet, even though he really does not need or desire the honor of men, they still ought to give it, and the reason that they do not is that they do not have the love of God in their hearts. Just as their lack of spiritual sensitivity caused them to reject the witness of the Father concerning His Son, so the complete absence of a real love for God causes them to turn from the Son in disdain rather than to receive

Him with open arms.

43 I am come in my Father's name, and ye receive me not: if another shall come in his own name, him ye will receive.

Jesus states that He has come in the name of His Father. To the Jews, one's name was an expression of his personality and essential character. "Thus, 'I am come in the Name of my Father' does not only mean 'I am come as His representative, having been sent by Him,' although it includes this; but it conveys the idea that the Incarnate Son reveals the Father in His character and power" (Bernard 255). Even though this is true, the Jewish authorities have utterly rejected Him. Their rejection at this point is part of a general pattern that runs all through the Fourth Gospel (e.g. 1:11; 3:11,32; 12:37).

Jesus goes on to say that, while they have rejected Him who has come in His Father's name, if anyone were to come in his own name (i.e. making boastful claims about himself), they would believe him. While these words are spoken generically with no particular person in view, they certainly are applicable to Simon Bar-Kochba, the leader of the Second Jewish Revolt (A.D. 132-135), whose claim to be the Messiah was widely accepted and who led the Jews to a disastrous defeat at the hands of the Romans. These words may point, for their ultimate fulfillment, to Antichrist.

44 How can ye believe, which receive honour one of another, and seek not the honour that *cometh* from God only?

Now Jesus attacks the real basis of the Jewish leaders' unbelief. Their problem is pride. They refuse to accept the truth of Christ's words because they are unwilling to submit themselves to God's will. They are unwilling to conform their lives and their religion to His truth. Deep down they do not want to please God but themselves (each other). They deliberately choose not to believe Jesus. To do so would necessitate modifications of their religion and life style, changes they have no intention of making. Therefore, as long as they persist in this attitude, it is impossible for them to believe (see Brown).

45 Do not think that I will accuse you to the Father: there is *one* that accuseth you, *even* Moses in whom ye trust.

Jesus has shown that the Scriptures, which the Jews wrongfully suppose to substantiate their own position, actually bear witness to Him. Now He turns to another special focus of their Jewishness, their pride in Moses. He says that it is not He who shall accuse them on the day of judgment, but Moses. His words are filled with irony. He does not say that there will not be such a day of judgment. He implies very strongly that there will. He does not say that He will play no role at all in that judgment. He has already made it clear that He will. He only says that He will not be their accuser. He leaves unsaid at this point that He will be their judge. He does not say that no one will accuse them. He only says that their accuser will be Moses rather than Himself. They will be accused by the very authority they mistakenly appeal to against Christ, the very Moses whose disciples they so haughtily claim to be (9:28). Moses is (Greek present tense) their accuser even at this moment. His inscripturated witness accuses them.

46 For had ye believed Moses, ye would have believed me: for he wrote of me.

However, it is obvious that the Jews do not rightly understand or believe Moses. If they did then they would believe in Christ, because He is the central theme of Moses' writings. Whether this should be taken as a reference to a specific passage (like Dt. 18:18) or as a general reference to the whole meaning of the Pentateuch is uncertain (see Brown). Either way, the meaning is the same.

47 But if ye believe not his writings, how shall ye believe my words?

Again there is sharp irony in Jesus' words. There tends to be a uniformity to people's behavior. Willful ignorance at one point will more than likely express itself at another. Never mind all their protestations to the contrary; if the Jews do not actually believe Moses (as Jesus has demonstrated), how can they believe Jesus? Their problem is not just an innocent confusion over the facts about Jesus; it is a total and willful rejection of God's truth—all of God's truth, that which comes through Moses just as much as that which comes through Christ.

**Summary
(5:17-47)**

In this third discourse Jesus further defines His own identity by demonstrating His unity and equality with the Father. He claims the same immunity from Sabbath restrictions as God whom He calls His Father. This is equivalent to claiming that He is God. His words are thus understood by the Jewish leaders. They consider His claim blasphemous and are, from this moment on, determined to eliminate Him.

Jesus defends Himself at length against the charge of Sabbath desecration and blasphemy. He states that there is a total identity of purpose between the Father and Himself. This identity exists because the Father loves the Son (Jesus) so completely that He reveals to Him all of His counsel. However, this is not the only effect of the Father's love for the Son. The Father is also going to demonstrate His love for the Son by committing to Him even greater powers than have yet been evident. To the Son are committed the divine prerogatives of resurrection and judgment. The Father's purpose in committing these powers to the Son is that men will honor and worship the Son just as they do the Father.

To believe Jesus' words is actually to believe the Father and to possess eternal life. It is Jesus who will soon speak the word of power that will raise the dead, for He is an independent and autonomous source of life just as is the Father. He will also judge the world, for He is the apocalyptic "Son of Man" spoken of by Daniel. While these truths may seem amazing, they will be obvious to all on the day of the Lord. Jesus goes on to explain that it is impossible that His judgment should ever deviate from His Father's, for He thinks the same way as His Father.

Jesus insists that He has evidence other than His own word as to His identity. There is another that bears testimony. This one is not John the Baptist, although John certainly was such a witness. This other witness is greater than John; in fact, this witness is superhuman. This witness is the Father Himself, who has given His testimony through the miracles which Jesus has performed and through the inner voice of His Spirit. Yet none of this testimony can have any effect on the Jews because they are totally insensitive to it. They are not attuned to hear God's voice, nor do they properly understand the Scriptures. They turn away from Jesus and seek eternal life by means of a pedantic study of the O.T., not realizing that the O.T. is in its very essence about Him. Yet while they search so diligently for eternal life where it cannot be found, they will not accept it from the only one whose it is to give.

They willfully refuse to believe on and worship Christ; yet that is not really surprising. They have no love for God within them; therefore they spurn God's Son. Jesus has come into the world as Immanuel only to be totally rejected; yet if one comes boastfully claiming to be something in himself, they will receive him. Their depraved, proud natures guarantee it.

In the final instance it will not be Jesus who will condemn them. It will be Moses himself. This is the ultimate irony. The very one they claim to follow, the one they quote to justify their rejection of Jesus, will be the one who will testify against them. The reason that they reject Christ is that they have rejected Moses. They have completely misunderstood his message.

Application: Teaching and Preaching the Passage

This section might very well be entitled, "Jesus' Claim To Be God." First, the claim is stated unequivocally in vv. 17 and 18. Jesus claims to be God in two ways. He claims that God is His Father, which in the minds of His hearers is equivalent to saying that He is God. He claims an authority analogous with the Father's by saying that He is no less entitled to work on the Sabbath than is the Father. He applies an exemption allowed for the Father to Himself.

Second, the claim is expounded logically, and in detail, in vv. 19-30. Jesus explains that there is a total unity of perspective and purpose between the Father and Himself (vv. 19, 20 and 30). He also explains that there is an equality of authority and function which He shares with the Father (vv. 21-29).

91

Third, the claim is attested irrefutably in vv. 31-47. Jesus Himself attests to the truth of His claim (v. 31) although, for the sake of argument, His own witness will be discounted. John the Baptist attests to the truth of His claim but will not be cited on the grounds of best evidence (vv. 32-36a). The Father Himself attests His claim by means of the miracles that He has empowered Jesus to perform while upon earth (v. 36b), by means of His inward witness to the hearts of those who truly know and love Him (vv.37,38), and by the O.T., especially the writings of Moses, through which He has revealed His will to men (vv. 39-47).

K. The Fourth Sign: Feeding the Multitude (6:1-15)

1 After these things Jesus went over the sea of Galilee, which is *the sea* of Tiberias.

There is apparently some lapse of time between the healing of the impotent man in Jerusalem and the present episode (see comments on "after these things" 5:1). Jesus is back in Galilee but there is no explanation of how He has come to be there. Some (e.g. Bernard and Schnackenburg) reverse the order of chapters five and six, thinking thereby to provide a more logical geographical sequence, with Jesus not going up to Jerusalem until after the Galilean events of chapter six. This suggestion creates as many problems as it solves and is quite arbitrary. There is no good reason for abandoning the original sequence. It is certainly feasible that Jesus goes up to Jerusalem alone and then returns to Galilee, rejoins His disciples, and begins a new, more public phase of His ministry.

The feeding of the 5,000 begins with Jesus crossing the Sea of Galilee, going from the northwestern shore near Ca-

pernaum to some unspecified point on the northeastern shore. John further identifies the Sea of Galilee as the Sea of Tiberias, the name by which it came to be known in the second half of the first century and the name by which it would be known to his readers. (The name came from the city on its western shore named in honor of the Roman emperor Tiberius, founded by Herod Antipas in about A.D. 20.) John is the only one of the Gospel writers to refer to the Sea of Galilee in this way.

2 And a great multitude followed him, because they saw his miracles which he did on them that were diseased.

Jesus is being continuously followed (Greek imperfect tense) by a great crowd of people. They follow Him only because they are impressed by the many "signs" or miracles which He has been doing, not because they truly understand or believe on Him. John does not give the details of these miracles other than to mention that most of them are healings. He seems to assume that his readers are familiar with the Synoptics where these miracles are delineated.

3 And Jesus went up into a mountain, and there he sat with his disciples.

Jesus goes up with His disciples into the heights to the east of the Sea of Galilee now known as the Golan Heights. Mark 6:31 indicates that He wishes to provide a time of rest and spiritual renewal for Himself and the Twelve. They have just returned from their preaching mission while Jesus, Himself, has been involved in His great Galilean ministry (Mk. 2-5) and has only recently been informed of the execution of John the Baptist. These circumstances make such a time of retirement desirable. That Jesus "sits" with the disciples indicates that He is teaching and instructing them. Perhaps He is explaining to them the significance of John's death and its implications for His own ministry and theirs.

4 And the passover, a feast of the Jews, was nigh.

John pauses to point out that it is the season of the Passover. This is the second of three Passovers mentioned in the Fourth Gospel (2:13; 11:55). Both of the other two are spent in Jerusalem, but for this one Jesus remains in Galilee. This may be one of those incidental details which John often provides, or it may be mentioned purposely to establish an appropriate context for the events which follow.

5 When Jesus then lifted up *his* eyes, and saw a great company come unto him, he saith unto Philip, Whence shall we buy bread, that these may eat?

The Synoptics reveal that a great crowd of people followed Jesus out to His place of retreat, that He healed many of them, and that He taught them concerning the kingdom of God. Toward the end of the day as Jesus observes that the people keep on coming (Greek present tense) and that the crowd is growing larger and larger, He says to Philip, "Where shall we buy bread so that all these people may have something to eat?"

6 And this he said to prove him: for he himself knew what he would do.

Philip, a native of Bethsaida (1:44), the nearest village (Lk. 9:10), is a logical choice for such a question; however, John lets his readers in on a secret. He points out parenthetically that Jesus al-

ready knows what He is going to do and that He only asks this question to test Philip. Does Philip really understand who Jesus is? Will He be able to approach the question from the perspective of Christ's supernatural power? These are the questions which Christ is seeking answers to.

7 Philip answered him, Two hundred pennyworth of bread is not sufficient for them, that every one of them may take a little.

Philip's answer reveals a complete lack of the true perspective. His summary of the situation reflects only a pragmatic naturalism and is not at all modified by the fact that He is speaking to the incarnate Son of God. He merely points out the insurmountable practical difficulties and flippantly assumes that they preclude any further discussion. Needless to say, Philip fails the test.

The *denarius* was a typical day's wage for a common laborer. In our terms, then, Philip was speaking of 200 days' earnings; thus NIV: "eight months wages."

**8 One of his disciples, Andrew, Simon Peter's brother, saith unto him,
9 There is a lad here, which hath five barley loaves, and two small fishes: but what are they among so many?**

At this point the disciples, apparently in response to an earlier instruction from Jesus that they should ascertain exactly what food is available (Mk. 6:38), report that, for all practical purposes, there is none. Andrew, however, in the interest of precise accuracy, mentions that He has found one lad who has five barley loaves and two small fish. He hastens to add that, of course, he does not suppose this fact to be especially relevant.

Perhaps Andrew's words imply a faint glimmer of faith yet a reluctance to appear ridiculous by expressing it directly.

10 And Jesus said, Make the men sit down. Now there was much grass in the place. So the men sat down, in number about five thousand.

His efforts at stimulating the faith of the disciples having come to naught, Jesus begins preparations for the miracle He has been planning all along (v. 6). His first instruction is for the disciples to seat all the people upon the ground.

John's mention that there is "much grass" corresponds with Mark's reference to the "green grass" upon which the multitude sits (Mk. 6:39). This correspondence of incidental detail lends credibility to both accounts. John also agrees with all three Synoptists in placing the number of the men at 5,000 (plus women and children).

11 And Jesus took the loaves; and when he had given thanks, he distributed to the disciples, and the disciples to them that were set down; and likewise of the fishes as much as they would.

Jesus' next action is to take the loaves and the fish, offer thanks for them, and give them to the disciples; they, in turn, give them to the multitude. While some manuscripts of John do not mention the intermediary step of Jesus' giving the loaves and fish to the disciples, the Synoptics make clear that He did so and that they actually distributed the food to the multitude.

It has been suggested that there was nothing miraculous about this episode at all. Some believe that what actually transpired on this occasion was on the order of a sacramental meal with each person receiving only a small, symbolic portion.

Such an interpretation is ruled out by the fact that everyone is said to have eaten as much as he wanted. This indicates that what was provided was a fully satisfying meal and not merely a symbolic portion. Christ's whole purpose for feeding the crowd was that they were hungry.

Another naturalistic explanation is that when the people saw the generosity of the lad in sharing his bread and fish, they all opened up the food that they had selfishly been concealing and in doing so found that there was plenty for all. This interpretation is, of course, completely at variance with the writer's purpose in relating the episode and the effect which he says it has upon the crowd. It is unlikely that the crowd would develop the (superficial and materialistic) attitude toward Jesus which they did (v. 26) on the basis of a "miracle" which consisted of nothing but their own acts of inspired generosity.

The actual miracle apparently occurred as Jesus blessed the loaves and fishes before He distributed them to the disciples. The somewhat peculiar wording of the last part of v. 23 seems to connect the miracle with Christ's action of giving thanks. It is hard to understand how Christ could distribute the five loaves and two fish to the Twelve if they had not already been, at that point, miraculously multiplied. There may also have been further miraculous multiplication as the disciples distributed to the multitude.

12 When they were filled, he said unto his disciples, Gather up the fragments that remain, that nothing be lost.
13 Therefore they gathered *them* together, and filled twelve baskets with the fragments of the five barley loaves, which remained over and above unto them that had eaten.

These verses confirm that a miracle did, indeed, take place. After everyone has eaten all he wants, the disciples gather up 12 large baskets (Greek *kophinos*) of fragments—the number 12 perhaps indicating a basket for each disciple. Neither of the alternative explanations for this miracle (see v. 11) account for this surplus. John may also wish to convey the idea that there is always a superabundance in God's grace.

14 Then those men, when they had seen the miracle that Jesus did, said, This is of a truth that prophet that should come into the world.

This event is not perceived by the people who are present as a sacramental rite or an object lesson in generosity in which they have played a key role, but as a miracle performed by Jesus. They equate Jesus' miraculous provision of bread with Moses' miraculous provision of manna in the wilderness and come to the conclusion that Jesus must be the "prophet like unto (Moses)," the Messiah (see comments on 1:21; 6:40,41).

15 When Jesus therefore perceived that they would come and take him by force, to make him a king, he departed again into a mountain himself alone.

This great miracle, intended primarily to strengthen and clarify the faith of the disciples (v. 6), has the secondary effect of compounding the misguided enthusiasm of the Galilean public. They are so convinced that Jesus is the Messiah that they are ready to proclaim Him their king right on the spot.

Of course, this is not the Father's plan. This is not the way Jesus is to redeem Israel. Instead, it is but another form of Satan's subtle temptation that Jesus accept earthly authority from him rather than the Father (Mt. 4:8,9). As such it is immediately and unequivocally rejected. Jesus withdraws from the throng and retreats to the isolation of one of the nearby mountains.

Summary
(6:1-15)

At some point in time after the events of chapter five, Jesus crosses from the northwestern to the northeastern shore of the Sea of Galilee. A great throng of people follows Him. They follow Him only because of a superficial attraction to His miracles rather than from a true belief. Jesus seeks to escape from the crowd by going with His disciples up into the mountains for a time of relaxation, instruction, and discussion. John points out that this episode occurred just prior to the Passover.

Toward the end of the day, as Jesus observes that the crowd which has followed Him is growing larger and larger, He says to Philip, "Where are we going to buy food so that we may feed all these?" Jesus asks this solely for the purpose of testing Philip's faith. He has already determined His course of action. Philip totally misses Jesus' point. He understands the question only in earthly terms and answers that the problem is pragmatically insurmountable. Andrew then reports that there is a lad who has a small lunch with him but hastens to add that he really doesn't think that this will be of help.

Jesus gives up on getting the disciples to understand the full significance of what He is about to do and proceeds with the miracle. He instructs the disciples to seat the people upon the grass. He then takes the lad's lunch, blesses it and distributes it to the disciples who in turn distribute it to the people. Everyone has all that he wants, and when all have eaten the disciples gather up 12 large baskets of leftovers.

The people who are present understand this event as a supernatural miracle. They interpret it as indicating that Jesus is the Messiah and are ready to declare Him their king. Jesus refuses their offer, however, for He knows the shallow and superstitious nature of their commitment. He withdraws to a mountain to be alone.

Application: Teaching and Preaching the Passage

This episode underscores the supernatural identity and power of Christ as He transforms the five loaves and two fish into enough food to feed a vast multitude, but it does more than that. Two facts essential to a full understanding of it are that it occurs just before Passover and that in v. 48 Jesus clearly identifies Himself as the "bread of life." Both indicate that this event is an object lesson demonstrating that Jesus is God's only provision for the salvation of mankind. Just as men must depend upon Him for food in the wilderness, so must they rely upon Him for eternal life.

There is also the lesson that, though Christians do not have in themselves the ability to meet people's needs, when they make what they have available to God, He can bless and multiply it and make it more than enough.

Finally, there is the lesson that Jesus will not consent to be accepted by men on their own terms. The Galilean multitude wanted to structure Christ's ministry along the lines of their own priorities. They wished to reject that aspect of His identity which is most central (His having come to seek and to save the lost and to offer Himself as a sacrifice for sin) and to accept that which was only peripheral (His ability to perform beneficent miracles). They wanted Him to become their earthly king, a provider of their physical needs, a source of temporal security, rather than their Savior and Lord.

L. The Fifth Sign: Walking On Water (6:16-21)

The disciples may very well have been discouraged by Jesus' refusing the kingship which the people had offered Him. This event was no doubt intended to bolster their morale and their confidence in their master. A fuller account of the incident is related in Mt. 14:22-33 and Mk. 6:45-52.

**16 And when even was *now* come, his disciples went down unto the sea,
17 And entered into a ship, and went over the sea toward Capernaum. And it was now dark, and Jesus was not come to them.**

At some point late in the afternoon of the same day Jesus has fed the 5,000, the disciples, in obedience to Christ's previous instruction (Mk. 6:45), board their ship (Mk. 6:32) to go back to Capernaum, apparently by way of Bethsaida (Mk. 6:45). While the particulars of their plans are not clear, apparently they intended to meet Jesus at some point along the way and take Him on board for the remainder of the journey. They apparently waited for Him at that point until well after dark before finally deciding to go on without Him.

**18 And the sea arose by reason of a great wind that blew.
19 So when they had rowed about five and twenty or thirty furlongs, they see Jesus walking on the sea, and drawing nigh unto the ship: and they were afraid.
20 But he saith unto them, It is I; be not afraid.
21 Then they willingly received him into the ship: and immediate-**

ly the ship was at the land whither they went.

Their progress is greatly impeded, however, by a strong and contrary wind, so that the journey takes them much longer than it normally would have. In fact, by the time of the fourth watch (i.e. almost morning: Mt. 14:25) they have only covered about three miles and are still "in the midst of the sea" (Mk. 6:47,48).

At this point they see what they at first think to be an apparition (Mk. 6:49) approaching them across the water and are frightened. As this form draws nearer, however, it speaks to them saying, "It is I; be not afraid" (Mk. 6:50), and they know that it is Jesus. Just as soon as the disciples can eagerly take Jesus on board, the storm abates (Mk. 6:51), and in almost no time at all they are at Capernaum.

Some have attempted to eliminate the miraculous element of this episode by suggesting that Jesus was actually walking along the shore rather than upon the water. This contradicts the express statement of all three Gospel accounts that Jesus was "walking on the sea." It also presupposes an extreme credulity and lack of attention on the part of the disciples. It is unreasonable that these men, many of whom had fished these very waters from their childhood and were therefore perfectly aware of their position, could become so completely disoriented as this theory supposes. Furthermore, Matthew's account of Peter's attempt to join Jesus on the water (Mt. 14:28-30) renders any such naturalizing explanation wholly untenable.

Summary
(6:16-21)

Late in the afternoon the disciples embark on their journey back to Capernaum. A contrary wind greatly impedes their progress and as morning approaches, they are still far from their destination when Jesus comes walking toward them on the sea. At first they think Him to be an apparition and are very much afraid, but when He speaks to them they perceive His identity and welcome Him into the ship. In a very short time they reach Capernaum and their ordeal is over.

Application: Teaching and Preaching the Passage

Jesus' purpose in instructing the disciples to return without Him by sea to Capernaum is to demonstrate that He will always be with them as they carry out His commands. He wants them to understand that, no matter how many difficulties they encounter and no matter how unequal to the task their own strength may be, He will not allow them to fail. He wants them to understand that His power is greater than any obstacle they will ever encounter and that they are to rely upon Him totally and trust Him implicitly even as they obey Him absolutely.

M. The Fourth Discourse: The Bread of Life (6:22-71)

There are two very different ways of interpreting and understanding this discourse. Some believe that it is primarily an explanation of the meaning of the Lord's Supper or Eucharist. They believe that John, who does not mention its initiation at the chronological point at which it occurs, prefers to give his account of it in somewhat allegorized form here. "Little evidence is cited for this view. It is accepted as axiomatic that language like that used here refers to the sacrament" (Morris 352).

Others interpret this discourse as analogous with that of chapter 4. They understand that Jesus used figurative language to convey spiritual truth. Eating His flesh and drinking His blood refer, not to the Eucharist as such, but to the act of receiving Christ into one's innermost being by faith. Even so, Jesus was conscious of the future institution of the Lord's Supper, and He may well have intended that many of the principles which He gave here be applied to it. This is certainly the better of the two ways of understanding the passage.

22 The day following, when the people which stood on the other side of the sea saw that there was none other boat there, save that one whereinto his disciples were entered, and that Jesus went not with his disciples into the boat, but *that* his disciples were gone away alone.

The next morning as Jesus and the Twelve arrive at Capernaum, a remnant of the five thousand are resuming their search for Him on the eastern shore (other side) of the Sea of Galilee. They remember that on the previous day the only ship available was the one Jesus and His disciples had arrived in. Since they saw the disciples leave in that ship without Jesus being with them, they assume that Jesus must still be nearby.

23 (Howbeit there came other boats from Tiberias nigh unto the place where they did eat bread, after that the Lord had given thanks.)

At this point John inserts parenthetical information that is necessary for a proper understanding of v. 24. He explains how it was possible for the remnant of the multitude to embark on ships for Capernaum when he has just said that there were no ships available except the one belonging to the disciples. Some ships from Tiberias had ar-

rived on the scene after the disciples left. The circumstances and exact timing of the arrival of these ships is not explained. Some believe that they may have been blown in during the night by the same wind that had hindered the disciples' progress, but that is only speculation. Obviously the people did not consider it possible that Jesus had left the eastern shore on one of these ships. All of them are either still there or otherwise accounted for.

The adverbial clause, "after that the Lord had given thanks" modifies the verb "eat" rather than the word "came." The sentence means that the multitude ate the miraculous bread "after the Lord had given thanks," not that the ships had come "after the Lord had given thanks." The whole phrase, "where they did eat bread, after that the Lord had given thanks," simply refers to the miracle of the feeding of the 5,000. As noted above (see v. 11) this may bear upon the precise timing of events since it associates the miracle directly with Jesus' offering of thanks. No special eucharistic significance should be attached to the wording.

24 When the people therefore saw that Jesus was not there, neither his disciples, they also took shipping, and came to Capernaum, seeking for Jesus.

When the people are satisfied that neither Jesus nor His disciples are still on the eastern shore, they apparently decide that He must have somehow returned to Capernaum though they are at a loss to explain how. Therefore, they embark upon some of the ships referred to in v. 23 to seek Jesus in Capernaum.

25 And when they had found him on the other side of the sea they said unto him, Rabbi, when camest thou hither?

The implication is that the people find Jesus without any difficulty once they reach Capernaum. They are puzzled as to how Jesus has come to "the other side of the sea." John is obviously focusing upon the miracle of the night before and sharing an "insider's" viewpoint with his readers. It is as if he says, "Ah, but we know how He got there, don't we?"

Upon finding Jesus, they ask Him, "Rabbi, when did you come here?" Some have thought that their use of the term "Rabbi" implies a cooling of ardor, a lessening of their desire to have Him as their king. This need not be the case. The title "Rabbi" would be appropriate for such a person as they supposed Jesus to be. The qualities that attracted them to Jesus (teaching, healing, miracles) were more those of a Rabbi than a warrior prince.

There are also those who think it strange that the people asked Jesus "when" rather than "how" He came to Capernaum. It is probably best to translate their question with the emphasis, "When did You come to be *here*?" "When" is, therefore, logically equivalent to "how." Although there is a connection between the two, the crowd's interest is focused more on the *means* by which Jesus has come to be in Capernaum than on the precise *time* He arrived.

26 Jesus answered them and said, Verily, verily, I say unto you, Ye seek me, not because ye saw the miracles, but because ye did eat of the loaves, and were filled.

Jesus' reply leads into His long discourse on the bread of life. He makes no effort to satisfy their curiosity about how He has gotten to Capernaum. He tells them that their motives for seeking Him are wrong, that they are not interested in the spiritual blessing of eternal life which He has come to bring them, and that they are interested only in the physical and material benefits which He can provide. They have totally missed the spiritual implications of His miracles. They understand them in grossly physical terms. They are trying to trivialize Jesus. They want to utilize the glorious power of Immanuel for the mundane purpose of providing themselves free meals. Jesus cannot allow Himself to be trivialized and demeaned so.

27 Labour not for the meat which perisheth, but for that meat which endureth unto everlasting life, which the Son of man shall give unto you: for him hath God the Father sealed.

Jesus warns His hearers not to waste their labor on food which perishes (i.e. physical food). Rather, He says they should be concerned about the supernatural food which only He, the Son of Man, can give to them—the food which will impart eternal life to those who eat it. Only He can give them this life-giving food because only He has been authorized ("sealed") by the Father to do so. He is the sole source of this spiritual food. Men can provide physical food for themselves, but only He can provide eternal life. Only to do this has He come.

This contrast between the food that perishes and that which endures to everlasting life is analogous to that which Jesus has drawn between the physical water from the well and the "living water" which He would give (4:10-14).

28 Then said they unto him, What shall we do, that we might work the works of God?

The legalistic Jews immediately pounce upon Christ's exhortation to *labor* for the food which imparts eternal life. They want to know precisely which *work* He refers to. What godly *work* is it that they must do in order to partake of this blessing? They are so smugly confident of their own sufficiency that they have no doubt that they can do it, once they understand what it is. They, like the Rich Young Ruler, will add but one more item to their already extensive list of righteous deeds.

29 Jesus answered and said unto them, This is the work of God, that ye believe on him whom he hath sent.

Jesus answers that the only "work" which God requires of those who would receive eternal life is to believe on that one whom God, Himself, has sent into the world. There is no holy deed that men can do to earn for themselves eternal life. There is an intentional irony as Jesus makes and John records the statement that the only "work" that men can do is to trust in and depend upon Jesus Christ, God's Son. John seems to enjoy recalling these carefully nuanced words of Jesus and sharing them with his readers. There was never such a nuanced speaker as Jesus and no one understood Him or caught on quite so well as John.

30 They said therefore unto him, What sign shewest thou then, that we may see, and believe thee? what dost thou work?
31 Our fathers did eat manna in the desert; as it is written, He gave them bread from heaven to eat.

Somewhat surprisingly, the crowd understands that Jesus is saying that He Himself is the one whom God has sent. But they answer with a wooden obtuseness which they suppose to be great shrewdness: "What proof do you offer of your assertion? What miracle will you perform before us so that we may be convinced of the truth of your claim?"

They will even go so far as to suggest what miracle might be effective in convincing them. Jesus has given them bread, but only earthly bread given once. Moses, on the other hand, gave to the Children of Israel the heavenly manna on a daily basis over an extended period (see Ps. 78:24). If Jesus can match Moses as a miraculous bread-giver, if He can give them heavenly bread on an ongoing basis over an extended period, then they just might be willing to believe in Him. They are trying to manipulate Jesus. They will continue to "believe" in Him only as He continues to justify their belief by a never-ending succession of ever more gaudy and mundane miracles.

32 Then Jesus said unto them, Verily, verily, I say unto you, Moses gave you not that bread from heaven; but my Father giveth you the true bread from heaven.
33 For the bread of God is he which cometh down from heaven, and giveth life unto the world.

Jesus replies, using the formula of solemnity "Verily, verily" to indicate the importance of His words: "The bread which Moses gave to your fathers in the wilderness was not the true bread from heaven." It was "heavenly" in only the very limited sense that it was supernaturally provided. It was entirely earthly in that it was completely physical in its composition and in that its effect on those who ate it was merely to sustain physical life. "On the other hand," He continues, "my Father is now in the process of giving to you the *truly* heavenly bread, a person. This person is of heavenly origin and has the capacity to introduce the life of heaven (eternal life) into this earthly realm, to make this eternal life available to everyone."

100

34 Then said they unto him, Lord, evermore give us this bread.

The crowd responds in much the same spirit of pedantic literalism as did the woman at the well (4:15). Christ's whole point, that the true bread from Heaven is not at all like manna, is wasted on them. Their wrongheaded preoccupation with the physical and the material blinds them completely to any spiritual reality or truth. They still understand this whole conversation in terms of Jesus' providing them with manna to eat. They speak with an obtuseness which they mistake for great solemnity, "Sir (probably the proper sense of the Greek *kurios* in this context; see 4:11,49; 5:7), always give us this bread."

35 And Jesus said unto them, I am the bread of life: he that cometh to me shall never hunger; and he that believeth on me shall never thirst.

Jesus speaks to the crowd in no uncertain terms, using the emphatic form, "I, myself am (Greek *ego eimi*), the bread of life." The idea that the heavenly bread which produces eternal life is some physical substance like manna He entirely rejects. The fact, which should have been clear all along, that Jesus has been speaking figuratively of Himself is now made crystal clear. He not only *gives* eternal life (v. 27), He *is* eternal life (vv. 32,33,35). To have Jesus is to have eternal life. All that one must do to have eternal life is to come to Jesus and believe on Him. He will never hunger or thirst again.

This is the first of seven such "I am" statements in the Fourth Gospel, each of which points up some important aspect of Christ's person and work. Jesus also uses this formula to refer to Himself as: the light of the world (8:12); the door (10:7); the good shepherd (10:11); the resurrection and the life (11:25); the way, the truth, and the life (14:6); and the true vine (15:1).

36 But I said unto you, That ye also have seen me, and believe not.

The meaning of this rather complicated sentence is approximately as follows, "However (in spite of the fact that I am the bread of life and that all who come to me will have eternal life), it is just like I told you before, that you also have seen me, and yet have not believed on me." Jesus may refer to some unrecorded previous statement of His or to what He has said in v. 26. At any rate, He wishes to impress these words upon His hearers as being particularly descriptive of their present attitude in rejecting Him. They have seen Him feed the five thousand, yet they do not believe. Jesus' statement stands in marked contrast to His words to Thomas in 20:29. The Gospel seems to imply that three levels of reaction to Christ are possible: seeing yet not believing, seeing and therefore believing, and not seeing but believing anyway.

37 All that the Father giveth me shall come to me; and him that cometh to me I will in no wise cast out.

In the face of their stubborn unbelief, Jesus declares to the crowd that their action is not to be the final word on the subject. If they will not believe, there are those who will. This is rendered certain by the fact that all whom the Father gives to Jesus will in fact come to Him. This "coming" includes, as the parallel in v. 35 shows, belief/faith in Him. The clear implication is that those who believe in Christ do so because of the Father's action of giving them to Him, that this crowd is not among that number, and that this explains their unbelief. Jesus is telling these people that there is a frightening aspect to their refusal to believe in Him. It marks them as being outside that chosen number who will inherit eternal life.

Of course, Jesus will receive those who come to Him because they have been given to Him by the Father; but the meaning is deeper than that. The point is that those who come to Jesus need not fear that they will be rejected as not being among the chosen number who are given to Christ. While it is certain that all who are chosen will come, it is just as certain that all who come are chosen. The method of God's working in the heart ensures it. Men come to God only when He draws them (v. 44); therefore, those who come have of necessity been drawn. The last part of the verse balances the first part. "There are difficulties as we try to reconcile the two parts of this verse. But whether we succeed in that or not we dare not abandon the truth in either part" (Morris 367,368). (See further the editor's note on v. 44, below.)

38 For I came down from heaven, not to do mine own will, but the will of him that sent me.
39 And this is the Father's will which hath sent me, that of all which he hath given me I should lose nothing, but should raise it up again at the last day.

The reason it is certain that Christ will receive all whom the Father gives Him as they come to Him is that there is a perfect cooperation between His Father and Himself (5:19). Jesus has come down from Heaven for the express purpose of doing the Father's will (4:34), and His Father's will in regard to those whom He has given to Christ is quite specific. He wills that Christ should not lose any of them and that He should

exercise His own resurrection authority (5:21, 25, 26) to raise all of them at the last day.

40 And this is the will of him that sent me, that every one which seeth the Son, and believeth on him, may have everlasting life: and I will raise him up at the last day.

For emphasis and clarity, Jesus once more specifies the will of the Father who has sent Him into the world. That will is that everyone who truly sees and believes on the Son should have everlasting life and that Jesus should raise Him up at the last day. The believer has eternal life now as his present possession, but its fullest expression will not be his until he is raised up by Christ at the last day.

"The seeing of the Son spoken of [here] is much more than the superficial seeing of Him, unaccompanied by faith, which [was] mentioned in v. 36; it is that divinely imparted vision which discerns the Glory of God in the Word become flesh" (Bruce 154).

41 The Jews then murmured at him, because he said, I am the bread which came down from heaven.
42 And they said, Is not this Jesus, the son of Joseph, whose father and mother we know? how is it then that he saith, I came down from heaven?

Until this point the group Jesus has been speaking to has been called "the people" (vv. 22, 24) and simply "they." Does the fact that those who answer Jesus are now referred to as "the Jews" mean that this is a different group and/or that the scene has changed, perhaps to the synagogue? One cannot be sure. Perhaps the conversation started near the lake, between Christ and the crowd who followed Him to Capernaum, has shifted to the synagogue and has been joined by some of the local Jewish leaders.

At any rate, "the Jews" begin to murmur at this point. They do not confront Jesus directly; they express their resistance to one another in subdued tones. The cause of their dissatisfaction is that Christ has said that He is the bread which came down from Heaven. They have likened Him to Moses, who gave them manna from Heaven (but who was, himself, clearly a human being of earthly origin), but Jesus has claimed a heavenly origin and, therefore, a heavenly identity for Himself. This is too high a claim for them to accept.

To them it was obvious that Jesus was not from Heaven. His origin was well known: He was Jesus the son of Joseph. They knew His parents. How could He, in the face of such clear proof to the contrary, claim that He came from Heaven? Again, it seems that John is sharing a private perspective on these words with his reader. The Jews, though very sure of themselves, did not have their facts straight. Jesus was not really the son of Joseph and He was much more than just the son of Mary.

43 Jesus therefore answered and said unto them, Murmur not among yourselves.
44 No man can come to me, except the Father which hath sent me draw him: and I will raise him up at the last day.

Either because He overhears them or because He perceives their thoughts (see 2:25), Jesus commands that they cease murmuring among themselves and confronts the objections which they are expressing. To do so He restates negatively the same principle that He stated positively in the first part of v. 37.

He says that no man can come to Him unless the Father who has sent Him draws him. In other words the initiative in salvation rests with God. Unless God draws a man to Himself, he will not—indeed, he cannot—come to Him by faith.

Taken alone, this verse might seem to indicate that God assumes the entire responsibility for salvation and that man has no responsibility at all in the matter. That this is not the case is inherent in the very nature of the gospel as a challenge to personal commitment (e.g. 3:16,18,20, 21) and in the teaching that men are responsible for their own failure to believe (e.g. 3:19; 5:40). While the decision to trust in Christ is a real one and the responsibility for doing so rests solely upon the individual, it is also true that one may not believe apart from the supernatural drawing and convicting power of God.

Christ again refers to the last day resurrection theme of v. 39. The ultimate impact of the decision to put one's trust in Christ is that he will be among those who will be restored to life on the last day by Christ's resurrection power.

EDITOR'S NOTE ON JOHN 6:44: THE DRAWING OF SINNERS

In stating that no person can come to Christ unless the Father "draws" him, pastor Stallings has expressed the original Arminian doctrine. The truth is that man's depravity is such that no person can accept the gospel offer or choose to put faith in Christ unless God's Spirit does this work *first*.

This "drawing" is what we often call *conviction*. And conviction is nothing more than a way of saying *convincement* or *persuasion*. Apart from it, no person would ever exercise saving faith.

This work of the Holy Spirit is what Arminius called "prevenient" (or "preventing") grace—using this now out-of-date word in the sense of "that which comes before." In full agreement with Calvinists (and Luther's classic *The Bondage of the Will*), Arminius and the original Remonstrants were forthright in acknowledging that the depraved sinner is helpless, without this work of grace up front, to believe. The depraved sinner, "dead in trespasses and sins," cannot even hear the truth as truth, much less reach out to it in faith, without this drawing. The true Arminian, no less than the Calvinist, believes in total depravity.

These days, we might better call this work of the Spirit "enabling" or "pre-regenerating" grace. The Remonstrants even thought of it as "the motions of (in the sense of the early stages of) regeneration." The key difference between the Reformation Arminian and the Calvinist, then, is that the Arminian understands this work of "drawing" to be co-extensive with the proclamation/publishing of the gospel, and thus potentially universal. The Holy Spirit "enables," in this way, those who are presented with the choice of the gospel, both the elect and the non-elect, both those who will believe and those who will not.

In other words, this work of grace is not irresistible; it does not overpower the human will. But it does truly "free" the sinner's will from its bondage and enable him to put faith in Christ. Still, not all who are thus enabled finally believe to the salvation of their souls. And there lies their own responsibility, which is the basis of the blame John assigns them, throughout the gospel, for their unbelief.

45 It is written in the prophets, And they shall be all taught of God. Every man therefore that hath heard, and hath learned of the Father, cometh unto me.

These words should be paired with those in v. 44 where Jesus says that none may come to Him unless they are drawn by God. He reiterates the truth of v. 37 that all of those who have been given to Him by the Father will in fact come to Him. He begins by quoting Is. 54:13 to the effect that all who are included in the kingdom age (the context of the passage) will be taught by God: that is, they will have the truth revealed to them from within (see comments 5:38). On the authority of the O.T., therefore, Jesus insists that everyone who is hearing the voice of God and is having the truth revealed to him from within by the Father accepts Him as the Messiah and comes to Him (believes on Him).

46 Not that any man hath seen the Father, save he which is of God, he hath seen the Father.

However, Christ's words are not to be interpreted as meaning that an individual may experience a direct mystical relationship with the Father apart from Himself. There is a difference between this inner "hearing" of God's voice and actually "seeing" Him. To hear God's inward voice is subjective and incomplete in itself. It must be accompanied by objective truth and is nothing more than a divinely wrought sensitivity to and comprehension of that truth. To see God, on the other hand, is to experience Him objectively, intimately, and comprehensively. Only Christ, who originates in and comes forth from God, has such an experience and knowledge of Him. Men may know God in this ultimate sense only through the intermediation of Christ (see comments 1:18).

47 Verily, verily, I say unto you, He that believeth on me hath everlasting life.

With the previous truth in mind, Jesus now goes on to say solemnly (Greek *amen, amen*) that, though one can never independently know the Father for himself, he can know Him through Christ and know Him in such an effective way as to obtain eternal life by that knowledge. Here is one of the underlying themes of the Fourth Gospel: belief in Christ as the key to eternal life (3:16, 20:31, etc.). "It is to the believer that the Son mediates that vision of God which He Himself enjoys immediately and uninterruptedly; and with the vision of God eternal life is bestowed" (Bruce 157).

48 I am that bread of life.

Jesus reasserts His claim (v. 35) to be "the bread of life" in the context of what He has just said. In effect He says, "It is in this context that you should understand my earlier statement that I am the bread of life. I am the bread of life in the sense that whoever believes in me (partakes of me by faith) will have everlasting life."

49 Your fathers did eat manna in the wilderness, and are dead.

Jesus quotes the people's earlier statement (v. 31) that their fathers ate manna in the wilderness, but He adds to their words the ominous phrase, "and are dead." The people originally said these words as a part of a challenge to Jesus to provide them with physical food miraculously (see comments v. 31). To them, the manna represented the epitome of miraculous provision. Jesus repeats their words in an entirely different light to demonstrate the complete inferiority of the wilderness manna to the bread of life which He offers.

50 This is the bread which cometh down from heaven, that a man may eat thereof, and not die.

Those who ate the manna in the wilderness all died there under the judgment of God, but whoever will eat of (believe in) Jesus, the true bread of life who comes down from Heaven, will not die but have everlasting life. Jesus "came down from heaven" in a far greater sense than did the manna. The manna came from heaven in the sense that it was supernaturally provided by God and that it fell from the sky. Jesus comes from Heaven in that He is a person who is, Himself, of heavenly origin, the very embodiment of Heaven come down to dwell among men, one who has the capacity to introduce the life of Heaven (eternal life) into this earthly realm (see comments vv. 33,38; 3:13,31).

51 I am the living bread which came down from heaven: if any man eat of this bread, he shall live for ever: and the bread that I will give is my flesh, which I will give for the life of the world.

Now Jesus summarizes and states succinctly the point He has been making throughout this long discourse: that He is the living bread which comes from Heaven (vv.33, 35, 38, 48, 50), and if anyone will eat of (believe in) Him, he will have everlasting life (vv. 39,40,44,47, 50). In the last part of the verse Jesus explains what He means by referring to Himself as the bread of life. He is the bread of life in a direct way since it is His *flesh* (i.e. His life) which He will give to provide the bread of life. Jesus has come to die, to give His life in order to provide eternal life for mankind (Mt.20:28). This is Jesus' third enigmatic (but clear) reference to His death, the others being in 2:19 and 3:14.

52 The Jews therefore strove among themselves, saying, How can this man give us *his* flesh to eat?

The crowd's response to Jesus' words is to quarrel (Greek *machomai*, to strive) among themselves. This clearly indicates a division among them, and it seems reasonable to suppose that some of them (a minority, no doubt) are beginning to lean toward believing Jesus. The quarrel centers around the thought of Jesus' giving them His flesh to eat. How is this possible? Some of them are willfully blind to the truth and, taking His words literally, consider them ridiculous. Others understand that He is speaking figuratively, but they do not understand the figurative meaning. None of them really understands how Jesus can give them His flesh to eat.

53 Then Jesus said unto them, Verily, verily, I say unto you, Except ye eat the flesh of the Son of man, and drink his blood, ye have no life in you.

Jesus' use of the "verily, verily" formula indicates that He is speaking with great care and deliberation. He has already said in v. 51 that whoever eats of the living bread (which is His flesh) shall live forever. Now He builds upon that thought, first negatively and then positively. He adds to the phrase "eat (my) flesh" the even more graphic and shocking, "and drink (my) blood." He says that whoever does not do so has no life within him, that he does not possess eternal life. Positively, whoever does do so has eternal life and will be among those who will be raised up by Christ's own power on the last day (see comments vv. 39,40,44). In v. 40 those who "see the Son and believe on Him" have eternal life and are to be raised up on the last day, whereas here the same thing is promised those who "eat (His) flesh and drink (His) blood." Eating His flesh and drinking His blood are parallel (and, therefore, equivalent) to seeing and believing on Him.

54 Whoso eateth my flesh, and drinketh my blood, hath eternal life; and I will raise him up at the last day.
55 For my flesh is meat indeed, and my blood is drink indeed.

Christ now explains why eating His flesh and drinking His blood have such glorious effect: because His flesh and blood are the ultimate food and drink. They are food in the truest sense, the food of the spirit, the food of the soul. Man's deepest hunger can be satisfied only by belief in and communion with Christ. The true food ("bread indeed") is neither the miraculously provided bread of the previous day nor the manna that was provided in the wilderness. They cannot satisfy man's deepest hunger. Only Christ can do that by giving His body to die for sinners. Only He is the true bread.

56 He that eateth my flesh, and drinketh my blood, dwelleth in me, and I in him.

Christ uses the physical process of digestion to teach a spiritual truth. Just as food taken into the body is digested and becomes a part of the body, so it is that when one appropriates Christ by faith, Christ begins to dwell in him and he in Christ. There comes to be a mystical union and fellowship between Christ and every believer. John will return to this theme in chapter 15.

57 As the living Father hath sent me, and I live by the Father: so he that eateth me, even he shall live by me.

Here Christ develops and expands His statement of v. 38. He has been sent into the world (see e.g. 3:34; 6:38) by the "living Father," i.e. the Father who has life in Himself (5:26a), whose most basic attribute is autonomous life (Ex. 3:14). He exists in a state of complete identification and cooperation with the Father (see e.g. 4:34; 5:19, 20, 30) even to the point of sharing with the Father the attribute of autonomous life (5:26b). Just as the preceding facts are true, so it is also true that the person who eats of (believes in) Christ shall live (truly and eternally) because of Christ and the relationship he bears to Him (v. 56).

58 This is that bread which came down from heaven: not as your fathers did eat manna, and are dead: he that eateth of this bread shall live for ever.

Now Jesus summarizes the preceding section. In v. 27 Jesus began to turn His hearers' thoughts away from the loaves and fish of the previous day to the "food which endureth unto everlasting life." He subsequently (v. 32) referred to this food as the true bread and then (v. 33) to Himself as the bread of God which comes down from Heaven and finally as the bread of life (v. 48). Now He reiterates the teaching of vv. 49 and 50 that, while the Israelites who ate the manna in the wilderness are dead, the one who eats of "this bread" (the bread that has been in focus since v. 27) shall live forever. The second phrase, "not as your fathers..." is something of an analogy by contrast on the order of Rom. 5:15,16.

59 These things said he in the synagogue, as he taught in Capernaum.

At this point John adds one of his almost incidental details. He states that Jesus said these things in the synagogue as He taught in Capernaum. It may be that the whole episode from v. 25 onward took place within the Synagogue, or it may be that the scene shifted to the Synagogue at some point subsequent to

that (see comments v. 41). At any rate the major portion of this confrontation took place within the Synagogue at Capernaum.

60 Many therefore of his disciples, when they had heard *this* said, This is an hard saying; who can hear it?

Jesus' teaching on this occasion offends not only the Jews (vv. 41,42,52), but also many of His own disciples. It is difficult to evaluate the exact nature of these "disciples." That they do not include the Twelve is obvious from v. 67. While the degree of their commitment may not be very great, they obviously have taken some action in regard to Christ which makes it appropriate for them to be called His disciples. The term is not indiscriminately applied to the general populace.

The reaction of these disciples is not unlike that of the other Jews. They also "murmur" back and forth to each other (v. 61). They are just as offended by Jesus' words as was the unbelieving crowd. When they say that Jesus' teaching is a "hard" (Greek *skleros*, rough, hard, harsh, unpleasant, difficult) saying, they do not just mean that it is mysterious and difficult to understand— although, no doubt, it is. They mean that it is very harsh and demanding. They are not able to "hear" (accept, tolerate) such teaching easily. Nor do they simply think Jesus' metaphor uncouth; they are offended by His claim to be the only source of eternal life, the only means of access to the Father.

61 When Jesus knew in himself that his disciples murmured at it, he said unto them, Doth this offend you?

Again, Jesus is able to perceive what people are thinking. He perceives that

107

many of His own disciples are expressing resistance to what He has told them. Previously (v. 41), only "the Jews" murmured, now some of His own disciples. Jesus confronts this negative, rebellious, unbelieving spirit directly. He says to them, "Does this (teaching) offend you?"

62 *What* and if ye shall see the Son of man ascend up where he was before?

Christ's question is incomplete. He leaves it for the disciples to finish. Does He mean to imply that seeing Him ascend back to Heaven would remove all their present difficulties or that it would create even greater problems for them? The answer to this question seems to lie in the interpretation of the word "ascend" (Greek *anabaino*). Is it to be understood as referring specifically to Christ's ascension to Heaven after His resurrection? Or as being analogous to "lifted up" in 3:14 and referring to the whole process of His glorification in which, ironically, the suffering of the cross is to play a prominent role? The most natural interpretation is to understand it as referring to the ascension itself (see Godet) and to understand Christ as saying somewhat cryptically, "What if you were to see the Son of Man ascend up (to Heaven) where He was before, would it then be easier for you to believe these things that I have taught you about myself? If you saw me ascend up to heaven would it then be easier for you to believe that I came down from Heaven (v. 38)?"

63 It is the spirit that quickeneth; the flesh profiteth nothing: the words that I speak unto you, *they* are spirit, and *they* are life.

The first part of this verse is to be understood in light of 3:6 and 1 Cor. 2:14 as affirming the inherent superiority of that which is spiritual, unseen, and eternal to that which is fleshly, seen and temporal (see Plummer). The apprehension of such spiritual realities conveys eternal life. "The flesh" which profits nothing is not to be confused with "my flesh" in the preceding verses. Christ is not contrasting His "flesh which (He) will give for the life of the world" with the things of the spirit.

In the second part of the verse, Jesus goes on to say that the words that He has spoken to them (and which have so offended them) are spiritual words, words from the spiritual realm which cannot be fathomed by the natural mind of man, but that they are also words which mean eternal life to those who understand and believe them.

64 But there are some of you that believe not. For Jesus knew from the beginning who they were that believed not, and who should betray him.

Jesus goes on to say that, in spite of all this and contrary to all that is reasonable, even some of those who claim to be His disciples do not actually believe on Him. John explains that Jesus fully understood from the time that they first started to follow Him which of His disciples truly believed on Him and which did not. Their rejection at this point does not catch Him off guard. He is prepared for it. In fact, He probably says these things purposely so as to separate those who truly believe from those who do not. To emphasize his point John goes on to say that Jesus even knew who would betray Him.

65 And he said, Therefore said I unto you, that no man can come unto me, except it were given unto him of my Father.

Jesus concludes His conversation

with these pseudo-disciples by saying that it was with just such persons as themselves in mind that He said that no man could come unto Him unless the Father enabled him to do so (v. 44). The obvious implication is that these have not been so enabled and that this is the explanation for their behavior.

66 From that *time* many of his disciples went back, and walked no more with him.

After (and because of) this whole episode, many of those who have thought of themselves as Jesus' disciples decide that they have been mistaken and are not really such after all. They "go back"— both to their homes and to their old ways. They will walk with Jesus no more, neither outwardly upon the byways of Galilee nor inwardly within their spirits. Walking with Him has turned out to mean something very different than they supposed.

67 Then said Jesus unto the twelve, Will ye also go away?

Very soon after this Jesus is apparently alone with the Twelve. The Greek words John uses make it clear that Jesus expects a negative answer to the question He poses to them: "You are not going to go away too, are you?" Jesus speaks to challenge their faith. Though the mass defection of so many disciples has greatly saddened Him, He does not despair.

68 Then Simon Peter answered him, Lord, to whom shall we go? thou hast the words of eternal life.
69 And we believe and are sure that thou art that Christ, the Son of the living God.

At least one of the Twelve is equal to the occasion. Peter takes it on himself to speak for the whole group and answers with a precision which must thrill Jesus' heart: "Lord, to whom shall we go? thou hast the words of eternal life." Peter quotes Jesus' own words (v. 63) and demonstrates that he has understood and accepts completely all that Jesus has been saying. Even though there are those who "believe not" (v. 64), Peter assures Jesus that the Twelve are not among them. They believe to the point of being certain of what others cannot accept: that Jesus is the Messiah, and, much more than that, that He is the Son of God. It is as if Peter cannot affirm it strongly enough, "No, Lord, we are not going anywhere."

70 Jesus answered them, Have not I chosen you twelve, and one of you is a devil?

This poignant and beautiful moment cannot last. Jesus Himself must destroy it. In spite of Peter's obvious sincerity, what he says is not true. They do not all feel as Peter does. Judas shares the very spirit that has just driven so many away, but the road of desertion is not open to him. He is too close, too involved. He must stay on in hypocrisy, pretending to believe what he does not believe, pretending to feel what he does not feel, pretending to be what he cannot be. Jesus cannot sanction this hypocrisy. He must confront Judas with the truth even if not directly. He is pleading with Judas to turn from his evil course as He will do on other occasions. But Judas will not hear. He hardens his heart in rebellion and forces his way toward disaster.

71 He spake of Judas Iscariot *the son* of Simon: for he it was that should betray him, being one of the twelve.

Many years later, as he recalls this scene, John shares with his readers what he did not comprehend at the time, that Jesus was speaking of Judas, the one who would ultimately betray Him; Judas, one of the Twelve.

Summary
(6:22-71)

On the morning after Jesus has fed the 5,000, a remnant of that multitude begins to search for Him. When they cannot find Him on the eastern shore they decide to look for Him in Capernaum. Upon finding Him there they ask Him when (how) He came there. Jesus' reply leads into the discourse on the bread of life.

Jesus rebukes the inquirers for their sensationalist and materialistic motives. He challenges them to forget about physical food and to become concerned about the bread which brings eternal life. The crowd wants to know what good work they must do to gain this eternal life. Jesus answers that they must believe on the one whom God has sent into the world, meaning Himself. Their response is to ask for a sign to assist them in believing in Him. Something like the manna which Moses provided in the wilderness will be sufficient. Jesus replies that the manna which God (not Moses) gave them was not the true bread from Heaven. This true bread from Heaven is the one who comes down from Heaven and gives life to the world.

The crowd (still thinking of physical food) responds that they want to receive this bread from now on. Jesus tells them that He is the bread of life and that those who believe on Him will, indeed, never hunger or thirst. He hastens to add, however, that they are not among those who believe even though they have had ample opportunity. All those whom the Father has given to Him will believe on Him and will be received by Him for He is in perfect agreement with the Father's will, which is that all those who come to Him shall be raised up at the last day to inherit eternal life.

By this time the scene has probably shifted to the synagogue and some of the Jewish authorities have joined the conversation. The Jews begin to murmur among themselves. Jesus' claim to have come down from Heaven offends them. They believe Him to be an ordinary human being for whom such a claim is blasphemous. Jesus confronts them directly by reiterating His claim and stating that the reason they do not come to Him is that they are not being taught by God.

Jesus says solemnly that, although one cannot know the Father independently, he can, through Christ, know the Father sufficiently to obtain eternal life. Jesus reiterates that He is the bread of life and that if they will "eat" of Him they, unlike their fathers who ate the manna in the wilderness only to die afterward, shall never die. Jesus explains that the bread He is talking about is His own flesh which He will give (in death) for the life of the world.

The Jews are confused and argue among themselves as to what Jesus means by saying that He will give them His flesh to eat. Jesus again responds with great solemnity that, if they do not eat His flesh and even drink His blood, they will not have eternal life or be raised up at the last day. Jesus goes on to say that those who do eat His flesh and drink His blood will become (mystically) united with Him. He climaxes His discourse by pledging that, as the living Father has sent Him and as He, Himself, lives by the power of the Father, so those who partake of Him shall have eternal life through Him. Jesus then summarizes His whole argument: "I am the bread that God has sent from heaven which, unlike those who ate the manna and died, if a man eats, he shall live forever." At this point John informs his readers that the preceding discourse (at least the latter part) was delivered in the synagogue in Capernaum.

These "hard sayings" offend even some of Christ's professed disciples. They, too, begin to murmur and doubt. Jesus confronts their murmuring with the challenge, "If you see the Son of Man ascend up to (Heaven) where He was before, will you believe me then?" Jesus warns His hearers that it is spiritual understanding rather than earthly observation which is the key to ultimate truth. He explains that His words, when spiritually interpreted and understood, lead to eternal life. He also warns them again that, although this is perfectly true, it has no meaning for some of them because they do not believe on Him. As He has told them earlier, no one can believe on Him except those to whom it has been given by the Father. As a result of this discourse, many of Christ's disciples forsake Him.

In the face of this great defection, Jesus asks the Twelve if they too are going to desert Him. Simon Peter assures Him that they are not. Such an action would be pointless since only Jesus can grant eternal life and since only He is the Messiah, the Son of God. While Peter speaks for all the Twelve, one does not share his unqualified faith. Even one of the Twelve does not really believe in Christ. Jesus, although He does not call him by name, rebukes Judas' unbelief and challenges him to repentance. But Judas will persevere in his rebellion and unbelief and ultimately betray his Master.

Application: Teaching and Preaching the Passage

Again, the basic inability of the Jews to think in anything but the most literal and physical terms underlies and shapes this discourse just as it has the ones with Nicodemus and the woman of Samaria. The peoples' minds are so focused on the physical aspects and implications of the miracle of the loaves and fish that they simply cannot focus upon the spiritual reality represented by that miracle. Throughout the discourse, they persistently misunderstand Jesus' teaching that He is the "bread of life." They seem not to have the vaguest notion that there is any figurative (spiritual) significance in His words.

The other underlying theme of this discourse is unbelief. The Jews are simply unwilling to accept that Jesus is the sort of heavenly personage He claims to be. They must have a sign (v. 30) if they are to believe. Their supposed knowledge of His earthly background (v. 42) entirely rules out the possibility of their believing. Jesus reacts to their unbelief by explaining that it is indicative of the fact that they are not part of the true people of God, that they have not been taught by Him (vv. 44,45; see also 5:38). He emphasizes that this unbelief and rejection of Him are very tragic for only by believing in and partaking of Him (eating His flesh and drinking His blood) can men have eternal life (vv. 47-58).

N. Confrontation With Unbelief (7:1-36)

1 After these things Jesus walked in Galilee: for he would not walk in Jewry, because the Jews sought to kill him.

As a background for the events of this chapter, John informs his readers that Jesus is unable to move about openly in Judea and must confine Himself to Galilee. He is unable to walk about teaching according to His normal custom in Judea because of the murderous intentions of the Jerusalem authorities who have been determined to eliminate Him ever since their confrontation with Him over His healing the lame man on the Sabbath (5:18). This period of confinement to Galilee corresponds with the great Galilean Ministry as recorded in the Synoptics. The events of chapter six have transpired during this period.

2 Now the Jews' feast of tabernacles was at hand.

It has been approximately six months since the feeding of the 5000, that being the time lapse between Passover (6:4) and the Feast of Tabernacles. The Feast of Tabernacles had two important themes. It was a feast of thanksgiving for the harvest which had just been gathered in, but it was also a time when Israel thanked God for His protection and provision for them during their wilderness wanderings. The people constructed small shelters of branches and leaves and lived in them during the course of this feast to remind themselves of their time in the wilderness and to contrast that time of deprivation with their current happy circumstances.

3 His brethren therefore said unto him, Depart hence, and go into Judaea, that thy disciples also may see the works that thou doest.
4 For *there is* no man *that* doeth any thing in secret, and he himself seeketh to be known openly. If thou do these things, shew thyself to the world.
5 For neither did his brethren believe in him.

Now, as the Feast of Tabernacles draws near, Jesus' brothers challenge Him to appear publicly in Jerusalem at the feast. Their advice is utterly carnal. Verse 5 makes it clear that they do not truly believe that He is the Messiah. They are challenging Him, if He is the

Messiah, to take action appropriate to His claim. Instead of remaining isolated in Galilee and performing His miracles for the benefit of a few provincials, He should go to Jerusalem, perform His miracles before the authorities, and formally declare His Messiahship to the whole Jewish world. His brothers are exasperated with Jesus. To the extent that they believe in Him at all, they have grown impatient with His lack of bold action. His hesitant conduct does not seem Messianic to them. They are saying in effect, and in a spirit of disbelief, "Either follow through with these Messianic pretensions of yours or forget about them."

6 Then Jesus said unto them, My time is not yet come: but your time is alway ready.
7 The world cannot hate you; but me it hateth, because I testify of it, that the works thereof are evil.
8 Go ye up unto this feast: I go not up yet unto this feast; for my time is not yet full come.
9 When he had said these words unto them, he abode *still* in Galilee.

Jesus' answer to His brothers is filled with irony and double meaning. He says that His time (Greek *kairos*) has not yet come (see comments 2:4). His brothers understand Him to refer to the timing of His going up to the feast. This is true, as far as it goes. Jesus intends to delay His arrival at the feast until after the people have assembled and an air of expectancy has been established (vv. 11-13). But there is an even deeper meaning to Jesus' words. He means that the time when He will openly reveal Himself to the world as the Messiah has not yet come. "Going up" to Jerusalem will ultimately involve His being "lifted up" (3:14; 8:28; 12:32,34) in crucifixion. Only in His death will He be fully revealed as

Messiah. Jesus can fulfill their request to reveal Himself to the world as the Messiah only by being crucified, and God's timing for that has not arrived. Only in this sense is Jesus' statement that He is not (some manuscripts read "not yet") going up to this feast to be understood. It is to another feast, the Passover, that He must go up in the ultimate sense and at which He must die.

Christ's brothers may go up at any time. No such considerations apply to them. There is no plot to crucify them. The authorities are not filled with hatred toward them. They have no strategic role to play in God's plan of redemption. But Christ is in danger of death. The authorities hate Him because He reveals their wickedness. He carries the responsibility for the whole world. His actions must be more circumspect. He has far more at stake than do His brothers, far more than they realize. So when His brothers go up to Jerusalem for the feast, Jesus remains (temporarily) behind in Galilee.

10 But when his brethren were gone up, then went he also up unto the feast, not openly, but as it were in secret.

After Jesus' brothers go up with the great caravan of worshippers to Jerusalem, Jesus also goes up unobtrusively. He does not, however, go up in the sense that his brothers have advised. They have exhorted Him to go up and "show himself" (Greek *phaneroo*) "to the world." But when Jesus does go up, He makes a special point to go "secretly" rather than "openly" (Greek *phaneros*). This does not mean that absolutely no one was aware that He was going (He was almost certainly accompanied by the Twelve), but that He was not following His brothers' advice to declare His mission publicly in Jerusalem upon the occasion of this particular feast.

11 Then the Jews sought him at the feast, and said, Where is he?

The Jewish authorities seem to be in agreement with Christ's brothers that this feast would be an appropriate time for Jesus to manifest Himself as the Messiah. At any rate, they expect Him at this feast. The precise reason for this is not known. Perhaps they reason that, since He has not attended the previous Passover (6:4), He will be certain to attend this feast. Their conversation centers on His absence: "Where is He? Why is He not here? What is He up to? Do you think He will come?"

12 And there was much murmuring among the people concerning him: for some said, He is a good man: others said, Nay; but he deceiveth the people.
13 Howbeit no man spake openly of him for fear of the Jews.

The common people, the great "uninformed majority," are also preoccupied with Jesus. They "murmur" among themselves: that is, they converse discreetly in hushed tones and out of the officials' hearing about Jesus. Opinion is divided. Some believe Jesus to be "a good man." While their feeling toward Jesus is essentially positive, they have no real comprehension of His identity and mission. Others believe Him to be a false prophet whose miracles and good works are only devices by which He deceives the people. Whichever view they hold, however, they are very careful what they say and to whom they say it, for they know that the authorities would condemn any discussion of Him at all.

14 Now about the midst of the feast Jesus went up into the temple, and taught.

113

15 And the Jews marvelled, saying, How knoweth this man letters, having never learned?

About halfway through the feast, Jesus emerges from His seclusion and begins to teach publicly in the Temple precincts. The content of His teaching is not given, but it seems reasonable to assume from the similarity of the reaction produced (see Mt. 7:28,29), that it was basically the same as the Sermon on the Mount. Those who hear Jesus are amazed. He has had no rabbinical training, yet His mastery of the Scripture and His erudition are obvious. What is the explanation? How has He come by this remarkable knowledge? One wonders if any of them recall the young lad who had visited the Temple some 20 years previously (see Lk. 2:46,47).

16 Jesus answered them, and said, My doctrine is not mine, but his that sent me.

Jesus' response has an initial appearance of self-denigration. He, like the rabbis, does not speak His own thoughts but the thoughts of another, the One who has sent Him. But who is this One who has sent Him and from where has He been sent? Jesus means, of course, that it is the Father who has sent Him from Heaven. He is actually reiterating His claim to be the divine heavenly messenger of God (see 3:13; 5:30,37; 6:29,38,39).

17 If any man will do his will, he shall know of the doctrine, whether it be of God, or _whether_ I speak of myself.

Jesus goes on to say that whoever does the will of the One who has sent Him (God the Father) will understand that His teachings come from God and are not just His own personal opinions.

Jesus is reaffirming His earlier teaching (5:38; 6:45) that those who are of God will recognize the truth when they hear it.

18 He that speaketh of himself seeketh his own glory: but he that seeketh his glory that sent him, the same is true, and no unrighteousness is in him.

Jesus sets forth a practical test for telling a true prophet from a deceiver. A deceiver, a false prophet who has no message from God but simply speaks out of his own thoughts, will always speak in such a way as to exalt himself, whereas the true prophet always speaks in such a way as to exalt the One who sent him (God). Jesus clearly implies that His own message is authenticated by this test. His teaching has not exalted Himself; it has exalted the Father who has sent Him (4:34; 5:30,43; 6:38; 17:4).

19 Did not Moses give you the law, and _yet_ none of you keepeth the law? Why go ye about to kill me?

When Jesus speaks of the Jews' desire to kill Him, He obviously has in mind the events of chapter five and the plot initiated at that time (5:16,18). This verse is often interpreted as a rebuke of the hypocrisy of the Jewish leaders who seek to kill Jesus for a minor infraction of the law of the Sabbath while they themselves are breaking the law in a much worse way by their murderous desire. However, the interpretation proposed by Godet and Bernard seems best. According to this view, Christ is saying in effect, "Even you Jews who value the Law of Moses above all things must occasionally violate the exact letter of the law (e.g. by pulling one's ox out of the ditch on the Sabbath, Lk. 13:15; 14:5), yet you desire to put me to death for doing no more than you yourselves do, for healing the lame man on the Sabbath."

20 The people answered and said, Thou hast a devil: who goeth about to kill thee?

It is the multitude (apparently those who have come up to Jerusalem for the feast) who break in to rebuke Jesus. Their statement that He "has a devil" may be idiomatic, the equivalent of, "You must be crazy," rather than an actual accusation of demon possession. The plot of the authorities may not be widely known, and these people could be sincere in their assurance that there is no plot against His life, but v. 13 is against such a view. It is more likely that their words reflect the rage that so often rises up when one is confronted with irrefutable logic which he is, nevertheless, determined to reject.

21 Jesus answered and said unto them, I have done one work and ye all marvel.

Jesus ignores the taunt about being demon possessed and returns to His point of v. 19 that it is unreasonable to insist that the law must be kept with literal exactness in every circumstance. When Jesus says that He has done one work and they marvel at it, He is not referring to the fact that they are greatly impressed by a supernatural miracle (by v. 23 it is obvious that Jesus has the healing of the lame man in mind from v. 19 onward). Rather, He is saying, "I have done one work (just one act of labor on the Sabbath) and you all are astonished (same sense of Greek *thaumazo* as in 3:7 and 4:27) by it. You are ready to stone me because I have performed just one solitary act of labor on the Sabbath."

22 Moses therefore gave unto you circumcision; (not because it is of Moses, but of the fathers;) and ye on the sabbath day circumcise a man.
23 If a man on the sabbath day receive circumcision, that the law of Moses should not be broken; are ye angry at me, because I have made a man every whit whole on the sabbath day?

Jesus now proceeds to demonstrate the illogical and inconsistent nature of His opponents' position. He points out that, in obedience to the command of Moses (which he, in turn, had received from the patriarchs), they circumcise male children on the eighth day even if that means doing so on the Sabbath. If it is proper for them to circumcise a child on the Sabbath (as it obviously is) is it not also permissible on the Sabbath to heal a man of a terrible malady that he has endured for 38 years? The law itself contains provisions that are contradictory if both are followed with the literal exactness that Christ's opponents are insisting on.

Had [the Jews] understood the significance of what they were doing [when they circumcised an infant on the eighth day] they would have seen that a practice which overrode the sabbath in order to provide for the ceremonial needs of a man justified the overriding of the sabbath in order to provide for the bodily healing of a man. This is a most important point for an understanding of the sabbath controversy between Jesus and His legalistic opponents. He was not arguing simply that a repressive law be liberalized. Nor did He adopt an anti-sabbatarian attitude, opposing the whole institution. He pointed out that His action fulfilled the purpose of the original institu-

115

tion. Had they understood the implications of the Mosaic provision for circumcision on the sabbath they would have seen that deeds of mercy such as He had just done were not merely permissible but obligatory. Moses quite understood that some things should be done even on the sabbath. The Jews had his words but not his meaning. They misinterpreted the significance of the sabbath. Jesus draws them back to the basic reason for its institution. He inquires why, if a ritual act must be performed, they should be wrathful when He has done a deed of mercy (Morris 409).

24 Judge not according to the appearance, but judge righteous judgment.

Jesus commands His hearers to stop judging important matters in this superficial, simplistic, and legalistic manner, and to start judging them correctly. Jesus contrasts their legalism with righteousness. Their interpretation of the law is not merely incorrect; it is actually wicked. "Righteous judgment would penetrate beneath surface appearances and judge according to the spirit and purpose of the law" (Bruce 177). The Jews' pedantic literalism, far from being the extreme holiness they supposed it to be, was actually wickedness in God's sight.

25 Then said some of them of Jerusalem, Is not this he, whom they seek to kill?
26 But, lo, he speaketh boldly, and they say nothing unto him. Do the rulers know indeed that this is the very Christ?
27 Howbeit we know this man whence he is: but when Christ cometh, no man knoweth whence he is.

Apparently these words make a favorable impression upon those who hear them for, at this point, some of the "Jerusalemites" (permanent residents of Jerusalem) ask the rhetorical question, "Isn't this the one whom they (the authorities) want to kill?" Clearly these Jerusalemites are aware of the plot against Jesus' life even if the multitude in v. 20 were not. Yet, if this is the one whom the authorities want to kill (as it obviously is) why are they allowing Him to speak in this way without challenging Him? Do they themselves now know Him to be the Messiah?

The negative particle (Greek *mepote*) indicates that they suppose the answer to their question to be "no." They do not really believe this to be the explanation of the authorities' behavior, but are emphasizing the strangeness of their failure to take action against Jesus. Of course, this Galilean cannot possibly be the Messiah because they know where He comes from (see 6:42); as everyone knows, when Messiah comes no one will know anything about His origins. The current belief of the Jews at the time (apparently based upon such O.T. texts as Mal. 3:1 and Is. 53:2,3,8; see also Morris 412, note 50) was that the Messiah would arise suddenly and mysteriously. As they saw it, this man obviously did not conform to this pattern and, therefore, could not be the Messiah.

28 Then cried Jesus in the temple as he taught, saying, Ye both know me, and ye know whence I am: and I am not come of myself, but he that sent me is true, whom ye know not.

Christ's response to this skepticism is to "cry out" (Greek *krazo*) in frustration and irony, "Oh, yes, you know me and you know where I come from." They know Him yet they do not know Him. They know just enough to miss the truth. They know certain superficial facts about His earthly background which serve only to lead them astray. They know, for example, that He is from Nazareth, but they do not know that He was born in Bethlehem. They mistakenly suppose other things to be true and are thereby misled; they suppose, for example, that He is the natural son of Joseph. They do not know as much as they think they do, and they misconstrue even those things about which they are correct. They do not know Him at all in terms of His true nature and origin.

Jesus now issues a very solemn warning. He presupposes His true origin and, contrasting it with (Greek adversative *kai*) their mistaken conception, assures them that He has not come simply on His own authority. He has come at the behest of another whose authority authenticates His mission. The Jews may not recognize that such is the case (much to their own misfortune), but it is, nevertheless. The one on whose authority He comes is the only "true sender" (i.e. the only one whose authorization really matters). The reason the Jews do not understand any of this is that they have no real knowledge of or relationship with the One who has sent Him— the Father (see v. 17; 5:38; and 6:45).

29 But I know him: for I am from him, and he hath sent me.

In contrast to His hearers, Jesus does know God. He knows Him personally and intimately. He knows Him because He is from Him and has been sent by Him. In this short sentence Jesus brings together three interrelated and recurring themes of His teaching concerning Himself. The first is His intimate knowledge of the Father (hinted at in 5:20 and recurring in 8:55; 10:15; and 17:25). The second is the fact that He comes forth from God, that He has a heavenly origin (3:13; 6:38,41, 42,46,51,58). The third is

the fact that it is God who has sent Him into the world (3:17,34; 4:34; 5:23, 24, 30, 36-38; 6:29, 38-40, 44, 57).

30 Then they sought to take him: but no man laid hands on him, because his hour was not yet come.

When they hear this, some of those present seek to arrest Jesus. They understand that He is claiming an intimacy with God that is inappropriate for a mere man. They are unable to accomplish their purpose, however, because Christ's hour has not yet come (i.e. the point in God's plan for Jesus to be arrested has not yet been reached; see comments on "hour" 2:4). This first effort to arrest Jesus seems improvised and somewhat disorganized. The authorities will make a much more systematic attempt beginning in v. 32.

31 And many of the people believed on him, and said, When Christ cometh, will he do more miracles than these which this *man* hath done?

In contrast to the utter rejection of Christ by some, others believe on Him (see comments 1:12 for meaning and 2:11,23; 4:39, 41,50 for other instances). Those who believe ask the rhetorical question, "When Christ comes, can he possibly do any more miracles than this man has done?" (expecting the answer "No"). These words may express the basis of their own faith, that they believe because of the miracles. If so, they are not criticized on that account. It is more commendable to believe without seeing miracles (20:29), but it is perfectly permissible to believe because of the miracles. And it is certainly better to believe because of the miracles than to remain unbelieving in spite of them (6:36). On the other hand, their words may not be intended to express the basis of their own faith, but as a rhetorical challenge to others to believe.

32 The Pharisees heard that the people murmured such things concerning him; and the Pharisees and the chief priests sent officers to take him.

The fact that such quiet conversations (for the meaning of "murmuring" see v. 12) are going on does not escape the Pharisees. They recognize the threat that such ideas pose to the established order, and they realize that something must be done before things get out of hand. Accordingly, they arrange to convene the Sanhedrin and, in concert with the high priests (who were Sadducees), send officers (of the Jewish Temple police) to arrest Jesus.

**33 Then said Jesus unto them, Yet a little while am I with you, and *then* I go unto him that sent me.
34 Ye shall seek me, and shall not find *me*: and where I am, *thither* ye cannot come.**

In the meantime Jesus continues to teach in the Temple. His words have reference to the fact that His time upon earth is growing short and that He is soon to return to His Father who has sent Him. There is an irony in Jesus' words as He continues. He is aware that the authorities are "seeking" Him for the purpose of arresting Him, but the time will come when they will seek for Him in a very different sense (i.e. as their Messiah and Deliverer) and shall not find Him. They will not be able to find Him for He will be in a place that (because of their very refusal to believe on Him) is inaccessible to them—Heaven (see e.g. 3:36 and 5:40).

35 Then said the Jews among themselves, Whither will he go, that we shall not find him? will he go unto the dispersed among the Gentiles, and teach the Gentiles? 36 What *manner of* saying is this that he said, Ye shall seek me, and shall not find *me*: and where I am, *thither* ye cannot come?

In keeping with their usual pattern of pedantic literalism, the Jews miss Jesus' point entirely. They speculate as to where this place, where He is going and they cannot find Him, could be. The best they can come up with is that perhaps He is talking about going to preach to Jews of the Diaspora—Jews scattered abroad and living among the Gentiles—or even to the Gentiles themselves. These words seem to indicate that there was a belief current among the Jews at the time, perhaps based upon such O.T. texts as Is. 42:1,6; 49:6; and 60:3, that the Messiah would conduct such a ministry. It is ironic that, though they did not have the sequence and particulars exactly right, they were basically correct in their understanding. This was to be the basic plan followed (by Paul, for example) in bringing the gospel to the Gentiles. Yet this scene closes with the Jews once again puzzled and unbelieving, wondering at the meaning of Jesus' words.

Summary
(7:1-36)

Jesus confines His ministry to Galilee for about a year because of a plot against His life by the Jewish authorities at Jerusalem. About six months after the feeding of the 5,000 and just before the Feast of Tabernacles, His brothers challenge Him to go up to Jerusalem and publicly declare Himself to be the Messiah to the many Jews who will be present for the feast.

Jesus explains to them that it is not

yet time for Him to take such a step. He tells them to go ahead to Jerusalem without Him. He is not going up to this feast, at least not in the public way that they suggest. That will come later. He goes up to this feast privately and does not arrive until it is about half over.

Prior to His arrival there has been a great deal of speculation about whether or not He will make an appearance. The people are divided in their opinions concerning Him. Some suppose Him to be a good man but others believe Him to be a charlatan. However, none voice their opinions publicly because they know the authorities are opposed to Him.

Soon after He arrives in Jerusalem, Jesus begins to teach in the outer court of the Temple. Everyone is amazed at His knowledge and wisdom, especially in light of the fact that He is not a trained rabbi. Jesus answers that His doctrines do not originate with Him but that they have been given to Him by God who has sent Him. He assures His hearers that if they will do God's will they will know that this is so. He tells them that they may know that He is a reliable teacher by observing that His message glorifies God rather than Himself.

Christ confronts the opposition by referring back to His healing of the lame man on the Sabbath. He says that they all realize that there are times when one is justified in violating the exact letter of the law, but that they are ready to kill Him for one small and technical violation. Moses himself acknowledged that the Sabbath might be technically violated to circumcise a child if the eighth day fell on the Sabbath. How much more legitimate it is, therefore, for Him to heal the lame man on the Sabbath. The reason they do not understand any of this is that they have missed the whole point of the Sabbath.

As they hear Jesus say these things, the people are puzzled by the lack of any action by the authorities to silence Him. They ask facetiously if perhaps the authorities themselves have accepted that He is the Messiah. Yet they do not really think that He is the Messiah. The Messiah will arise suddenly and mysteriously as from nowhere, whereas everyone knows that Jesus is from Nazareth in Galilee.

Christ responds to their sarcasm with an irony of His own. In a loud voice He tells them that, while they think they know Him, they really do not. He is a far different person than they suppose, and there are aspects of His being of which they are totally ignorant. He tells them that He has been sent by God and that the reason they do not accept Him is that they do not know God. These words so anger some of the crowd that they attempt (unsuccessfully) to arrest Christ. But many believe on Him and suggest that the Messiah could not possibly do greater miracles than Jesus has done. When the Pharisees realize that Jesus is having this sort of impact, they decide that He must be arrested and, with the collaboration of the high priests, send officers to do so.

Jesus responds to the effort to arrest Him by saying enigmatically that He is soon going to leave and return to the place from which He came. He says that they will then search for Him in a very different sense than they suppose but that they will not be able to find Him, for He will have gone to a place inaccessible to them. The Jews do not understand that He is speaking of His death and return to Heaven and wonder if He is speaking about a preaching mission among the Gentiles. Indeed, they realize that they do not know what He means.

Application: Teaching and Preaching the Passage

In chapter six the strength of the unbelief which Jesus faced was illustrated by the fact that even some of those who called themselves His disciples really did not believe. Now in the first few verses of chapter seven John calls to the reader's attention that even Jesus' own brothers did not believe in Him. There is certainly a lesson in this for the Christian. The servant is not greater than his Lord. If Christ experienced such rejection from those of His own family, the Christian must not be discouraged when he encounters a similar response.

In the running dialogue of vv. 10-36 one can get a feeling for Jesus' manner of conversing with the people of His time and also for their mind-set and peculiar ideas (this is also true for the rest of chapter seven and for chapters eight, nine, and ten). If one reads carefully, he can piece together a very interesting picture of the popular Judaism of the day, its reaction to Christ, and of His method of dealing with it. There were many confused beliefs and false ideas about the Messiah. They are instructive as to how a truth can be twisted so as to miss the whole point.

There were many opinions about Jesus. Some thought Him a good man, some a deceiver. Some were amazed at His knowledge. Some thought Him a blasphemer and a dangerous enemy of the truth. Some even believed on Him as the Messiah. The personality, intelligence, authority, and majesty of Jesus are clearly in focus in this section and in the rest of chapters seven through ten.

O. The Fifth Discourse: The Water of Life (7:37-52)

37 In the last day, that great *day* of the feast, Jesus stood and cried, saying, If any man thirst, let him come unto me, and drink.

The Feast of Tabernacles climaxed on the eighth day with a great ceremony (see Lev. 23:36). Over the years a ritual had grown up where water was brought from the Pool of Siloam and poured out before the altar to symbolize both thanksgiving for the rain of the previous year and a prayer for rain in the year to follow. In the context of this ceremony involving water, Jesus stands in the court of the Temple and calls out that anyone who thirsts should come to Him and drink. This is obviously another of Christ's enigmatic statements and is intended by Him to convey a spiritual truth. He expands upon such O.T. texts as Is. 12:3; 44:3; 55:1; and 58:11 which speak figuratively of salvation as water, to say that all who have a spiritual need should come to Him. He designates Himself as the source of the water of salvation (see 4:10, 14).

38 He that believeth on me, as the scripture hath said, out of his belly shall flow rivers of living water.

The one who believes on Jesus (i.e. drinks) will not only satisfy his own spiritual thirst but will become a conduit through which the water of life will flow to others. This expands upon the idea of 4:14. There the believer will have a constant supply of the water of life bubbling up within him. Here he will actually become an intermediate source of this water for others although, of course, its ultimate source is Christ. Jesus apparently does not quote just one verse here but draws upon and summarizes several O.T. texts (e.g. Zech. 14:8; Ezek. 47:9; and Joel 3:18).

39 (But this spake he of the Spirit, which they that believe on him should receive: for the Holy Ghost was not yet *given*; because that Jesus was not yet glorified.)

John parenthetically explains that when Jesus speaks of the "living water," He is speaking of the Holy Spirit. This helps one to understand His usage in 4:10-14. The living water which Jesus refers to can be thought of either as eternal life or as the Holy Spirit who conveys that life as He indwells the believer. There is no conflict between identifying the living water as eternal life and as the Holy Spirit who is life and produces life. When John says that the Holy Spirit "was not yet," He means that Pentecost had not yet occurred. The Holy Spirit was present in the world prior to Pentecost (e.g. 1:32 and 3:5) but not in the same sense as afterward. When he says that the reason the Holy Spirit had not yet come was that Jesus had not yet been glorified (i.e. crucified, risen and ascended), John anticipates Jesus' teaching of 14:26 and 16:7 that the Holy Spirit will not come until Christ has returned to Heaven.

40 Many of the people therefore, when they heard this saying, said, Of a truth this is the Prophet.
41 Others said, This is the Christ. But some said, Shall Christ come out of Galilee?
42 Hath not the scripture said, That Christ cometh of the seed of David, and out of the town of Bethlehem, where David was?

Jesus' words have quite an impact on His listeners. In fact, they convince some of them that He must be some sort of apocalyptic personage, either the prophet like unto Moses (6:14) or the Messiah Himself. It should be noted that these people differentiate between these two figures and do not view them as one and the same (see 1:19-22 for similar discussion concerning John the Baptist). It is also interesting that it is Christ's words, rather than His miracles, which produce this effect on this occasion. However, others respond that He obviously is not the Messiah because, as everyone knows, the Messiah is to be a

descendant of David and is to come from Bethlehem (1 Sam. 20:6; 2 Sam. 7:12-16; Mic. 5:2). Once again John's sense of irony calls silent attention to the fact that the very bases of these peoples' rejection of Jesus would be bases for acceptance if they only knew all the facts.

43 So there was a division among the people because of him.
44 And some of them would have taken him; but no man laid hands on him.

Once again, the general populace is divided in its opinions of Jesus, with some believing Him to be either the prophet or the Messiah, others believing such to be precluded by the facts of the case, and some still trying to arrest Him.

45 Then came the officers to the chief priests and Pharisees; and they said unto them, Why have ye not brought him?
46 The officers answered, Never man spake like this man.

With the mention of the desire of some to arrest Jesus, John turns again to the group of Temple police sent out earlier by the authorities to arrest Jesus (v. 32). They return to the Sanhedrin at this time, having failed to arrest Jesus. Asked the obvious question, "Why have you not brought Him?" their reply indicates that they themselves have been very much impressed by Jesus. Instead of referring to any difficulty in arresting Jesus (e.g. the large number and hostility of those among the crowd who were inclined to believe in Jesus), they simply say that no one ever spoke like this man.

Here is an astounding fact. The very Temple officers who were sent out to arrest Jesus are so impressed by Him that they not only refuse to arrest Him, but actually defend Him to the authorities. An interesting sidelight is that approximately four days have passed since they were sent out (vv. 14,37), apparently without any communication with the Sanhedrin. One wonders what transpired in this interim.

47 Then answered them the Pharisees, Are ye also deceived?
48 Have any of the rulers or of the Pharisees believed on him?
49 But this people who knoweth not the law are cursed.

The impact of the officers' words is not lost upon the authorities. They ask rhetorically and in utter amazement, "You are not also deceived, are you?" Their question assumes that Jesus is a deceiver and acknowledges that some have been deceived, but assumes that surely members of the Temple constabulary are not to be counted among that number. They point out that none of the rulers (chief priests) or Pharisees believe on Christ. (Nicodemus apparently has kept his own counsel.) They suppose that this observation will settle the matter once and for all, their self-confidence being so complete as to regard their own opinion as the ultimate confirmation of itself. As for this people, this unwashed rabble, these illiterate peasants, they are so utterly ignorant of the Law as to be accursed of God. Their opinion is completely irrelevant.

50 Nicodemus saith unto them, (he that came to Jesus by night, being one of them,)
51 Doth our law judge *any* man, before it hear him, and know what he doeth?
52 They answered and said unto him, Art thou also of Galilee? Search, and look: for out of Galilee ariseth no prophet.

At this point, Nicodemus, who came to Jesus by night and who is a member of the Sanhedrin and a Pharisee, objects rhetorically: "Does our law (in which, of course, we are all great experts) judge a person without allowing him to explain his own actions?" His point is obvious and cannot be avoided except by sarcasm: "Are you also of Galilee?" The Law is not a standard by which these men examine the propriety and ethics of their own actions. It is rather a device by which they enforce their will upon others.

They set forth what they suppose to be an irrefutable argument against the possibility that Jesus could really be the Messiah or any other Messianic personage, the fact that He is from Galilee. Their statement that no prophet comes from Galilee should not be taken to mean that there has never been a prophet from Galilee but rather in a more limited sense that there is no prediction that any Messianic personage will come from there. It is easy to fault Nicodemus for not making a bolder defense of Jesus at this point, but even the small effort he does make may require a great deal of courage. John does not seem to imply that there was anything dishonorable about Nicodemus' conduct.

Summary
(7:37-52)

On the last day of the feast, Christ cries out that whoever thirsts should come to Him and drink and that whoever believes on Him will, as the Scripture says, have the living waters flowing out from him to others. John explains that Jesus is speaking of the Holy Spirit that is to be poured out upon the church in a special way at Pentecost after Jesus' ascension.

These words of Christ have quite an impact on His hearers. Some suppose Him to be "the prophet like Moses" while others suppose Him to be the Messiah Himself. Others, however, object that He could not possibly be the Messiah since He comes from Galilee rather than Bethlehem. The people remain divided in their opinion of Christ, with some still trying to arrest Him.

At this point John relates that the officers sent out by the authorities to arrest Jesus return, having failed for four days to do so. When asked for an explanation of their failure, these officers indicate that they have, themselves, been much impressed by Jesus' teaching. This, of course, very much angers the authorities who sarcastically reproach the officers for their supposed gullibility. This provokes Nicodemus to ask if it is lawful for anyone to be condemned (as they are condemning Jesus) without his being allowed to answer the charges against him. His barely concealed rebuke prompts the rest of the Sanhedrin to turn their sarcasm on Nicodemus by asking if he also is a Galilean, pointing out once more the absurdity of the idea that the Messiah could possibly be a Galilean.

Application: Teaching and Preaching the Passage

In vv. 37,38 Jesus teaches that those who drink of Him will not only receive great blessing themselves but will become a source of that blessing for others. In Gen. 12:2, God promised Abraham that, by obedience, he would not only be blessed but be a blessing. So it is when one trusts in Christ and, consequently, is indwelled by the Holy Spirit. He is not only blessed, he becomes a conduit of blessing. God's purpose in saving any individual is larger than his own personal salvation. He saves him to reach others (e.g. Acts 9:15).

In vv. 40-44 one can observe the tremendous negative impact of just one small error of fact. Many of the people are so impressed by Jesus' answers that they decide that He must, indeed, be the Messiah, the great Prophet. But others totally reject this conclusion. They interpret (correctly) that the Messiah was to be born in Bethlehem. They assume (incorrectly) that Jesus does not meet this condition. Then they conclude (incorrectly) that Jesus cannot be the Messiah. Even though they are correct in their interpretation of Scripture, these people reject Jesus because of a small error of fact. Christians must always be careful to get the facts. Since Christianity is founded upon facts, no one should be more interested in precise truth than Christians.

In vv. 45-52 can be observed the great contrast between the power of light and the power of darkness. The power of light can be seen in that the very Temple police are so impressed with Jesus that, far from arresting Him, they seem almost to believe on Him. But the power of darkness is apparent in the wrongheaded, sarcastic attitude of the Pharisees, who are determined to destroy Jesus, no matter what.

P. The Woman Taken In Adultery (7:53-8:11)

This section is not found in the oldest manuscripts of the Gospel, and this raises a question whether it was part of the original text (see Morris, Bruce, Brown, Bernard, and especially Godet). (In a few of the manuscripts that include this section, it is marked in such a way as to differentiate it from the rest of the text.) Nevertheless, it seems to be a genuine account of an episode in the life of Christ. If not original, it was probably inserted by some scribe because he thought it should be preserved and this was an appropriate place to include it. Various interpreters have observed that its style is more like that of the Synoptics than John (in fact, one Latin manuscript places it after Lk. 21:38 rather than in John). The context of the incident seems to fit better with the events of Christ's last week (see the comments on vv. 1, 2 below) rather than the Feast of Tabernacles. Indeed, the passage appears to break the flow of this section, as 8:12 very naturally follows 7:52.

53 And every man went unto his own house.
8:1 Jesus went unto the mount of Olives.
2 And early in the morning he came again into the temple, and all the people came unto him; and he sat down, and taught them.

The statement that "everyone went home" would naturally come at the end of a section of narrative and seems to indicate that this section was once part of a larger narrative and followed upon another episode. If not the episode related in 7:45-52, then precisely which episode is unknown; but it could well have been during the last week of Christ's life, perhaps the very day when the authorities tried to trap Him by questions concerning tribute to Caesar and the resurrection (e.g. Lk. 20:20-40). The Synoptics describe Jesus' pattern during that time as coming into the Temple area during the day and retiring to the Mount of Olives each evening (Lk. 21:37; 22:39). (Mark says Bethany (11:11), but since Bethany is located on the Mount of Olives, there is no contradiction.) Here Jesus goes out to the Mount of Olives, presumably at evening, and early the next morning returns to the Temple to teach. This clearly seems to fit the pattern of His last week.

3 And the scribes and Pharisees brought unto him a woman taken in adultery; and when they had
set her in the midst.

As Jesus is teaching the people, He is approached by a group of "scribes and Pharisees." (This pairing, which is often used in the Synoptics but not by John, who never even mentions the scribes and who, when he pairs the Pharisees with anyone, pairs them with the "chief priests," seems to indicate that this passage is more synoptic than Johannine.) They bring to Him a woman whom they say has been taken in adultery and "set her in the midst," i.e. as the defendant in a judicial proceeding.

4 They say unto him, Master, this woman was taken in adultery, in the very act.
5 Now Moses in the law commanded us, that such should be stoned: but what sayest thou?
6 This they said, tempting him, that they might have to accuse him. But Jesus stooped down, and with *his* finger wrote on the ground, *as though he heard them not.*

Those who bring the woman to Jesus say, "Master, this woman was caught in the very act of adultery. Now it is very clear that Moses, in the law, said that she should be stoned (Lev. 20:10; Deut. 22:22-24), but what do you say should be done to her?" Lest any should miss the obvious, John shares with his readers that these people have no other purpose in this affair than to try to trap Jesus into saying something that they may use against Him. While John does not explain the exact nature of their trap, it would seem to be that they assume that Jesus will oppose stoning the woman and thus be technically in violation of the law.

Jesus does not immediately respond to them. Instead, He stoops down and begins to write or draw (Greek *katagra-*

pho) on the ground. John gives no clue as to the nature of what Jesus writes. One supposes that he would supply this information if it were pertinent. The point seems to be that Jesus deliberately ignores them.

7 So when they continued asking him, he lifted up himself, and said unto them, He that is without sin among you, let him first cast a stone at her.

Christ's opponents are very sure of themselves. They consider that they have Him trapped, and they press their advantage by repeating their supposedly unanswerable question. Finally Jesus stands up and says, "Let the one among you who is himself sinless cast the first stone."

One must emphasize that Jesus' statement is not a blanket condemnation of the punishment of crime by properly constituted authorities. The Jews were not such and had no official responsibility or right to punish this woman themselves (see Westcott). Since their whole action was a charade designed for no purpose but to discredit Him, Jesus disposed of it by an *ad hominem* logic before which their supposed paradox fell to the ground. He refused either to oppose Moses or to acquiesce in their cruel cynicism. He frustrated the designs of these hypocrites by turning upon them what seems the most unlikely of weapons: their own consciences. They were totally unprepared for this tactic, and it confounded them absolutely. A major point of this episode is that nobody can match wits with Jesus.

8 And again he stooped down, and wrote on the ground.
9 And they which heard *it*, being convicted by *their own* conscience, went out one by one, beginning at the eldest, *even* unto

the last: and Jesus was left alone, and the woman standing in the midst.

After this devastating reply, Jesus again kneels down and resumes His writing on the ground. Slowly, as the force of His argument hits them and their own consciences convict them, Christ's would-be inquisitors slip away one by one, beginning with the oldest and most respected, until every one of them is gone and Jesus is left alone with the woman. Ironically she still "stands in the midst" (i.e. in the place of the accused) even though there are no longer any accusers present.

10 When Jesus had lifted up himself, and saw none but the woman, he said unto her, Woman, where are those thine accusers? hath no man condemned thee?
11 She said, No man, Lord. And Jesus said unto her, Neither do I condemn thee: go, and sin no more.

Jesus has remained kneeling and writing until now. Finally, when the last one has left, He stands and, looking around and seeing that no one but the woman remains, says to her, "Woman, where are your accusers? Did no one condemn you?" Jesus, of course, is speaking tongue in cheek. Obviously there have been accusers; the point is that they are now gone. The woman picks up on Jesus' meaning and answers, "No one (Greek *oudeis*), Lord."

Since the focus of this episode is the hypocritical crowd rather than the woman, no explanation of her experience is given. Therefore, it is difficult to know what is going on in her heart. Jesus' words do not necessarily imply forgiveness. He may simply refer to the fact that condemnation is not His purpose for coming into the world (3:17). Perhaps her reference to Him as "Lord" or "Sir" (Greek *kurios*) implies some perception of His identity and character, even an incipient faith. But this is not clear. At any rate, Christ accepts her guilt as a matter of course, and His refusal to condemn does not imply any tendency to condone her sin, merely a refusal to assume judicial responsibility for it. He sends her away with the stern warning to stop her sinning.

Summary
(7:53—8:11)

The Jews bring to Jesus a woman who has been taken in the very act of adultery. They try to place Him in a situation where He will either have to take the lead in and assume the responsibility for stoning the woman or contradict the Law of Moses. Jesus escapes this dilemma by tacitly conceding that the woman should be stoned (thus conforming to the law) but requiring that the one who is to assume judicial responsibility by casting the first stone must be completely innocent himself (thus avoiding any complicity in this brutal charade).

Not even the hypocrisy of the Pharisees can withstand this appeal to conscience. They are forced to withdraw in humiliating defeat. When they are gone, Jesus kindly informs the woman that she is no longer accused and condemned. Her original accusers have departed and, by implication, withdrawn their charges. This leaves Jesus alone to judge her, and He is not going to press charges either. Even as He allows her to go away in freedom, He warns and exhorts her to cease her sinful ways.

Application: Teaching and
Preaching the Passage

This episode demonstrates the sheer brilliance of Jesus' mind. His enemies, as on so many occasions, suppose that they have completely outwitted Him only to find Him too smart for them. This episode must be understood in the context of a match of wits between Jesus and His enemies. The situation is a contrived one, designed for no purpose other than to confound and embarrass Jesus. Jesus' answer should not be understood as an attempt to impose complete justice on a complex situation, but as an agile escape from the logical trap which the Jews have set for Him. Some have supposed that Jesus' action undermines the authority of the civil authorities to enforce the Law and that it condones sin. This is not the case. Christ's refutation of the logical position for stoning the woman is not directed at properly constituted officials who are conscientiously and consistently trying to enforce the Law, but at conniving hypocrites. His refusal to condemn the woman after their dispersal is not a condoning of her sin but a refusal to assume temporal power while here upon earth (see 18:36).

Q. The Sixth Discourse: The Light of the World (8:12-59)

12 Then spake Jesus again unto them, saying, I am the light of the world: he that followeth me shall not walk in darkness, but shall have the light of life.

The exact timing of this event is not certain. It probably takes place shortly after the Feast of Tabernacles. The great crowds seem to be gone, leaving only the Pharisees and Jerusalem officials to confront Christ. The setting still seems to be the Temple precincts. Jesus has said that He is the bread of life (6:35) and (by implication) that He is the water of life (4:10,14; 7:37,38). Now He states that He is the light of the world.

This is the second of the seven great

"I am" sayings of Christ (see 6:35). In the O.T., light is the symbol of knowledge, truth and salvation (e.g. Ps. 27:1), and Jesus' words should be understood in this sense. John has referred to Jesus as the light, the true light, that lighteth every man (1:4,5,9). John's usage there is apparently based upon Christ's statement here.

Jesus is reasserting His claim to be the only source of the truth of God (5:19,20). He is the source of that knowledge by which men may come to possess eternal life. Those who follow Him (i.e. walk in His light) will no longer be in spiritual darkness but shall come into the full illumination of the truth and, thereby, eternal life.

13 The Pharisees therefore said unto him, Thou bearest record of thyself; thy record is not true.

The Pharisees, of course, reject Jesus' claim. They say that His own affirmation is not a sufficient basis for His contention. They make reference to the general principle, which Jesus Himself has earlier recognized (5:31), that the testimony of one man cannot establish the truth beyond all doubt. Their point is simply that Jesus' mere statement of fact, as far as they are concerned, does not mean that it is so. They are implying that His self-confirming testimony is false.

14 Jesus answered and said unto them, Though I bear record of myself, *yet* my record is true: for I know whence I came, and whither I go; but ye cannot tell whence I come, and whither I go.
15 Ye judge after the flesh; I judge no man.

Before going on to make His main point that His testimony is not unsubstantiated, Jesus advances a lesser argument to the effect that even unsubstantiated testimony may be true. In fact, such is the present circumstance. Jesus knows His own testimony to be absolutely true. He is aware of His own origin. He remembers being in Heaven. He is fully cognizant of His own identity. Whether His words are believed or not, they are true.

However, in contrast to His perfect knowledge of the facts of the case, His opponents know nothing about them. They have no informed opinion, for they can perceive only the outward appearances and are oblivious to the inward realities; yet they do not hesitate to judge Jesus a liar. This is ironic: in spite of their total incompetence to do so, they are eager to judge Jesus; while He, who knows all things and could judge them with complete accuracy, refrains from doing so. There is an ominous note in Christ's words, however, for the day is coming when the situation will be reversed and they will all stand before Him for His omniscient and devastating judgment.

16 And yet if I judge, my judgment is true: for I am not alone, but I and the Father that sent me.

The Pharisees have said (v. 13) that Jesus' testimony about Himself is not true. Jesus says that, if He were to judge, His judgment, in marked contrast to their present judgment of Him, would be true, true in a sense which they do not understand (i.e. accurate, incisive, and drastic). The implication is that someday there is going to be such a judgment, a judgment which Christ will conduct and in which the Pharisees are not going to fare well.

At this point Jesus' preliminary argument that His testimony, even though unsubstantiated, is true, converges with His major point that it is, in fact, substantiated by God Himself. Jesus' judgment, if He were to judge, would be true because it would be conducted in cooperation with His Father who has sent Him into the world and with whom He is in complete harmony (5:19,30; 6:38; 10:30). Just as Jesus would not be alone in that judgment, so He is not alone now in His testimony as to His own identity. Though Jesus appears to the Pharisees to be the only witness to the truth of His words, the Father is at this very moment in Heaven bearing witness to their truth. Jesus can hear His words of confirmation whether they can or not. This foreshadows the logic that Jesus will use with Philip (14:9-12), that ultimately the matter comes down to whether one believes Christ's testimony about Himself.

17 It is also written in your law, that the testimony of two men is true.
18 I am one that bear witness of myself, and the Father that sent me beareth witness of me.

Jesus says that even their own Law—the Mosaic Law, which they are bound to abide by—requires that the testimony of two men must be accepted as establishing the truth (Deut. 17:6; 19:15). Jesus says that, on the basis of this principle, the truth of His words is established beyond all doubt because He has the two witnesses: Himself and His Father who has sent Him.

19 Then said they unto him, Where is thy Father? Jesus answered, Ye neither know me, nor my Father: if ye had known me, ye should have known my Father also.

The Pharisees zero in on what they consider to be the obvious flaw in Jesus' logic. Jesus is speaking for both Himself and the Father. They want to hear the Father's testimony from His own mouth rather than second-handedly from Christ. They want Jesus to produce the Father and let Him testify for Himself. Obviously, this is an *ad hoc* argument on their part, the purpose of which is to force Jesus to abandon His claim to the Father's confirming testimony. Jesus replies with the same argument as in 5:37,38 (which see for comments). One can hardly avoid the impression that Jesus is toying with His pompous, overly confident interrogators.

20 These words spake Jesus in the treasury, as he taught in the temple: and no man laid hands on him; for his hour was not yet come.

At this point John supplies another of those incidental details which characterize his account. He reports that the incident just related transpired "in the treasury." The "treasury" was an area within the Court of the Women where there were 13 containers to receive various kinds of offerings. (Later in the same area, Jesus observed the widow offering her two mites; see Mk. 12:41-44.)

The "treasury" was very near the chamber where the Sanhedrin met, and this may be the reason John mentions the location. Ironically, Jesus is preaching right outside the Sanhedrin chamber and yet (adversative use of the Greek *kai*) the rulers do not arrest Him. The only reason John offers for their failure is that His hour has not yet come. This theme has already been introduced (2:4 etc.) and will recur several more times (12:23,27; 13:1; 17:1). It refers not only to Christ's death, but also to His glorification. John mentions this now because, as the next verse reveals, it is in Christ's mind and is the psychological backdrop for this whole section.

21 Then said Jesus again unto them, I go my way, and ye shall

seek me, and shall die in your sins: whither I go, ye cannot come.

At some point not long after claiming to be the light of the world, Jesus makes another enigmatic statement. The chronology of this section is somewhat indefinite. There is no clear note of time between 7:37 when it is October and 10:22 when it is December. Obviously the intervening events stretch over two months, but there is no way of knowing the precise timing of any of them.

The pronoun "them" indicates that Jesus is still addressing the same group as in v. 13, the Pharisees. He tells them that He is going to go away, that they will seek for Him after He is gone, that they will die in their sins, and that they will not be able to come to where He is. When Jesus says that He is going away, He is obviously speaking of His death and return to Heaven. His statement that they will then (unsuccessfully) seek for Him could be understood as meaning that they will continue their efforts to arrest Him even after He has departed from this world; however, it is best to understand these words as having an eschatological tone (see e.g. Zech. 12:10; Mt. 23:39; 24:30; 26:64). There will come a time when the Jewish people will recognize Jesus as their Messiah and desire His salvation. In the meantime, however, they will die in their sin (i.e. with their sin— singular—of rejecting Christ unconfessed and unforgiven). Not only will they be unable to follow Jesus to Heaven immediately upon His leaving; they will also be unable to follow Him there later when they die, their rejection of Him barring them forever.

22 Then said the Jews, Will he kill himself? because he saith, Whither I go, ye cannot come.

Again, the Jews miss Jesus' point entirely. Previously (7:35) the crowd interpreted a similar statement to mean that Jesus was going to leave Israel and go and preach to those of the Diaspora and the Gentiles; now these people are puzzled by His words and ask, "He isn't going to kill Himself, is He?" They sense the ultimacy of Christ's words, but they refuse to consider them seriously. There is a sarcastic tone to their rhetorical question.

23 And he said unto them, Ye are from beneath; I am from above: ye are of this world; I am not of this world.

Jesus interrupts them by saying that He is a being of an entirely different order than they. He is from above while they are from beneath. He is heavenly while they are earthly. This explains why they cannot understand His words and why they cannot follow Him where He is going. He is returning to the realm from which He came (3:13; 6:38,62) and in which He will be perfectly at home, but for which they are not at all fitted. By rejecting Him they lose for themselves all possibility of ever entering that realm.

24 I said therefore unto you, that ye shall die in your sins: for if ye believe not that I am *he* , ye shall die in your sins.

The Jews are essentially earthy. Jesus is essentially heavenly. The reason the Jews will die in their sins is that they do not comprehend either of these truths. They do not comprehend their own depraved, earthy nature; therefore, they do not understand their own guilt before God. On the other hand, they do not comprehend the heavenly identity of Christ, so they refuse the salvation that God offers them through Him. They do not suppose they need salvation because they misunderstand themselves, and they reject the only provision of that salvation because they misunderstand Jesus.

Jesus says, "If you do not believe that I am [who I am], you will die in your sins." If they do not accept Him as the Messiah, the Son of God, then they will be eternally lost, because believing in Him is the only way to be forgiven of their sins.

25 Then said they unto him, Who art thou? And Jesus saith unto them, Even *the same* that I said unto you from the beginning.

Jesus has said that they must believe that He is who He is; therefore, the Jews derisively ask Him, "You! (placed first in the Greek for emphasis) Who are you?" They reject entirely the idea that Jesus is anyone special. It is not that they are unaware of His claims; they *reject* them. In reply to their taunt, Jesus says, "I am just what I have been saying all along." (While the Greek at this point is very difficult, this seems to be the sense of what Jesus says.) In other words, Jesus is reaffirming His claims to be from Heaven and to be the Son of God.

26 I have many things to say and to judge of you: but he that sent me is true; and I speak to the world those things which I have heard of him.

Once again Jesus sounds an ominous note. The Jews are pressing Him to speak to them about His own identity. Jesus, while refusing to speak any more "to" them about His identity, says that He has many things to say "about" them, the implication being, in judgment. Jesus goes on to say that His words of judgment will not be His alone. His judgment will be in accordance with the true, righteous judgment of His Father, the

One who sent Him into the world (see 5:19,20,30). That judgment will be drastic and unsparing. Jesus implies that, although He is not saying as much as His interrogators demand on this occasion, the day will come (at the judgment) when He will say far more than they care to hear.

Jesus continues by saying that, just as He will speak the words of the True One (the Father) in Heaven when He someday judges the world, so He speaks the truth of God even now as He tells them over and over again of His own identity. Though they do not recognize or accept them, Jesus' present words are just as true and have just as much import as the words He will someday speak at the judgment.

27 They understood not that he spake to them of the Father.

Of course, the Jews miss Jesus' point entirely. They do not understand that He is speaking of the Father. The implication is that if they do not understand that Jesus' reference to "the one who sent me" is to God, then they do not understand that He is speaking enigmatically of the judgment either. They miss Jesus' whole point, not just the fact that it is the Father who has sent Him into the world.

**28 Then said Jesus unto them, When ye have lifted up the Son of man, then shall ye know that I am *he*, and *that* I do nothing of myself; but as my Father hath taught me, I speak these things.
29 And he that sent me is with me: the Father hath not left me alone; for I do always those things that please him.**

Jesus continues by making reference to His approaching death, using the same term, "lifted up," that He used in

3:14 (which see for comments). When He is "lifted up" His audience will come to understand that He is the Messiah, that He is in intimate fellowship and agreement with the Father (v. 26), that He takes no action without the Father, that everything He says has the Father's sanction, and that the Father, who has sent Him, is always with Him and never leaves Him alone.

The basis and proof of all this is that Jesus never says or does anything that is not pleasing to the Father (see v. 46 below). Jesus says that all of this will become apparent to His hearers when He is "lifted up." Does He refer to His crucifixion or to His exaltation? There may be an element of each. Perhaps He is thinking of the day of Pentecost. Perhaps He is thinking of the time when all eyes shall behold Him, coming in the clouds of glory.

30 As he spake these words, many believed on him.
31 Then said Jesus to those Jews which believed on him, If ye continue in my word, *then* are ye my disciples indeed.

Surprisingly, John says that many believe on Jesus as they hear these words. This is not what one would expect. The reaction to Jesus in this context has been monotonously negative. Who are these people who believe on Him? Are they Pharisees? Are they merely bystanders? Do they believe in the fullest sense (6:69) or only in a superficial and generalized way (2:23)? Apparently, their belief is more like that of 2:23 than 6:69, for Jesus admonishes them that they must continue in His words if they are to be among His "disciples indeed," rather than (by implication) among those "who go back and walk no more with Him" (6:66).

32 And ye shall know the truth,

and the truth shall make you free.

This is a much-quoted and much-misunderstood verse. It does not mean "that truth in a philosophical sense exercises a liberating function, and that adherence to the school of Jesus procures such intellectual insight that men are delivered from the bonds of ignorance" (Morris 456). It means that as men come to know Jesus, both the source and embodiment of ultimate truth, they will be freed from the presence, power, and penalty of sin. They will, for the first time, be free men rather than slaves of sin and Satan.

33 They answered him, We be Abraham's seed, and were never in bondage to any man: how sayest thou, Ye shall be made free?

There is a question about the identity of those who address Jesus at this point. Some (e.g. Morris) believe them to be those Jews who believe on Him. Others (e.g. Bruce) believe them to be Jews other than those who believe. These latter suggest that Jesus is addressing a mixed group; that, at the beginning, the believers are more in focus; then, as the conversation progresses, the unbelieving Jews monopolize the conversation and Jesus converses primarily with them from this point onward. It does not seem likely that Jesus (or John) would refer to people with such an attitude as is indicated here as being in any sense whatever Christ's disciples. Christ's statement in v. 37 that they are seeking to kill Him seems to rule out such a possibility.

These Jews respond to Jesus' claim that belief in Him will make them truly free by saying that being made free does not apply to them. They are the descendants of Abraham and are, therefore, in bondage to no man. How can anyone who is already wholly free be made free? Jesus is talking nonsense! Of course, their statement is grossly inaccurate. They had been slaves in Egypt, they had been carried captive to Babylon, and at this very moment they were living under Roman domination.

34 Jesus answered them, Verily, verily, I say unto you, Whosoever committeth sin is the servant of sin.

Jesus does not challenge this historical inaccuracy; rather, with great solemnity (Greek *amen, amen*), He points out the self-evident truth that every person who sins is the slave (Greek *doulos*) of sin. The obvious implication is that Jesus considers His antagonists to be sinners and, therefore, in this sense, slaves. He is speaking of something far more serious than political bondage or freedom.

35 And the servant abideth not in the house for ever: *but* the Son abideth ever.

Jesus goes on to challenge their claim to be Abraham's (and, therefore, God's) children. He relegates them to the status of servants while reserving to Himself alone that of a son. He is so uniquely and essentially a son that He is *the* Son. In comparison to His unique (see 1:14) Sonship, all others are but servants.

36 If the Son therefore shall make you free, ye shall be free indeed.

Therefore, if this unique Son declares one free, he is truly free. This statement presupposes the Jews' sinfulness, the absolute authority of the Son, and the glorious nature of the freedom which He is empowered to confer. The person whom Christ makes free is truly free, for He is free from the greatest of all slavemasters, the tyranny of sin.

37 I know that ye are Abraham's seed; but ye seek to kill me, because my word hath no place in you.

Jesus concedes that, physically, the Jews are the children of Abraham, but insists that their desire to kill Him proves that, in spite of this, they are sinners and, therefore, the slaves of sin (and not *really* Abraham's children; vv. 39,40). The reason they hate and reject Him is that His word (i.e. His teaching) does not register with them. They do not understand or accept the truth of His teaching. They are not on His wavelength.

38 I speak that which I have seen with my Father: and ye do that which ye have seen with your father.

Jesus refers again to His heavenly origin (v. 23; compare 5:30,37; 6:38,46) and to the fact that His teachings do not originate with Him but with the Father (v. 28; 5:19; 7:16). Then He contrasts Himself, His Father, and what He speaks with His hearers, their father and what they do. He teaches as He does because of who He is, who His Father is, and what He has learned from intimate association with Him. They reject His teaching as they do because of who they are, who their father is, and what they have learned from intimate association with him. Jesus' Father is God. He clearly implies that their father is Satan.

**39 They answered and said unto him, Abraham is our father. Jesus saith unto them, If ye were Abraham's children, ye would do the works of Abraham.
40 But now ye seek to kill me, a man that hath told you the truth, which I have heard of God: this did not Abraham.**

The Jews may not understand just what Jesus is getting at, but they know that He is implying something about their ancestry. They stay on what they suppose to be safe ground by reiterating the stock answer that Abraham is their father.

Jesus replies that this cannot be the case because, if they were Abraham's children, then they would do the works of Abraham. Yet, instead of doing the works of Abraham, they are trying to kill Him, one who has simply told them the truth which He has heard from God. Abraham would never have acted like that. It is not Abraham who is their father.

41 Ye do the deeds of your father. Then said they to him, We be not born of fornication; we have one Father, *even* God.

Having eliminated Abraham as a possibility, Jesus again focuses upon the question of their ancestry. He repeats His contention of v. 38 that they do the works of their father. If their father is not Abraham then who is he?

The Jews still do not quite understand what Jesus is getting at. They reply, "First, that if it is being suggested that they are not the legitimate descendants of Abraham and Sarah, it is not true; and secondly, that if it is spiritual and not physical descent that is in question, then their Father is God. The sentence is very much compressed" (Bernard 311).

42 Jesus said unto them, If God were your Father, ye would love me: for I proceeded forth and came from God; neither came I of myself, but he sent me.

Just as Jesus rejected the Jews' previous contention that Abraham was their father, so now He rejects the idea

that God is their father. If God were their father (as, by implication, He is not; in Greek, the "condition" is assumed untrue), then they would love Him (as they obviously do not) because He has come forth from God. He has not come on His own but has been sent by God. Jesus' logic is very similar to that in 5:38 (which see for comments). If there were really any familial bond between these Jews and God the Father, then they would sense that same bond with Jesus, God's unique Son. Their hatred for Jesus belies their love for the Father (see 1 Jn. 5:1).

43 Why do ye not understand my speech? even because ye cannot hear my word.

There is a play on words in this statement. Jesus says that the reason they cannot understand His *speech* (Greek *lalia*, i.e. His outward speech, His way of expressing Himself) is that they do not understand His *word* (Greek *logos*), His teaching as expressing a rational meaning. They are unable to understand what Jesus is talking about because they have no understanding of, or sensitivity to, such concepts as He refers to. It is, to them, as if He spoke in a foreign language.

**44 Ye are of *your* father the devil, and the lusts of your father ye will do. He was a murderer from the beginning, and abode not in the truth, because there is no truth in him. When he speaketh a lie, he speaketh of his own: for he is a liar, and the father of it.
45 And because I tell *you* the truth, ye believe me not.**

Jesus has hinted at the truth long enough. Now He comes right out with it. The problem is that their Father is neither Abraham nor God, but the devil.

Their evil propensities are traceable to their ancestry. The reason they act as they do, that they reject Christ so utterly, is that they are children of the devil. Like father, like son. His evil characteristics are expressed in them.

Why are they possessed with this manic desire to kill Jesus? Because their father the devil is first and foremost a murderer, and His murderous spirit finds expression in his children. Why are they so adverse to truth which Christ expounds to them? Because their father, being the first and original liar, hates and utterly rejects the truth. These characteristics are expressed in his children. That the children of the father of falsity should be allergic to truth is only natural. They have inherited this allergy from their father.

The reason, therefore, that they do not believe Jesus is that He is telling them the truth (v. 45). The very truth of His words is the reason for their rejection of them.

46 Which of you convinceth me of sin? And if I say the truth, why do ye not believe me?

Jesus continues His rebuke with a challenge: "Which of you (is able to) convict me of sin?" "Convict" (Greek *elegcho*) means to bring to light, to expose, to set forth. Jesus challenges His enemies to state, if they can, any sin of which they know Him to be guilty. Jesus speaks these words almost casually, as part of a logical demonstration of the Jew's inconsistency in failing to believe Him. It is illogical not to believe one against whom no charge of wrongdoing can be laid, to assume that such a person is not speaking truthfully. The Jews must admit that Jesus is such a person, and yet they refuse to believe Him. This is absurd.

It would be easy to miss the monumental claim that Jesus makes for Himself here. He assumes His own sinlessness to be incontrovertible and then uses it as logical proof of His veracity.

47 He that is of God heareth God's words: ye therefore hear *them* not, because ye are not of God.

This argument is essentially the same as in v. 42 and 5:38 (which see for comments). The only explanation for the Jews' stubborn refusal to believe Jesus, in the face of irresistible evidence of the truth of what He says, is that they are not of God. If they were of God, they would believe Him.

48 Then answered the Jews, and said unto him, Say we not well that thou art a Samaritan, and hast a devil?

The Jews' reply makes no attempt to counter Jesus' logic. It is simply a resort to invective. They speak as though it is a common saying among them that Jesus is a Samaritan and is demon possessed and that His words prove this saying to be accurate.

The exact implication of their use of "Samaritan" is not clear. Perhaps they considered Jesus' challenge of their claim to be the true children of Abraham as an essentially Samaritan argument since the Samaritans characteristically challenged this claim. In that case, they were attempting to shame Jesus who, though a Jew, would be siding with His people's worst enemies in their slander of the Jewish nation. Or perhaps they were simply using "Samaritan" as an insulting epithet, being the worst thing they could think of to call anybody. Or they may have viewed "Samaritan" as the equivalent of "having a demon," with which they paired it. In accusing Jesus of "having a demon," they apparently had in mind insanity rather than diabolical wickedness (see Bernard).

49 Jesus answered, I have not a devil; but I honour my Father, and ye do dishonour me.

Jesus does not respond to the charge that He is a Samaritan, which may indicate that He interprets "Samaritan" as the equivalent of "having a demon." On the other hand He may purposely refuse to respond to the taunt to show that He does not consider Samaritans inherently odious.

At any rate, Jesus responds only to the charge that He has a demon, simply denying it. His rejection of their claim to be the children of God and of Abraham does not arise from demonic dementia but from simple conformity with the wishes of His Father. It is the Father who has rejected them as His children, and Jesus is simply relating to them the facts. He must do no less if He is to be faithful to the wishes and instruction of the Father, if He is to honor the Father. Jesus is saying that He gives honor where it is due while they do not, for they are even now refusing to honor Him whom the Father has sent—and, indirectly, the Father who has sent Him.

50 And I seek not mine own glory: there is one that seeketh and judgeth.

Jesus is not seeking His own glory. He does not need to do so for there is another who seeks to glorify Him, the Father. Furthermore, He does not need to receive glory from the Jews. Such glory as mere men can give Him is utterly meaningless. They are incompetent to confer any meaningful glory. Only from the one truly righteous judge is He interested in receiving glory. Only that glory which the Father gives has any meaning for Him.

51 Verily, verily, I say unto you, If a man keep my saying, he shall never see death.

Using the formula of solemnity (Greek amen, amen) to introduce His words, Jesus restates in slightly different form the basic truth which He has set forth in vv. 31,32. Instead of saying that they will be His disciples indeed if they continue in His word, He says that they will never really die if they keep His saying. Jesus is summarizing His entire argument to this point. This is the climax toward which He has been moving. The words "see death" mean to experience death. He refers, of course, to eternal death rather than physical death. This is the same theme of eternal life which Jesus has reiterated so many times already.

52 Then said the Jews unto him, Now we know that thou hast a devil. Abraham is dead, and the prophets; and thou sayest, If a man keep my saying, he shall never taste of death.

The Jews, with their wooden literalness, suppose Jesus to mean that those who obey His words will not experience physical death. They consider such a statement to be patently absurd. Even Abraham is dead. The prophets are dead. These men kept faithfully the very words of Jehovah and yet even they have died. In light of this, how can Jesus dare to suggest that those who obey His words will not die? Indeed, He must be demented to make such a preposterous claim.

53 Art thou greater than our father Abraham, which is dead? and the prophets are dead: whom makest thou thyself?

Is Jesus actually claiming to be

greater than Abraham and the prophets? That is the inescapable implication of His statement. If obedience to His words exempts one from death, then He must be greater than Abraham and the prophets, who are dead. The Jews suppose that they have reduced Jesus' claim to an absurdity. They consider it self-evident that He is infinitely inferior to Abraham and the prophets. Their words, "Whom makest thou thyself?" are a sarcastic rebuke of His supposed presumption rather than a request for further enlightenment. Again, John's use of irony is in view. It never occurs to the Jews that what they consider to be patently absurd is, in fact, the sober truth: that Jesus really is infinitely superior to both Abraham and the prophets.

54 Jesus answered, If I honour myself, my honour is nothing: it is my Father that honoureth me; of whom ye say, that he is your God.

Jesus does not deny the charge that He is claiming to be superior to Abraham and the prophets. He does not deny that His words imply great honor for Himself. Instead, He submits that it is not He who honors Himself (such honor being, inherently, meaningless, see e.g., 5:31 and v. 13), but His Father who honors Him. To eliminate any possibility of misunderstanding, He further identifies His Father as the one whom they say is their God. This is an unequivocal claim to deity of the same magnitude as 5:17. It is interesting to note that Jesus implies that God is not really their God in spite of their confident assumption that He is.

55 Yet ye have not known him; but I know him: and if I should say, I know him not, I shall be a liar like unto you: but I know him, and keep his saying.

In spite of the fact that the Jews claim that Jesus' Father is their God, they do not really know Him at all. In contrast to them, however, Jesus, Himself, knows the Father perfectly (see v. 14). There is sharp irony in Christ's words. For Him to say that He did not know the Father would make Him just as much a liar as the Jews in claiming that they did know the Father. Jesus knew the Father in the most intimate and complete manner possible (see comments 7:29). This intimate fellowship between Christ and the Father produced a complete unanimity of spirit between them (see v. 16; and 5:19,20). Jesus always acted in harmony with the will of His Father.

56 Your father Abraham rejoiced to see my day: and he saw *it* and was glad.

The Jews, in v. 53, have attempted to use Jesus' assumed inferiority to Abraham as an argument against His claims. Now, having refuted their false logic, Jesus will demonstrate the real bearing of Abraham upon the subject. The fact is that Abraham, from whom the Jews so proudly claim descent, rejoiced to see Jesus' day.

The question which may puzzle modern minds is when and under what circumstances did Abraham do this. There is no clear answer. The important thing to remember is that the Jews did not question Jesus as to whether Abraham did, in fact, foresee and rejoice in the Messiah's coming. They accepted that as established. The point of contention was that Jesus applied Abraham's vision to Himself: "Abraham rejoiced to see *my* day." Jesus was not merely asserting that Abraham had a vision of the Messiah, but that the vision of the Messiah (which they all conceded Abraham to have had) was actually a vision of Himself. This saying is exactly analogous with that of 5:39.

57 Then said the Jews unto him, Thou art not yet fifty years old, and hast thou seen Abraham?

The Jews interpret Jesus' words to mean that He is claiming to have been alive at the time of Abraham. They point out the obvious fact that this is impossible since Jesus is still a relatively young man (not yet 50 years old), whereas Abraham has been dead for many centuries. This is not, of course, what Jesus means; actually He claims that Abraham has seen Him and not that He has seen Abraham. It may be a deliberate misunderstanding on their part. If so, it is an ironic twist that Jesus turns their sarcasm upon them and answers their rhetorical challenge with a quiet affirmation.

58 Jesus said unto them, Verily, verily, I say unto you, Before Abraham was, I am.

In effect the Jews have offered a sarcastic rejoinder: "You don't really claim to have seen (i.e. to have been alive at the same time as) Abraham, do you?" Jesus answers with the calm, sober affirmation: "Verily, verily, I say unto you, Before Abraham was, I am." Jesus solemnly affirms what they sarcastically put forward as inherently ridiculous: that He was, in fact, alive at the time of Abraham. Indeed, He was alive even before that, alive from all eternity.

This is the clear indication of Jesus' use of the present tense "I am" rather than "I was." This use of "I am" is also reminiscent of the name by which God identified Himself to Moses (Ex. 3:14) and is another claim on Christ's part to deity, understood as such by His hearers (v. 59). This is the climax of this long discourse, a clear affirmation by Christ of His own deity, a claim to possess eternal being as one of the primary attributes of God.

59 Then took they up stones to cast at him: but Jesus hid himself, and went out of the temple, going through the midst of them, and so passed by.

This affirmation, if not true, is blasphemous, and thus do the Jews interpret it. Their anger is so aroused that they take up stones to stone Jesus on the spot. They have neither the time nor the inclination for the formality of a trial. His guilt is obvious.

The last part of the verse says that Jesus escaped unharmed from their midst. The exact nature of this escape is uncertain. Was it a miraculous event or a providential deliverance? The evidence is inconclusive. For similar events see 10:39; 12:36; and Lk. 4:30. (The last phrase, "Going through the midst of them, and so passed by," is not found in many good manuscripts; some suggest that it comes from Lk. 4:30.)

Summary
(8:12-59)

Shortly after the Feast of Tabernacles, Jesus proclaims that He is the light of the world and that those who follow Him will no longer walk in darkness but will have the light of eternal life. The Pharisees reject this claim on the basis that it is uncorroborated. Jesus responds, first, that uncorroborated testimony is not, necessarily, false and His, in fact, happens to be true. Then He affirms that He does have a corroborating witness, His Father in Heaven, who has sent Him into the world. The Jews challenge Jesus to produce the Father and let Him testify, but Jesus replies that it would be useless to do so, given their total lack of rapport with the Father.

Soon Jesus makes another enigmatic statement. He is going to go away and they, seeking but unable to find Him, will die in their sins. In response to the Jews' sarcastic question whether He means to kill Himself, Jesus states that He is of an entirely different order of being than they and that this is the reason they cannot follow Him and will die in their sins. The Jews reject Christ's claim to any transcendent identity by asking: "Who are you?" Jesus responds quietly that He is just who He has been claiming to be all along. He ominously implies that they are going to be hearing a great deal from Him in the future. They will stand before Him in judgment. It will then be quite clear that He is in perfect agreement with the Father. These words cause many, at least outwardly, to believe on Jesus.

Jesus tells these new "believers" that they must continue in His words if they are truly to be His disciples. If they will do this, they will know the truth and thereby be free. This reference to freedom prompts some of the Jews to retort, "What do you mean by saying that we shall be free? As the children of Abraham we are already free." Jesus replies that anyone who sins is in bondage to sin, implying, of course, that this applies to them. They are slaves, not sons, but He is the Son; and if He were to grant them their freedom, they would be truly free.

Jesus concedes that they are, physically, the children of Abraham, but that their rejection of Him proves that they are not Abraham's spiritual descendants. Just as Jesus speaks those things which He has heard from His Father, so the Jews speak those things which they have heard from their father, the devil. The Jews continue to insist that Abraham is their father, but Jesus counters that this cannot be so for, if they were truly Abraham's children, they would act like Abraham. Instead their actions are obviously not those of Abraham. Abraham would not be trying to kill a man who was attempting to tell the truth which he has heard from God. No, whoever their father is, it is not Abraham.

Thus pressed, the Jews state that, ultimately, their Father is God. Jesus counters that, if that were the case, they would love and receive Him, for He has come forth from God and has been sent by Him into the world. The reason they reject Jesus is that what He says is totally alien to them, and this is because they are the children of the devil rather than of God. They do not believe Jesus even though He tells them the truth and even though He is obviously a trustworthy witness. They refuse to believe the words of God because they are not the children of God.

The Jews can but retort that Jesus is a demented Samaritan. Jesus assures them that He is perfectly sane and that it is the Father Himself who has rejected them as His children. He is merely delivering to them the Father's verdict. With great solemnity, Jesus goes on to say that, if one will keep His saying, he will never really die, but have eternal life.

Again the Jews level their charge of insanity. Even Abraham is dead, and yet Jesus claims that people who keep his saying will never die. Does Jesus consider Himself to be greater than Abraham? Just who does Jesus suppose Himself to be? Jesus quietly replies that whatever honor these claims imply for Him does not come from Himself but from His Father, the one whom the Jews themselves say is their God. While they do not really know God at all, Jesus knows Him intimately, and all that Jesus says or does is at the Father's behest.

Jesus continues, "As for Abraham, from whom you so proudly claim descent, even in antiquity he rejoiced that someday I should come into the World." The Jews object that Jesus could not possibly have known Abraham; Jesus replies that He was alive before Abraham was ever born. This response prompts the Jews to attempt to stone

Jesus for blasphemy, but Jesus escapes them unharmed.

Application: Teaching and Preaching the Passage

William Hendriksen sees this section as a sort of running dialogue between Jesus and the Jews in which Jesus repeatedly reveals some truth about His own identity only to have it immediately rejected by the Jews. This dialogue runs roughly as follows: (1) Jesus says, "I am the light of the world." The Jews flatly contradict Him, "Your testimony is not true." (2) Jesus says, "My judgment is true, for I am not alone....the Father that sent me bears witness of me." The Jews demand that He produce the Father and allow Him to testify: "Where is this father of yours?" (3) Jesus says that He is going to depart this world and go where they cannot follow. The Jews retort, "He's not going to kill Himself, is He?" (4) Jesus says that if they will not believe that He is [the Messiah] they will die in their sins. They respond, "You, who are you?" (5) Jesus claims to come from God: "He that sent me is true, and I speak to the world [only] those things which I have heard from Him." The Jews fail to understand that He is speaking of the Father. (6) Jesus says that when they have "lifted up" the Son of Man, then they will know that He is the Messiah. While many "believed" on Him at this point, it seems that they were a minority and/or that their belief was less than totally sincere, for the opposition intensifies. (7) Jesus says, "If you continue in my word, you will know the truth and the truth will make you free." The Jews retort, "We are the descendants of Abraham and have never been slaves to anyone. What do you mean when you say that we will be made free?" (8) Jesus states that if they were the children of Abraham, then they would act like Abraham. The Jews reply

that they are not born of fornication, that they have one Father, God. (9) Jesus says that He has come forth from God and has been sent by Him, but they are of their father, the devil. They reply with blind hatred, "Are we not correct in saying that you are a Samaritan and are demon possessed?" (10) Jesus insists that He is not demon-possessed and that if anyone will keep His saying, he will never see death. The Jews reply, "Now we know that you have a demon ....You are actually claiming to be greater than Abraham. Just who do you think you are?" (11) Jesus replies that, actually, Abraham had looked forward to His coming. The Jews reply incredulously, "You are not even fifty years old, and you claim to have seen Abraham?" (12) Finally, Jesus makes a claim to one of the primary attributes of deity—eternity—by saying, "Before Abraham was, I am." The Jews' response to these words is to prepare to stone Jesus. Jesus has claimed to be the Messiah, to be God. His claim has been thoroughly rejected.

R. The Sixth Sign: Healing the Man Born Blind (9:1-41)

1 And as *Jesus* passed by, he saw a man which was blind from *his* birth.

The timing and exact location of this episode are uncertain. It probably takes place some little time after Christ's escape from the mob in the Temple rather than immediately upon His exit while He was still being hotly pursued. Jesus' actions are those of a man maintaining a low profile, but not those of a man in immediate danger. This view is substantiated by the fact that the blind man is healed on a Sabbath (v. 14), while there is no indication that the escape from the mob took place on a Sabbath. The proximity of the Pool of Siloam, as well as the general conditions, indicate that the episode takes place in Jerusalem, most likely in the Temple environs.

In chapter eight, Jesus has referred to Himself as the light of the world. The restoring of sight to the man born blind is a graphic and symbolic object lesson of this truth. As Jesus walks about, He observes this unfortunate man and calls attention to him in some way.

2 And his disciples asked him, saying, Master, who did sin, this man, or his parents, that he was born blind?

Apparently there is some discussion as to the man's sad plight, during which the disciples ask Jesus whether the man's blindness is caused by his own or his parents' sin. In keeping with the accepted wisdom of the day, they assume that it is one or the other. No other explanation is even considered. There is no hope that people who limit their options to variations of error will ever arrive at truth.

3 Jesus answered, Neither hath this man sinned, nor his parents: but that the works of God should be made manifest in him.

Jesus rejects their formulation of the problem and says that the reason for the man's blindness is neither of the two they suggest but something entirely different. "But" (Greek *alla*) is a strong adversative and indicates great contrast. The man has, in the providence of God, been born blind so that His mighty power can be demonstrated through him. Simply put, he has been born blind so that Jesus can heal him. God, in His wisdom and power, has deemed to turn one of the many results of the curse (sin being the ultimate, but not immediate, cause of the man's blindness) to His own purpose. In doing so He both glori-

fies His Son and increases (rather than lessens) the ultimate happiness of the man involved. God has not caused the man's blindness (ultimately, Satan has done that), but He uses it to achieve ultimate good. From the eternal perspective, the man is better off to have endured many years of blindness and to be gloriously healed as he is, than to have lived out a life of normal vision.

4 I must work the works of him that sent me, while it is day: the night cometh, when no man can work.
5 As long as I am in the world, I am the light of the world.

Jesus now offers a preliminary explanation for the miracle He is about to perform. He says that He must do the works which have been assigned to Him by His Father who has sent Him into the world, because the time allotted for these works is limited and will soon come to an end. He will only remain in the world for a finite time before He returns to Heaven. His function while He is here, as He has previously stated, is to serve as the light of the world. He is saying, by implication, that the miracle which will follow is an aspect of His function as the light of the world.

6 When he had thus spoken, he spat on the ground, and made clay of the spittle, and he anointed the eyes of the blind man with the clay,
7 And said unto him, Go, wash in the pool of Siloam, (which is by interpretation, Sent.) He went his way therefore, and washed, and came seeing.

Jesus' action of spitting on the ground, making clay, and then daubing the clay upon the blind man's eyes is somewhat strange. Scholars are divided in their understanding of this action. Some suppose it to be an aid to the man's faith since spittle was assumed, in the ancient world, to have curative powers. The more likely explanation seems to be that Christ utilizes this method so as to require an act of obedience and faith from the man. Like Naaman of old, he is required to carry out an apparently arbitrary action and thereby demonstrate faith and obedience. John seems to imply that this is correct by emphasizing to his readers that Siloam means "sent."

Jesus' sending of this man to the pool to wash is presented as an important aspect of the event, not just an incidental detail. John also stresses that the man did, in fact, carry out Christ's instructions and that it was not until he had done so that he received his sight. It may also be that Christ's action of making clay, anointing the man's eyes, and requiring him to go to Siloam was a deliberate, technical violation of the Sabbath designed to antagonize the Pharisees and to draw attention to the miracle.

Significantly, Jesus is the only person presented in Scripture as healing the blind. (Ananias' action in regard to Saul of Tarsus is of another sort, entirely.) The healing of the blind was prophesied as being an activity of the Messiah (Is. 29:18; 35:5; 42:7). Jesus referred to it, in answer to the query of John the Baptist, as an indication that He really was the Messiah (Mt. 11:5).

8 The neighbours therefore, and they which before had seen him that he was blind, said, Is not this he that sat and begged?

John's description of the reaction to this miracle seems true to life. The man's neighbors and those who are accustomed to seeing him at his post begging say among themselves, "This is the fellow who [formerly] sat and begged, isn't it?" They know that it is, yet he is so drastically changed that he hardly seems like the same person.

9 Some said, This is he: others said, He is like him: but he said, I am he.

The change in the man is so drastic that a controversy arises as to whether he is the same man or not. Some are convinced that he is, while others do not think so. His bearing and manner are so radically altered that some, while admitting that he is very similar to the blind beggar they used to know, are convinced that he must be someone else. The man himself soon settles the controversy. He is not at all confused about the matter. He says with absolute certainty, "I am he." John clearly appreciates the humor of the situation.

10 Therefore said they unto him, How were thine eyes opened?

The controversy about his identity now resolved to everyone's satisfaction, the people inquire of the man how he has received his sight. Obviously, they were not present when Jesus anointed his eyes and sent him to Siloam.

11 He answered and said, A man that is called Jesus made clay, and anointed mine eyes, and said unto me, Go to the pool of Siloam, and wash: and I went and washed, and I received sight.

The man's reply is brief and precise. A man called Jesus made clay, anointed his eyes with it, and told him to go and wash in the pool of Siloam. Doing as he was told, he went to Siloam, washed his eyes in the pool, and received his sight. The man knows little about Jesus except His name at this stage, yet he already must sense that He is not an ordinary man. It is interesting to note the progression of his understanding of Christ's identity as the account proceeds.

12 Then said they unto him, Where is he? He said, I know not.

The crowd wants to know where this Jesus is. The man seems to assume that they will have heard of Jesus, but they do not seem to be very familiar with Him. Their question seems to be more, "Where is this Jesus you speak of?" than, "Just where is Jesus at the moment?" Regardless, the man can only reply that he does not have any idea where He is.

13 They brought to the Pharisees him that aforetime was blind.

The crowd, apparently, continues to discuss the matter and decides that, since this is essentially a religious question, the proper action is to take the man to the Pharisees. They are the religious experts; let them get to the bottom of this.

14 And it was the sabbath day when Jesus made the clay, and opened his eyes.

At this point John shares with his readers the important detail that Jesus healed the blind man on a Sabbath. Some believe that the people brought the man to the Pharisees because of this, but there has been no indication that they were concerned about the Sabbath. Their discussion has centered upon the miracle, the blind man's identity, and the identity of his healer. It seems preferable to understand that John mentions the Sabbath at this point to prepare the reader to understand the dialogue which will follow.

15 Then again the Pharisees also asked him how he had received his sight. He said unto them, He put clay upon mine eyes, and I washed, and do see.

Once more the formerly blind man is called on to give an account of his healing, this time to the Pharisees. Probably he gave a full account and the terse, "He put clay upon my eyes, I washed, and do see," is but John's summary of his statement. However, some believe that these were his exact words. Under the latter assumption, his words may indicate either a circumspect precision to avoid self-incrimination or a growing impatience at being repeatedly asked to reiterate the obvious.

16 Therefore said some of the Pharisees, This man is not of God, because he keepeth not the sabbath day. Others said, How can a man that is a sinner do such miracles? And there was a division among them.

When some among the Pharisees become aware that this miracle transpired on the Sabbath, they know all they need to know. Jesus obviously cannot be of God because He does not keep the Sabbath. They have already condemned Jesus as a desecrator of the Sabbath (5:16), and this latest action serves merely to vindicate their previous verdict. Others of the Pharisees, however, are not so certain. They cannot see how a man who is a sinner could perform such miracles as this one. Apparently this latter group constitutes a very small minority since nothing more is heard from them in the dialogue which follows.

17 They say unto the blind man again, What sayest thou of him, that he hath opened thine eyes? He said, He is a prophet.

At this point, the Pharisees do something contrary to their usual practice: they ask for a non-Pharisaical opinion. They will soon be back at themselves, however, this momentary lapse having been completely rectified (v. 34). For the moment, though, the man's special position as the subject of such an undeniably profound miracle renders his opinion relevant. The Pharisees ask "What do *you* (emphatic in the Greek order) have to say about Him, since you are the one who had his eyes opened?"

The man gives his considered opinion that Jesus is a prophet. Undoubtedly, he has reflected upon this "man called Jesus" who has bestowed upon him the wonderful gift of sight after a lifetime of blindness. With his limited information and understanding, he has arrived at the conclusion that Jesus is a prophet. His designation of Jesus as a "prophet" indicates that he holds an extremely high view of Him, but he does not yet comprehend the fact of His deity. The Samaritan woman also referred to Jesus as a "prophet" with approximately the same implications (4:19).

18 But the Jews did not believe concerning him, that he had been blind, and received his sight, until they called the parents of him that had received his sight.

The Pharisaic majority, now referred to as "the Jews," refuses to accept the man's account that he has been healed of blindness. They cannot deny that he can now see, so they set about to prove that he has never been blind. They must have the testimony of his parents as to this alleged blindness. The absurdity of this inquiry (and the desperation of the Pharisees) is apparent. This august body will hear evidence as to whether or not the blind man has really been blind, after all.

19 And they asked them, saying, Is this your son, who ye say was born blind? how then doth he now see?

When the man's parents appear, the Pharisees ask them, "Is this your son, whom ye say was born blind? How then does he now see?" The question is phrased as negatively as possible. The first part, "Is this your son?" seems to challenge the fact that the man now standing before them is the one who was formerly blind, who "sat and begged," and who was known to be the son of these parents. The second part, "Whom you say was born blind," challenges the parents' claim that their son was, indeed, born blind even as it acknowledges that this is, in fact, their claim. This is cynicism at its worst. The question both assumes and challenges what it purports to be trying to ascertain. The third part, "How then does he now see?" begs the question and is intended only to intimidate. The unassailable fact is that the man does now see. The parents can only testify as to whether this man is, in fact, their son and as to whether he was actually born blind.

20 His parents answered them and said, We know that this is our son, and that he was born blind:
21 But by what means he now seeth, we know not; or who hath opened his eyes, we know not: he is of age; ask him: he shall speak for himself.

The Pharisees' attempt at intimidation is entirely successful. The man's parents are intimidated to the point of disassociating themselves from their own son (v. 21b). Even so, they state clearly that this man is their son and that he was born blind. For all their servile bowing and scraping, for all their disavowal of any knowledge of the means by which

143

their blind son has been made to see, their testimony destroys the Pharisee's case.

22 These *words* spake his parents, because they feared the Jews: for the Jews had agreed already, that if any man did confess that he was Christ, he should be put out of the synagogue.
23 Therefore said his parents, He is of age; ask him.

John points out, as if to make some excuse for the parents' cowardly betrayal of their own son, that the reason they acted as they did is that they were afraid of the Jewish authorities who had made it known that anyone who confessed that Jesus is the Messiah would be put out of the synagogue. They must be very careful not to say anything which might be construed to mean that they thought Jesus was the Messiah. This hardly justifies their conduct, but it does explain it.

24 Then again called they the man that was blind, and said unto him, Give God the praise: we know that this man is a sinner.

Having failed to prove that the man was never blind in the first place, and therefore having to admit that a great miracle has taken place, the Jews try to disassociate the miracle from Jesus. They use the argument that God can use even sinners to accomplish His will. They recall the man and tell him to give God, rather than this Jesus, the glory for restoring his sight. They assure him that Jesus is a sinner.

Originally they denied that any miracle had actually taken place and accused the man of only pretending to have been blind. They did this because they knew that such a miracle would be very strong evidence that Jesus was, in fact, the

Messiah. Now they pretend that there is no such implication, that there is no connection between the miracle and Jesus' claim to be the Messiah. If that is the case, then what has all the commotion been about? If the miracle has no implications for Jesus' identity, then why did they deny that it took place? Why did they not just tell the man that Jesus was a sinner and that it was God who was responsible for this wonderful miracle when he was first brought to them?

25 He answered and said, Whether he be a sinner *or no*, I know not: one thing I know, that, whereas I was blind, now I see.

The formerly blind man may not be able to match the Pharisees in subtle rationalizing, but when it comes to simple logic he beats them hands down. The force of his reply is irresistible: "I cannot speak definitively as to whether he is a sinner or not; such things as that must be left to you experts. But there is one thing I am absolutely certain of: whereas I used to be blind, now I can see. I know that to be a fact. Even such an ignoramus as I can discern the difference between blindness and sight."

26 Then said they to him again, What did he to thee? how opened he thine eyes?

The Pharisees do not choose to stand and fight on this issue. They know when they have been bested. Rather, they make a tactical withdrawal. They want to discuss the procedures, the actual process by which Christ has given the man his sight. Perhaps there is some clue to the mystery to be found there. Perhaps, if the event is recounted often enough, they can find some flaw, some impropriety, some technical violation of proper miracle-working procedure, something they can use against Jesus.

27 He answered them, I have told you already, and ye did not hear: Wherefore would ye hear it again? will ye also be his disciples?

The formerly blind man sees what the Jews are trying to do and answers that he has already been through it all with them. Contrary to the obvious evidence, they have refused to accept (hear) his testimony. What good will it do to go through it all again? At this point he adds a touch of irony. He asks them if they "also" wish to become disciples of Christ.

There are two ways the word "also" (Greek kai) can be used here. There is the ascensive use in which it is translated "even," and there is the adjunctive use in which it is translated "also." If it is translated "even," then the man would be saying, "Are even you Pharisees going to become His disciples?" If it is translated "also," then he is saying, "Are you going to believe in Him, too?" Either way, the man assumes that Jesus does have some disciples and sarcastically questions whether the Pharisees are going to join them. The man may or may not include himself among Christ's disciples. Morris supposes that he does in fact include himself and sees this as an indication of a great progression in his attitude toward Christ.

28 Then they reviled him, and said, Thou art his disciple; but we are Moses' disciples.

This answer stirs up the Pharisees' anger and hatred, and they begin to speak contemptuously and abusively to the man, "You are his disciple; but we are Moses' disciples." Do they really understand the man to be claiming to be Jesus' disciple, or do they purposely twist his words so as to ridicule him? Whichever, they draw a sharp contrast between themselves, the disciples of the venerable and ancient Moses, and the man who is, in their view at least, the disciple of this rabble-rouser, Jesus.

29 We know that God spake unto Moses: as for this fellow, we know not from whence he is.

The Pharisees consider Moses' legitimacy as a spiritual authority to be beyond all doubt, but as for this Jesus, they know nothing about Him. He is an obscure and insignificant nobody. They are not seriously considering the question of Jesus' origins; they are simply belittling Him and calling attention to His lack of legitimacy as a religious leader. Only in John's mind does the irony of their words, especially in light of the man's reply, come to bear. It is only too true that they do not know where He comes from. They have no idea of His heavenly origin, His identity, His majesty, or His authority.

30 The man answered and said unto them, Why herein is a marvellous thing, that ye know not from whence he is, and yet he hath opened mine eyes.

Once again the man uses sarcasm to respond to the Pharisees. He tells them that the real miracle in the whole affair (literally, "in this is the marvel") is their complete lack of knowledge of such a person as Jesus obviously is. That Jesus is a great personage of some sort is inherent in His healing the man's blindness. The thing that astounds the man is that they, the leaders of the Jews, the religious authorities who are supposed to know about such things, have no explanation for Jesus' miraculous powers.

31 Now we know that God heareth not sinners: but if any man be a worshipper of God, and doeth his will, him he heareth.

In v. 16 some of the Pharisees concluded that since Jesus did not keep the Sabbath, He was a sinner and, therefore could not have performed this miracle. Others saw it quite differently. They concluded that Jesus could not be a sinner if He could perform such a miracle as this. The formerly blind man now adopts the second position. He says that all must agree that God would not hear a sinner (i.e. that He would not, at the sinner's request, perform a miracle), and that it is only such people as worship God and do His will whom God hears (and, by implication, to whom He grants the power to perform miracles). The miracle which Jesus has performed is, in and of itself, clear evidence that He is not a "sinner" as the Pharisees insist (v. 24).

32 Since the world began was it not heard that any man opened the eyes of one that was born blind.
33 If this man were not of God, he could do nothing.

The formerly blind man continues by stating that it is completely unheard of for anyone to give sight to one who has been born blind. Jesus clearly could not have performed such a wonderful miracle except by God's power. The miracle proves more than that Jesus is not a sinner; it proves that He is a godly person, that He has God's blessing and approval.

The man's understanding of Jesus has clearly progressed. In v. 11 he referred to Him as simply "a man called Jesus." In v. 17 he called Him "a prophet." Now he says that He is a man "of God."

34 They answered and said unto him, Thou wast altogether born in sins, and dost thou teach us? And they cast him out.

The Pharisees are angered by this impertinent reply. Their anger pours forth in a stream of invective: "You were born totally in sin, and do you [dare] to instruct us [on matters of who is righteous and who is a sinner]?" In their anger, the Pharisees have forgotten themselves. When they say that the man was born in sin, they refer (by the same logic as the disciples in v. 2) to the man's congenital blindness and thereby admit that he was, indeed, born blind.

In light of the threat mentioned in v. 22, the phrase, "cast him out" apparently indicates that the Pharisees, in addition to unceremoniously kicking him out of the present assembly, actually excommunicated the formerly blind man from the synagogue.

35 Jesus heard that they had cast him out; and when he had found him, he said unto him, Dost thou believe on the Son of God?

When Jesus hears that the Pharisees have cast him out of the synagogue, He finds the formerly blind man and asks him (in a way that clearly expects an affirmative reply and lays emphasis on the word "you"), "You (at least) believe on the Son of Man, don't you?" (The oldest manuscripts have "Son of Man" rather than "Son of God." This does not alter the meaning, since it is Christ's Messianic identity which is in view in either set of terms.) Jesus, on the basis of the answers the man has given the Pharisees, perceives that the man has come, by reflection, to understand a great deal about Him and, to a great degree, to believe on Him. He means, by His question, to encourage and stimulate this belief. The question is also a subtle instruction that Jesus is, indeed, the Messiah. Jesus suggests the resolution to the quandary in the man's mind about His identity: He is the Messiah. He gives Him the last piece of the puz-

146

zle, and this makes all the other things he has figured out for himself make sense.

36 He answered and said, Who is he, Lord, that I might believe on him?

There is a subtle, knowing quality about the man's response that is not apparent in the KJV. His words are, "And who is He, Lord, that I may believe on Him?" Just as Jesus' question has presupposed that the man does, in fact, believe on "the Son of Man," the man's reply suggests that he already knows who "the Son of Man" is. He only awaits formal confirmation from Jesus' lips before declaring his faith openly.

37 And Jesus said unto him, Thou hast both seen him, and it is he that talketh with thee.
38 And he said, Lord, I believe. And he worshipped him.

Jesus' answer does not disappoint the man. He says, "You are looking at Him (a Greek intensive perfect, which indicates strong emphasis rather than past time), and it is He who is speaking with you." There is a special significance in the fact that the man is "looking" at Him. He has not done any "looking" before meeting Jesus. The wonderful fact that He has received his sight at Jesus' word is clearly in view. There can be no doubt in the man's mind now; he responds immediately, "Lord, I believe," and begins to worship Him.

39 And Jesus said, For judgment I am come into this world, that they which see not might see; and that they which see might be made blind.

Jesus now interprets the symbolic meaning of this whole episode. In it a

judgment may be perceived. It is not so much a judgment which He actively pronounces upon men, as one which His very presence provokes them to bring upon themselves by their response to Him. He has come in order that those who do not see may see. By this He refers, not only to the restoring of physical sight to the physically blind, like the man in this episode, but also to the granting of spiritual vision to the spiritually blind. The formerly blind man has not only been granted physical sight; more important, he has also been enabled to perceive the spiritual reality that Jesus is the Messiah.

In marked contrast to the blind whom Christ enables to see are those who suppose themselves to have perfect vision but whose rejection of Christ reveals them to be completely blind. This is the meaning of Christ's ironic and enigmatic reference, "that they which see might be made blind." The Pharisees confidently assume their own spiritual infallibility even as they reject their Messiah.

40 And *some* of the Pharisees which were with him heard these words, and said unto him, Are we blind also?

Some Pharisees who are nearby, apparently monitoring Jesus' teaching, respond sarcastically: "You are not saying that we are blind, are you?" Clearly they suspect that He is. (The Greek wording indicates their utter rejection of the notion that they might also be blind.)

41 Jesus said unto them, If ye were blind, ye should have no sin: but now ye say, We see; therefore your sin remaineth.

The Pharisees, apparently, expect Christ to reply that they are, indeed, spiritually blind. His answer does not conform to their expectation, however.

It is even more confrontational and condemning than they expect.

Jesus' answer is in two parts, each involving bitter sarcasm and harsh judgment. First, if they were completely blind, their sin would be less than it is. In fact, they are not completely blind and they understand enough to render their rejection of Him inexcusable. Second, if they admitted their blindness and were not so presumptuously certain of their spiritual vision, then there would be some hope of their receiving their sight. But, since they refuse to admit their blindness and insist that their vision is perfect, there is no help for them and they remain in their sin. Unlike the man born blind, *their* (spiritual) blindness *is* the result of their sin.

Summary
(9:1-41)

As Jesus is walking about, He observes a man who has been blind from birth. The disciples wrongheadedly ask whether it is the sin of the man himself or that of his parents which has caused him to be born blind. Jesus answers that neither of these is the case and that the man was born blind in order that the power of God may be revealed through him. Jesus explains the significance of the miracle He is about to perform by stating that He must soon accomplish His task of bringing light into the world since His time for doing so is limited. Jesus spits on the ground to make clay and, after daubing some of it on the man's eyes, commands him to go and wash it off in the pool of Siloam. The man obeys Jesus' instruction and, as a result, receives his sight.

When the man's neighbors and those who have previously seen him begging observe that he is able to see, a controversy arises. Some believe him to be the man whom they know to have been born blind, while others believe him to

be an impostor. When the man assures them that he is the man born blind, they ask him how he has come to receive his sight. He answers that a man called Jesus is responsible. When pressed for further information about his benefactor, he must admit that he knows very little about Him.

For whatever reason, the crowd brings the man to the Pharisees, who ask him again how he has come to receive his sight. The man recounts the event to them, but when they become aware that he has been healed on the Sabbath, the great majority of them pronounce that Jesus is obviously a sinner since He has violated the Sabbath. Others among them retort that it is not reasonable to suppose that one who can perform such a miracle is a sinner. At this point, the Pharisees ask the man born blind for his opinion of Jesus. He states that he believes Him to be a prophet.

The Pharisees call the man's parents to testify, in the hope that they can discredit the miracle by proving that the man was never really blind in the first place. This tactic fails miserably as the parents, in spite of being totally intimidated, confirm that the man is their son and that he was, in fact, born blind. Thus rebuffed, the Pharisees exhort the man to give the glory for his healing to God rather than to this Jesus, who is (as they see it) obviously a sinner.

At this point there begins a dialogue between the formerly blind man and the Pharisees, which will end in his excommunication from the synagogue. The man states that he is not competent to speak to the point of whether Jesus is a sinner, but that there is one point on which he is uniquely qualified to expound: whereas he used to be blind, now he can see. In reply, the Pharisees can but weakly suggest that he, once more, recount the episode. The man suggests that this is quite pointless since he has nothing to add to what he has already told them. He asks, ironically, if they, themselves, are considering becoming Christ's disciples.

This sarcasm quite angers the Pharisees. They revile him by saying that, while he is Christ's disciple, they are Moses' disciples. They consider it quite respectable to be Moses' disciples, but as for this Jesus, He is a nobody. The man retorts, "Why this is a great wonder, that my eyes should be opened by a nobody. It is obvious that a sinner could not perform such a uniquely glorious miracle as giving sight to one born blind. If this man were not of God, He could not do such a thing." Unable to resist this logic, the Pharisees can only insult and excommunicate this one who dares defy them.

Later, Jesus finds the formerly blind man and knowingly says, "You, at least, believe on the Son of Man, don't you?" Just as knowingly, the man replies, "Who is He, Lord, that I may believe on Him?" Jesus assures the man that He is the Son of Man. The man immediately responds, "Lord, I believe," and worships Jesus.

Jesus explains the meaning of this episode to those around Him by saying that His coming has brought a judgment upon the world, a judgment which involves sight for the blind and blindness for those who will not see. The Pharisees sense that He has them in mind and challenge Him, "Do you mean us?" Jesus answers them by saying that, since they are not completely blind, they are sinning against knowledge and that, since they are so confident of their own vision, there is nothing He can do to help them.

Application: Teaching and Preaching the Passage

This chapter consists of a miracle, Christ's healing of the man born blind,

and a series of dialogues concerning it. The miracle, itself, is important simply because it is such a tremendous and undeniable one. Its obvious reality lends an almost surrealistic aspect to all that follows. It is almost comical the way everyone goes about establishing whether or not the obvious has, in fact, occurred; and then, once this is established, the way they attempt to deny its implications.

The first dialogue takes place between the formerly blind man, his neighbors, and those who have known him as a beggar. The question they debate is whether the man with whom they speak is, in fact, the man whom they have known as a blind beggar. Some believe that he is. Others believe that he is not the blind beggar at all, but an impostor who looks just like him. Ultimately the question is too complex to be resolved by such simplistic evidence. It must be referred to some competent authority, such as the Pharisees.

The second dialogue involves the formerly blind man and the Pharisees. The contribution of the majority of the Pharisees to the discussion, after hearing the facts of the matter, is that the man who performed this miracle (if, in fact, there was a miracle) is not of God, because a true man of God would not perform such a miracle on the Sabbath. Thus, they settle the matter to their own satisfaction without ever dealing with the question of whether a miracle has actually transpired or if this is the man who has formerly been blind. They intend to avoid ruling on the merits of the case, as such.

But some of their number insist that they actually deal with the evidence. They state that no sinner could possibly perform such a miracle as this, apparently accepting the man's (obviously factual) contention that he is the formerly blind beggar and that he does now see. The question of the man's identity and the validity of the miracle are set aside while the more pressing question of Christ's character is settled. The man's own opinion is accepted as being of some value at this point, so he is asked what he thinks of the one who has opened his eyes. He replies that he believes Him to be a prophet, but since his view does not conform to their own, the Pharisees ignore it and decide to focus the inquiry once again upon the man's identity and the validity of the miracle. In keeping with this purpose, they decide to get the testimony of this alleged man's alleged parents as to his alleged blindness. The rule governing these proceedings seems to be that only evidence which appears to sustain the Pharisees' predetermined verdict will be accepted.

The third dialogue transpires between the Pharisees and the man's parents. In it the Pharisees have no other purpose than to try to catch these frightened people in some contradiction. Their questions do not seek information; they simply try to confuse and intimidate. In spite of this, however, the parents' testimony establishes beyond all doubt that this man is actually the blind beggar and no impostor, and, therefore, that he has in fact been made to see.

In the fourth dialogue, the participants are, once again, the formerly blind man and the Pharisees. The Pharisees are determined to ignore the findings of their own investigation, which they tacitly concede has verified the facts as they have been presented to them. Having heard evidence that establishes beyond any doubt that Jesus has performed a great miracle, they rule that this evidence is irrelevant to the issue at hand and determine the issue on the basis of their own *a priori* assumption that Jesus is a sinner and therefore could not be responsible for the miracle. Since it is obvious that a miracle has happened and that Jesus has nothing to do with it, the man should simply thank God for it

and join the Pharisees in their condemnation of Jesus as "a sinner." The formerly blind man rejects this logic and argues the issue skillfully and at length. At last, the Pharisees, in frustration, reprimand and excommunicate him.

The fifth dialogue is between the man born blind and Jesus. In it Jesus subtly challenges the man to faith in Himself as the Messiah and the man responds with an unreserved belief in Him.

The sixth and last dialogue involves Jesus and the Pharisees. Jesus explains the spiritual implications of this miracle only to be challenged by the Pharisees. In reply, He rebukes them for their willful blindness to the truth and pronounces upon them a terrible doom.

In this series of dialogues can be seen the parallel themes of emerging faith in Christ as the Messiah and determined resistance to Him. They serve as a microcosm of the two entirely different reactions of the Jewish people to Christ which John described in the Prologue (1:11,12).

S. The Seventh Discourse: The Good Shepherd (10:1-18)

1 Verily, verily, I say unto you, He that entereth not by the door into the sheepfold, but climbeth up some other way, the same is a thief and a robber.

There is no break between the events at the end of chapter 9 and this discourse on the good shepherd. Jesus never uses the words "Verily, verily" (Greek *amen, amen*) to introduce a completely new thought, but always to solemnly emphasize and apply some previous teaching.

This discourse on the good shepherd is in the form of an allegory and is based on the O.T. conception of Israel as a flock of sheep and God as their Shepherd (see e.g. Ps. 23; Is. 40:11). Jesus seems to refer specifically to Ezekiel's prophecy that a descendant of David (the Messiah) will be the One True Shepherd of Israel (34:23). In identifying Himself with this prophetic figure, Jesus is making a clear claim to be the Messiah.

Jesus begins His allegory with a representation of the Pharisees as thieves and robbers who enter into the sheepfold by some means other than Himself as the true door. Though they claim to be religious authorities, the Pharisees actually have no real knowledge of God (5:38). Therefore, they reject Jesus' claim to be His Son, the only source of eternal life (5:40). Their attempt to enter Heaven by any means except Jesus Christ, the one official door which He has provided, angers and alienates God.

2 But he that entereth in by the door is the shepherd of the sheep.

Jesus contrasts these thieves and robbers with the shepherd of the sheep, who is recognizable by the fact that he always enters the sheepfold through the door. He has no need to climb over the fence and sneak into the sheepfold, for he has every right to enter by virtue of his identity as the shepherd. Jesus implies that the Pharisees are mere usurpers with no legitimate claim to spiritual authority, whereas He is the True Shepherd who will be instantly recognized as such by all in a position to truly know about the matter.

3 To him the porter openeth; and the sheep hear his voice: and he calleth his own sheep by name, and leadeth them out.

The doorkeeper recognizes the voice of the true shepherd and opens to him the door. The sheep also recognize the voice of their shepherd and follow him

willingly as he calls them by name. Apparently, Jesus means to liken the doorkeeper to His Father (although some suppose this a veiled reference to John the Baptist) who recognizes and endorses Him as His Son and who immediately grants His every wish. The sheep are those true believers within whom the Spirit of God bears witness that Jesus is, indeed, the Son of God.

4 And when he putteth forth his own sheep, he goeth before them, and the sheep follow him: for they know his voice.

Every morning, when the shepherd takes his sheep out of the fold and leads them forth to pasture, they willingly follow him because they recognize his voice. Christ's implication is that those who are truly of the fold of God will recognize the voice of His Son, their true shepherd, when they hear it (5:38, etc.).

5 And a stranger will they not follow, but will flee from him: for they know not the voice of strangers.

The sheep, however, will not by any means (Greek *ou me*, two negatives for emphasis) follow a stranger. They will run from him because they do not recognize his voice. Just as those who are truly of God's flock will recognize and respond to the voice of their true shepherd, so they will refuse to hear and will reject the teachings of false shepherds (teachers).

6 This parable spake Jesus unto them: but they understood not what things they were which he spake unto them.

John refers to the previous verses as an "allegory" or "proverb" (Greek *paroi-*

mia). While the KJV translates this word as "parable," it is different from the word usually rendered "parable" (Greek *parabole*). A "parable" is an extended simile, while this word indicates an extended metaphor or an allegory. Jesus' hearers, the Pharisees (9:40, v. 19), do not understand the meaning of this allegory, so it must be explained to them.

7 Then said Jesus unto them again, Verily, verily, I say unto you, I am the door of the sheep.

In vv. 7-18 Jesus explains His allegory of the sheepfold, the sheep, and the shepherd. He assigns to Himself a dual role in His allegory. He is both the Door and the Shepherd. The two roles are complementary rather than contradictory. The first symbolic role Jesus assigns Himself is that of the Door. By this Jesus intends to say that He is the only means by which the sheep may enter the sheepfold, the only means by which one may enter the Kingdom of God (see 14:6). Men may come to God only through His Son, Jesus. This is the third of the great "I am" statements of Jesus (see 6:35).

8 All that ever came before me are thieves and robbers: but the sheep did not hear them.

It seems that the reason Jesus speaks first of Himself as the Door is that the door is mentioned at the very beginning of the allegory; however, He suspends His commentary on the meaning of the fact that He is the Door until v. 9. In this verse He refers to Himself primarily as the Shepherd, in contrast with the thieves and robbers who have refused to enter in by the door and have, instead, tried to climb up over the wall and into the sheepfold some other way. These "thieves and robbers" are all those who have come before Him (i.e. claiming to

be the Messiah, a prophet, or a religious authority). The sheep have not heard them, however, because they were not their true shepherds. The true people of God have not received these false prophets, false Messiahs, and religious leaders (like the Pharisees) because they have failed to recognize the true voice of God in their message.

9 I am the door: by me if any man enter in, he shall be saved, and shall go in and out, and find pasture.

Now Jesus focuses upon His role as the Door (for the significance of this term, see comments v. 7). The special emphasis on the words "by me" indicate that it is only through Jesus that men may enter into the fold of God. The word "saved" (Greek *sozo*) seems to be used as a comprehensive term for the whole process of coming to have eternal life by believing in Christ and as synonymous with "have everlasting life" (see 3:16,17). The last phrase, "shall go in and out and find pasture," has no deep, hidden meaning and should be understood as referring, quite generally, to a happy, contented, and secure life. Its meaning is explained in the last part of v. 10.

10 The thief cometh not, but for to steal, and to kill, and to destroy: I am come that they might have life, and that they might have *it* more abundantly.

The thief comes only to steal, to kill, and to destroy. He cares nothing for the sheep. He is concerned only for himself. Jesus, on the other hand (the "I" is emphasized for contrast), has come so that the sheep may live—live even more abundantly and happily than they would have otherwise. Jesus is contrasting His own attitude toward the people of Israel with that of the Pharisees. Their motives are wholly selfish. They wish only to gain power and position for themselves. They are using the sheep for their own purposes. He, on the other hand, has come into the world for one purpose only, to bring happiness and eternal life to mankind.

11 I am the good shepherd: the good shepherd giveth his life for the sheep.

The second role which Jesus assigns Himself in His allegory is that of the Shepherd. He has spoken, in vv. 2-5, of "the shepherd of the sheep" who came in by the door, was admitted by the doorkeeper, and was known and followed by the sheep. Here He refers to that personage as "the good shepherd" and identifies this One as Himself.

To the qualities already attributed to the good shepherd, Jesus now adds that he gives his life for the sheep. As Jesus says that the good (true) shepherd will protect his sheep at all cost, even die for them if necessary, He is speaking of Himself and His willingness to give His own life for those who believe in Him. This is the fourth of Jesus' seven "I am" statements (see 6:35).

12 But he that is an hireling, and not the shepherd, whose own the sheep are not, seeth the wolf coming, and leaveth the sheep, and fleeth: and the wolf catcheth them, and scattereth the sheep.
13 The hireling fleeth, because he is an hireling, and careth not for the sheep.

In marked contrast to the self-sacrificing love of the true shepherd is the selfish unconcern of the hireling. The sheep are not his. He cares nothing for them. Therefore, whenever there is danger he deserts the sheep, leaving them to fend for themselves, and flees, thinking only of his own safety. He is but a hireling. Jesus speaks this of the Pharisees. The people are, to them, merely a means to an end, a way to achieve the position of respect and authority they desire. They care nothing for the people themselves or their welfare.

14 I am the good shepherd, and know my *sheep* , and am known of mine.

In the allegory Jesus has said that the shepherd calls his own sheep by name (v. 3), implying that he knows them well and that the sheep know their shepherd's voice and follow him (v. 4). Now Jesus says that, as the Good Shepherd, He knows His sheep and is known by them. Jesus is saying (1) that there are those who are His sheep (i.e. His disciples who have come to have eternal life by believing in Him), (2) that He knows each one of them, and (3) that each of them, as he is instructed by the Father, recognizes in Christ his own True Shepherd.

15 As the Father knoweth me, even so know I the Father: and I lay down my life for the sheep.

The relationship of reciprocal familiarity that exists between Christ and His individual disciples is like that which exists between Him and His Father (see 5:19,20). The act by which Jesus will submit entirely to His Father's will (the crucifixion) will also be the act by which he will completely identify Himself with His sheep. He will willingly give His life for them (see vv. 17,18).

16 And other sheep I have, which are not of this fold: them also I must bring, and they shall hear my voice; and there shall be one fold, *and* one shepherd.

At this point Jesus interjects a truth which is not fully understood by His hearers, but which will be clearly intelligible in light of later events. He says that He has other sheep that are not part of "this fold" (i.e. Israel) which He must also gather into His flock. He is, of course, referring to the Gentiles who are to be included in the new flock which He is gathering, the Church. They, too, will hear His voice, which is to say that the Father will work in their hearts the same supernatural response and recognition of His Son that He has worked in the hearts of believing Jews. In that future time there will be but one flock (the literal meaning of the Greek *poimen*, translated "fold" in the KJV). And there will be but one shepherd over both Jews and Gentiles in that one flock (see Eph. 2:14-16).

17 Therefore doth my Father love me, because I lay down my life, that I might take it again.

Jesus has already mentioned twice that He will lay down His life for His sheep (vv. 11,15). Now He says that His Father has a special love for Him because of this willingness to sacrifice His own life for His flock. This willingness emphasizes the complete unity of purpose between the Father and the Son, the perfect love that exists between them.

At this point, however, Jesus introduces a new element into the discussion of His voluntary death on behalf of His sheep. Not only is He going to lay His life down, He is also going to take it up again. Not only is Jesus going to die, He is also going to rise from the dead.

18 No man taketh it from me, but I lay it down of myself. I have power to lay it down, and I have power to take it again. This commandment have I received of my Father.

There is an autonomous sovereignty in Christ's laying down His life for His sheep. He does so because He chooses to do so and for no other reason. No exterior necessity can compel Him to do so. No power in the universe can take His life from Him. He gives it willingly for His sheep. By the same token, He has power to take it up again, to rise from the dead. Yet even in this confident expression of His own authority, Jesus reveals that He is in perfect agreement with and submission to His Father, for it is in obedience to His Father's command that He lays down His life. This is the second time that Christ has predicted His own resurrection from the dead (see 2:19).

Summary
(10:1-18)

Jesus continues His rebuke of the Pharisees by means of an allegory. He represents the Pharisees as thieves and robbers who sneak into the sheepfold by some means other than the door. He contrasts them with the true shepherd who, by virtue of his identity, is recognized by the doorkeeper and enters boldly and openly by the door. The sheep also recognize him and follow him willingly as he leads them forth every morning. The sheep will not follow a stranger, however, because they do not know his voice.

The Pharisees do not understand Jesus' allegory so He proceeds to explain it to them. Jesus assigns to Himself a dual role. He is both the Door and the Good Shepherd. As the Door, He is the only entrance into salvation and happiness. As the Good Shepherd, He is contrasted with the false religionists, the hirelings, who have preceded Him and have been rejected by the people and who have only their own selfish purposes in mind. He thinks only of the sheep and is willing to give His life for them.

Jesus explains that He has other sheep of another fold (an oblique reference to the Gentiles) whom He intends to combine with His Jewish sheep to make one homogeneous flock. When He gives His life for His sheep, it will not be taken from Him, but He will give it willingly. Not only will He give it; He will take it again. This is a prophecy of His resurrection as well as His death. Jesus makes plain that all of His actions are in accordance with His Father's will.

Application: Teaching and Preaching the Passage

There are three basic figures in this allegory: the true (good) shepherd, the false shepherds, and the sheep. The true shepherd loves his sheep and gives his life, if necessary, to protect them (v. 11). He knows his sheep and calls them by name (v. 3). He owns the sheep. They are his own possession (vv.3,4). He has a personal stake in each one.

The false shepherds are thieves and robbers. They have no right in the fold and do not own the sheep. They are strangers: they do not know the sheep nor do the sheep know them. They are hirelings and do not love the sheep or have any real interest in their welfare.

The sheep will listen to and follow their shepherd, but they will not hear, nor will they follow a stranger. They enter by faith through the one door to salvation (Christ) and thereby obtain a life of abundance and happiness. They are not all of the same fold, but they all comprise one great flock. They are totally subordinate to and dependent upon their shepherd.

T. Controversy Concerning Christ (10:19-42)

19 There was a division therefore again among the Jews for these sayings.

As in 7:43, Jesus' words again produce division among His hearers. They take sides for and against Him. His claims that He is the Good Shepherd and, more important, that He will rise from the dead, do not allow for neutrality. They force people to decide how they feel about Jesus, whether they are for or against Him.

20 And many of them said, He hath a devil, and is mad; why hear ye him?

As in 7:20 and 8:48, some take the position that Jesus is insane. The word translated "is mad" (Greek *mainomai*) is a verb which carries the idea of raving. They see no point in listening to and taking seriously the ravings of a maniac.

21 Others said, These are not the words of him that hath a devil. Can a devil open the eyes of the blind?

Others reject this thinking as inconsistent with the facts. Jesus' words (apparently the immediately preceding discourse is in their minds) are not the words of a madman. Furthermore, a demon could not open the eyes of a blind man as Jesus has. These diverse opinions of Jesus should be fitted into the same general context as 7:40-43 and 9:16 where the people seem confused and divided regarding Christ's identity. It does not necessarily follow that those who are hesitant to condemn Jesus as insane actually believe in Him as the Messiah.

22 And it was at Jerusalem the feast of the dedication, and it was winter.

155

It may be that this verse marks a break in the sequence and the beginning of a new episode, or it may be that John merely pauses in the midst of his narrative to parenthetically inform his readers that these events occurred at the time of the Feast of Dedication. This feast, also called Hanukkah, celebrated the rededication of the Temple by Judas Maccabaeus in 164 B.C. after its desecration by Antiochus Epiphanes. That the feast began on December 9 squares with John's comment that it was winter.

23 And Jesus walked in the temple in Solomon's porch.

Since it is winter (i.e. the rainy season) Jesus is walking in a covered portico in the Temple complex called Solomon's colonnade. This colonnade ran along the eastern side of the outer court and was mistakenly thought to be a remnant of the original Solomonic Temple, thus the name. Compare Acts 3:11; 5:12.

24 Then came the Jews round about him, and said unto him, How long dost thou make us to doubt? If thou be the Christ, tell us plainly.

As Jesus walks in the Temple, He is surrounded by a group of the Jews. Apparently, the encounter is not accidental or spontaneous. They are purposely trying to force Jesus' hand. They want to force Him to take a public stand as to whether He is the Messiah. They ask Him how long He is going to keep them in suspense (literally, how long He is going to "lift up their soul," similar to the English usage "keep us hanging," or "up in the air"). They challenge Him, if He is the Christ, to tell them straight out. The implication is that they have understood His previous statements to imply that He is the Christ, but that they want Him

to say so in an unequivocal way, in unambiguous words that can be quoted against Him.

25 Jesus answered them, I told you, and ye believed not: the works that I do in my Father's name, they bear witness of me.

Jesus responds to their challenge (much as in 8:25) by saying that He has already told them that He is the Messiah. While He has not, to this point, told the Jewish leaders in so many words that He is the Messiah, the whole tone of His many statements to them is inexplicable on any other assumption. While He has used veiled, cryptic language, His statements have clearly implied that He is the Messiah (see e.g. 5:17, 39; 6:33,38; 8:42), and only those whose hearts are so blinded by unbelief that they are determined not to understand can have missed His implication.

Jesus goes on to say that, even if His words have been inconclusive, His miracles, which He has performed in His Father's name, prove beyond all doubt that He is the Messiah. This is the same logic He used in 5:36 and in His reply to the emissaries of John the Baptist (see Mt. 11:2-6).

26 But ye believe not, because ye are not of my sheep, as I said unto you.
27 My sheep hear my voice, and I know them, and they follow me.

In marked contrast to what their reaction to Christ's words and deeds should be ("but," Greek *alla*, indicates a strong contrast), these Jews are not convinced. That they do not believe that Jesus is the Messiah is obvious: the question is *why*. Jesus says that they do not believe because they are not among His sheep. His sheep, as He has pointed out in vv. 3,4 and 14, hear, recognize, and respond to His voice. Jesus has already made the point (see 5:38; 6:45; 7:17; and 8:37) that God speaks directly to the hearts of those who are sensitive to His voice; now He makes it clear that these Jews are not among that number.

28 And I give unto them eternal life; and they shall never perish, neither shall any *man* pluck them out of my hand.

Unto those who are His sheep, who hear His voice and believe on Him, Jesus gives eternal life. This is the thirteenth of John's 17 usages of the term "eternal/everlasting life" (Greek *zoe aionios*, 3:15,16; 4:14,36; 5:24,39; 6:27, 40,47, 54, 68; 10:28; 12:25, 50; 17:2, 3). It refers to the life of the age to come, a life that will never end. Here, as in 3:16, "eternal life" is contrasted with "perishing" (Greek *apollumi*). One who possesses eternal life shall never perish, nor shall any be able to pluck him from Christ's hand.

Many have seen in this verse the doctrine of unconditional final perseverance. Bishop Westcott speaks to this question as follows:

We must carefully distinguish between the certainty of God's promises and His infinite power on the one hand, and the weakness and the variableness of man's will on the other. If man falls at any stage in his spiritual life, it is not from the want of divine grace, nor from the overwhelming power of adversaries, but from his neglect to use that which he may or may not use. We cannot be protected against ourselves in spite of ourselves. He who ceases to hear and to follow is thereby shown to be no true believer, I Jn. 2:19. The difficulty in this case is only one form of the difficulty involved in the relation of an infinite to a finite being.

The sense of the divine protection is at any moment sufficient to inspire confidence, but not to render effort unnecessary (II:67).

EDITOR'S NOTE ON JOHN 10:27-29: IS THE BELIEVER'S SECURITY UNCONDITIONAL?

This passage is often used by those who teach the doctrine of the unconditional security of the Christian. Commentator Stallings' quotation from Bishop Westcott (who did not believe that doctrine) goes a long way toward showing the assumptions implicit in the verses.

We should look at what Jesus says here from both sides. On the one hand, the strong words provide us with assurance. The destiny Christ has promised His sheep is eternal life; that is what He has planned for them. And no force outside the personal relationship between the believer and his God has the power to remove him from Christ's, or the Father's, hand. (This assurance is exactly the same as in Rom. 8:35-39, which is to be understood in the very same way.) A part of the Good Shepherd's responsibility is to protect the sheep from any "wolves" (v. 12) that threaten to seize them. He can be counted on to do this absolutely; there is no force—not even Satan himself—that can overpower Christ to take His sheep against His and their will. The sheep are altogether safe in His hand. And since faith is the first and final condition of justification, the one who maintains faith has full assurance of salvation now and hereafter.

But even the Calvinist understands that this does not allow the believer to be careless of his faith or conduct. The responsible Calvinist insists that perseverance is found *in the use of the means* God has provided and *not outside them*, and that the warnings against apostasy are part of the means of assuring that

157

the believer will not apostatize. The difference is that the Calvinist believes God has guaranteed that the elect will use those means and persevere, while the Arminian holds open the real possibility that a true believer may turn away from faith and cease to be one of the sheep who has been promised such protection. The sheep are safe, but not apostates from the fold. The words of assurance do not invalidate the words of warning found elsewhere.

The promise of v. 28, then, is to be interpreted in exactly the same way as that in 5:24, and throughout this Gospel. See the Editor's Note on 5:24, which emphasizes that there are two sets of promises that characterize the Gospel of John, and which must be interpreted in the same manner. To unbelievers (those who persevere in unbelief) is promised eternal condemnation; they "will not see life" (3:36). To believers (those who persevere in faith) is promised eternal life; they "will not perish." Neither promise means that the person referred to can never change his status.

Perseverance in faith, then, is not unconditionally guaranteed—as the Book of Hebrews, for example, makes abundantly clear. The believer must be warned of the possibility of apostasy. He must make use of the means of grace which God has provided in order to maintain saving faith. As Westcott has said, in the quotation above, we are not protected "against ourselves in spite of ourselves."

29 My Father, which gave *them* me, is greater than all; and no *man* is able to pluck *them* out of my Father's hand.
30 I and *my* Father are one.

The first part of v. 29 may be understood either as saying that the Father, who has given (the sheep) to Christ, is greater (more powerful) than any other force, or that what the Father has given to Christ (the sheep) is greater (more important to Christ) than anything else. Probably the second of these interpretations is to be preferred. Jesus is truly the Shepherd of His sheep. No one will be able to injure or harm them while He guards them, for He will guard them with His life (vv. 11,15).

The word translated "pluck" (Greek *harpazo*) in vv. 28,29 is the same word that is translated "catch" in v. 12 and should be thought of as having that meaning here. In this verse Jesus says that the sheep will not be stolen from His Father's hand, while in v. 28 He said that they would not be stolen from His own hand. This should be understood of as illustrative of the principle set forth in v. 30, "I and my Father are one." The Father and the Son share the role of protecting the sheep. Jesus functions coequally with the Father (5:17; 8:54). With these words Jesus reaches the climax of His answer to the question of whether He is the Messiah. He goes farther than that: He is actually equal with the Father. He is God. If the Jews want Jesus to say something that they can use against Him, they have accomplished their purpose. His words, if not true, are clearly blasphemous.

31 Then the Jews took up stones again to stone him.

Upon hearing these words, the Jews are again ready to stone Jesus (see 8:59). The word translated "took up" (Greek *bastazo*) is not the same as in the previous episode (Greek *airo*). In addition to "take up," this word may mean "carry or bear." Perhaps the Jews went out of the Temple complex and returned, bearing stones with which to stone Him; or it may even be that they had purposely brought stones with them, in the hope that they would have the opportunity to stone Him. At any rate, as intimated by the use of this word, there is something left unexplained about this attempt to stone Jesus within the Temple precincts. Such activity was totally inappropriate there, and a ready supply of stones would not normally be there.

32 Jesus answered them, Many good works have I shewed you from my Father; for which of those works do ye stone me?

As they prepare to stone Him, Jesus calmly confronts the Jews with the absurdity of their action. He says that He has performed many "good works" (i.e. miracles) in their midst and asks them (rhetorically) for which of these they wish to stone Him. Obviously, one should not be stoned for such "good works" as healing the lame and the blind. Jesus subtly calls attention to the evidence, which they refuse to accept, that He really is the Messiah. He calls attention to the illogical nature of their unbelief.

33 The Jews answered him, saying, For a good work we stone thee not; but for blasphemy; and because that thou, being a man, makest thyself God.

The Jews reply that it is not because of one of His "good works" that they are about to stone Him, but because of His blasphemy in claiming to be God when He is just a man. It is interesting to note that both of the previous attempts to kill Christ were occasioned by such "blasphemous" claims (5:17,18; 8:38,42,58, 59). The real reason the Jews hate Jesus and want to kill Him is His claim to be the Messiah, to be the Son of God. This "blasphemous" claim (as they see it) will be the charge against Him when He is crucified (Mk. 14:61-64).

34 Jesus answered them, Is it not written in your law, I said, Ye are gods?
35 If he called them gods, unto whom the word of God came, and the scripture cannot be broken;
36 Say ye of him, whom the Father hath sanctified, and sent into the world, Thou blasphemest; because I said, I am the Son of God?

Jesus answers by using a particularly Jewish form of reasoning. He says that even the Jews' own law calls men gods. The reference is to Ps. 82:6; thus "law" is being used, in the broadest sense, of the whole Old Testament. Since the Scripture, obviously, cannot be mistaken in its usage, it is not inherently incorrect to speak of men as gods, and it cannot be automatically assumed that Christ's claim to be God's son (i.e. actually God, v. 33; 5:18) is blasphemous. If it is appropriate to refer to mere men as gods, how can it possibly be considered blasphemous for the One whom the Father has consecrated and sent into the world (5:36,37; 6:38; etc.), the One who is the Father's only unique Son (1:14,18; 3:16) to refer to Himself as the Son of God? It should be noted that Christ refers off-handedly to the doctrine of the infallibility of Scripture. This doctrine was, for Him, so obvious as to require no defense or even delineation.

37 If I do not the works of my Father, believe me not.
38 But if I do, though ye believe not me, believe the works: that ye may know, and believe, that the Father *is* in me, and I in him.

Having established that it is not inherently impossible that He could be the Son of God, Jesus now challenges His hearers to consider the question in the light of the evidence. He asks them to objectively evaluate Him. If He has not done works (performed miracles) befitting the Son of God, then they need not believe His claim; but if He has, then they should believe Him. This is the same logic He has used in v. 25 and in 5:36. It was also the logic of the man born blind (9:31-33). Even if they do not find Jesus subjectively believable (there is an extreme irony here), they should believe Him on the basis of an objective evaluation of the evidence. Jesus desperately wants them to believe that He is the Son of God, that He is one with and equal to the Father ("the Father is in me and I in Him" is equivalent to "I and my Father are one," v. 30). He wants them to believe all this because He knows that they will die in their sins if they do not. Jesus' argument is the same that He will use with Philip in 14:11 and the very same which John uses for having written his Gospel (20:31).

39 Therefore they sought again to take him: but he escaped out of their hand.

Jesus' deep concern for these Jews and His attempts to persuade them are all for nought. They hear nothing but the blasphemous words of a charlatan, a religious impostor. They respond only with an attempt to arrest Him. Previously, they have taken up stones to stone Him (v. 31). Does "arrest" imply a less impassioned reaction here or are they simply going to arrest Him to carry Him out to be stoned? One cannot be sure. The question is academic because Jesus escapes. As in 8:59, John does not specify the nature of this escape; whether it involves anything miraculous we are not told.

40 And went away again beyond Jordan into the place where John at first baptized; and there he abode.

At this point Jesus leaves Jerusalem (not to return until Palm Sunday, more than three months later) and returns to Bethabara/Bethany (see comments 1:28) where John the Baptist was baptizing when Jesus first encountered him (as opposed to Aenon near Salim where he later baptized, 3:23). He will remain there until He goes up to Bethany to raise Lazarus.

41 And many resorted unto him, and said, John did no miracle: but all things that John spake of this man were true.
42 And many believed on him there.

Many of the inhabitants of the area come out to hear Jesus and to observe His miracles. Memories of and comparisons with John the Baptist are inevitable. They recall John's statements about Jesus (1:26-36; 3:22-30) and affirm that they were accurate. Even though John performed no miracles to attest them, Jesus' own miracles confirm John's words about Him. Many, therefore, having had their hearts prepared by John's ministry, readily believe on Jesus when they encounter Him. This is the last mention of John the Baptist in the Fourth Gospel, and it is interesting to note that, though dead, his voice still bears witness to Jesus in the memories of those who heard him.

Summary
(10:19-42)

Jesus' description of Himself as the Good Shepherd causes a division among His hearers. Some assert that He is insane, but others reject this idea as inconsistent with His teachings and miracles. John interrupts his narrative to inform his readers that these events occur at the time of the Feast of Dedication (December) as Jesus walks in Solomon's colonnade in the Temple.

The Jews confront Jesus and ask Him to state clearly whether He is the Messiah. Jesus responds that He has already told them. By this He means that all His previous teachings, properly understood, indicate that He is the Messiah. He also insists that the miracles which He has performed prove that He is the Messiah. He says that the reason these Jews do not believe in Him is that they are not among His sheep: that is, they have no God-given sensitivity to His voice. Jesus gives to His sheep eternal life. Since the Father has given them to Christ, they are of utmost importance to them both. Therefore, neither of them will allow the sheep to be snatched away from them by any other force. Jesus and the Father are as one in their determination to protect the sheep. With this claim to a shared role with the Father, Jesus reaches the climax of His answer to the Jews' question. Not only is He the Messiah, He is equal with God.

Jesus' words so provoke the Jews that they wish to stone Him. Rhetorically, Jesus asks which of His good works they wish to stone Him for. They reply that they are not stoning Him for any of His good works, but for His blasphemous claim to be God. Jesus counters that such a claim is not inherently blasphemous since even the O.T. calls men gods. How, then, can it be blasphemous for Jesus, whom the Father has consecrated and sent into the world, to refer to Himself as God's Son? Having eliminated their *a priori* objections, Jesus challenges the Jews to consider His claims in the light of the evidence. Does the evidence substantiate His claims? If so they should believe Him, even though they are prejudiced against Him.

Jesus' plea has no effect, however. The Jews' only response is to try to arrest Him. Somehow, He escapes them and flees to the eastern side of the Jordan where He was baptized by John the Baptist. Many of the inhabitants of that area come to hear Him. They remember all that John has said about Him and believe on Him.

Application: Teaching and Preaching the Passage

This section serves as a microcosm of all of the first half of the Gospel of John, especially chapters 7-10. First, there is a division among the people about Christ. Some are prone to consider Him an insane, demon-possessed blasphemer. Others are not so sure, perhaps even leaning in the direction of accepting Him as the Messiah. This division among the people is a recurring and constant theme. Christ always creates division.

Second, there is a confrontation between Jesus and the Jewish leaders. They want Jesus to "put up or shut up." They want Him to declare specifically that He is the Messiah so that they can charge Him with blasphemy. All through the Gospel of John, this same spirit of confrontation prevails. There is a diabolical antagonism toward Christ in the minds of the Jewish leaders. It is as if their "father the devil" is actually speaking through them to issue his challenges to Jesus.

Third, Christ makes an unmistakable claim to deity. He claims equality and union with the Father, as well as saying that He is the Son of God. There can be no doubt about the point of contention between Jesus and the Jews. It is His claim to be God.

Fourth, there is an absolute rejection of Christ by the Jews. Their response to His attempt to reason with them is to attempt to arrest Him. He has no recourse except to escape and flee their city.

U. The Seventh Sign: The Raising of Lazarus (11:1-57)

Many critics do not accept the historicity of John's account of the raising of Lazarus. Some reject it because they simply do not believe in the possibility of miracles, others on the more subtle grounds that it is not mentioned in the Synoptics. They think that the Synoptists would not have omitted such a striking and well-publicized (see e.g. 11:45,46; 12:9,17-19) event. Against this view must be urged: (1) The vividness and detail of the account itself. It certainly has all the earmarks of an eyewitness account (places and persons specifically named, distance from Jerusalem, graphic details, etc.). (2) The extreme improbability that John would invent such an episode as a sort of parable to illustrate that Jesus is the resurrection and the life. (3) The obvious fact that none of the Gospel writers felt it necessary to include every event from Christ's life (only Luke, for example, mentions the well-publicized incident of the raising of the widow of Nain's son; see Lk. 7:17). It should be noted that neither the healing of the lame man (ch. 5) nor that of the man born blind (ch. 9) is mentioned in the Synoptics. (4) This episode is a part of the Judean ministry which, as has already been noted, the Synoptists do not cover. This would certainly be reason enough for them to omit it. There is no good reason for supposing that John's account of the raising of Lazarus is not perfectly genuine.

1 Now a certain *man* was sick, *named* Lazarus, of Bethany, the town of Mary and her sister Martha.

Not long after fleeing Jerusalem, Jesus receives word that His friend Lazarus is sick. This is John's first mention of Lazarus and his two sisters, Mary and Martha. They are inhabitants of Bethany, a small village about two miles east of Jerusalem across the Mount of Olives on the road from Jerusalem to Jericho.

2 (It was *that* Mary which anointed the Lord with ointment, and wiped his feet with her hair, whose brother Lazarus was sick.)

John mentions that this is the Mary who anointed Jesus with ointment and wiped His feet with her hair. Although John will not actually relate this incident until the following chapter, he assumes that his readers are familiar with it. Apparently Jesus' prophecy (Mt. 26:12) that her deed would be known wherever the gospel is preached was fulfilled.

3 Therefore his sisters sent unto him, saying, Lord, behold, he whom thou lovest is sick.

Soon after Lazarus becomes ill, his sisters send word to Jesus (they must know where He is; see 10:40) of his condition. The exact nature of his illness is not specified, but its seriousness is apparent: they suppose that he will soon die. That Mary and Martha felt confident in describing Lazarus as "he whom You love" indicates that there was a very close bond between Jesus and this family.

4 When Jesus heard *that* , he said, This sickness is not unto death, but for the glory of God, that the Son of God might be glorified thereby.

When Jesus receives the message, He responds by remarking somewhat enigmatically, "This sickness will not lead to or result in [literally, is not toward] death, but [it will be] for the glory of God [specifically], that the Son of God may be glorified through it."

The most natural understanding of Jesus' words to those who heard Him is that Lazarus was not going to die. This is not, of course, how Jesus meant them. Jesus meant that, although Lazarus would die, death would not be the ultimate outcome. Once again John shares with his readers a special insight into the meaning of Christ's words that was not apparent to those who first heard them. As with the man born blind (9:3), God had a purpose in this seemingly tragic event. He intended by it to gain glory for Himself and His Son, Jesus. It was God's purpose that, through this sickness (and the miracle it occasioned), the identity and authority of Jesus should be manifested for all to see.

5 Now Jesus loved Martha, and her sister, and Lazarus.

John interrupts his narrative with the parenthetic remark that Jesus loved Martha, Mary, and Lazarus. John's use of the verb here (Greek imperfect tense) seems to indicate that, even as He spoke these words, even as He delayed going immediately to aid them, Jesus' heart was filled with love for them. John assures his readers that the reason for Christ's delay was not any lack of love for those who were in the midst of a great trial.

6 When he had heard therefore that he was sick, he abode two days still in the same place where he was.

It seems best to take "therefore" (Greek *oun*) as adversative ("however," rather than the more common "therefore"). John is saying, "However (in spite of the fact that Jesus loved this family), when He received the message that Lazarus was sick, He still remained where He was for two days." Jesus did not delay *because* of His love for these people, but *in spite of* it.

The reason for His delay was the purpose of God to glorify Him as His Son through raising Lazarus from the dead. Jesus delayed so that Lazarus, by the time He arrived at Bethany, would have been dead long enough (four days) that there could be no doubt that he really was dead and that Jesus' act of bringing him back to life was a *bona fide* miracle. No doubt the disciples, based on their misunderstanding of Christ's words in v. 4, supposed that Jesus was not going to risk going back into Judea to see Lazarus, since he was not terminally ill.

7 Then after that saith he to *his* disciples, Let us go into Judaea again.

After this two-day delay, Jesus says to His disciples, "Let us, again, return to Judea." The delay has apparently convinced the disciples that Jesus is not going to go to Bethany to see Lazarus at this point. Perhaps they are just a little disappointed in Jesus; more likely, they agree with what they suppose to be His opinion that discretion, in this instance, is the better part of valor.

8 *His* disciples say unto him, Master, the Jews of late sought to stone thee; and goest thou thither again?

Jesus' statement surprises the disciples, who reply respectfully but insistently, "Rabbi, the Jews were [just] now seeking to kill You, and You are going to go back there [knowing that]?" It should be noted that Jesus does not specifically mention going to see Lazarus, but simply going back to Judea. The disciples may have allowed Lazarus' sickness to slip from their minds after two days and may not have realized that it was because of him that Jesus was proposing to return to Judea.

9 Jesus answered, Are there not

163

twelve hours in the day? If any man walk in the day, he stumbleth not, because he seeth the light of this world.
10 But if a man walk in the night, he stumbleth, because there is no light in him.

Jesus answers the disciples with a somewhat enigmatic parable or proverb. He says that there are 12 hours in a day, that the one who walks in the day does not stumble because there is plenty of sunlight. On the other hand, if a person walks at night he will stumble because he will not be able to see since he has no light (literally, has no light in him).

What does Jesus mean by this strange saying? With 9:4 apparently in mind, He means to say that there is a certain time allotted to Him in which to fulfill His mission (12 full hours), and that until that time for work is fully ended (all 12 hours of it) it is still "day" and, therefore, still safe for Him to continue His work. Only when the "day" of His work is ended and the night comes will there be any danger. Jesus intends to take full advantage of even the last of His 12 hours. John may also intend his readers to perceive a second meaning by which Jesus, Himself, is the light and Christians remain perfectly safe, as long as they walk in His light, but face certain disaster apart from Him (see e.g. 1 Jn. 1:5-7).

11 These things said he: and after that he saith unto them, Our friend Lazarus sleepeth; but I go, that I may awake him out of sleep.
12 Then said his disciples, Lord, if he sleep, he shall do well.

John's phrase, "He said these things," seems more than just a redundant statement of the obvious. It seems, rather, to be intended to give the reader pause, to

cause Him to reflect on the fact that it was with these enigmatic words that Jesus explained why He was going back to Judea.

Jesus now says (still somewhat mysteriously) that Lazarus is "asleep" and that He is going to him so that He can awaken him. The disciples, missing His point entirely and supposing Him to mean that Lazarus is literally asleep, suggest naively that sleep may be the best thing for him in his illness.

13 Howbeit Jesus spake of his death: but they thought that he had spoken of taking of rest in sleep.
14 Then said Jesus unto them plainly, Lazarus is dead.

John clarifies for his readers what he is undoubtedly embarrassed to admit: that he, himself, did not originally understand that Jesus was not speaking of mere sleep but of death. Jesus is forced to tell them plainly that Lazarus is dead. They simply do not follow His figurative language. (Jesus must have often felt like an Oxford scholar trying to teach literature to fifth-graders.) He has obviously been waiting for Lazarus to die before going to Bethany. Now that He (supernaturally) knows him to be dead, He is ready to go.

15 And I am glad for your sakes that I was not there, to the intent ye may believe; nevertheless let us go unto him.

Jesus says that He is glad, for the disciples' sake, that He was not there when Lazarus died. He thus implies that Lazarus would not have died if He had been present. Had He been there He would have miraculously healed Lazarus, but since He was not there, He will now perform the much greater miracle of raising him from the dead. Raising

Lazarus from the dead will have the effect of producing faith in the disciples. Though they already believe, this great sign will strengthen and deepen their faith. Very soon they will need this sign and the faith it has produced, for they will see death come to Jesus Himself. Jesus concludes His statement by saying that, in spite of the fact that He was not there when Lazarus died, He does intend to go there now that he is dead.

16 Then said Thomas, which is called Didymus, unto his fellow-disciples, Let us also go, that we may die with him.

Unexpectedly, it is Thomas (also called Didymus; both *Thomas* in Aramaic and *Didymus* in Greek mean "the twin") who speaks up to urge his fellow disciples to go to Judea with Jesus. He evaluates Christ's chances of escaping arrest and execution as very slim, thus disregarding completely Christ's assurance that no harm will befall them. But he does not want Jesus to go and face His fate alone, so he pessimistically and resignedly suggests that they go and share it with Him.

17 Then when Jesus came, he found that he had *lain* in the grave four days already.

When Jesus arrives in the area of Bethany, He is informed that Lazarus has been in the grave for four days. There is a later Rabbinical tradition that the spirit remained near the body for three days after death. Some suggest that this belief may have prevailed at the time of Christ. If so that may help explain the significance of the fact that Lazarus had been dead for four days. This is very speculative; it is better to understand the significance of the four days as removing all doubt that Lazarus was dead.

Had Jesus not delayed two days (v. 6), Lazarus would have been in the grave only two days upon His arrival at Bethany. Accordingly, Jesus would not have arrived before Lazarus' death even without the two-day delay. Jesus did not delay so as to allow Lazarus to die so that He could then raise him from the dead, but to allow enough time to establish beyond all doubt that Lazarus really was dead.

18 Now Bethany was nigh unto Jerusalem, about fifteen furlongs off:
19 And many of the Jews came to Martha and Mary, to comfort them concerning their brother.

John informs his readers that, since Bethany is just under two miles (15 furlongs) from Jerusalem, many of the Jews (from Jerusalem) have come out to comfort Martha and Mary in their grief at their brother's death. Apparently John uses the term "Jews," in this instance, to refer to the population at large, rather than just to the authorities opposed to Jesus. It should also be noted that, according to v. 45, many of these Jews will believe on Jesus because of the raising of Lazarus, the implication being that they have not previously been believers.

20 Then Martha, as soon as she heard that Jesus was coming, went and met him: but Mary sat *still* in the house.

When Martha hears that Jesus is approaching, she goes out to meet Him, but Mary remains seated in the house (the normal procedure for receiving visitors during a time of mourning). These actions conform with the personalities of the two women presented by Luke (10:38-42). Martha is impetuous, active, and outgoing, while Mary is sedentary, reflective, and introverted.

**21 Then said Martha unto Jesus, Lord, if thou hadst been here, my brother had not died.
22 But I know, that even now, whatsoever thou wilt ask of God, God will give *it* thee.**

Martha's words express a deep faith in Christ's power. She believes not only that He could have healed Lazarus had He arrived in time, but that "even now" (now that Lazarus is dead) the situation is not totally beyond His power. This can only mean that she believes Jesus is able to raise Lazarus from the dead if He desires. She is indirectly asking Jesus to raise Lazarus. Assuming that she has been informed by the messenger (v. 3) of Jesus' assurance (v. 4) that Lazarus' sickness was not unto death, Martha may vaguely suppose that this affair is not yet over with, that the final word has yet to be spoken.

**23 Jesus saith unto her, Thy brother shall rise again.
24 Martha saith unto him, I know that he shall rise again in the resurrection at the last day.**

When Jesus responds to Martha that her brother is going to rise again, does He simply offer the conventional consolation that Lazarus will be resurrected in the last day, or does He refer to His intention to raise Lazarus immediately and miraculously? Jesus is speaking of the impending miracle, but, realizing how He will be understood, He uses words usually associated with the future resurrection as the starting point for explaining what is about to happen. Martha obviously assumes that He refers to the resurrection of the last day and, while she accepts that her brother will indeed rise then, the thought provides her little comfort in her present bereavement.

**25 Jesus said unto her, I am the resurrection, and the life: he that believeth in me, though he were dead, yet shall he live:
26 And whosoever liveth and believeth in me shall never die. Believest thou this?**

In response to Martha's mention of the resurrection, Jesus says, in effect: "But don't you see, Martha, *I* am the resurrection; when you speak of the resurrection, you are speaking of *Me*." By this Jesus means that He controls the resurrection, that it is only by His power and at His word that it will occur, that there is no resurrection apart from Him (see 5:21,24-29; 6:39,40,44,54). If Lazarus is to be raised some day in the resurrection, it will be Jesus who will raise him. The power necessary to raise him then is sufficient to raise him now. The One who controls the future resurrection of the dead stands present now before Martha. This marks the fifth of Christ's seven great "I am" sayings (see 6:35).

Not only is Jesus the resurrection; He is also the life (eternal life, see 3:16; 4:14; 5:24; 6:40; 10:28). Just as Jesus alone can raise men from the dead, so only He can give them eternal life. There is obviously a connection between the resurrection and eternal life, but the fine distinction which Jesus intends to draw between them can best be understood by pairing each of them with one of the following clauses. Thus, since Jesus is the resurrection, one who believes in Him, even though he should die, will live again (be resurrected). Similarly, since Jesus is the life, one who is alive and believes in Him will never die. Jesus is the hope of resurrection for the believer at the moment of death and the hope of never ending life for the believer while he lives. The phrase "shall never die," is literally, "shall never die unto the ages (or into eternity)."

Jesus has stated that He is the resurrection, that only by His agency will men survive death and experience eternal life. Now Jesus asks Martha whether she believes that all of this is so. Does she, in principle, believe that He has the power to raise the dead? Jesus intends to lead Martha from the general principle that He is able to raise the dead, to the specific understanding that He is able to raise Lazarus.

27 She saith unto him, Yea, Lord: I believe that thou art the Christ, the Son of God, which should come into the world.

Some suppose that Martha attempts to sidestep Jesus and answer His direct challenge (as to whether she believes that He has the power to raise the dead) with indefinite and noncommittal cliches. This could not be more wrong. Martha says that, yes, she does believe that Jesus has resurrection power. Then she adds, not as an irrelevant, temporizing cliche, but as the logical justification of her confidence, "I believe that You are the Christ (etc.)" She believes that Jesus can raise the dead because of who and what she believes Him to be. She is saying in effect, "Yes, obviously You can raise the dead. You are the Christ!" Martha's affirmation includes all the central aspects of Jesus' teaching concerning Himself: that He is the Messiah (1:41; 4:25, 29,42; 6:69; etc.), that He is the Son of God (i.e. actually equal with God, 1:34; 1:49; 3:16,17; 5:17,18; 5:25; etc.), and that He is the one who has been promised to come into the world (1:15,27; 3:2,31; 5:43; 7:27, 28; etc.).

28 And when she had so said, she went her way, and called Mary her sister secretly, saying, The Master is come, and calleth for thee.
29 As soon as she heard *that*, she arose quickly, and came unto him.

30 Now Jesus was not yet come into the town, but was in that place where Martha met him.

After her great confession of faith in Christ, Martha, at Jesus' instruction, goes back home and tells Mary that "the Rabbi" has arrived and is asking for her. Mary quickly arises and goes out to meet Jesus, who has remained where He conversed with Martha. Jesus' motives for remaining outside the village are uncertain. He might have been trying to avoid the Jews, He might have wished to speak privately with Mary just as He had with Martha, or He might have been near the place where Lazarus was buried and wished to remain there rather than coming on into the village. The probable reason why Martha does not speak to anyone but Mary is that Jesus has so instructed her.

31 The Jews then which were with her in the house, and comforted her, when they saw Mary, that she rose up hastily and went out, followed her, saying, She goeth unto the grave to weep there.

At any rate, when the Jews, who are in the house with Mary, see her quickly get up and leave, they follow. They suppose that she is on her way to the grave to mourn there. This certainly seems to indicate that, as she went to meet Jesus, Mary was headed in the general direction of the grave. If so, this reenforces the idea that the place where Jesus halted was somewhere near Lazarus' grave.

32 Then when Mary was come where Jesus was, and saw him, she fell down at his feet, saying unto him, Lord, if thou hadst been here, my brother had not died.

When Mary reaches Jesus, she falls at His feet (characteristic of her humble spirit, see 12:3 and Lk. 10:39) and repeats the same words Martha had used earlier. Her state of mind very closely approximates that of her sister (see comments vv. 21, 22).

33 When Jesus therefore saw her weeping, and the Jews also weeping which came with her, he groaned in the spirit, and was troubled.

As He observes Mary and the Jews who are with her weeping, Jesus Himself is overcome with emotion. The word translated "groaned" (Greek *embrimaomai*, here and in v. 38) usually refers to anger and many believe that it does so here. They suggest that Jesus was angry with sin and Satan, the ultimate causes of death. However, this does not seem to fit the situation here. Jesus was not so much angry as sharing Mary's deep sorrow.

This understanding of "groaned" is confirmed by the fact that it is paired with "was troubled" (Greek *tarasso*). Whenever John uses this word (in the derived sense with reference to the emotions) he always refers to a state of sorrow and perplexity, never to anger (see 12:27; 13:21; 14:1, 27). It is also confirmed by the fact that in v. 35 Jesus will burst into tears, an action much more appropriate to sorrow than anger. Furthermore, those who observed Him evaluated His mood as sorrow rather than anger (v. 36).

Some may suppose such emotion to be incompatible with Christ's divine nature as well as with His settled purpose to raise Lazarus (vv. 4,11,15, 23, 25). Actually, it demonstrates Christ's humanity. His human nature was overcome with the sorrow of the situation, even though He knew as God that He was about to eliminate the occasion for the sorrow.

34 And said, Where have ye laid him? They said unto him, Lord, come and see.

Overcome as He is with emotion, Jesus asks where Lazarus has been buried. Some in the crowd, perhaps Mary and Martha themselves, volunteer to lead Him to the grave. They probably suppose that Jesus wishes to go there to weep for His dead friend.

35 Jesus wept.
36 Then said the Jews, Behold how he loved him!

At some point as they are leading Him to Lazarus' tomb, Jesus begins to weep (Greek ingressive aorist). This action causes some of the Jews (see v. 19) to remark about His love for Lazarus. These people do not quite know what to make of Jesus. Is He a charlatan, as the Pharisees insist, or is He really the Messiah? Regardless what else may be said of Him, no one can deny that He certainly did love Lazarus. Would one expect such a love as this from a deceiver?

37 And some of them said, Could not this man, which opened the eyes of the blind, have caused that even this man should not have died?

As they observe His great sorrow, some within the group venture to suggest that perhaps, if He had arrived in time, this one who had opened the eyes of the blind could have prevented Lazarus' death. These words reveal a very real, if not totally satisfactory, belief in Christ (the Greek question is phrased positively). Like Martha and Mary, they believe Jesus' powers to be considerable, even if they are not able to think in terms of His raising Lazarus from the dead.

38 Jesus therefore again groaning in himself cometh to the grave. It was a cave, and a stone lay upon it.

Jesus is still overcome with emotion as He arrives at the grave. It is a cave (perhaps man made) with a stone lying against the door. One cannot miss the fact that the arrangement is very similar to that of the tomb in which Jesus Himself will soon be buried and from which He will victoriously arise. Even in this small detail does Christ's raising of Lazarus prefigure His own resurrection.

39 Jesus said, Take ye away the stone. Martha, the sister of him that was dead, saith unto him, Lord, by this time he stinketh: for he hath been *dead* four days.

Arriving at the burial site (apparently without delay) Jesus commands that the stone be removed from the entrance to the tomb. Martha objects that, since Lazarus has been dead for four days and His body has already begun to decompose and stink, it will be inappropriate to remove the stone. Is Martha naively, even somewhat impatiently, informing Jesus of the obvious, or is she knowingly and suggestively probing Jesus to discern His intentions? In light of vv. 21, 22, 27 and John's propensity for such subtleties, the latter seems likely; but Martha may not have discerned Jesus' purpose in removing the stone. One cannot be certain.

40 Jesus saith unto her, Said I not unto thee, that, if thou wouldest believe, thou shouldest see the glory of God?

Jesus rebukes Martha's lack of faith by reminding her of what He has told

her earlier: that if she would believe, she would see the glory of God. The problem is that John has not recorded such a statement. The words seem to combine what Jesus said to His disciples upon hearing of Lazarus' illness (v. 4) and His words to Martha in v. 26. Obviously, John's is a summary account and not every word of each conversation is recorded. It is very possible that Jesus made this statement in His earlier conversation with Martha (vv. 21-27) even though John did not record it.

41 Then they took away the stone *from the place* where the dead was laid. And Jesus lifted up *his* eyes, and said, Father, I thank thee that thou hast heard me.

Jesus' words apparently remove all objection, for the Jews now remove the stone as He has requested. Jesus lifts His eyes to Heaven and begins to pray. He addresses God as His "Father," implying that He bears a special relationship to Him which no others share. He thanks God that He "heard" (Greek aorist tense) Him. This is a dramatic use of the tense of the verb: a present reality (in this case, perhaps, an immediately future one) is spoken of with the certitude of a past event. It emphasizes Jesus' absolute confidence that God is going to grant His request.

42 And I knew that thou hearest me always: but because of the people which stand by I said *it,* that they may believe that thou hast sent me.

Jesus continues His prayer by saying that He knows (Greek pluperfect used like the aorist in the previous verse) that God always hears Him (Greek present indicates ongoing action). He says that He is saying all these things out loud, not because He feels He needs to remind God of them, but because He wants those standing by to hear them so that when they see the great miracle which He is about to perform, they will have no doubt that He has done it through the power of God. Then they will be able to believe that He is, indeed, God's Son whom He sent into the world.

43 And when he thus had spoken, he cried with a loud voice, Lazarus, come forth.
44 And he that was dead came forth, bound hand and foot with graveclothes: and his face was bound about with a napkin. Jesus saith unto them, Loose him, and let him go.

Having thus explained the significance of what He is about to do, Jesus now cries with a loud voice, "Lazarus, come forth!" No sooner has Jesus spoken (notice how matter-of-factly John relates it) than (literally) "the one having died" comes forth from the tomb still bound with the graveclothes, His face still wrapped in a napkin. John gives all this detail so as to leave no doubt that Lazarus was really dead. Lazarus having hobbled out as best he can under the circumstances, Jesus commands the stunned observers to cut the bindings from him, uncover his face, and let him go.

45 Then many of the Jews which came to Mary, and had seen the things which Jesus did, believed on him.
46 But some of them went their ways to the Pharisees, and told them what things Jesus had done.

This is obviously a great miracle and, because of it, many of the Jews who have come with Mary to the grave are convinced that Jesus is the Messiah and believe on Him. Yet, even in the face of this stupendous miracle, some will not believe. These harden themselves and go to tell the Pharisees in Jerusalem what has happened.

47 Then gathered the chief priests and the Pharisees a council, and said, What do we? for this man doeth many miracles.

As soon as they learn of this latest of Jesus' miracles, the chief priests and Pharisees call a meeting of the Sanhedrin. While this word (Greek *sunedrion*) can be used generically to mean any "council," it probably refers, in this context, to the Sanhedrin *per se* (even taking into account the lack of the definite article). They are quite disturbed. Their question, "What are we doing?" should be understood as rhetorical. By it they mean to reproach themselves for their failure to deal decisively with Jesus to this point. It is as if they say, "Here He is working all these miracles and what are we doing about it?" They acknowledge the validity of Jesus' miracles, but these, rather than motivating them to believe in Him, are a motive for moving all the more quickly and effectively to destroy Him.

48 If we let him thus alone, all *men* will believe on him: and the Romans shall come and take away both our place and nation.

The Jewish authorities were afraid that, if they continued to let Jesus perform His miracles and propound His message, "everyone" would soon believe on Him. They further reasoned that, if a majority of the Jewish people should become followers of Christ, there would be grave consequences. First of all, their own place of leadership would be endangered. If the Romans came to believe that Jesus, rather than they, represented the dominant strain of Judaism, they might very well recognize Him as the official head of Judaism and allow Him to assume the position of authority then held by the Sanhedrin. Secondly, they were afraid that the Romans would see Jesus' Messianic function as a political rebellion against Roman rule and move to destroy the whole Jewish nation. That such an idea was not completely unrealistic is revealed by the events of A.D. 70 and 132.

49 And one of them, named Caiaphas, being the high priest that same year, said unto them, Ye know nothing at all.

At this point, John relates what he considers to be a most ironic incident. Caiaphas, the High Priest, voices His opinion as to the appropriate course of action and, in doing so, unknowingly makes an official comment upon the significance of Christ's approaching death. John draws attention to Caiaphas' being High Priest "*that* year." Because of this, some suggest that John mistakenly supposed that the High Priests were appointed annually. Of course, this is not the case at all. John's point is that Caiaphas was the High Priest in this fateful year, *the year in which Christ was to die*. He thinks it remarkable that the High Priest, whose duty it is to enter the holy of holies and offer the atonement for this year, should unconsciously utter a prophecy of the efficacy of the Atonement which Christ was soon to accomplish on the cross (see Bernard).

Some believe that Caiaphas manifests an obnoxious and domineering spirit as he speaks to the other members of the council, that he is saying that they—quite unlike himself!—completely misunderstand the whole situation. While this is certainly possible, it seems more likely that Caiaphas, rather than speaking condescendingly to his compatriots, is speaking ironically.

50 Nor consider that it is expedient for us, that one man should die for the people, and that the whole nation perish not.

Caiaphas continues by saying that, even though they do not realize it, there is an obvious solution to their dilemma. That solution is that one man should die on behalf of the people, rather than that the whole nation should perish. Why does Caiaphas use such language? He may very well be drawing on the language of Lev. 16 (especially v. 33) which deals with the Day of Atonement. He is speaking sarcastically, of course, making a pun of sorts. He supposes himself to be frightfully (one might say, diabolically) clever. The fact that he is the High Priest adds a particularly bizarre and irreverent note. In effect he says, "Speaking as High Priest, I will give a bit of priestly advice." Such pseudo-sophisticates as Caiaphas often derive great pleasure from intentional irreverence. Caiaphas was no doubt accustomed to making puns on the language of Leviticus.

51 And this spake he not of himself: but being high priest that year, he prophesied that Jesus should die for that nation;
52 And not for that nation only, but that also he should gather together in one the children of God that were scattered abroad.

Though Caiaphas does not realize it, the "joke" is on him. While he has his own reasons for speaking as he does, these do not completely explain why he does so. God is controlling him and achieving His own purposes quite apart from Caiaphas' intentions. God wills that Caiaphas, in his official capacity as High

Priest and in spite of himself, should make an official pronouncement concerning the efficacy and substitutionary nature of Christ's impending death. Caiaphas means his words for evil, but God means them for good. Jesus will indeed die for the nation of Israel, but not for them alone. He will die for (those who are to become) God's children who are (presently) scattered abroad. Christ's death will make of all God's children, both Jew and Gentile, one great new body, the Church. Caiaphas would certainly be mortified if he had any idea of his words' true import.

53 Then from that day forth they took counsel together for to put him to death.

The Jewish leaders have wanted to kill Jesus ever since He healed the lame man at Bethesda (see 5:16,18; 7:1,19, 20, 25; 8:37,40, 59; 10:31; 11:8). Now this generalized inclination becomes a serious plan of action which will actually result in His crucifixion.

54 Jesus therefore walked no more openly among the Jews; but went thence unto a country near to the wilderness, into a city called Ephraim, and there continued with his disciples.

When the leaders' plans become known to Him, Jesus ceases to circulate openly among the Jews and goes into hiding in the small town of Ephraim. The exact location of this town is uncertain, but it is thought to have been about 15 miles northeast of Jerusalem. This was a very sparsely inhabited area where Jesus was not likely to be discovered.

55 And the Jews' passover was nigh at hand: and many went out of the country up to Jerusalem before the passover, to purify themselves.

Since the Passover is near, many Jews go up to Jerusalem from the surrounding countryside to purify themselves. The regulations for ceremonial purity were very complex and as much as a week might be required to purify oneself. John informs his readers of this situation so as to explain the presence of large crowds in Jerusalem at this time.

56 Then sought they for Jesus, and spake among themselves, as they stood in the temple, What think ye, that he will not come to the feast?

A major topic of conversation among the people assembling in Jerusalem just prior to the feast is whether Jesus will come up to the feast. The situation is reminiscent of that described in 7:11.

57 Now both the chief priests and the Pharisees had given a commandment, that, if any man knew where he were, he should shew it, that they might take him.

This time the Jewish leaders are prepared. They have put out the word that if anyone locates Jesus, they are to report His whereabouts to them so that they can arrest Him. They do not intend for Jesus to escape them this time. They are determined to deal with Him once and for all. So the end of this eleventh chapter finds Jesus in approximately the same situation as the beginning—in hiding from the Jews. The scene is set for the final confrontation between Jesus and the Jewish authorities.

Summary
(11:1-57)

Not long after fleeing Jerusalem, Jesus receives word that His friend Lazarus is sick. His first reaction to the news is to remark that this sickness will not end in death and that God has allowed it to come about for His own glory. In spite of His great love for Martha, Mary, and Lazarus and contrary to what one might expect, Jesus does not immediately go to Bethany but remains where He is for two days. When He finally does indicate His intention to go into Judea, His disciples remind Him of the great danger in doing so. Jesus reassures them, however, that until the day of His ministry is ended they will be perfectly safe and informs them that He is going into Judea to wake Lazarus from his sleep. The disciples misconstrue Christ's reference to Lazarus' death and suggest that it might be best to let him sleep since he is sick. Jesus is forced to tell them bluntly that Lazarus is dead. He explains that it is actually best that He was not present at Lazarus' death because his death is going to have the effect of causing them to believe more completely in Him. The disciples resignedly determine to go with Him into Judea.

When Jesus arrives at the edge of Bethany, He is told that Lazarus has been dead for four days. Since Bethany is near to Jerusalem, many of the Jews are present to comfort Mary and Martha in their sorrow. When Martha learns that Jesus has come, she goes to meet Him and says that if He had been present her brother would not have died. She adds, somewhat mysteriously, that even now God will give to Jesus whatever He asks. Jesus assures Martha that her brother will rise again. She replies that she knows that this will be so at the time of the great resurrection of the end time. Jesus insists that He is the resurrection and the life and that those who believe in Him will live forever. He asks Martha if she believes this, and Martha replies that indeed she does. She believes that He is the long-expected Messiah, the Son of God.

Having thus spoken, Martha goes and quietly informs Mary that Jesus is asking for her. When Mary hears this she goes immediately to Jesus, followed by some of the Jews who suppose her to be going to Lazarus' tomb. When she reaches Jesus she repeats Martha's statement that if Jesus had only been present, Lazarus would not have died. Jesus is deeply saddened by Mary's sorrow. He asks where Lazarus is buried and, as He is taken there, bursts into tears. Even the Jews are moved by His obvious love for Lazarus and suggest that, if He had been present earlier, He might well have done something to keep Lazarus alive.

When they arrive at the tomb, Jesus, still overwhelmed by grief, commands that the stone be removed from the entrance to the tomb. Martha objects that, since Lazarus has been dead for four days, the odor will be unbearable. Jesus reminds her of His previous assurance that, if she can believe, she will see the glory of God. When the stone is removed, Jesus thanks God in advance for the great miracle that is about to transpire and for the faith that it will provoke in those who will see it. Then He cries, "Lazarus, come forth," and Lazarus comes hobbling out of the tomb still bound in his grave clothes. Jesus commands those standing by to unbind Lazarus and let him go. When they see this great miracle, many of the Jews believe on Jesus, but some go and inform the Pharisees of what has transpired.

When they are informed of this miracle, the Jewish leaders call a meeting of the Sanhedrin to discuss their response to this provocation. They realize that they must do something, or Jesus is going to gain the upper hand on them and usurp their position of religious authority. Caiaphas, not realizing the full import of his words, suggests that the best thing is that Christ should die, rather than the whole nation. From this point on the Jews actively plot to kill Jesus.

Learning of their intentions, Jesus withdraws to the small village of Ephraim.

As the Passover approaches, many Jews come into Jerusalem, and the main topic of discussion among them is whether Jesus will show up for the feast. For their part, the authorities are determined that Jesus will not escape them this time. If He comes, He will be arrested.

Application: Teaching and Preaching the Passage

This section may be comprehended under the following headings. First, a problem is brought to Jesus. It is an extreme problem for which there seems to be no solution apart from Him. It seems natural and appropriate to bring the problem to Him.

Second, Christ's response does not conform to expectations. Men usually have a particular solution in mind when they bring their problems to Jesus. In this case, everyone expects Him to go to Bethany and heal Lazarus so that he will not die. However, that which men expect may not be that which Christ knows to be wisest and best. Sometimes His great purposes are not discernible to men. Therefore, as Jesus sets about doing what is ultimately best, but what does not conform to men's expectations, His actions seem pointless, even irrational to men. Men must learn that they are not competent to understand, let alone evaluate, the actions of God.

Third, Christ's solution proves to be more than adequate. All of the concerns of the people are taken care of even more wonderfully than they could have imagined. In addition, the overriding purpose of God for allowing this event to transpire in the first place is achieved. Christians must be careful not to try to impose their very limited perspective upon God.

Fourth, men's reactions to this miracle are quite diverse. Some have their faith in Christ confirmed and strengthened (Martha, Mary, Lazarus and the apostles). Some of the Jews are moved to believe for the first time. Others, however, are hardened in their rejection of Christ. This includes those who go and tell the authorities and the authorities themselves. The same event has opposite effects upon people of diverse spiritual inclinations.

V. THE CLIMAX OF THE PUBLIC MINISTRY (12:1-50)

All four gospels mention Jesus' being anointed by a woman (Mt. 26:6-13; Mk. 14:3-9; Lk. 7:36-50; Jn. 12:1-8). The connection between these accounts seems to be that Matthew, Mark, and John all refer to the same episode, but that Luke refers to a separate incident that occurred in Galilee early in Jesus' career (see Morris 571574). John mentions the supper at the time it actually occurred (Saturday), while Matthew and Mark mention it when they relate that Judas went to the priests to betray Jesus (Wednesday). The connection is that the plan which eventually culminates in Judas' betrayal first began to take shape in his mind at the supper in Bethany.

1 Then Jesus six days before the passover came to Bethany, where Lazarus was which had been dead, whom he raised from the dead.

Having ended His seclusion in Ephraim, Jesus comes to Bethany (apparently by way of Jericho, Mk. 10:46-52) six days before the Passover. (The chronology seems to be that Jesus arrived late Friday evening as the Sabbath was beginning, that the "supper" took place on Saturday, and that "on the next day" [v. 12], Sunday, He entered triumphantly into Jerusalem.) John also reminds his readers that Bethany is the place where

Jesus previously raised Lazarus from the dead.

2 There they made him a supper; and Martha served: but Lazarus was one of them that sat at the table with him.

Jesus apparently spends the Sabbath (i.e. from sundown Friday until sundown Saturday) quietly, probably in the company of Lazarus, Martha, and Mary. Then Saturday night (the Sabbath being ended), certain of the inhabitants of the village hold a supper in His honor. While the exact details of this supper are not known, the general circumstances seem clear enough. Matthew and Mark relate that it was held in the house of Simon the Leper. John states that Martha, as ever, was in charge of the serving and that Lazarus himself was one of those who ate with Jesus.

3 Then took Mary a pound of ointment of spikenard, very costly, and anointed the feet of Jesus, and wiped his feet with her hair: and the house was filled with the odour of the ointment.

At some point during the meal, a strange incident transpires. Mary anoints Jesus' feet with ointment and wipes them with her hair. There are several points to consider about this action. Perhaps her motive can be understood if the conjunction (Greek *oun*) is given its full causative force as "therefore," rather than simply "then." This would tie Mary's act to the fact that Lazarus is one of those eating with Jesus. It is because Lazarus is alive, restored from the grave, that Mary pours out her heart in gratitude to Christ by her symbolic and extravagant act of worship.

That the act is extravagant is emphasized by John. She uses an unusually large amount (slightly less than 12 ounces avoirdupois) of a very expensive perfumed oil (called "nard") to anoint Jesus. Matthew and Mark state that she anoints His head while John says that she anoints His feet. Both are accurate, though incomplete, statements. She probably pours the anointing oil upon the whole length of Jesus' body as He reclines at the meal, starting at His head and moving downward. There is so much that it literally drips upon the floor. Mary spontaneously loosens her hair and begins to wipe the excess from the only part of Jesus' body which she dares to touch, His feet.

Even as he writes, John remembers the episode vividly: the room was filled with the pungent sweetness of the perfume. This is another of those incidental observations of detail which mark this Gospel as the work of an eyewitness.

Mary's action is doubly offensive to those present, appearing to be garishly excessive, in poor taste, undignified, and wasteful. The oil is very expensive and there is much of it. A small amount poured out in a dignified manner on the head would be one thing, but for the whole bottle to be poured on His whole body is too much. Her loosening of her hair and using it to wipe Christ's feet is also objectionable— unbecoming, even vulgar, embarrassing everyone in the room except Jesus. Only He understands her motives and is impressed by her effusive love and gratitude.

4 Then saith one of his disciples, Judas Iscariot, Simon's *son*, which should betray him.

Mary's action provokes "indignation" among the disciples (Mt. 26:8; Mk. 14:4), but John recalls that it was Judas who was the most upset and acted as spokesman for the group in expressing this "indignation." John cannot mention Judas without remembering that it was he who was to betray Christ (see 6:71).

His act of betrayal renders all other facts about him irrelevant. For this alone John remembers him.

5 Why was not this ointment sold for three hundred pence, and given to the poor?

Judas (with the other disciples apparently in agreement) proceeds to rebuke Mary's generous act of love by saying that this ointment should have been sold and given to the poor rather than so lavishly and foolishly wasted. He estimates (and who would know better than he?) it to be worth 300 denarii, about a year's wages for the working man of the time. (The N.T. "penny" translates the Greek/Latin *denarius*, the standard laborer's day's wage at the time.) This is just too much money to waste. Very likely, Judas is rebuking not only Mary for making such an extravagant gesture, but also Jesus for allowing it. At the very least, he is totally oblivious to any validity or appropriateness in Mary's action. He does not share her unrestrained gratitude and love. His heart is not stirred by any such emotions as those which animate her.

6 This he said, not that he cared for the poor; but because he was a thief, and had the bag, and bare what was put therein.

John parenthetically informs his reader at this point that Judas' motive was not concern for the poor. He could not care less about them. His real purpose lay in the fact that he was the "treasurer" for the group, that all monies contributed to the cause came under his supervision, and that he was stealing from these funds for himself.

This verse also provides an insight into a mundane aspect of Jesus' life on this earth—His financial arrangements. Jesus and His disciples were in possession (at times at least) of funds. The source of these funds is not stated but may be assumed to include donations (see e.g. Lk. 8:2,3). That financial concerns were not given high priority is indicated by the fact that responsibility for them was assigned to Judas, one of the lesser apostles, and by the fact that he was able to embezzle these funds undetected (or at least unconfronted).

7 Then said Jesus, Let her alone: against the day of my burying hath she kept this.

Jesus has remained quiet as Judas and the other disciples have condemned and berated Mary, but now He speaks in her defense. Surely it is enough for Mary that Jesus approves, that He understands, though everyone else on earth should criticize and scorn her.

Some interpret Jesus' words to mean that Mary "kept" some of the ointment and should be allowed to keep that remaining portion to anoint His body when He is dead. This interpretation seems to be precluded by the fact that, according to Mark (14:3), Mary actually broke the container; that all three accounts use language which implies that the whole container full, the whole "pound," was poured over Jesus (Mt. 26:7; Mk. 14:3; Jn. 12:3); that the whole reason for the outrage over Mary's action was that she had wasted 300 denarii (implying that all the ointment was used); and that John emphasizes that the whole house was filled with the aroma of the ointment.

A better way of understanding Jesus' meaning is to understand Him as saying that Mary has kept back this precious ointment *until now* (in contrast to having sold it and given the proceeds to the poor, as the disciples have suggested) for the purpose of anointing His body at this time. Whether she understands it or not, she is anointing Jesus' body for burial.

One need not suppose that Mary fully understood the significance of her action, although it seems quite possible that she did. She is presented as being perceptive and sensitive to Jesus' meanings as He taught. She was perhaps Jesus' best pupil. Certainly the great blessing that Jesus pronounced upon her (Mt. 26:13; Mk. 14:9) implies that her action was especially significant and suggests that she comprehended (to some degree at least) this significance.

8 For the poor always ye have with you; but me ye have not always.

Jesus now focuses directly upon the hypocrisy and insensitivity of Judas' words by saying that the poor will always be available if the disciples wish to help them, but that He will not always be with them so that they can express their love and devotion to Him. When Jesus says that the poor will always be present, He does not offer a normative teaching on the universality and inevitability of poverty; rather, He draws attention to the shortness of the time that He has left upon the earth and to the obvious insensitivity of the disciples to this fact and to the poignancy and beauty of Mary's symbolic act. To suggest that these words indicate a *laissez-faire* view of economics is to miss the point entirely.

9 Much people of the Jews therefore knew that he was there: and they came not for Jesus' sake only, but that they might see Lazarus also, whom he had raised from the dead.

Those who have come up to Jerusalem for the feast (11:55,56) are very curious about Jesus. They have heard that He is in Bethany and is scheduled to appear there at the dinner at Simon's.

They come out from Jerusalem to see Him, just as the sun goes down ending the Sabbath. As an added bonus Lazarus, the man whom Jesus has restored to life, is also present.

10 But the chief priests consulted that they might put Lazarus also to death;
11 Because that by reason of him many of the Jews went away, and believed on Jesus.

The Jewish authorities' reaction is in marked contrast to this idle curiosity. They have already determined to do whatever is necessary to eliminate Jesus (11:53). Now they decide that it may be necessary to kill not only Jesus, but also Lazarus, since many are believing on Christ because of him. Just by being alive, Lazarus bore witness to Christ's identity and power. It would be hard to condemn and execute Jesus as an impostor and fraud while Lazarus remained alive and well.

12 On the next day much people that were come to the feast, when they heard that Jesus was coming to Jerusalem,
13 Took branches of palm trees, and went forth to meet him, and cried, Hosanna: Blessed *is* the King of Israel that cometh in the name of the Lord.

On the next day, Sunday (five days before the Passover; see v. 1), the morning after the feast in Bethany, many of the people who have come to Jerusalem for Passover go forth to meet Jesus, whom they have heard is actually coming into Jerusalem. They do not just happen to be on hand when He arrives; they purposely go to meet Him. Their purpose is to proclaim Jesus King of Israel.

While the palms might simply have

signified joyous celebration, another explanation is more likely. Since the time of the Maccabees the palm seems to have become the national symbol of Israel, a symbol of Jewish nationalism. This being the case, these Jews were expressing their belief and hope that Jesus was the Messiah who would free Israel from the yoke of Roman rule. This explanation ties in very well with the chant, "Hosanna, blessed is the King of Israel who comes in the name of the Lord." Their chant reflected Ps. 118:26a, but the people themselves declared Jesus to be "the King of Israel." Many of these people were from the outlying areas like Galilee and really believed that Jesus was the Messiah. They had been waiting for Him to assert Himself and to assume His Messianic prerogatives. Now, at long last, He was doing so— they thought—and they were overjoyed. They were ready to proclaim Him king and follow Him into battle against Rome, against the Jerusalem authorities, or against whomever He might lead them.

14 And Jesus, when he had found a young ass, sat thereon; as it is written,
15 Fear not, daughter of Sion; behold, thy King cometh, sitting on an ass's colt.

There is deliberate significance in Jesus' decision to ride into the city on a young donkey. His action is intended to correct the false impression of the crowd that He is about to lead them into battle and to symbolize that He has not come for war, but for peace. The horse is the mount associated with war, but the donkey is used only for mundane and peaceful purposes. John informs his readers that this action fulfills the prophecy of Zechariah (9:9). It is interesting that this prophecy actually makes the exact point that the Messiah, the King, will be a man of peace, not of war (see

especially Zech. 9:10).

16 These things understood not his disciples at the first: but when Jesus was glorified, then remembered they that these things were written of him, and *that* they had done these things unto him.

The symbolic significance of Jesus' riding into Jerusalem on a young donkey is not immediately apparent to the disciples. Only later, after His glorification (i.e. His death, resurrection, and ascension; see commentary 7:39), will they come to understand it. Only then will they comprehend how literally these events have fulfilled the O.T. prophecies.

17 The people therefore that was with him when he called Lazarus out of his grave, and raised him from the dead, bare record.
18 For this cause the people also met him, for that they heard that he had done this miracle.

While all this is going on, those residents of Jerusalem who were actually present when Jesus raised Lazarus from the grave are giving their testimony (Greek *martureo*; the imperfect tense indicates a continuing action). They tell about this great miracle to those who have come up for the feast (11:55; 12:12) and take the lead in escorting Jesus into Jerusalem as their king. Their knowledge of this miracle serves to intensify their enthusiasm.

19 The Pharisees therefore said among themselves, Perceive ye how ye prevail nothing? behold, the world is gone after him.

As they observe the enthusiasm with which Jesus is greeted and proclaimed king, the Pharisees comment among themselves that the situation is getting out of control. Their plans to neutralize Jesus do not seem to be working. To the contrary, "the whole world" (i.e. everyone; a slight hyperbole) seems to believe in Him and accept Him as the Messiah. The situation seems to be getting completely out of hand.

20 And there were certain Greeks among them that came up to worship at the feast.

Among those in attendance at the feast are certain "Greeks" (Greek *Hellen*). They are clearly Gentiles (the same word is translated "Gentiles" in 7:35) rather than Greek-speaking Jews (Greek *Hellenistes*). They are apparently "God-fearers" or "proselytes of the gate" who, while they are attracted to the monotheistic Jewish religion, have not actually taken the step of being circumcised and becoming full-fledged converts (proselytes) to Judaism. Such "God-fearers" often came up to the feasts. They were allowed into the outer court of the Temple, the "Court of the Gentiles," and they were allowed to participate in the worship of God so long as they did not overstep the restrictions placed on them.

21 The same came therefore to Philip, which was of Bethsaida of Galilee, and desired him, saying, Sir, we would see Jesus.
22 Philip cometh and telleth Andrew: and again Andrew and Philip tell Jesus.

The Greeks approach Philip and tell him that they wish to see (i.e. talk with) Jesus. Why they approach Philip is unclear. Some have supposed that it is because of his Greek-sounding name or because he is from Galilee, but one cannot be sure. At any rate, Philip shares their request with Andrew (they have collaborated before, see 6:5-9) and together they relate it to Christ.

23 And Jesus answered them, saying, The hour is come, that the Son of man should be glorified.

Jesus' response is directed not to the Greeks, but to Philip and Andrew. He remarks, somewhat enigmatically, that the hour of His glorification has finally arrived. Previously it has been said that Jesus' "hour" (Greek *hora*, 2:4; 7:30; 8:20) or "time" (Greek *kairos*, 7:6,8) had not yet come, but now, at last, it has arrived. For the significance of "glorified," see comments on v. 16.

To understand Jesus' response is to understand the meaning and significance of this whole episode. John is the only Evangelist to mention these Greeks' request, and it is the only occurrence he places between the triumphal entry and the Last Supper. He clearly supposes it to be significant, yet he does no more than mention that it occurred. There is no indication that the Greeks actually got to see Jesus or that they heard the discourse of vv. 23-36. The importance of this event seems to be symbolic. As Jesus' life drew to a close, as He was about to be finally and decisively rejected by the Jews, these Gentiles arrived upon the scene as the symbolic representatives of their race and expressed their desire to converse with Him. They prefigure all those from among the Gentiles who were to be reconciled to God by Christ's impending death upon the cross. Their coming brought all of this to Jesus' mind and prompted Him to remark that the time of His sacrifice, that action which would make it possible for Gentiles to come into fellowship with God, had arrived. His response to their request to talk with Him was not to talk with them but to remark upon the fact that the barrier between them and Himself (and the Father) was about to be once and forever removed. The time during which His ministry was to be confined to the lost sheep of Israel was almost at an end.

24 Verily, verily, I say unto you, Except a corn of wheat fall into the ground and die, it abideth alone: but if it die, it bringeth forth much fruit.

The only hope for these Greeks who want to speak with Jesus— indeed, the only hope for all mankind—is that He will give Himself to die for their sins. Talking to them will not help. Jesus expresses this truth somewhat enigmatically by use of the figure of a seed. The purpose of a seed is the bringing forth of a new plant which will, in turn, produce much grain. In order for this purpose to be accomplished, the seed itself must die. Only by death will new life come to be. So with Jesus and humanity: He must die that men may live (eternally). Jesus is not insensitive to the need of the Greeks, but the means by which He can help them most is not by talking with them, but by dying for them. (Of course, it may be that Jesus *did* speak to the Greeks in some way, but the fact that John fails to mention such indicates that what He said was not important to the meaning of the incident.)

25 He that loveth his life shall lose it; and he that hateth his life in this world shall keep it unto life eternal.

Having spoken it parabolically, about His own approaching death on behalf of mankind, Jesus now puts the principle that life comes through death in the form of an axiom. Anyone who loves his life will lose it, but anyone who hates his earthly life (i.e. deems it less important than his eternal destiny) will keep it for eternity (i.e. he will not only preserve his

earthly life but, through the proper use of it, come to possess eternal life as well). Jesus has stated essentially this same axiom before (Mt. 16:25; Mk. 8:35; Lk. 9:24). This is a recurring theme in His teaching (see e.g. Mt. 10:39).

26 If any man serve me, let him follow me; and where I am, there shall also my servant be: if any man serve me, him will *my* Father honour.

Jesus has expressed the principle that life comes through death as a parable (v. 24) and as an axiom for all men (v. 25). Now He states it as a rule of life for His disciples. If anyone is going to serve Him, then he must follow Him all the way; he will have to share all the hardship and suffering that is a part of His mission. Again, Jesus states this same principle in the Synoptics (Mt. 16:24; Mk. 8:34; Lk. 9:23). On this occasion, however, Jesus adds the reassuring promise that those who do thus share completely in the suffering and hardship will be appropriately honored and rewarded for their faithfulness and sacrifice by the Father.

27 Now is my soul troubled; and what shall I say? Father, save me from this hour: but for this cause came I unto this hour.

John does not record the agony in Gethsemane, and these words of Jesus seem to be roughly equivalent to His prayer in Mk. 14:36. As He faces the impending horror of the cross, Christ is troubled in His spirit. His human nature shrinks from its agony. What is He to say in the face of this gruesome prospect? How is He to deal with this, His ultimate crisis?

Some believe the phrase "Father, save me from this hour" is a continuation of Christ's previous rhetorical question (e.g. Morris and Godet). They believe this to be a hypothetical rather than an actual prayer. Others (e.g. Bruce, Bernard, and Hendricksen) believe it to be an actual prayer which approximates Christ's prayer in Gethsemane.

The second view is to be preferred. While His words in no way imply rebellion against God's purpose, they do express an actual desire to be delivered from the terrible agony of the cross "if it be possible" (Mt. 27:39). However, Jesus is totally resigned, even committed, to fulfilling the Father's purpose for Him. He is fully aware that He has come into the world for the express purpose of dying vicariously for others (see e.g. vv. 23, 24, 32; and especially 18:11).

28 Father, glorify thy name. Then came there a voice from heaven, saying, I have both glorified it, and will glorify it again.

While at one level of His being Jesus wishes to escape the horror of the cross, at the deepest level His wish is only to fulfill the Father's will and thereby facilitate the Father's own glorification of Himself. He knows that His death is directed to that great goal, and in this knowledge He finds deep satisfaction even as He recoils from the approaching cross.

The Father answers this prayer by means of a supernatural, audible voice from Heaven. He says that He has already glorified His own name and is going to glorify it again. The reference to a past glorification may be to Christ's baptism and/or His transfiguration; at both of them God audibly pronounced approval upon His Son. On the other hand, the reference may be to Jesus' whole life, which was in its totality a revelation of God's glory (1:14), or to His miracles (2:11), especially the raising of Lazarus (11:4,40). The likelihood of

the latter interpretation is increased by the fact that John does not mention either the baptism or the transfiguration.

The future glorification is obviously that of the cross, which is at once both Christ's greatest humiliation and ultimate triumph (see 3:14). In effect the Father recalls this ironic truth to His Son at this particular moment so as to encourage and reassure Him in the face of the cross: "Remember that it is by the very means of this horrifying death that You are to achieve for Me [and for Yourself] the ultimate glory."

29 The people therefore, that stood by, and heard it, said that it thundered: others said, An angel spake to him.

That this is no private subjective experience of Jesus is clear from the fact that those who stand nearby actually hear the audible sound. Some say that it has thundered, indicating the unusually loud nature of the voice. Others suggest that an angel has spoken to Christ, indicating that they perceive what they hear to be meaningful speech rather than mere sound. These comments apparently indicate a sincere perplexity, and John means to imply that the bystanders did not understand the actual content of the message. This occurrence is analogous to Paul's experience on the road to Damascus, when those traveling with him did not understand what Christ said to him (Acts 9:7; 22:9). The identity of these bystanders and the circumstances and timing of their arrival upon the scene are not specified. Apparently Christ's discourse has drawn a crowd.

30 Jesus answered and said, This voice came not because of me, but for your sakes.

Jesus tells the bystanders that God has spoken in this manner for their sake rather than His. This is not to say that God's words had no relevance for Jesus. But they were not intended for Him exclusively or even primarily; they were for the bystanders' benefit. How can this be if they did not actually understand the words and, therefore, the content of the message? The sound actually came from Heaven, and in immediate response to Christ's prayer. These were sufficient indications that the voice was from God and that it was intended as a divine acknowledgement of Jesus and attestation to His claims.

31 Now is the judgment of this world: now shall the prince of this world be cast out.

Jesus' mind remains focused on the approaching cross, and He continues to speak of it just as if there had been no interruption. He speaks of it as already present. He may speak of it so simply because it is so near (see 4:23), but it may be that He means to imply that the Jews' present act of rejection is more strategic than they know and that, with this rejection, the crucifixion and all its momentous consequences become inevitable.

Jesus says that very soon there will be a judgment rendered. The world will direct that judgment against Him, but in doing so, they will actually be judging themselves. There is a play on "of this world," so that it is both objective and subjective (as a genitive noun in Greek). It is subjective in the apparent sense that the Jews are judging Christ. It is objective in that, ultimately, they are judging themselves and will be judged by God.

Not only is the world to be judged, but the "prince of this world" (Greek *ho archon tou kosmou*) is to be "cast out." This is an obvious reference to Satan. He is, by usurpation, the prince of this world, and he is able to control the world's verdict concerning Christ; but

his authority does not extend beyond this world, and he cannot control the verdict of Heaven. Therefore, since the ultimate impact of the world's verdict is to condemn itself, so also it is to condemn Satan as its ruler and guiding influence. "Cast out" (Greek *ekballo*) should probably be understood in the context of the figure of a prince who is deposed or forced from his throne. Jesus is saying that there is to be a revolution against Prince Satan and that his regime of terror is to be swept away. That revolution will trace its legitimacy to Christ's cross; it will begin at Calvary.

32 And I, if I be lifted up from the earth, will draw all *men* unto me.

"Lifted up" (Greek *hupsoo*) is a word which John uses to refer both to Christ's crucifixion and to His exaltation (see 3:14 and 8:28). Here he has His death primarily in mind (see v. 33). The "if" should not be understood as casting any doubt on whether Christ will, in fact, be crucified; rather it simply means that the (still future) event is being considered from a theoretical perspective as a means of focusing upon its special significance.

Christ's crucifixion is going to have a very different consequence for Him (the "I" is emphatic) than for the world and its prince. For Christ the result will be that He will "draw all men unto" Himself. This last phrase must be understood in the light of the context. Jesus has been approached by the Greeks. He has expressed the idea that His talking to them will not really help them and that only His substitutionary death can actually help them. Now He says that, when He has been crucified, He will draw all men, including Greeks, to Himself. This drawing, apart from which none may be saved (6:44), will be extended to include even the Gentiles. The point of "all" is not that every single individual will be convicted and regenerated, but that all sorts and classes of men will be.

EDITOR'S NOTE ON JOHN 12:32: THE MEANING OF ALL

To identify the "drawing" referred to here with that of 6:44 is probably correct; the same Greek word is used. In that case, both here and there the drawing is conviction of sin and of the truth of the gospel, not regeneration as such. See the Editor's Note on 6:44: the drawing is the work of the Spirit of God that enables the sinner, despite his depravity, to grasp and appropriate the truth and thus to put faith in Christ. Salvation must be initiated by God; man who is spiritually dead can only respond to the gospel as he is enabled by this drawing.

Then how is this drawing for "all"? Calvinists are convinced that "all" does not mean all individuals of mankind, here, but that the elect come from all peoples, without distinction. Some Arminians agree that the context in this passage—given the inquiry of the "Greeks" (vv. 20ff)—supports the idea that Jesus is not so much thinking here about every single individual as about the fact that His work will break down the old Jew-Gentile distinction and result in the drawing of people from every race and class. According to this view, then, the effect of Jesus' words is: "I will draw *from among* all *peoples* to myself." This is certainly a possible understanding of the words and will not negate the all-inclusive meaning of "all" in some other passages.

Still, one wonders if this does justice to "all." There is the context of the whole Gospel to consider, and a deliberately universalistic tone characterizes John's report. This universalism is seen, for example, in God's love for the entire world, as in 3:16; see the Editor's Note on that passage, and compare 1:29; 8:12; 12:46. Furthermore, the other times an unqualified "all" occurs in the Gospel, it apparently means all individuals (see 2:24; 5:23; and compare 1:9).

But if "all men" is truly all-inclusive, here, how can it be said that Jesus draws all to Himself? As pastor Stallings has noted, not every individual is actually brought under conviction, much less regenerated and saved. The answer is that the only limitations on the drawing are those imposed by the proclamation of the gospel. As already indicated in the note on 6:44, conviction (that is, enabling grace) is "co-extensive with the gospel." The potential of the gospel is as wide as the atonement itself, that every person should hear and be drawn. And all who respond to that enabling work of grace in faith are actually saved. The difference between the potential and the actual, therefore, is exactly the same as in Tit. 2:11: "The grace of God that bringeth salvation hath appeared to all men." But the actual communication of this grace, and the persuasion/attraction involved in the "drawing," while potentially for all, is limited to those who come under the sound of the gospel of Christ. By the gospel and the co-extensive work of enabling grace, Christ draws all to Himself.

33 This he said, signifying what death he should die.

While Jesus' primary purpose is not to communicate that the manner of His death will be crucifixion, His words do constitute a prophecy to that effect. John draws attention to them as an example of the irony and hidden significance which he so often observes in Christ's words.

34 The people answered him, We have heard out of the law that Christ abideth forever: and how sayest thou, The Son of man must be lifted up? who is this Son of man?

183

For the first time during His long discourse, Christ's hearers (see v. 29) interrupt Him (the speculations of v. 29 were not actually addressed to Jesus). They express their confusion (either real or contrived) as to His statement that He is to be "lifted up," which term they correctly understand to refer to His death. They understand from the law (i.e. the O.T. as a whole, not just the Pentateuch) that Christ will abide forever (i.e. establish an eternal kingdom). They have apparently formed this belief on the basis of such Scriptures as Ps. 110:4; Is. 9:7; Ezek. 37:25; and Dan. 7:14. They wonder then how Jesus, who obviously claims to be the Christ, can say of Himself that He is to die.

There is no doubt in their minds that by the term "Son of Man" Jesus means Himself. He has used the term this way in v. 23, apparently in their hearing. Furthermore, they are undoubtedly aware that He has characteristically used it to refer to Himself. They do not see how He can be "lifted up" if He is actually the Messiah. Almost as an afterthought they ask Jesus just who this "Son of Man" is. Are they correct in assuming this to be another designation for the Messiah? Are they correct in assuming that Jesus means Himself? They want Jesus to clear up these difficulties.

35 Then Jesus said unto them, Yet a little while is the light with you. Walk while ye have the light, lest darkness come upon you: for he that walketh in darkness knoweth not whither he goeth.

Jesus answers with a solemn warning. He implies that their problem is not that they do not understand, but that they are willfully rejecting His teaching. He warns them that the light (i.e. Himself) is only going to be with them for a little while, for He is soon to return to His Father (see 7:33,34). He warns them

that they had better make use of the light while it is available to them. If they do not, darkness will descend upon them, a darkness so great that they cannot possibly find their way (see 11:9,10).

36 While ye have light, believe in the light, that ye may be the children of light. These things spake Jesus, and departed, and did hide himself from them.

He urges them to make use of the light while they have it and thereby to become, themselves, children of light. Jesus is telling these Jews that He is the only truth and that if they will believe in Him, on the basis of their present understanding, then they will come to know all the truth. As one accepts and submits to the truth He does comprehend, He is transformed into a child of the truth and the whole realm of truth opens up before him.

With these final words, Jesus' public ministry to the Jewish nation is concluded. He therefore withdraws from the public for the purpose of privately instructing and encouraging His own disciples. The remaining verses of this chapter are a sort of epilogue to the public ministry, the Book of Signs.

37 But though he had done so many miracles before them, yet they believed not on him.

In spite of the fact that He has performed so many convincing miracles in their sight, the reaction of the vast majority of the Jewish people to Jesus is rejection and unbelief. They do not believe that He is the Messiah, and they will not accept His message about Himself and about their own need of salvation. As John sees it, the whole purpose for Christ's miracles is to provoke and inspire personal belief and trust in Christ, and thereby to convey eternal life (20:31). In the case of these Jews, that purpose has not been achieved. Although they have seen the miracles, they do not believe in Christ.

38 That the saying of Esaias the prophet might be fulfilled, which he spake, Lord, who hath believed our report? and to whom hath the arm of the Lord been revealed?

Such complete rejection of the Messiah, by the very people who have been prepared for no other purpose than His coming, demands an explanation. Why do they reject so utterly their Messiah? For the answer John turns to the prophet Isaiah. They do so in conformity with God's sovereign purpose. The central significance of Christ's coming (i.e. His vicarious death for sinners) presupposes complete rejection by the Jews. Their rejection, then, is not all that puzzling. It has been included in God's plan all along. He has even revealed that it was to be so through the prophets. Isaiah, for instance, predicted such a rejection (Is. 53:1). John does not mean to say that the Jews' unbelief has no other purpose than to fulfill the prophecy of Isaiah. Rather, he means to say that it is to accomplish the eternal purpose of God as expressed in the prophecy of Isaiah.

39 Therefore they could not believe, because that Esaias said again,
40 He hath blinded their eyes, and hardened their heart; that they should not see with *their* eyes, nor understand with *their* heart, and be converted, and I should heal them.

John continues explaining why the Jews have rejected their own Messiah. He says that they are actually not able to believe, that it is not possible for them

to believe. He grounds this assertion in another of Isaiah's prophecies (6:9,10). Just as God intensified the original hardness of Pharaoh's heart and directed it to His own purposes, so He did with O.T. Israel and so He is doing with these Jews who have rejected Christ. While they are totally responsible for their great sin of rejecting Him, they are actually fulfilling God's plan as they do so. Peter explains this principle very clearly in Acts 2:23.

41 These things said Esaias, when he saw his glory, and spake of him.

The context of Is. 6:9,10 is Isaiah's vision of Jehovah in 6:1-4. This must surely be what John has in mind as he writes these words: that Isaiah actually saw *Jesus'* glory in his vision. John's exact implication is uncertain. Does he mean that Isaiah expressly spoke these words with Jesus' "glorification" in mind, or does He simply mean to say that Isaiah was aware of Christ's glory even as He spoke these words? Probably the latter view is to be preferred.

42 Nevertheless among the chief rulers also many believed on him; but because of the Pharisees they did not confess *him*, lest they should be put out of the synagogue:
43 For they loved the praise of men more than the praise of God.

In spite of the fact that most of the Jews completely reject Christ, there are some even among the chief rulers (i.e. members of the Sanhedrin) who believe in Jesus. Yet, while they believe in Him, they are not willing to acknowledge Him openly for fear of the Pharisees. They are afraid that if they openly confess their belief they will be excommunicated from the synagogue (see 9:22, 34) by the zealous Pharisees. They are more concerned to maintain their standing and prestige among men than to secure for themselves the commendation and reward of God. Certainly John must have both Nicodemus and Joseph of Arimathaea (19:38-40) in mind at this point.

The question whether the faith referred to is a genuine but weak faith, or a mere intellectual assent rendered totally insufficient by the refusal to confess it openly, is difficult to answer. Certainly some do "believe" in a way that falls short of full commitment to Christ (2:23-25), but it seems from a later reference (19:38) that John regards Joseph of Arimathaea as a true, if weak, believer. Certainly, John does not condone this cowardly course, however the question is answered.

44 Jesus cried and said, He that believeth on me, believeth not on me, but on him that sent me.
45 And he that seeth me seeth him that sent me.

This last section (vv. 44-50) is a final summary of the public ministry of Jesus. That it presents an actual discourse of Christ, given on a particular occasion, seems to be indicated by the reference to a circumstantial detail (i.e. that Jesus "cried out"). John has chosen to place it here because it effectively summarizes and concludes Christ's public ministry. In these words, all of which draw upon His previous teachings, Jesus challenges all men everywhere to believe on Him.

Jesus assures men that to believe on Him is not just to trust in Him alone or in Him as a mere human being, but is to trust in the Father as well. He refers to the Father as the one who has sent Him and with whom He shares an intimate unity (see 5:19, 30; 6:51; 7:16; 8:19, 42). The unity between Christ and the Father is so complete that to see Christ is to see the Father (see e.g. 5:18; 8:19;

10:30,38). This truth will be forcefully expressed again in 14:9.

46 I am come a light into the world, that whosoever believeth on me should not abide in darkness.
47 And if any man hear my words, and believe not, I judge him not: for I came not to judge the world, but to save the world.

Christ refers to Himself as a light that has shone forth into the darkness so that those who believe in Him need not remain in darkness (see e.g. 1:5,9; 8:12; 9:5; and vv. 35,36). He has come to bring salvation, not judgment, into the world (see e.g. 3:17). The Father is the One who will judge those who reject the Son (see e.g. 5:45; 8:16-18, 50).

48 He that rejecteth me, and receiveth not my words, hath one that judgeth him: the word that I have spoken, the same shall judge him in the last day.

On those who reject Him and do not receive His words the Father is going to pronounce judgment according to those very words (see 5:24, 45-47; 6:63; 8:31,51). Jesus will return to this theme in 14:23, 24.

49 For I have not spoken of myself; but the Father which sent me, he gave me a commandment, what I should say, and what I should speak.
50 And I know that his commandment is life everlasting: whatsoever I speak therefore, even as the Father said unto me, so I speak.

Jesus' teachings do not originate with Him, but He is simply relaying the message which has been given Him by the Father (see 3:11; 7:16; 8:26, 28). He will mention this again in 14:10 and 17:8. The whole purpose of the message which the Father has given to Him and which He, in turn, has delivered to men is to make possible eternal life for those who will receive it (see e.g. 3:16; 5:24; 6:63; 8:51; 20:31).

Summary
(12:1-50)

Having ended His seclusion in Ephraim, Jesus comes to Bethany late on Friday afternoon. He spends a quiet Sabbath (Saturday) and then, after sundown, attends a banquet in His honor. During this banquet, Mary anoints Jesus with very expensive ointment and wipes His feet with her hair. Mary's "extravagant" action provokes "indignation" among the disciples. Judas, who is especially indignant, asks why this ointment was not sold and the proceeds donated to the poor. Judas' motive is not concern for the poor, however, but avarice and jealous hatred of Jesus. Jesus defends Mary's action as being a perceptive and meaningful gesture in light of His approaching death. He informs His disciples that there will be ample opportunity to help the poor after He has been taken from them.

When those in attendance at Passover learn that Jesus, the one who raised Lazarus, is nearby, they go out to Bethany to see Him. This provokes the authorities to put Lazarus' name alongside that of Jesus on their death list, since his being alive from the dead is causing many to turn to Christ. On Sunday many go out to meet Jesus and escort Him triumphantly into Jerusalem. Those who had been present when He raised Lazarus recount the event, adding to the excitement. The welcome and celebration are such that the Pharisees remark bitterly that it seems as if the whole world is going after Jesus.

Among those at the feast are certain Greeks who come to Jesus' disciples expressing a desire to speak with Him. Christ does not meet with them, but remarks somewhat enigmatically that the barrier between Himself and them is about to be removed through His death. Christ's death is to provide the only hope for such Gentiles as these. Jesus states the axiom that life (i.e. eternal life) comes only through death (in this case, His own) and tells His disciples that if they are to truly follow Him, they must be prepared to go all the way with Him.

Christ reveals His agony of spirit by praying to be delivered from the cross if it is possible, yet He is completely submissive to the Father's will in the matter. His real concern is that whatever is about to transpire will bring glory to His Father. God responds to this prayer by an audible voice to say that He has already glorified Christ and is going to glorify Him further. The voice is audible and provokes a controversy among those nearby. Some say that it has thundered, others that an angel has spoken. Jesus insists that the audible voice signifies God's seal of acceptance and approval upon Him and that God has spoken not so much for His benefit as for theirs. Jesus remains focused on the approaching cross. Its essential significance is that it will provide salvation for all men, even Greeks.

Jesus' hearers interrupt Him at this point to express their confusion as to how He can be the Messiah and yet be "lifted up." The two are not compatible in their view. Jesus answers with the solemn warning that He is only to be with them a short while and that they had best accept the light He offers them while they may, before He is taken away. With this warning He ends His public ministry to the Jews.

In spite of the many miracles which He has performed in their presence, most of the Jews have refused to believe in Jesus. John says that their rejection is in keeping with God's eternal purpose as revealed in the O.T. and that it actually is being used by God to facilitate His purpose. John points out that there are exceptions to this pattern of rejection. For instance, even some members of the Sanhedrin have inwardly and secretly believed in Christ although they are too intimidated to acknowledge Him openly. John closes this section with a sermonic discourse of Christ's which both summarizes and epitomizes His public ministry. Every point is drawn from His previous teachings.

Application: Teaching and Preaching The Passage

Mary's anointing of Jesus (vv. 1-11) presents a vivid contrast between the carnal and the spiritual mind-sets. Mary represents spiritual fervor and sensitivity while the disciples represent wooden insensitivity to such motivations. Carnality always brands such actions as Mary's impractical and extravagant. Nothing seems more pointless and absurd (to those with a carnal mind) than spiritually motivated actions, especially costly and sacrificial ones.

In the triumphal entry into Jerusalem (vv. 12-19), Jesus presents Himself as a spiritual Messiah as opposed to the great national leader whom Israel expected and desired. The crowds, while they demonstrate a superficial willingness to accept Him, do so on their own terms. The Pharisees' fears that Jesus has stolen the people's hearts are not well-founded, for no one comprehends the meaning of Jesus' symbolism as He rides into the city on a donkey—not even His own disciples. When their exuberant but shallow emotions have subsided, the multitude will abandon Jesus to His fate.

In vv. 20-36 Jesus delivers a discourse in response to the request of some Greeks to speak with Him. This dis-course represents Jesus' final words to the Jewish public. In vv. 23-29 Jesus explains that only by dying for them can He be of real help to these Gentile inquirers. He explains that He is therefore determined to see His mission through to the bitter end in spite of His own apprehensions and, thereby, to glorify His Father. The Father expresses His approval of these motives by an audible voice from Heaven. In vv. 30-36 Jesus explains the significance of His approaching death and warns His hearers not to squander their opportunity to achieve the eternal life which He offers them. This solemn warning constitutes His last word to the Jewish public.

In vv. 37-43 John explains that Jesus' rejection by the Jewish nation, though superficially incomprehensible, is actually in keeping with the eternal purpose of God as revealed in the Old Testament. He also points out that this rejection is not so absolute as it appears. In fact, many of the Sanhedrin members, themselves, believe on Him, but only secretly for fear of persecution.

Finally, vv. 44-50 constitute a final discourse which is drawn from and summarizes His previous teachings. It is an accurate characterization of Jesus' public preaching while upon this earth.

III. THE BOOK OF GLORY: CHRIST REVEALED IN HIS DEATH AND RESURRECTION (13:1—20:31)

A. The Last Supper (13:1-30)

1. The Footwashing (13:1-17)

1 Now before the feast of the passover, when Jesus knew that his hour was come that he should depart out of this world unto the Father, having loved his own which were in the world, he loved them unto the end.

188

This verse marks the transition from the Book of Signs, in which Christ's ministry has been directed to the public at large, to the Book of Glory, in which He will deal privately with the inner core of His disciples.

In vv. 4,5 John is going to relate what he considers to be an astounding event, Jesus' washing of His disciples' feet. In vv. 1-3 he gives all the circumstances of the event. He begins with a rather indefinite reference to its timing. He says simply that it transpired prior to the Passover proper. It seems reasonable to assume, in spite of the objection that 18:28 may indicate otherwise, that the meal referred to by John was the "Last Supper" referred to by the Synoptists and that it was a true Passover Meal (see comments 18:28).

John now begins to list the circumstances which, in His mind, are significant. They render the scene inherently unlikely and, thereby, the more remarkable, glorious, and poignant. He notes that, even though Jesus knows that His "hour" (see 2:4; 5:25,28; 7:30; 8:20; and 12:23, 27) has arrived and that He is about to be crucified and, thus, to depart this world and return to His Father, His thoughts are focused upon His little group of disciples whom He loves to the bitter end and to the most extreme degree. He loves them even as He realizes that to love them means to die for them.

"His own" refers to those who truly and completely received and believed on Him (i.e. His closest disciples), in contrast to the second "His own" of 1:11 which referred to the Jewish nation (i.e. His own people or kindred) who as a group had now completely rejected Him.

2 And supper being ended, the devil having now put into the heart of Judas Iscariot, Simon's son, to betray him.

John continues recounting the signifi-

cant circumstances by mentioning that the episode occurs after (or during) the meal rather than at the usual time for the washing of guests' feet, when they first arrive. Jesus' love and humility seem the more remarkable to John in light of the fact that, even as He washed their feet, Satan was already working in Judas' mind, convincing him to betray Jesus.

3 Jesus knowing that the Father had given all things into his hands, and that he was come from God, and went to God.

Jesus fully comprehends His own identity and authority as He undertakes this action of self-abasement. He knows that He is the only begotten of the Father. He is fully aware that all the universe will someday kneel before Him and own Him Lord. He knows that He has come forth from God and that He will soon return to Him. He is completely cognizant of His own glorious majesty as He prepares to wash His disciples' feet. Never did John "behold His glory" (1:14) more brightly than at this moment. Never did Jesus "manifest forth His glory" (2:11) more than now.

4 He riseth from supper, and laid aside his garments; and took a towel and girded himself.
5 After that he poureth water into a bason, and began to wash the disciples' feet, and to wipe *them* with the towel wherewith he was girded.

Jesus now rises from the table and, in the most graphic manner possible, illustrates that He has come to minister rather than to be ministered unto (Mt. 20:28), that He is among men as a servant (Lk. 22:27), and that He has taken upon Himself the form of a servant (Phil. 2:7), by washing the disciples' feet. The scene is still vivid in John's mind: Jesus' rising, laying aside His outer garments, taking the towel and girding it around His waist, pouring water into the basin and then proceeding to wash the disciples' feet and dry them with the towel. His attitude is in marked contrast to that of the disciples. They have just been arguing about which of them shall be greatest (Lk. 22:24) while He, the incomparably great one, willingly humbles Himself before them. None of this is lost on John as he recalls that night.

6 Then cometh he to Simon Peter: and Peter saith unto him, Lord, dost thou wash my feet?

As Jesus proceeds around the table washing each of the disciples' feet, there is, apparently, a complete silence. The disciples are taken completely aback by Jesus' action. When He comes to wash Peter's feet, however, that exuberant soul cannot contain himself. "You, my feet are going to wash?" he exclaims. (This somewhat awkward translation conveys the emphasis of the Greek.) Peter can neither comprehend nor accept that Jesus, whom he knows to be the Messiah, the very Son of God (6:69; Mt. 16:16), will wash his feet. He comprehends that this is completely inappropriate and absurd. He fully understands the vast gap between himself and Jesus.

7 Jesus answered and said unto him, What I do thou knowest not now; but thou shalt know hereafter.

Jesus replies that, though Peter does not presently understand the significance and, therefore, the necessity of Jesus' action, he will do so "hereafter," i.e. after Jesus' death, resurrection, and ascension.

8 Peter saith unto him, Thou shalt never wash my feet. Jesus answered him, If I wash thee not, thou hast no part with me.

Peter is adamant, however, and refuses to consider the idea that Jesus will wash his feet. At this point Jesus states enigmatically that if He does not wash Peter, then Peter will have no part with Him. Jesus obviously does not mean to say that Peter will be lost unless He washes his feet. Salvation comes by grace through faith, not by means of any outward, ceremonial action. Therefore, Jesus must use the word with a dual meaning and refer by it not just to the act of washing Peter's feet, but to the washing of the soul by His atoning death. This washing of the disciples' feet is symbolic of the whole process of Christ's humiliation which climaxes in the cross and by which He will cleanse from sin the souls of all those who trust in Him.

9 Simon Peter saith unto him, Lord, not my feet only, but also *my* hands and *my* head.

Peter, mistakenly supposing Jesus to mean that if He does not wash his feet, he will be lost, says with characteristic rambunctiousness, "Then wash not only my feet, but my hands and my head also." Peter certainly does not want to be cut off from Christ for lack of sufficient washing. Better too much than not enough.

10 Jesus saith to him, He that is washed needeth not save to wash *his* feet, but is clean every whit: and ye are clean, but not all.
11 For he knew who should betray him; therefore said he, Ye are not all clean.

Jesus explains to Peter that the person who has already had a bath (Greek *louo* which means to wash the entire body) only needs to have his feet washed when he arrives at the home of his host, since only his feet will have become dirty on the journey. The spiritual meaning is that the person who has been regenerated, justified, and cleansed of His sins by trusting in Christ as Savior does not ever need to be "saved again" but only needs to be cleansed, from time to time, of his sins. The footwashing, therefore, not only symbolizes Christ's humiliation but also the ongoing sanctification of the believer. Jesus adds that the disciples have already been cleansed (i.e. regenerated) and are, therefore, clean—but, He adds ominously, not all of them. Some are not in the state of grace which He describes. Of course, Jesus had Judas in mind as He spoke these words. He knew that Judas was soon to betray Him, and therefore He said that not all of them were clean.

12 So after he had washed their feet, and had taken his garments, and was set down again, he said unto them, Know ye what I have done to you?

When He has completed His task, Jesus again dons His outer garment and reclines at the table. Rhetorically asking them if they comprehend the significance of His washing their feet, He begins to explain that significance to them.

13 Ye call me Master and Lord: and ye say well; for so I am.
14 If I then, your Lord and Master, have washed your feet; ye also ought to wash one another's feet.

Jesus reminds them that they refer to Him as "Master" (Greek *didaskalos*, teacher/rabbi) and "Lord" (Greek *kurios*) and assures them that they are correct in so doing since those words accurately reflect His true identity and stature. If He, their Lord and Master, has so humbled Himself as to wash their feet, then, certainly, they ought to be willing to wash one another's feet.

15 For I have given you an example, that ye should do as I have done to you.
16 Verily, verily, I say unto you, The servant is not greater than his lord; neither he that is sent greater than he that sent him.
17 If ye know these things, happy are ye if ye do them.

Jesus tells the disciples that He has acted as He has as an example for them. He wants them to develop the same spirit of humility which they have just seen Him manifest. Since they willingly and correctly acknowledge that He is their rightful Lord and Master, it is altogether inappropriate for them to refuse to do as He has done. A servant is not superior to his master; he cannot demand to be treated more preferentially than his master. These apostles, these who are to be sent (Greek *apostello*) by Jesus to the world with His message, are not above Jesus Himself. They, too, are to manifest Christ's spirit of humility as they go forth to finish His work. Jesus assures them that since (the correct sense of the Greek *ei*) they understand this principle of self-humbling, implementation of it will bring them true happiness.

EDITOR'S NOTE ON JOHN 13:1-17: IS FOOTWASHING AN ORDINANCE?

Did Jesus mean to establish an ordinance of footwashing here, or did He mean only to exhort His disciples to manifest the same spirit of humility and self-abasement they saw in Him? Most Christian groups resist the idea that Jesus meant for the practice to become a regular ordinance of the church. They are confident He meant His action as a dramatic illustration of a principle, and that practicing humble service in other ways more appropriate for our culture is adequate fulfillment of His exhortation.

The wording of v. 14, however, is both literal and emphatic (literally): "You are obligated to be washing one another's feet." ("You ought" is the Greek *opheilo*, to be bound, obligated, to owe as a debt.) Verse 15, following this immediately, must surely mean that the disciples should maintain His example in that very act. Jesus does not say, for example, that they should emulate His example of humility, but that if He washed their feet they must wash one another's feet, and that "as I did to you you also do."

One objection to making the practice an ordinance is that this was merely the customary act of the host in the culture of that day. It is true that a host would either wash the guests' feet or (much more likely) provide a servant to do it. But that courtesy came when the guests entered the house, not after the meal had already gotten under way (see the comments on v. 2). There is something special about this particular footwashing; Jesus used it at a time and in a way that was not part of the custom of the time.

Another objection is that the washing of one another's feet does not point to one of the major truths about the redemptive work of Christ. Baptism points to His death, burial, and resurrection (which is the reason for immersion). The Lord's Supper points to His atoning death, His broken body and shed blood. But (they argue) footwashing does not.

There are two answers for this. For one thing, it is "arguing in a circle." It amounts to choosing baptism and the Lord's Supper as the only two ordinances, then observing that both of them point to a major truth about Christ's

redemptive work, and then ruling out footwashing since it presumably does not meet that criterion. But if Jesus actually meant for it to be practiced regularly by the church, it should be recognized as such. There is no prior restraint on what of value an ordinance may teach.

The other point to be made is that, in fact, the footwashing may indeed point to Christ's great self-humbling as manifested in the entire period that the theologians call His humiliation, beginning with His incarnation and climaxing in His atoning death. One can hardly think of the passage here in John without recalling the great hymn of Philippians 2:5-11. Indeed, there are several parallels between the two passages that are suggestive; see that commentary on Philippians for further discussion.

Still another objection is that we have no record of the practice of the ordinance in the early church. Insofar as the N.T. is concerned, 1 Tim. 5:10 may, after all, be such a record. And there is ample evidence of the practice in some of the apostolic and church fathers.

Finally, some object that the lesson is more important than the act itself. Certainly the practice of footwashing is meaningless apart from a genuine spirit of self-humbling that will find many outlets of service in various, practical ways. That being true, the reality pointed to by the ordinance is obviously more important than the symbol. But that is true of *any* ordinance, and so is no argument at all.

As has been made clear in the comments on the passage, the footwashing represents Christ's own humiliation and the believer's commitment to follow His Lord's example in humbly serving others. It also represents the believer's continued need for confession of sin and cleansing; and that is, after all, a part of his humility.

Summary
(13:1-17)

Before relating the events of the Last Supper, John tells his readers of Jesus' strong and boundless love for His disciples. He loves them even though He is aware of the nearness of the cross, even though He knows that Judas is about to betray Him. At some point in connection with this last meal Jesus, being fully aware of His heavenly identity and origin, performs an act which embodies the very essence of humility: He washes the disciples' feet.

He arises from the table, lays aside His outer garment, girds Himself with a towel, pours water into a basin, and begins to wash the disciples' feet. Soon He comes to Peter who, realizing his complete inferiority to Christ, resists. Jesus explains that while Peter may not understand this action presently, it will become clear to him later. He tells him that it is essential for him to be washed. Peter, mistakenly supposing that the washing is essential to his salvation, wants to be washed all over. Jesus then explains that this is not necessary, that washing the feet will suffice. He calls attention to Judas' wicked condition by mentioning that not all of the group are clean.

After resuming His place at the table, Jesus explains the meaning of His action to the disciples. He calls attention to His own exalted station and says that if He, exalted as He is, can manifest the spirit of humility by this servant's action, then certainly these disciples ought to be able to do likewise. His actions are an example for them. Since they understand this principle, putting it into practice will bring them true happiness.

Application: Teaching and Preaching the Passage

The footwashing is an enacted para-

ble wherein Jesus illustrates His self-emptying and humbling to redeem fallen man. His act of washing the disciples' feet pictures and epitomizes His larger self-abasement. Only in the sense that this action pictures Christ's humbling of Himself on men's behalf, even to the point of dying for them on the cross (see Phil. 2:7,8), is it necessary to Peter's salvation.

The footwashing demonstrates the need for renewed cleansing after the initial and determinative cleansing of justification. The Christian needs to confess and be forgiven of his sins on a continuing basis even after he is regenerated.

The footwashing is an example in humility for the Christian. If his Lord and Master was not above even the most menial service to others, then, certainly, he should be willing to humble himself as well. Contrary to all expectation, in this attitude of self-abasement and humble service to others true happiness is to be found.

2. The Prediction of Judas' Betrayal (13:18-30)

18 I speak not of you all: I know whom I have chosen: but that the scripture may be fulfilled, He that eateth bread with me hath lifted up his heel against me.

Jesus now states that His promise of happiness is not applicable to all the disciples, that there is one among them to whom it can never apply in that he is a traitor. He has knowingly chosen each of His disciples, even the traitor, for His own purposes. In fact, the traitor has been chosen for the very reason that he is a traitor. His choosing and his impending treachery are all part of Christ's purpose and plan. It has happened, in fact, so that "the scripture may be fulfilled."

The Scripture which Jesus had in

mind is Ps. 41:9, which was spoken by David, apparently with Ahithophel in mind, but which Jesus obviously applied to Judas. It speaks of one "who eats bread with me" (further identified in the Psalm as "my own familiar friend in whom I trusted") having "lifted up his heel against me." The figure "lifted up his heel" seems to refer to the kick of a horse and conveys the idea of purposeful and severe injury. The meaning, then, is that a trusted companion treacherously, viciously, and without provocation directed what he supposed to be a lethal blow at Jesus.

19 Now I tell you before it come, that, when it is come to pass, ye may believe that I am *he*.

Jesus says that He is telling the disciples about this now, believing (Greek present subjunctive) in Him. Jesus does not want His betrayal by Judas to appear as though it takes Him by surprise. He does not want His disciples' belief in Him to be weakened by this event when it occurs. He does not want their belief in His Messiahship to be overwhelmed by apparent evidence that He has been caught off guard, that He was unprepared for what is about to transpire. He knows that their faith is to be sorely tested in the hours that lie ahead, and He wants to help them as much as possible.

20 Verily, verily, I say unto you, He that receiveth whomsoever I send receiveth me; and he that receiveth me receiveth him that sent me.

The connection between this verse and the preceding one is not immediately apparent. That there is such a connection is the key to its interpretation. Apparently Jesus is continuing to offer the disciples encouragement with the

impact of His approaching betrayal and death in mind. In effect He is saying, with the utmost solemnity (Greek *amen, amen*), "No matter what happens, do not forget that he who receives whomever I send receives me; and he who receives me receives my Father who sent me. Never forget that you are my representatives, the representatives of the Son of God who has come down to earth from Heaven. Never, therefore, allow yourselves to be intimidated by men."

21 When Jesus had thus said, he was troubled in spirit, and testified, and said, Verily, verily, I say unto you, that one of you shall betray me.

Jesus has hinted (vv. 10,18) that there is a serious problem among the Twelve, that one of them is not "clean," that one of them has "lifted up his heel" against Him. He has, undoubtedly, been trying to communicate discreetly with Judas, to arouse his conscience and his love, to turn him from his deadly course. Now, seeing that Judas is not going to be deterred from his wicked designs or salvaged for grace, He reluctantly and sorrowfully confronts the issue directly. He makes a formal statement ("testifies," Greek *martureo*), again using the formula of solemnity (Greek *amen, amen*), that one of those actually present, one of His own disciples, is going to betray Him.

22 Then the disciples looked one on another, doubting of whom he spake.

The disciples are dumbfounded. This comes to them as a bolt out of the blue. They have perceived that Jesus is unhappy and that He is, in some way, displeased with them (or with someone). But that He is actually to be betrayed and by one of them, they cannot fathom. What does He mean? Of whom does He speak? The Synoptics indicate that each suspects himself (e.g. Mk. 14:19). Obviously, they understand Jesus to refer to some unintentional act which has the effect of betraying Him. They cannot grasp that Jesus is speaking of deliberate betrayal.

23 Now there was leaning on Jesus' bosom one of his disciples, whom Jesus loved.

John, again at this point, provides his readers with one of those personal insights characteristic of his Gospel. (Inherent in the interpretation followed here is the assumption that "the disciple whom Jesus loved" is, indeed, John, the author of this Gospel. For the arguments for this identification see the Introduction.) He remembers vividly his own role in that which he is about to relate. He was "leaning on Jesus' bosom," i.e. reclining to Jesus' right (the place of honor), so that he could easily lean his head back against Jesus' chest (v.25). This clearly indicates a special relationship and closeness between John and Christ. (Apparently the Jews usually sat at table to eat, but reclined for special meals, including the Passover. They lay on their left sides, right hand free.)

24 Simon Peter therefore beckoned to him, that he should ask who it should be of whom he spake.
25 He then lying on Jesus' breast saith unto him, Lord, who is it?

Peter, always the inquisitive and precocious one, catches John's eye and by a gesture indicates that he should ask Jesus just which one of them is going to betray Him. He apparently supposes that the question is less likely to anger Jesus coming from John than from himself. He also may think that any rebuke produced by the question is better directed at John than him. At any rate, John guilelessly and directly asks Jesus, "Who is it, Lord?" There is something almost childlike in John, at least in his attitude toward Jesus. Perhaps this is the reason Jesus loves him so.

26 Jesus answered, He it is, to whom I shall give a sop, when I have dipped _it_. And when he had dipped the sop, he gave _it_ to Judas Iscariot, _the son_ of Simon.

Just as Peter expected, no rebuke is forthcoming. Jesus simply informs John (apparently so that he alone can hear) that the one who is to betray Him is the one to whom He will now give a sop. He then proceeds solemnly to dip a morsel of bread into the common bowl and to give it to Judas.

This was a clear indication to John that Judas was the traitor, as he would understand clearly in retrospect. It is not clear, however, that he fully understood it at the time. He may simply have been too shocked to comprehend it. At any rate, v. 28 seems to indicate that he did not convey the information to his fellow disciples. Jesus' gesture of giving the sop to Judas, apart from the special significance given to it by His remark to John, would be viewed as a mark of special honor for Judas. Perhaps it was, in fact, a last gesture of love, a final attempt to divert him from his evil purpose.

The view presented above need not conflict with the Synoptic account. Apparently Christ's remark in Mt. 26:23 and Mk. 14:20 should be understood as indefinite, simply informing the disciples that the traitor was one of their own number and not indicating Judas directly. Also Christ's positive response to Judas' question, "Is it I?" (Mt. 26:25), should be understood as spoken to Judas privately and not comprehended by the other disciples.

27 And after the sop Satan entered into him. Then said Jesus unto him, That thou doest, do quickly.

Upon his receiving the morsel of bread (perhaps it is also at this point that he asks Jesus if he is the traitor and receives an affirmative answer), a momentous change transpires within Judas. He consciously yields himself to Satan and is, henceforth, completely possessed by him. There is to be no turning back now.

Therefore (Greek, *oun*, i.e. because of His understanding that he is now completely under Satan's control), Jesus tells Judas to do quickly that which he is determined to do. This marks the end of Jesus' attempts to dissuade Judas from his evil course and His abandoning of him to Satan's power. It is a fearful and awesome moment.

28 Now no man at the table knew for what intent he spake this unto him.
29 For some *of them* thought, because Judas had the bag, that Jesus had said unto him, Buy *those things* that we have need of against the feast; or, that he should give something to the poor.

John informs his readers that "no one at the table" understood the true significance of Christ's words to Judas. Does he include himself in this oddly denominated group? One suspects that he does not, that, though his understanding was incomplete, he sensed that Christ's words to Judas were of great import, but that he held his peace for lack of certainty.

Apparently, it was this lack of complete certainty, along with the lack of

any overt action by Christ, which restrained John from openly expressing to the rest of the disciples that Judas was the traitor. At any rate, he relates that "some of them" thought that Jesus' words had to do with the fact that Judas, as "treasurer," might have some business matters to attend to on Christ's behalf. One cannot help but feel that John excludes himself from this misapprehension.

30 He then having received the sop went immediately out: and it was night.

Immediately upon receiving the sop from Jesus, Judas goes out finally and irrevocably from the Savior's presence. John remembers the circumstances. He remembers how sudden and drastic was Judas' act. He remembers the blackness of the night into which Judas went out from Christ for the last time. He clearly means to refer to more than the fact that it was dark outside when Judas left. He means to imply that, when Judas went out from "the light of the world," he went out into a darkness which no ray of light could ever penetrate. He went out into a darkness, a night, from which he would never return and in which he would remain forever.

Summary
(13:18-30)

Jesus states that the terrible fact that one of the disciples is a traitor does not take Him by surprise and does not mean that His purposes are in danger of being frustrated. He purposely has chosen all of His disciples, even the traitor, and his treachery is a part of that purpose. He warns them that the traitor is one of their own select number and explains that He is informing them of the fact beforehand so that his treachery, when it is revealed, will not destroy their faith but, rather, strengthen it. Jesus goes on to tell the disciples that, no matter what happens, they must not forget that they are the chosen ambassadors of the Son of God.

Seeing that His overtures to Judas have been completely rebuffed, Jesus must reluctantly confront the issue directly and say straight out that one of the disciples is the traitor. The disciples are shocked to learn that such could be true of one of their own intimate band. They naturally want to know the traitor's identity. Peter beckons to John to ask Jesus who it is. Jesus tells John that the traitor is the person to whom He will give a sop and then proceeds immediately to give such a sop to Judas. Upon receiving the sop, Judas consciously and finally yields himself to Satan who assumes complete control over him. When Jesus sees this, He gives up on salvaging Judas and tells him to go on and do what he intends to do. None of this is understood by the disciples (with the probable exception of John); they interpret Jesus' words as instructing Judas to take care of some business matters. As Judas goes out from the Savior's presence, he goes out into a night of darkness from which he will never return.

Application: Teaching and Preaching the Passage

The first person John focuses on in this passage is Jesus, who is "troubled in spirit." He is troubled for Himself because of His approaching passion. He is troubled for His disciples and the ordeal of sorrow which He knows is soon to challenge their faith. He is troubled for Judas whom He knows to be about to sell Him to the Jews and himself to the devil.

The second group John focuses on is the disciples who are perplexed and filled with self-doubt as Jesus tells them of the traitor in their midst. Each doubts himself. They all doubt each other. It saddens and confuses them to see their Master so troubled.

The last one John focuses on is Judas, who is possessed by Satan. He is filled with hatred and rebellion. He resists all Christ's overtures of love and forgiveness. He is determined upon a course of betrayal and self-destruction. He goes out from Jesus' presence forever. He goes out from the company of Christ and the apostles to the company of those who are plotting to kill Jesus. He goes out from being Christ's chosen and trusted servant to being Satan's slave. He goes out from "the light of the world" to the blackness of darkness forever. He goes out from everlasting blessedness to eternal doom.

B. The Farewell Discourses (13:31—17:26)

These farewell discourses should be understood as interpreting the final sign, Christ's glorification—His death and resurrection.

1. The New Commandment (13:31-38)

31 Therefore, when he was gone out, Jesus said, Now is the Son of man glorified, and God is glorified in him.

Judas' exit is a decisive event. His act of betrayal sets irrevocably in motion a course of events which will culminate in Christ's death and resurrection, so that Christ refers to His being "glorified" as if it were already accomplished (Greek *edoxasthe*, culminative aorist). Judas' exit also eliminates the cloud of suspicion and doubt which has been hanging over the group to this point. Now Jesus can relax and open up His heart. He is among friends.

His first words to them are words of encouragement to prepare them for the terrible events bearing down upon them. He reminds them again that His approaching death is not His defeat, not His destruction, but His glorification, His victory, His triumph. Not only so: it is also by His death that He will glorify God, His Father.

32 If God be glorified in him, God shall also glorify him in himself, and shall straightway glorify him.

This conditional sentence is assumed to be true (in Greek, a first class condition). It is not, therefore, in doubt whether God is glorified by Jesus' death. Such is the case: *since* Jesus' death will glorify the Father, the Father is also going to glorify Him in return. Furthermore, this glorification of Him by the Father is immediately imminent, which is the whole point. The glorification of Jesus by the Father is not some remote future prospect. It is to transpire right away, in the next few hours.

33 Little children, yet a little while I am with you. Ye shall seek me: and as I said unto the Jews, Whither I go, ye cannot come; so now I say to you.

Jesus has been emphasizing the extreme nearness of His departure. Now, tenderly referring to them as "little children" (Greek *teknion*) He informs the disciples that He is going to be with them only a short while longer. The close personal relationship which they have sustained to Him for these few years is about to be terminated. He is about to leave them and go to a place where they cannot follow. He reminds them that He has previously spoken these words to the Jews (7:33,34; 8:21) in their hearing, and they are as true now as when He first spoke them. Yet,

while they are the same words, they are spoken with a very different purpose. Whereas Jesus meant to rebuke and threaten the Jews, He means to comfort and encourage the disciples. He tells them tenderly that which He knows will bring them pain, but which He also knows to be in their long-term best interest (see e.g. 16:7a). This scene is not unlike that of a mother comforting and kissing her child as he is wheeled away for surgery.

34 A new commandment I give unto you, That ye love one another; as I have loved you, that ye also love one another.

In order to soften the blow of His leaving and to enable them the more easily to sustain the great loss, Jesus gives to His disciples His "New Commandment" (Greek *entole kainos*) that they love one another as He has loved them. He suggests that they become to each other what He has been to them all, that they render to each other that quality and degree of love which has previously come only from Him (see e.g. v. 1). "New" (Greek *kainos*) means not only "new," but also "previously unknown, remarkable, not previously present."

This commandment is new in at least two ways. It is new in its narrowed focus. While the disciples are to love all men, they are to love, in a special way, their brethren in Christ. It is especially important to Jesus that they do so. As He contemplates leaving them, His own great love for each of them sharpens His desire that they love one another on His behalf. He is as a father exhorting his (perhaps feuding) sons from his deathbed to forget their petty differences and, in deference to him and his love for each of them, love each other.

The command is new also in that it is motivated by a radical new model,

Christ's own love for them. The world has never seen a love like this before— such an utterly selfless and sacrificial love as Christ has manifested to men, especially these men. He has loved them to the end, to the fullest extremity, to the point of giving Himself as their dying substitute (13:1). The disciples do not fully comprehend His love at this point. Still, Jesus commands them, by way of anticipation, that when they do come to understand how radically He has loved them they will remember these words and pattern their love for one another after His own great love for them.

35 By this shall all *men* know that ye are my disciples, if ye have love one to another.

"It is precisely in your love for one another that men shall see my likeness in you," says Christ. Just as Christ's most outstanding characteristic has been His great love, so it is by manifesting love to one another that men may most definitively mark themselves as His disciples. The greatest witness to the reality of the salvation wrought by Christ is for Christians to live together in love. The world knows that this is not natural, that it must inhere in the fact that these people are Christ's disciples.

36 Simon Peter said unto him, Lord, whither goest thou? Jesus answered him, Whither I go, thou canst not follow me now; but thou shalt follow me afterwards.

Peter, apparently impervious to Christ's appeal to the disciples to love each other, returns to something Jesus has said which has puzzled him. He probably has not even heard the "New Commandment." He wants to know just where this place is, this place where Jesus is going and the disciples cannot follow. Jesus answers that they cannot

presently follow Him where He is going but that they will be able to follow Him in due course. He obviously refers to His approaching death and ultimate ascension to Heaven and means that, while they cannot follow Him immediately, the disciples will indeed follow Him by means of their own deaths.

37 Peter said unto him, Lord, why cannot I follow thee now? I will lay down my life for thy sake.

While slightly enigmatic, Christ's statement in v. 36 is, by no means, beyond understanding; yet Peter manages to miss the point entirely. He says, with his accustomed bravado, "Why cannot I go with You where You are going? There is not anywhere that I would not be willing to go with You. I will even die for You, if need be." Peter is wrong on two counts. He is not willing to die for Christ, as his actions will soon demonstrate; and it is not he who is to die for Christ but Christ who is to die for him. One may be certain that the irony of this statement is not lost upon John as he recounts it to his readers.

38 Jesus answered him, Wilt thou lay down thy life for my sake? Verily, verily, I say unto thee, The cock shall not crow, till thou hast denied me thrice.

Though He deeply loves Peter and is sensitive to his good intentions, Jesus cannot allow this patently false assertion to pass unchallenged. He remarks whimsically, "Will you really lay down your life for me, Peter? I think not. The fact of the matter is that, far from laying down your life for me, you will, before the cock crows tomorrow morning, have three times denied me." How many times Peter is, in retrospect, to rue his presumptuous impertinence one can only surmise.

Summary
(13:31-38)

Judas' exit eliminates the tension and suspicion that have characterized the evening thus far. Jesus is now able to speak encouragingly to the remaining disciples. He reminds them again that His approaching passion will be a triumph, not a tragedy. He assures them that His "glorification," His hour of victory, is very near. He informs them that He is going to be with them physically for only a short while longer and urges them, in light of this fact, to love each other on His behalf when He is gone. He assures them that, by doing so, they will give a clear-cut testimony to the world that they are, indeed, His disciples.

Peter's attention has been drawn to the fact that Jesus is going somewhere where he cannot follow. He wants to know where this place is. Jesus tells him that, though he cannot follow Him immediately, he will ultimately be able to do so. Peter asserts that there is nowhere that he will not follow Christ and that he is willing even to die for Him. Jesus answers this brash boast with the prediction that Peter will have denied Him three times before morning.

Application: Teaching and Preaching the Passage

In this brief section there are three basic emphases. The first and most basic of these is comfort (vv. 31-33). Jesus assures the disciples that the time of His glorification has arrived. He also prepares them to accept His absence.

The second emphasis is the commandment (vv. 34,35) to love each other with a love patterned after Christ's own and, thereby, to give witness to the fact that they are His disciples.

The third emphasis is a challenge to the presumption of Peter (vv. 36-38) who tries to impose his own agenda

upon Christ and grossly overestimates his own courage.

2. The Way, the Truth, and the Life (14:1-14)

1 Let not your heart be troubled: ye believe in God, believe also in me.

Jesus is fully aware of His disciples' state of mind. He knows how worried and perplexed they are. He understands that His statements about a traitor in their midst, His own departure, and Peter's prospective denial have upset and discouraged them. He knows, furthermore, that they will soon face challenges to their faith even more devastating than these. His words to them, therefore, convey not rebuke, but encouragement. He tells them to cease being troubled in their hearts.

Jesus does not, however, simply offer the empty platitude, "Cheer up." He urges their faith as a ground for hope even in this dark hour. The form of the word "believe" (Greek *pisteuete*, the same in both clauses) may be either indicative or imperative. All agree that the second is imperative, but there is disagreement as to the first. If the first "believe" is indicative, Christ is taking the disciples' faith in God for granted and, on the basis of that, urging them to believe in Him as well. If both are imperatives, Christ is urging the disciples to believe in God as well as in Him. The important emphasis, whichever way one takes the first "believe," is that the disciples should believe in Jesus. They must not lose confidence in Him. In spite of much that will tend to indicate otherwise, everything that He has told them is true. All of His promises to them will be fulfilled. He really is the Son of God and He really is able to give eternal life to all who trust in Him. Jesus exhorts His followers to trust Him no matter what

200

happens.

2 In my Father's house are many mansions: if *it were* not *so* , I would have told you. I go to prepare a place for you.

Jesus now moves to provide a basis for the faith and hope to which He has exhorted the disciples. First, He informs them that there are, in His Father's house, many individual dwelling places. (This is to be preferred over "mansions" as a translation of the Greek *mone*.) While these dwellings will undoubtedly be "mansions" in the fullest sense, this is not the literal significance of the word. Jesus says that if this were not so, He would have told them that it was not so. This rather complicated double negative can be better understood, "If this were not the truth, I would not have said it." Obviously, Jesus has not communicated falsehoods. The very fact that He has said something marks it as absolute truth. Jesus considers this argument to be absolutely conclusive so far as these men who have walked beside Him every day are concerned (see v. 9). His integrity is, for them, beyond all question. He does not ask them to "believe" Him on blind faith, but on the basis of His consistently demonstrated trustworthiness.

The disciples must not despair. The coming separation is not to be a permanent one. Far from it! The ultimate purpose of Christ's leaving is to make provision for them to join Him where He goes. While it is temporarily and partially true that where He goes they cannot follow (v. 36), it is not ultimately so. He must go on alone at this point, but His chief business in going is to make the necessary arrangements so that they may follow—to see to their lodgings, so to speak.

3 And if I go and prepare a place for you, I will come again, and re-ceive you unto myself; that where I am, *there* ye may be also.

The conditional form of Christ's reference to His going to prepare a place is not intended to call into question whether He shall go. Rather, it has a logical force only. Jesus is simply saying that it would be absurd to think that He would go and prepare a dwelling place for the disciples and then not actually take them to live in it. What would be the point in that? "You may depend upon it," Jesus says. "If I go and prepare you a dwelling place, I will come back and get you and take you to live in it." The disciples may be certain, then, that their separation from Christ is not to be permanent. He is going to go away and prepare a place for them and, someday, He is going to come back for them and take them to live with Him in that place which He is going to prepare.

Jesus' "coming again" clearly refers to His Second Coming. Only at the Second Coming will He receive His disciples to Himself so that they may be with Him where He is going to be (in Heaven). Attempts to equate this "coming again" with Christ's resurrection, the coming of the Holy Spirit, Christ's presence within the Church, or the Christian's going to be with Christ at death all fail on this count. Only the Second Coming itself meets the conditions specified by Christ.

4 And whither I go ye know, and the way ye know.

The best reading of this verse seems to be, "And where I go, ye know the way." The meaning is not affected since, whichever way one reads it, the emphasis is on the fact that the disciples know the way to where Jesus is going.

What does Jesus mean by telling the disciples that they know the way to the place where He is going? He apparently means to say that, although they do not realize it, they already know the way to where He is going, if they will just stop and think about it. He is urging them to reflect upon the matter, to put two and two together, to understand what He is telling them now in light of His previous teachings. They ought to be able to see the way to where He goes.

5 Thomas saith unto him, Lord, we know not whither thou goest; and how can we know the way?

Thomas seems to be Peter's only rival in both gall and insensitivity. With Peter temporarily silenced by Jesus' stinging rebuke (13:38), he must become the spokesman for obtuseness. Dutifully, therefore, he says, "Lord, we don't even know where You are going; how can we possibly know the way?"

6 Jesus saith unto him, I am the way, the truth, and the life: no man cometh unto the Father, but by me.

In response to Thomas' question, Jesus utters one of His best known and most beautiful sayings, the sixth of His seven "I am" sayings (see 6:35): "I am the way, the truth, and the life: no man cometh unto the Father, but by me." Jesus tells Thomas that He Himself, in His own person, is the way. This is very similar to Christ's saying in 10:9 that He is the "door" by whom men enter and are saved. Here, He is the way (Greek *hodos*, road, highway, path) by which men must journey if they wish to arrive at that place where He is going. The way to Heaven is not a plan, a principle, or a force, but a person. Men get to Heaven by means of a personal knowledge of and relationship with this person. Not only is Jesus the way; He is the only way. No man can come to God by any other. Only through Him may men approach God. All other ways of approaching God are useless. Only through Christ do men have the fellowship with the God of Heaven which they so desperately desire (Ps. 42:1).

Not only is Jesus the way, He is also the truth. He is the truth in that He is the "Word" (1:1 etc.), that which communicates the essential nature of God's being. What Jesus *says* is true, and He is truly what He claims to be. But He means more than that: He is the *embodiment* of truth. Truth inheres in Him. The very essence of reality derives from Him. To simply say, then, that Jesus is truthful and that what He says is accurate, though it is certainly correct, understates the case. Surely men can believe Him who is the very ground and essence of truth, truth personified.

Finally, Jesus is the life. This is not a new concept. There have been many references in this Gospel to Jesus as the One who can grant eternal life (1:4; 4:10,14; 6:51; 10:10; 11:25, which see for comments). Here Jesus draws upon all that has been said previously to emphasize to the disciples what Peter has already expressed (6:68), that Jesus is the only means by which they may attain eternal life.

7 If ye had known me, ye should have known my Father also: and from henceforth ye know him, and have seen him.

Jesus, as the truth, the Word, so completely communicates the essential nature of God's being, that to truly know Him is to know the Father as well. When Jesus says that, if the disciples had really known Him, they would have known the Father, He implies that they have not fully done either. Though He has lived among them on the most intimate terms, they have not really known Him. Jesus now uses something of the same logic as in v. 4. He says that, though they have not been aware of it, they have been learning about God. They have been learning about Him because they have been living with Him and watching Him day by day. They have been learning about God because they have been learning about Jesus, who is God. As 1:14 shows, this became perfectly clear to John in time.

8 Philip saith unto him, Lord, shew us the Father, and it sufficeth us.

It is now Philip's turn to reveal how completely he has missed Jesus' point. Jesus, of course, means that, since He, Himself, is God, to know Him is to know God. Philip wrongly supposes Him, however, to refer to an impending theophany in which the Father will physically manifest Himself to the disciples. He therefore says, in effect, "Why, that's a great idea. Show us the Father. Let Him materialize here before us. That will be more than sufficient. That should answer all our questions and alleviate all our doubts."

9 Jesus saith unto him, Have I been so long time with you, and yet hast thou not known me, Philip? he that hath seen me hath seen the Father; and how sayest thou *then*, Shew us the Father?

Christ's answer conveys, at once, sorrow, exasperation, rebuke and restraint. How can Philip have accompanied Jesus all through His earthly ministry and have failed to subjectively comprehend, as he obviously has, who Jesus really is? How can it be that he has not realized that he has been constantly in the company of the incarnate God? He has failed to comprehend the most basic and important reality of Christ's person.

Jesus now states more explicitly the truth of v. 7 by saying that anyone who

has seen Him has seen the Father. He has been trying all along to teach the truth that He and the Father are one (8:19; 10:30,38; 12:45)! To know Him is to know the Father as well. In light of all this, it is incomprehensible that Philip can so completely misconstrue Christ's words as to say, "Show us the Father."

10 Believest thou not that I am in the Father, and the Father in me? the words that I speak unto you I speak not of myself: but the Father that dwelleth in me, he doeth the works.

Jesus' next words are phrased so as to indicate the expectation of an affirmative answer. He says, "You do believe that I am in the Father and the Father is in me, do you not?" Jesus is certain that Philip actually does accept this proposition. He means to convey to Philip that to say this is to say that He shares an essential likeness and unity with the Father, which is logically equivalent to saying that to see Him is to see the Father. Even the Pharisees seem to have followed this logic (5:18; 10:33).

Jesus reminds Philip of His oft-repeated statement that His teachings do not originate with Him but with God (3:11; 3:34; 7:16; 8:26, 28; 12:44; 17:8). He also refers, rather obliquely, to the point which He will make more directly in the following verse, that His miraculous works are a clear indication of the truth of His words and of the Father's blessing and approval upon His teaching.

11 Believe me that I *am* in the Father, and the Father in me: or else believe me for the very works' sake.

Jesus now makes a personal appeal to Philip and the rest of the disciples. The imperative, "believe" (Greek *pisteuete*, as in v. 1), is plural and so commands all the disciples to believe Jesus and to take Him at His word. Jesus wants His disciples to focus upon the extended and intimate relationship which they have shared with Him. In that time have they not found Him to be one worthy of credence? Has He ever given them any reason to doubt Him? Is there any question at all as to His complete integrity? Is not the fact that He says a particular thing enough for them? Has He not earned their trust?

Jesus' next suggestion is that, if they cannot believe His testimony on the basis of His personal integrity, they should believe it on the basis of the empirical evidence. He does not mean to imply that the empirical evidence is superior to His own testimony; rather, He means simply that it is a second and confirmatory basis for belief. He has referred to the value of His miraculous works previously (e.g. 5:36; 10:25, 38 and v. 10).

12 Verily, verily, I say unto you, He that believeth on me, the works that I do shall he do also; and greater *works* than these shall he do; because I go unto my Father.

Again the formula of solemnity (Greek *amen, amen*) indicates that Jesus considers what He is about to say to be very important. He has just told Philip that His miracles, in and of themselves, are a sufficient basis for believing in Him. Now He promises the disciples that they are going to be able to do these very works themselves, even though He will be gone. In fact, they are going to be able to do greater works than He has done. By greater works Jesus apparently means that the spiritual work of salvation is greater than physical miracles. The miracles have as their purpose to lead men to salvation. The miracle of regeneration is the greatest of all. Christ's true emphasis on the

superiority of the miracle of salvation over all others is completely lost when one assumes Jesus merely to be saying that the disciples are going to perform more amazing miracles than He has.

Interestingly, the reason they are going to be able to do these greater works is that He is going to leave them and return to His Father. They are going to perform them not just in spite of the fact that Jesus is leaving them, but because of it. This seems to anticipate the teaching of 16:7 that Christ's going away is necessary for the Holy Spirit's coming.

13 And whatsoever ye shall ask in my name, that will I do, that the Father may be glorified in the Son.
14 If ye shall ask any thing in my name, I will do *it*.

These words are often misunderstood as an open-ended promise to answer any prayer accompanied by the formula, "This I ask in Jesus' name." Actually, there are some rather specific limitations placed on this promise. First, there is the limitation of the context. Jesus' words mean only what He intends them to mean. They refer only to what He is talking about. They must not be transformed into a universal maxim if that is not His intent as He speaks. It is clear in the context that Jesus is referring to the "greater works" of salvation in which the disciples are soon to be involved. The promise is given in connection with their accomplishing these "greater works." Jesus is saying that whatever needs the disciples may encounter as they carry out their task will be met, that whatever they ask for in connection with their grand mission will be given to them.

Second, there is the limitation that only those petitions made in Christ's name will be granted. To be in Christ's name, a prayer must be in accordance with what Christ is. His name represents His essential being and nature. One cannot ask something in Christ's name that is for his own selfish ends. Rather, a request made in Christ's name must be in accordance with God's purpose in sending Christ into the world. God's great purpose in sending Christ into the world (as, indeed, it has been for all His actions from all eternity) is His own glory. This is the most basic limitation: the request must have, as its ultimate goal, God's own glorification through His Son, Jesus.

It is interesting that Jesus promises to answer such prayers Himself, whereas it might have been expected that the Father would answer them. This seems to grow out of Christ's consciousness of a complete equality and identity with His Father as revealed in vv. 9-11 and elsewhere.

Summary
(14:1-14)

Realizing that His previous words have very much frightened His disciples, Jesus exhorts them to trust Him completely, no matter what may come. He assures them that His approaching separation from them will only be temporary and that He is going to make provision for them to join Him where He is going. He intends to return for them and take them to be with Himself. He adds that they already know the way where He is going even though they do not know that they know.

Thomas is quick to inform Jesus that he certainly does not know either where Jesus is going or the way to get there. Jesus responds by assuring Thomas that He Himself is the way, the only way to Heaven, where He is going. If the disciples really understood Him, they would realize that to know Him is to know the Father, that because they have known Him they have known the Father also.

Philip, supposing Jesus to refer to a theophany by the Father, says that to see the Father will certainly solve all their problems. Jesus must explain to Philip that, by knowing Him, they have been seeing the Father all along. He has revealed the Father to them in a way that a theophany could not match, let alone improve upon. Jesus reminds Philip that He shares an essential likeness and unity with the Father, as demonstrated by the many miracles which the Father enables Him to perform.

Jesus solemnly assures the disciples that they will, in the future, perform even greater miracles than He. By this He means to say that through the power of the Holy Spirit, they will bring about the greatest miracle of all—the salvation of lost souls. He promises them that whatever they ask for, in connection with their ministry of bringing the miracle of salvation to lost men, will be granted them.

Application: Teaching and Preaching the Passage

The theme of this section is reassurance and encouragement. Jesus gives the disciples three basic reasons they should cease being troubled in their spirits. First, He tells them that, although He is going away, He will return for them so that they may ultimately join Him where He is going (vv. 1-3). Second, He tells them that, though He is going away, He will still be the only means by which men may come to God and go to Heaven (vv. 4-11). Third, He tells them that, though He is going away, their ministries are not finished. In fact, the best is still ahead. They are going, by the Holy Spirit's power, to be part of the greatest miracle of all, bringing men to salvation (vv. 12-14).

3. "I Will Not Leave You Comfortless" (14:15-31)

Jesus has promised the disciples that they will do greater works than He (vv. 12-14); now He gives them the even more wonderful promise of the Comforter, the Holy Spirit.

15 If ye love me, keep my commandments.

There are three ways to take this brief verse. The first is to take the verb "keep" (Greek *tereo*) as an imperative. This makes the sentence read, as in the KJV, "If you love me, keep my commandments." The second is to take it as a future: "If you love me, you will keep my commandments." This seems to be the view of most commentators. The third way is to take it as a subjunctive and a continuation of the protasis or "if clause." This view would combine this verse with v. 16 and make it read, "If you love me and keep my commandments, I will also pray to the Father...."

While I believe the third view to be the correct one, the essential teaching is the same whichever view one adopts. Jesus clearly relates real love for Him to obedience to His commands. Love is not mere sentiment and emotion. It is commitment; it demands to be expressed in real, tangible ways. Jesus' own love for men involves His dying in their stead. By the same token, the disciples' love for Him involves obedience to His commands. Love is not just the way one feels; it is also the way one acts.

16 And I will pray the Father, and he shall give you another Comforter, that he may abide with you for ever.

Jesus tells the disciples that He is going to make a special request of His Father on behalf of those who demonstrate their love for Him by keeping His commands. He is going to request that the Father give to such another "Comforter" (Greek *parakletos*, paraclete, advocate, comforter; literally, one who is called alongside to speak for another, like a defense attorney, or to encourage). That this is to be "another" (Greek *allos*, another of essentially the same kind) Comforter indicates that Jesus, Himself, has been their Comforter to this point. Now that He is leaving them, this function will be assumed by the Holy Spirit. While Jesus has been their Comforter for only a short time, however, the Holy Spirit will remain with them forever. In fact, it is "in order that" (Greek *hina*) this Comforter may be with them forever (in contrast to Christ's temporary earthly ministry) that Jesus makes this request on the disciples' behalf. Indeed, this is even a part of His reason for going away in the first place (see v. 12; 16:7).

17 *Even* the Spirit of truth; whom the world cannot receive, because it seeth him not, neither knoweth him: but ye know him; for he dwelleth with you, and shall be in you.

Jesus describes this coming Comforter as the Spirit of truth. By this He means not only that the Holy Spirit is the very embodiment of truth (as is Christ Himself, see comments on v. 6), but that His special function will be to lead believers into a comprehension of the truth, especially the truth that is bound up in Christ.

The unregenerate world cannot receive or benefit from the ministry of this coming Comforter, for they have no spiritual vision or understanding by which to perceive or apprehend Him. Just as the Jews in 5:37, 38 were insensitive to the subjective voice of the Father, so the world will be insensitive to the Holy Spirit. On the other hand, the disciples will be able to see (i.e. know) Him because He will dwell among them, even within them.

The words "see" and "dwell," while present in form, are future in meaning. The evidence is divided as to whether "shall be" is present or future, but this really does not matter since Jesus' whole reference is to the future. He does not mean to contrast the Holy Spirit's *present* relationship to the disciples with what it will be in the *future* (after Pentecost). Indeed, He is simply referring to the Spirit's future role in the hearts of believers (see Brown, Plummer, Hendriksen).

18 I will not leave you comfortless: I will come to you.

John does not, in his Gospel, clearly differentiate between the various aspects of Jesus' "coming back again" (see Bruce). There are at least three aspects to the fulfilment of His promise to do so: Christ's post-resurrection appearances, His coming in the person of the Holy Spirit at Pentecost, and His Second Coming at the end of this age. John presents Jesus as including all of these aspects in His generalized reference to the fact that, rather than leaving His children (see e.g. 13:33) alone as "orphans" (Greek *orphanos*, rather colorlessly translated "comfortless" in the KJV), He is going to "come to them."

19 Yet a little while, and the world seeth me no more; but ye see me: because I live, ye shall live also.

Jesus reiterates a previous statement (7:33; 12:35; 13:33) that He has only a little while to remain among men before He leaves them. After He "goes away," the world in general will see Him no more. The disciples, however, will continue to see Him even after He is taken away. They will see Him again during His resurrection appearances to them (16:16,18-22), but they will also see Him by the eye of faith as He is revealed to them by the Holy Spirit. In fact, the Holy Spirit will grant to them a perception of His nature and significance which will be far superior to that which they have had heretofore (see e.g. v. 26 and 16:13-15).

That Jesus' previous words refer, at least in part, to His resurrection is obvious from His next statement. Because Jesus lives (i.e. is constantly and immutably alive; the present tense emphasizes ongoing action), the disciples also will live. Jesus' indestructible, never-ending life is the source of their life. They will have eternal life because He is eternally alive, as His resurrection will reveal (see e.g. 1:4; 5:26; 11:25; 14:6; Rev. 1:18).

20 At that day ye shall know that I *am* in my Father, and ye in me, and I in you.

Jesus' phrase "At that day" (Greek *en ekeine te hemera*) seems to refer to the same time which He has indicated by the phrase "a little while" in v. 19. It is interesting to note that the only other time this same phrase occurs in this Gospel (16:23,26), the context clearly relates it to Christ's resurrection. One must remember, however, that John presents Jesus as combining all the aspects of His "coming back again" into one concept (see comments v. 18). Jesus, therefore, is making a general reference to the time after the resurrection when the Holy Spirit will be working within Christians to lead them into all truth (see comment v. 19).

Jesus says that "at that day" they will come to understand a principle that He has been trying to explain to them for a long time, His absolute unity of essence and person with the Father. He has indicated (v. 10) that they should have already come to understand this truth which He has taken such pains to explain (8:19; 10:30,38; 12:45). Now He says that "at that day," they are finally going to comprehend it. But not only will they come to understand this truth which has puzzled them for so long, they will also come to understand the analogous truth of the relationship that exists between themselves and Christ.

Christ does not say that the Christian's unity with Him is *precisely* like that between Him and the Father. Rather, He implies that they are similar and that a true understanding of His unity with the Father will enable Christians to comprehend their own unity with Christ. There is between the Father and Christ an absolute unity of essence while there is between Christ and the believer an ethical and spiritual unity. The difficulty of precisely defining the unity between Christ and the believer is apparent in the fact that it has been traditionally referred to as "mystical." This union is apparently facilitated through the person and work of the Holy Spirit (v. 17).

21 He that hath my commandments, and keepeth them, he it is that loveth me: and he that loveth me shall be loved of my Father, and I will love him, and will manifest myself to him.

Jesus now restates the principle of v. 15 (see comments) that real love for Him involves obedience to His commands. This is a formal and universally applicable maxim: "The one who has and keeps my commandments, he it is who truly loves me." To "have" (Greek *echo*) Christ's commandments means to make them one's own, to understand them and to accept them. To "keep" (Greek *tereo*) them means to implement them in one's daily life. This is, of course, far more difficult. It is one thing to be aware of and to acquiesce in righteousness; it is quite another to incorporate it into one's own actions.

Obedience to His commandments is not only an indicator of one's true love for Christ, it also pleases the Father and provokes a reciprocal love on His part. Both the Father and Jesus Himself react in love to such loving obedience. This is not to suggest that God loves men because they first loved Him, but simply that He is pleased by and responds positively to loving obedience on the part of believers. God's love both provokes and reacts with pleasure to man's love for Him.

One aspect of God's reaction to those who manifest their love by obedience is that Christ will "manifest" (Greek *emphanizo*) Himself to them. This word means both to reveal or make visible and to explain or make clear. John may have both meanings in mind. Jesus will be made visible to the disciples once again by the resurrection. He will be more completely understood and appreciated as the Holy Spirit comes to indwell and instruct them (see comments v. 19).

22 Judas saith unto him, not Iscariot, Lord, how is it that thou wilt manifest thyself unto us, and not unto the world?

The following is an instance of what Westcott somewhere calls John's "habitual particularity" in the use of names. One of the disciples, Judas the son of James (Lk. 6:16; Acts 1:13; perhaps also called Thaddeus: Mt. 10:3; Mk. 3:18), who is carefully differentiated from Judas Iscariot, interrupts Jesus (the fourth such interruption, 13:37; 14:5,8) to ask what He means by saying that He is going to reveal Himself to the disciples but not to the world at large. He may simply wish clarification; more likely, the spirit of his question is essentially that of Christ's own brothers in 7:3,4. He supposes that Christ refers to a manifestation of Himself as the Messiah and he cannot imagine why Christ would want to keep that manifestation secret. If so, Judas' interruption is no more perceptive than those of Peter, Thomas, and Philip.

23 Jesus answered and said unto him, If a man love me, he will keep my words: and my Father will love him, and we will come unto him, and make our abode with him.

Jesus answers Judas by summarizing or paraphrasing what He has already said. If a man loves Jesus, he will obey Him (vv. 15,21). Such a one will be loved by the Father (v. 21) and both the Father and the Son will come and make their abode with him (vv. 18, 20, 21). Jesus is obviously speaking of His coming in the person of the Holy Spirit at Pentecost rather than of His post-resurrection appearances or His Second Coming. What He means to say is that, through the agency of the Holy Spirit, both the Father and the Son manifest themselves to the hearts of true believers in a way that enables them to perceive spiritual reality far more effectively than was ever possible previously (see comments on v. 17).

24 He that loveth me not keepeth not my sayings: and the word which ye hear is not mine, but the Father's which sent me.

On the other hand, those who do not love Christ will not keep His sayings, will not be especially loved of the Father, and will not have the Father and the Son make their abode with them. In other words, they will not have the Holy Spirit indwelling them and giving them special insight into spiritual reality. Christ will not "manifest Himself" unto them. Jesus adds that, just as He has said before (7:16, which see for comments), His sayings do not originate with Himself, but come directly from the Father who has sent Him into the world.

25 These things have I spoken unto you, being *yet* present with you.
26 But the Comforter, *which is* the Holy Ghost, whom the Father will send in my name, he shall teach you all things, and bring all things to your remembrance, whatsoever I have said unto you.

Jesus now summarizes all that He has been saying in this section. Referring to the many things which He has taught them while He has been present with them in the flesh, He tells the disciples that the Comforter not only is going to remind them of these things, but also will go on to teach them all things necessary to their understanding and happiness. The Comforter will recall to their minds Jesus' teachings; He will enable them to understand them truly and completely; and He will develop and expand them into new and more wonderful truths (see 16:13-15).

Jesus has referred to the coming Comforter as the Spirit of Truth (v. 17); now He designates Him "the Holy Spirit." Holiness is the predominant characteristic of this third person of the Trinity. Not only is He absolutely holy in His own being, but His primary function is the work of making men holy. This is the work we call sanctification.

In v. 16 Jesus has said that the Comforter is going to be provided to the disciples by the Father on the basis of His (Jesus') prayer that He should do so. Now He says that the Father is going to send the Comforter in His (Christ's) name. These statements are essentially identical and imply a joint action involving both Father and Son (see also 15:26).

27 Peace I leave with you, my peace I give unto you: not as the world giveth, give I unto you. Let not your heart be troubled, neither let it be afraid.

The normal Hebrew word for both greeting and farewell is "Peace" (*shalom*). Jesus expands on this normal farewell to describe His own legacy to the disciples He is about to leave behind. He leaves them peace (Greek *eirene*), not the mere absence of hostility which the world knows, but His own special peace which comes from right relation with and confident reliance upon the Father. Jesus, Himself, has experienced this peace as a result of His unity and identity with the Father. He grants it to His disciples on the basis of the promised ministration of the Holy Spirit. There is no need, therefore, for them to be agitated and afraid (Greek *deiliao*, to be afraid in a timid or cowardly sense). Christ's peace will sustain them in His absence.

28 Ye have heard how I said unto you, I go away, and come *again* unto you. If ye loved me, ye would rejoice, because I said, I go unto the Father: for my Father is greater than I.

Having warned the disciples not to be cowardly, Jesus now exhorts them not to be selfish. His words "if you loved me" should be understood as a figure of speech (either a hyperbole or a comparative negative). He does not question their love for Him. Rather, He wants them to allow this love for Him to focus their thoughts on His departure. His return to Heaven is a wonderful blessing so far as He is concerned. He will once again enjoy the glory that was His before He came to earth (see 17:5). Jesus does not expect them to completely forget their own loss at His leaving. He simply wishes them to allow thoughts of His happiness at returning to Heaven to temper their sorrow at losing Him. Christ's comment that the Father is greater than He does not imply an inherent inferiority of the Second Person of the Trinity to the First. Rather, it refers to the temporary and economic subordination of Christ to the Father during His ministry upon the earth (see Phil. 2:5-8; Heb. 2:7).

29 And now I have told you before it come to pass, that, when it is come to pass, ye might believe.

Jesus again expresses the thought of 13:19 (which see for comments) that He is predicting things beforehand so that their fulfillment will be an aid to the disciples' faith. This time, however, He relates the principle to the whole process by which He will return to Heaven rather than to Judas' betrayal.

30 Hereafter I will not talk much with you: for the prince of this world cometh, and hath nothing in me.

Some suppose that Jesus' statement that He is no longer going to discuss such matters with the disciples must indicate the end of His discourse and that chapters 15 and 16 should actually come before chapter 13 (see Bernard xx-xxii, 556). This need not be the case. The discourse is characterized from beginning to end with the sense of Christ's eminent departure and the cessation of His personal association with the disciples (e.g. 13:1,33; 14:19,28). This statement expresses the general sentiment of the entire discourse, on through ch. 17, and need not be woodenly interpreted as indicating that Jesus is terminating the discourse at this point.

The prince of this world is, of course, Satan (see comments 12:31). Jesus is very much aware of the activities which Judas and the Jewish authorities, even at this moment, are engaged in, but He sees past them to their master, Satan. He knows Himself to be matched against the great Adversary himself. He knows that He is battling Satan for control of the world and for the souls of men.

Christ's comment that Satan "has nothing in me" should be understood as meaning that Satan has no hold upon Jesus. Satan's hold upon men is sin; therefore, he has no hold at all upon Jesus, The Sinless One.

31 But that the world may know that I love the Father; and as the Father gave me commandment, even so I do. Arise, let us go hence.

Jesus has said that the way the disciples may prove that they truly love Him is by obedience to His commands. Now He says that He is about to prove His own love for the Father in the same manner. He is going to obey His Father's commandment that He give His own life for His sheep (see 10:18).

Christ's last words, "Arise, let us go hence," may be interpreted in at least three ways. Some interpret them to indicate the end of the discourse and have therefore placed chapters 15 and 16 prior to chapter 13 (see comments on v. 30). Another interpretation is that at this point Jesus and the disciples get up and start toward Gethsemane, the rest of the discourse taking place as they walk. Finally, some (e.g. Morris) believe that Jesus' words should be understood in a rather symbolic sense as if He said, "There now, since we all see our duty, let us be up and at it." Perhaps, in keeping with his penchant for double meanings, John intends his readers to understand that both of the latter two ideas are legitimate.

Summary
(14:15-31)

Jesus informs the disciples that, as they manifest their love for Him by obeying His commands, they will be given a Comforter (the Holy Spirit) to console them and to compensate for His leaving them. This Comforter, who is called the Spirit of truth, will remain with them always. While the world will be oblivious to Him because of its spiritual insensitivity, the disciples will have intimate fellowship with Him as He indwells them.

Jesus is not going to leave the disciples as orphans in the world. He is going to manifest Himself to them in the person of the Holy Spirit. Though He has only a short time left to be with them physically, Jesus assures the disciples that He is not going to abandon them altogether and that, because He is eternally alive, they will have eternal life as well. In fact, when the Comforter comes they will come to understand the true relationship between Christ and the Father and between themselves and Christ. Jesus again emphasizes that to truly love Him is to obey Him. He assures the disciples that one who so demonstrates such obedient love will be loved by both the Father and Himself and that He will manifest Himself to him.

Judas (not Iscariot) asks Jesus to explain what He means by saying that He is going to reveal Himself to the disciples but not to the world. Jesus answers that, through the agency of the Holy Spirit, He and the Father are going to manifest themselves to those who lovingly obey Christ. By the same token, those who do not demonstrate this loving obedience will not experience this spiritual manifestation.

Jesus explains that the Holy Spirit is going to build upon and expand all that He has been teaching them while He has been with them. He assures them that, through the agency of the Holy Spirit, they are going to enjoy the same inner peace which has been so characteristic of His own life among them. Therefore, there is no need for them to be unduly fearful. He tells them that His going away is really cause for rejoicing when viewed from His own perspective, since it means that He will be returning to Heaven and the fellowship of the Father.

Jesus explains again that He is telling them these things ahead of time so that their faith will be strengthened when they actually happen as He has predicted. He indicates that the time of His speaking to them of these things is almost over and that Satan is about to begin his attack. Just as the disciples reveal their love for Him by obedience, so He will reveal His love for the Father by following through with the Father's will for Him—the crucifixion.

Application: Teaching and Preaching the Passage

This passage contains two parallel and interwoven themes. The first of these is that real love involves obedience. Love is not simply sentiment and words. Love is obedient action. Jesus says that such obedient love is characteristic of a true disciple (vv. 15, 21, and 23). Even His own love for the Father is to be proved by His obedience to the Father's will (v. 31). Such love will be recognized and reciprocated by both the Father and the Son (vv. 21,23).

The second theme is the coming of the Comforter. Jesus says that the disciples are not to be left as orphans in the world after He leaves them, but that a Comforter, the Holy Spirit, is going to abide with them continually (vv. 16,18). This Comforter will actually indwell them (v. 17). He will teach them all truth (vv. 17, 26), recalling and expanding upon all that Christ has taught them. He will grant them the same inner peace

which Christ Himself experienced while He walked among men (v. 27). Finally, He will give them the glorious hope that, because Christ is eternally alive, they will have eternal life as well (v. 19).

4. The Vine and the Branches (15:1-11)

1 I am the true vine, and my Father is the husbandman.

In the last of His seven "I am" statements (see 6:35), Jesus says that He is the true vine. With these words He introduces an allegory to explain the relationship which will exist between Himself and His disciples after His return to Heaven.

The vine is used in the O.T. as a symbol of Israel (Ps. 80:8-16; Is. 5:1-7; Jer. 2:21; Ezek. 15:2; 19:10; Hos. 10:1). Maccabean coins used the image of a vine to represent Israel. Israel was intended to be God's own vine, His own special possession, but proved itself unworthy of that honor. Now Jesus is saying that He is actually the genuine (see 1:9 for comments on "true") vine, the true Israel, the personal embodiment of the purposes of God.

This is so because God's whole purpose for Israel was for it to be the channel through which Messiah would come into the world. Israel had no identity or significance of its own apart from Messiah. It is also true in that Israel failed to achieve God's purposes for her, purposes which Jesus Himself would accomplish. In the truest sense, Jesus is Israel.

In keeping with the same O.T. figure, the Father is the husbandman (Greek *georgos*; literally, "farmer," from which the common name George). The process by which men are united to Christ and redeemed from their sins is initiated and superintended by the Father.

It should be noted that Jesus identifies Himself as the vine, i.e. the whole plant, including the branches, not just as the trunk to which the branches are attached. The branches are actually part of the vine, i.e. Christians are actually a part of Christ.

2 Every branch in me that beareth not fruit he taketh away: and every *branch* that beareth fruit, he purgeth it, that it may bring forth more fruit.

Continuing His allegory of the vine, Jesus refers to two separate actions that may be taken in reference to the branches of a vine. In the early spring, the apparently dead and fruitless branches are pruned away. Later, during the growing season, all the tiny new shoots are pinched off so that all of the nourishment may go to the main branches which bear the fruit. The first pruning is a very severe act which involves the removal and complete destruction of branches involved. The second is much less so since only the tiny shoots are pruned away so that the branch itself may not only be preserved, but actually be enabled to achieve its highest potential. (John uses the Greek word *airo* to refer to the first, more drastic pruning and *kathairo* to refer to the second, milder action. There is clearly a play on the two very similar Greek words. The second word, while it can be used of pruning, more often means, simply, to cleanse.)

The second pruning (cleansing) apparently refers to a chastening process by which Christians are stimulated and equipped to produce the fruits of righteousness in their lives. As to the first, there is disagreement. Most commentators seem to tie their interpretation of the first, radical pruning to their viewpoint on the security of the believer. Those who believe in unconditional eternal security interpret it as meaning that those indicated are "in Christ" in some sense other than true saving faith and that their being removed from Him does not indicate a loss of faith by a true Christian. Morris says that the action of a branch's being taken away is but a parabolic detail with no spiritual significance at all. Those who believe in the possibility of apostasy, on the other hand, may see this cutting off as a final loss of salvation by truly regenerate individuals.

Admittedly, this text is difficult, but it seems that a proper exegesis must accept that Jesus uses the term "branches" of the disciples (v. 5); that the disciples are, in fact, true believers; and that His warning, while expressed in broad terms, is directed at them. At the same time, one must admit that Jesus very likely had Judas in mind as He spoke. Apparently, Judas was never truly regenerate (see 6:70).

3 Now ye are clean through the word which I have spoken unto you.

Jesus hastens to assure the disciples that they are in the second category, i.e. those who are being "cleansed" so that they may bring forth more fruit. In fact, His very words to them, though they have seemed hard at times, have been the means by which they have been pruned and cleansed.

4 Abide in me, and I in you. As the branch cannot bear fruit of itself, except it abide in the vine; no more can ye, except ye abide in me.

Although Jesus has assured the disciples that they are among those who are being "cleansed" so that they may bring forth more fruit, He warns them against presumption. He commands them to abide in Him as He abides in them. This is not a conditional promise to remain in them if they remain in Him but a simple command. They can remain in Christ only as He remains in them, enabling them to do so, yet they are responsible to do so and are here commanded to do so. They may simply take for granted Christ's remaining in them as they endeavor to remain in Him. Just as a branch cannot bear fruit unless it is attached to the trunk of the vine from which it receives the life-giving sap, so the Christian cannot bear fruit except as He is attached to and indwelled by Christ (see e.g. Phil. 2:13).

5 I am the vine, ye are the branches: He that abideth in me, and I in him, the same bringeth forth much fruit: for without me ye can do nothing.

Jesus now repeats His statement that He is the vine and adds what is clearly a summary of vv. 2-4, that the disciples are the branches. His purpose seems to be to emphasize that, while there is a definite unity between Himself and His disciples, there is a definite distinction also. He is the vine; they are but branches. They derive their identity and function only from Him. He is utterly and eternally self-sufficient. They are completely and forever dependent upon Him. Without and apart from Him, they are nonentities, but as they abide in Him, they will be very productive.

6 If a man abide not in me, he is cast forth as a branch, and is withered; and men gather them, and cast _them_ into the fire, and they are burned.

Jesus says that there are extremely negative consequences for the disciple who does not remain united with Him. He says that such a disciple will be like an unfruitful branch that is cut off of the vine. He will be cast forth (apparently, out of the vineyard); he will wither (and die); he will be gathered up, along with others such as himself, cast into the fire, and burned. This is undeniably very strong language. It almost certainly refers to eternal destruction in the lake of fire.

Those who reject the idea that a true disciple could ever be lost explain this passage in one of two ways. Some of them say that to be one of the branches and to be "in Christ" does not necessarily mean to be a truly regenerate person and that Christ has in mind, as He speaks these words, those who have had some connection with Him short of actual saving faith (see e.g. Hendriksen). Others suppose that the branches are disciples in the fullest sense, but they believe that the casting into the fire, etc., is but a part of the symbolic picture of what happens to a branch, that the fate of those disciples is much less drastic than "being cast into the fire" might seem to indicate, and that it involves temporal punishments rather than eternal reprobation (see e.g. Morris).

It seems to me that neither of these positions is tenable. The branches are apparently disciples in the fullest sense, and the fate implied for those who do not remain in Christ seems clearly to be final damnation. If one is to harmonize this passage with the position that no truly regenerate person will ever be finally lost, he would be best advised to follow a line of logic suggested by Hendriksen (but, in my opinion, not consistently applied) that these statements of Jesus view the matter of perseverance from man's perspective. He observes that "God does not keep a man on the way of salvation without exertion, diligence, and watchfulness on (the) man's part" (II:299); and that such warnings as this are the means by which He preserves him. This method has the advantage that it respects the integrity of the present passage and does not impose upon it an unnatural interpretation derived entirely from an *a priori* doctrinal commitment.

EDITOR'S NOTE ON JOHN 15:2,6: DOES JESUS REFER TO APOSTASY?

Commentators have long debated whether vv. 2,6 refer to the possibility of apostasy: "Every branch in me that beareth not fruit he taketh away"; "If a man abide not in me, he is cast forth as a branch, and is withered; and men gather them, and cast them into the fire, and they are burned." On the one hand, we are always best advised to be cautious about building theology on parabolic representations, like that of a vine and its branches. And there is no doubt that Jesus' *main* point, here, is not about apostasy but about fruit bearing. Still, the words are pointed and must be dealt with, even though with caution.

Those who believe that the security of the believer is unconditional usually take one or the other of two approaches (if they speak to the issue at all). Some, following the lead of Calvin, understand the passage to refer to those who are merely supposed to be disciples but are not really, those only outwardly related to Christ, hypocrites. Others suggest that being "taken away" or "cast out" does not mean loss of salvation but loss of usefulness. Pastor Stallings has correctly shown the inadequacy of both approaches. Indeed, Calvinist interpreters show this inadequacy, with those on each side showing how impossible the other approach is.

Consequently, pastor Stallings has indicated that a Calvinist will be better advised to regard the passage as a hypothetical warning to true believers against real apostasy. Careful expositors in the Reformed tradition have always taught that perseverance lies *in* the use of the means God has provided, and not *outside* them, and that such warnings as are found now and again in the Bible are a part of the means God has provided to ensure that the truly regenerate will persevere.

The weakness of this view is that, after all, the warnings are hypothetical. Either it really is possible for a true believer to commit apostasy or it is not; and the subtle distinction between God's perspective and man's perspective does not change this. We cannot afford to suggest that God wants us to perceive something in a way that is different from the way He perceives it. And the Calvinist view, finally, is that the perseverance of the believer is not only certain but *necessary*.

As Lenski observes, it is probably best to regard v. 6 as expounding v. 2. (And for that reason, the effort to retranslate "taketh away" by "lifteth up"—see Pink, for example—is not convincing.) That way, the one not bearing fruit (v. 2) is, in fact, the one not remaining/abiding in Christ (v. 6). And this is, clearly, a branch that is in life-giving union with Christ (v. 2). Furthermore, the removal of the branch (v. 2) involves being cast out (v. 6) to shrivel up and await the fire.

One should also note the parallelism of vv. 6,7. Following the affirmation of v. 5—"I am the vine, you are the branches"—Jesus introduces two grammatically equal possibilities: not abiding in Him (v. 6) and abiding in Him (v. 7). The two possibilities are presented by the same grammatical construction (Greek *ean* with the subjunctive, to introduce true conditions, conditions that are at least reasonable possibilities).

The truth of the position that apostasy is possible does not depend, of course, on finding every single passage that may teach the doctrine. If apostasy is taught here, it is a secondary rather than a primary point of the passage.

Even so, one finds it difficult to resist Lenski's conclusions, that "Some will, indeed, fail to remain in Jesus," and that vv. 2,6 refer to "disciples whose hearts have lost the faith and love that once dwelt in them and joined them to Christ."

7 If ye abide in me, and my words abide in you, ye shall ask what ye will, and it shall be done unto you.

Having warned of the dangers of failing to do so, Jesus now begins to explain some of the positive benefits of continuing to abide in Him. He says that as the disciples abide in Him and He (by means of His words) abides in them, they will have their prayers answered. This promise seems to combine two previous ideas: the teaching of 14:23 that Christ will manifest Himself to (abide with) those who love Him and keep His sayings, and the teaching of 14:14 that if anyone asks anything in Christ's name He will do it. Now Christ draws the two together—abiding in Him and allowing His words to abide within—and makes them the dual condition for having prayers answered. Obedience to Christ's words is the secret of abiding in Him, and abiding in Him is the secret of having one's prayers answered. Therefore, if a man both abides in Christ and manifests that he does so by obeying His words (as he meditates and reflects upon them), there can be no doubt that his prayers will be answered.

8 Herein is my Father glorified, that ye bear much fruit; so shall ye be my disciples.

The interpretation of this verse depends upon the meaning of "herein" (Greek *en touto*, literally, "in this"). It is usually thought to refer by anticipation to what follows, the meaning being, then, that it is in the disciples' bearing much fruit that the Father is glorified. The problem with this interpretation is that it leaves no real connection between this verse and the preceding one. A better explanation seems to be that "herein" looks back upon what has been said in v. 7 and then anticipates what follows in the present verse. The meaning is as follows, "The Father is glorified as, abiding in me and allowing my words to energize and control you, you find your prayers being gloriously answered. In fact, it is just this attitude, just this process, that will enable you to bear much fruit and to be my disciples indeed."

9 As the Father hath loved me, so have I loved you: continue ye in my love.
10 If ye keep my commandments, ye shall abide in my love; even as I have kept my Father's commandments, and abide in his love.

Jesus has been exhorting His disciples to abide in Him. He has told them that they must abide in Him if they are to avoid purging (vv. 2,6), bear fruit (vv. 4,5), have their prayers answered (v. 7), and glorify the Father (v. 8). Now He tells them that another reason for abiding in Him is that they may share His own wonderful experience of love. This includes His own experience of the Father's love for Him; His love for the disciples which is, in turn, patterned after the Father's love for Him; His love for the Father which has been manifested in His obedience to the Father's commands; and, finally, the disciples' love for Christ which manifests itself in their obeying His commands to them. Christ does not want this wonderful circle of love to be broken. He wants it to remain in effect. He wants the disciples to continue to experience it. Yet He reminds them that the real essence and evidence of love is obedience.

11 These things have I spoken unto you, that my joy might remain in you, and *that* your joy might be full.

Why is Jesus telling them all of this? It is because He wants them to have joy (to be happy). Even though He must leave them, He wants His joy to remain with them. The indestructible nature of this joy is apparent in that, even in the very shadow of the cross, His experience of it is so real that He wishes to share it with those whom He loves supremely. This joy transcends circumstance, is absolutely indestructible, and derives from God alone. For it Jesus is willing to endure all the horror and shame of the cross (see Heb. 12:2). Jesus has said much about "remaining," but there is one particular thing that He hopes will remain with His disciples when He is gone, His joy. Jesus wants them to abide in Him, His commandments, and His love, so that they may abide in His joy.

Summary
(15:1-11)

In the last of His seven "I am" statements, Jesus refers to Himself as the true vine. By use of this metaphor He means to reveal Himself as the only source of spiritual life and strength. He says that those "branches" which are part of Him but do not produce any fruit are cut off the vine, while those that do produce fruit are pruned so that they will produce even more. He assures the disciples that they are among those who are producing fruit and are being pruned.

Jesus exhorts the disciples to "abide in" Him. Just as a branch must remain attached to the vine if it is to bear fruit, so must the disciple remain attached to Christ. Apart from Christ, the disciple can do nothing. Jesus warns that what happens to severed branches will happen to disciples who do not remain attached to Him: they will be destroyed. On the other hand, Jesus states that great blessing comes to those who do remain in Him. Their prayers are answered, they bear much fruit, they share in the wonderful love that exists between Christ and the Father, and they will experience Christ's own wonderful joy.

Application: Teaching and Preaching the Passage

This three-part metaphor focuses upon Jesus as the vine, the Father as the husbandman, and the disciples as the branches of the vine. It is interesting to systematize what is said about each of them.

1. Jesus, the vine. First, He, rather than Israel, is the true vine (v. 1). Second, He is the source of spiritual life for His disciples; they share His life with Him (v. 2). Third, He is absolutely essential to any spiritual accomplishment by the disciples (vv. 3-5).

2. The Father, the husbandman. First, He cuts off and casts away those branches that do not bring forth any fruit (vv. 2,6). Second, He prunes producing branches so that they will produce even more (v. 2). Third, He answers the disciples' prayers (v. 7). Fourth, He dearly loves the vine (v. 9). Fifth, He takes pleasure in and is glorified by the fruitfulness of the branches (v. 8).

3. The disciples, the branches. First, they are part of the vine and can live only as they remain united with Him (v. 4). Second, they are able to produce fruit only through the strength which they receive from the vine (v. 5). Third, they find true happiness only as they remain a part of the vine (v. 11).

5. "My Friends" (15:12-17)

12 This is my commandment, That ye love one another, as I have loved you.

Having stressed that obedience to His commandments is the secret to experiencing His love (v. 10), Jesus now draws attention to the single most important of these commandments. This one comprehends all the others, the commandment which He has previously called a "new commandment," the commandment to love one another. In effect Jesus says, "The one thing that I really want you to do, the one thing that I require of you, is for you to love one another, to love one another with the same radical love with which I have loved you." (Christ's words are almost identical with 13:34, which see for comments.)

13 Greater love hath no man than this, that a man lay down his life for his friends.

Jesus says that there can be no greater love than His love for His disciples, a love which does not refuse even to die for them. It is this most extreme form of love which Jesus commands the disciples to bear toward one another. John expresses the truth of vv. 12 and 13 very well in 1 Jn. 3:16, "Hereby perceive we the love of God, because he laid down his life for us: and we ought to lay down our lives for the brethren."

14 Ye are my friends, if ye do whatsoever I command you.

Jesus returns to the principle that real love for Him involves obedience to His commands (cf. 14:15, 21, 23, 24; and v. 10). This is especially true in regard to the command to love one another. He tells the disciples that their loving one another verifies their love for Him. In 13:35 He has said that love for one an-

other will clearly demonstrate that they are, indeed, His disciples; now He says that their loving one another will prove that they are His friends. It is by loving each other that they truly love Jesus, that they enter into a new intimacy with Him, that they become His friends.

As in 14:3 (see comment there), the conditional form of the sentence is not meant to cast doubt on the disciples' obedience. While obedience to His commands is necessary to being classified as Jesus' friend, Jesus assumes that the disciples have kept His commands in the past and intend to continue doing so in the future. Therefore, He counts them, already, as His friends. He wants them to know just how dear to Him they are, how close to them He feels.

15 Henceforth I call you not servants; for the servant knoweth not what his lord doeth: but I have called you friends; for all things that I have heard of my Father I have made known unto you.

The requirement of obedience may, at first, seem incompatible with the status of "friend," but Jesus hastens to assure the disciples that it is not. Even though Jesus demands obedience from them, He still views them as friends rather than servants. One does not share his motives and purposes with servants. He simply gives them orders and expects them to obey without question. Jesus, however, has shared everything with the disciples. Nothing which the Father has shared with Him has been withheld from them. He has shared with them His innermost thoughts. He has not dealt with them condescendingly as servants (as He had every right to do); rather, He has taken them into His confidence as friends. Jesus assures the disciples that He does not consider them to be mere servants whom He only tolerates, but that He genuinely loves and values them, that He considers them to be His friends.

16 Ye have not chosen me, but I have chosen you, and ordained you, that ye should go and bring forth fruit, and *that* your fruit should remain: that whatsoever ye shall ask of the Father in my name, he may give it you.

That the disciples are very dear to Jesus is evident in that they did not choose Him but that He chose them. It is He, not they, who initiated the friendship between them. It has not come about by the normal process in which men are attracted to a great leader and decide to become His followers. Rather, it has come about as Jesus has searched them out individually and challenged them to follow Him and become His disciples.

The implication is that, because of their inferiority to Christ, the disciples could never have initiated a friendship between themselves and Him. Masters may initiate a friendship with their servants, but servants dare not attempt to do so with their masters. Any friendship, therefore, between Jesus and the disciples has necessarily been initiated by Him for His own purposes. The disciples need not fear, therefore, that their lives are to be failures. To the contrary, a successful ministry is part of Christ's purpose in choosing them. He has ordained that they shall have productive and eternally significant ministries and that they shall have from the Father those things which they shall ask in His (Christ's) name (see v. 7 and 14:13,14).

17 These things I command you, that ye love one another.

Jesus concludes the section by saying, in effect, "Let me repeat myself. My command to you, my friends, is that you must love one another. I love each of you too much to think of your failing to love each other" (see v. 12; and 13:34).

Summary (15:12-17)

Jesus says that the one thing above all others that He wants His disciples to do is to love one another. He sets forward as an example His own extreme love for them, a love that is willing even to die for them. He considers them to be His friends because they obey His commands. He will no longer refer to them as servants, but as friends. They are His friends simply because He has chosen to consider them as such and to treat them as such by taking them into His confidence and sharing with them all His privileged communication with the Father. That the disciples are very dear to Him can be seen in the fact that it was He, the Son of God, who chose them as friends rather than the reverse. In choosing them, Jesus ordained that they should have productive ministries and that their prayers should be answered. Finally, Jesus reminds the disciples that His highest priority for them is that they love one another.

Application: Teaching and Preaching the Passage

The theme of this passage is the glorious truth that Jesus considers those who trust and follow Him to be His friends. First, Jesus expresses His grave concern in the form of a commandment. The concern is that unity and love should characterize His disciples after His departure. Jesus loves each of His followers so much that for them to fail to love one another would bring Him great sorrow. The passage, therefore, both begins and ends with the expression of the command to love one another (vv.12 and 17).

Second, Jesus gives an example of the kind of love He has in mind (vv. 12b and 13). It is a love like His own, a love that accepts even death in the interest of its object. Jesus wants the disciples to love one another as deeply as He loves each of them, and He knows His own love to have no limitation whatsoever; He is about to lay down His life for them.

Third, Jesus announces a new relationship between Himself and His disciples: they are His friends (v. 14). This relationship is both present and potential. It is present in that the disciples are already proving themselves to be Christ's friends by obeying His commandments. It is potential in that, as they obey more completely the particular commandment to love one another, they will come to experience, in an ever more intimate way, true friendship with Christ.

Fourth, Jesus contrasts the disciples' status as friends with that of servanthood (v. 15). The disciples are not His servants, even though He does make demands of them. Rather, they are His friends. He has treated them as friends rather than servants in that He has not simply issued them commands but has taken them into His confidence and shared with them the reasoning and motives behind the commands.

Fifth, Jesus assures the disciples of His affection for them by reminding them that it is He who has initiated the relationship between them. He, not they, has made it possible for them to be friends. They may therefore be confident of the future. His choosing them to be His friends involves many wonderful privileges, among which are productive service and answered prayers (v. 16).

6. Warning of the World's Mindless Hatred (15:18—16:4)

18 If the world hate you, ye know

that it hated me before *it hated* you.

The great importance of the disciples' love for one another is to be seen in the fact that the world (used in the sense of human society organized in ignorance of and opposition to God) hates them. They will need one another's love as they encounter the world's hatred.

When Jesus says "if the world hate you," He does not mean to imply that the matter is in doubt. Here the conditional element is assumed to be true (a first-class condition in Greek). It is taken to be axiomatic that the world will hate the disciples of the One whom they hate supremely, if for no other reason than that they are His disciples. The hatred which the Christian experiences is directed primarily at Christ and at himself only secondarily as Christ's disciple. The Christian must realize that, just as there are wonderful blessings associated with being Christ's follower (e.g. the experience of Christ's own love and that of his fellow disciples), there are negative aspects as well. One of these is that he is going to experience the hatred of the world.

19 If ye were of the world, the world would love his own: but because ye are not of the world, but I have chosen you out of the world, therefore the world hateth you.

Jesus explains that the basic reason for the world's hatred of His disciples is their radical difference from the world and its essential antagonism to them. If His disciples were still of the world (i.e. if they still shared its perspectives, values, and alienation from God), then the world would love them as part of itself. But since Christ has chosen them out of the world to be His disciples and has so completely transformed them that they no longer share its essential character, the world hates them. The world hates and is infuriated by nonconformity, especially nonconformity that inheres in subjection to Christ. The Christian's acceptance of Christ's lordship in his life is, by definition, a rejection of the world's lordship, and that rejection brings upon him the world's wrath and hatred.

20 Remember the word that I said unto you, The servant is not greater than his lord. If they have persecuted me, they will also persecute you; if they have kept my saying, they will keep yours also.

Jesus reminds the disciples of His statement in 13:16 to the effect that a servant is not superior to his master and cannot demand treatment more preferential than that accorded his master. His point seems to be that His disciples must simply accept the fact that the world that persecuted their Master will, inevitably, persecute them. Indeed, it would be presumptuous for a Christian to expect to live without persecution in a world which has crucified Jesus. Jesus means to establish it as a maxim that persecution is to be the characteristic lot of those who follow Him. It is assumed to be obvious that the world persecuted Jesus and rejected His message. It is just as obvious that it will persecute His disciples and reject their message.

21 But all these things will they do unto you for my name's sake, because they know not him that sent me.

Jesus states that the world will persecute His disciples "for His name's sake" (i.e., simply because of their identification with Him and the fact that they are His disciples). This is essentially the same truth as v. 18, that the world's hatred is directed primarily at Christ and only secondarily at His disciples. What is really new in this verse is the added explanation that the motive behind men's hatred of Christ is their lack of knowledge of the Father who has sent Him into the world. Christ has previously explained that the inability to recognize and accept Him as the Son of God is due to a lack of knowledge of the Father (5:37, 38; 8:42,47; which see for comments).

22 If I had not come and spoken unto them, they had not had sin: but now they have no cloak for their sin.

Having demonstrated that the reason for the world's rejection of Him (and His disciples) is its lack of knowledge of the Father, Jesus now proceeds to show that this ignorance is inexcusable. It is inexcusable because it is a willful and arrogant rejection of the obvious. The Jews reject Jesus, not because what He says is incomprehensible to them, but because what He says condemns their sin (see 7:7). Their pride and self-righteousness will not allow them to either face or admit their own sinfulness, therefore they resent and despise one who reveals and rebukes their sin. Nothing infuriates the world quite so much as to be confronted with its own sinfulness. The more sustainable the charge and the more righteous the accuser, the more extreme the fury of the reaction. For such an extremely wicked and self-righteous people as the Jews to have such obviously accurate charges leveled against them by such a sinless accuser as Jesus was bound to produce an explosion of rage. This rage accounts for the world's original rejection of Jesus and for that of His disciples in every succeeding age.

When Jesus says that if He had not come and spoken to the world, they would not have had sin, He does not mean that men were not sinful or that they were not responsible for their sin prior to His coming. Rather, He means that their sin is clearly revealed and rendered inexcusable by His coming. For them to reject and despise Jesus, as the very incarnation of God, who communicates with precise accuracy the being of God, reveals once and for all their utter ignorance of and estrangement from God.

23 He that hateth me hateth my Father also.

Jesus' words here are a variation on the theme of His absolute unity and identity with the Father (see e.g. 8:19; 10:30, 38; 12:45; 14:9). On this occasion, He adapts that theme to His explanation of the world's hatred and rejection of His disciples and Himself. He has said (v. 18) that hatred of the disciples is but a manifestation of hatred for Him (Jesus). Now He says that hatred of Him is but a manifestation of hatred for the Father. The reason the world hates Him so intensely is that they actually harbor a deep-seated hatred for God Himself.

Jesus is not simply reiterating the general principle of His own unity with the Father. He is stating something much more profound. What the Jews most despise in Jesus are the very qualities which most accurately reflect the being and attributes of the Father. As they hate these attributes of deity in Jesus, they are actually hating the Father Himself.

24 If I had not done among them the works which none other man did, they had not had sin: but now have they both seen and hated both me and my Father.

Jesus has already explained (v. 22) that the world hates Him because His teaching has exposed their sin. Now He goes on to say that it is not only His teaching which exposes their sin and arouses their hatred, but also His works (miracles). As in His previous conversation with Philip (14:10,11), Jesus refers to His works as confirmatory evidence of His identity and the truth of His teaching (see also 5:36; 10:25, 38).

Again, as in v. 22, Jesus does not mean that men were not accountable for their sins until He came and performed His miracles, but that their refusal to believe is absolutely inexcusable in light of their having observed these miracles. Jesus has performed such glorious works among the Jews as to constitute undeniable evidence that He is the Son of God. Refusal to believe, in light of such overwhelming evidence, is a crime of immense proportions deserving of the most extreme punishment (see Mt. 11:20-24). Such willful rejection of the obvious emanates from a hatred so intense as to obliterate reason. Yet this is precisely the crime of which the world is guilty. They have seen Christ's miracles and yet they continue in their unbelief and hatred, a hatred directed at both Christ and the Father (v. 23).

25 But *this cometh to pass*, that the word might be fulfilled that is written in their law, They hated me without a cause.

Some explanation is required for the world's (Jews') incredible rejection of and wicked hatred for Christ. That explanation involves an extreme irony. On one level, the explanation is that this hatred is a part of God's sovereignly devised plan for achieving the salvation of mankind and, as such, has been prophesied in the Scripture (Ps. 69:4). This is in keeping with the idea that God often uses the sinful actions of men to achieve His purposes (see Acts 2:23).

On another level, the world's hatred is completely arbitrary, gratuitous, and without any cause whatever. The irony is that Jesus demonstrates that the world's hatred is part of God's sovereign plan by showing that it has been foretold in Scripture but that the actual statement of the Scripture He chooses to make this point (Ps. 69:4) is to the effect that the hatred is absolutely groundless and inexplicable.

26 But when the Comforter is come, whom I will send unto you from the Father, *even* the Spirit of truth, which proceedeth from the Father, he shall testify of me:
27 And ye also shall bear witness, because ye have been with me from the beginning.

Jesus wants the disciples to understand something beyond the fact that they are going to have to endure the hatred and persecution of the world. With the coming of the promised Comforter (see 14:16, 26), the Spirit of truth (see comments 14:17), they are going to become identified with Him (the Comforter) in a ministry of "witness" which will completely transcend their persecution and flourish even in the midst of it. The mission of the Comforter will be to carry on the ministry of "witness" which has been begun by John the Baptist (e.g. 1:7; 5:33) and carried forward by Jesus Himself (e.g. 3:31-34; 8:16). While Christ is to be replaced by the Holy Spirit as the agent of witness, He will continue to be the content of the witness.

Up to this point, Christ has borne the entire burden of communicating His "witness," but from this point on, this responsibility is to be assumed primarily by the Holy Spirit and secondarily by Christians. Christians "also" (i.e. additionally, supplementally, and subordinately) will bear witness. They may take comfort in the fact that they are but a constituent part of the great ministry of witness which the Holy Spirit is carrying forward in the world. While their role is significant, even essential, it is always subordinate and secondary. The ultimate success of the effort depends upon the Holy Spirit, not them. They can witness confidently as they conceive of themselves as the instruments of the Holy Spirit in His ministry of giving witness to the world of Christ.

16:1 These things have I spoken unto you, that ye should not be offended.

Jesus explains that His motive for telling the disciples all that He has been telling them is that they will not later be offended (Greek *skandalizo*), i.e. be disheartened and give up. Jesus refers primarily to what He has been saying about persecution. The only subject which He has been discussing which could reasonably be expected to have the effect of causing the disciples to lose heart is the coming persecution.

2 They shall put you out of the synagogues: yea, the time cometh, that whosoever killeth you will think that he doeth God service.
3 And these things will they do unto you, because they have not known the Father, nor me.

The persecution which Jesus warns the disciples to expect will vary greatly in degree and intensity. It will range from the relatively mild action of ostracism (being put out of the synagogue) to the most extreme intensity of being put to death.

Perhaps the greatest tragedy of all is that many of those who persecute them will suppose themselves to be doing God's will. Certainly, this will prove to be the case with Saul of Tarsus (Acts 8:1; 26:9,10; 1 Tim. 1:13). Though they will suppose themselves to be acting in obedience to God, those who are to persecute Christ's disciples will actually do so because they know neither the Father nor Christ (see comments 15:21). One of the ironies of history is that much of the persecution directed against Christians has come from those who claimed to be Christians and acted in the name of God. One notes that Jesus' prediction of the disciples' persecution is unconditional. It is not just that it *may* come about, but that it is certain.

4 But these things have I told you, that when the time shall come, ye may remember that I told you of them. And these things I said not unto you at the beginning, because I was with you.

Jesus statement here is essentially identical with v. 1 (which see for comments). The repetition is for emphasis. Jesus wants to impress firmly upon the disciples' minds that they are going to encounter persecution.

The reason He has not explained this to them before is that, to this point, He has always been with them. Now, of course, He is about to go away and wants to make sure they understand this truth before He goes. As long as Jesus has been with the disciples, the world's persecution has been directed primarily at Him rather than at them. Now that He is going away, this persecution will be aimed much more directly at them. In addition, He will not be present to counsel and encourage them. Therefore the disciples must be prepared to face the persecution which they are certain to encounter. He wants them to know beforehand that it is coming so that when it actually arrives they will remember that He has predicted it and understand that He knew that it was coming all along. To be forewarned

is to be forearmed. The impact of the persecution will be far less devastating if the disciples understand that it is a part of God's foreordained plan for them.

Summary
(15:18—16:4)

Jesus informs the disciples that a major reason for their loving one another is that the world is going to hate them. It will hate them precisely because they are His disciples, and because they are so utterly different from itself. As the world has persecuted Him, so will it persecute them. They must simply accept that this is so. Men will hate the disciples because they hate Christ, and they hate Christ because they do not know the Father. The world's hatred of Christ is inexcusable because it is willful. It hates Jesus because His teaching reveals its sin. (When men hate Jesus, they are hating the very qualities of the Godhead; they are hating the Father Himself.)

Not only does the world hate Jesus because of His teaching, it hates Him in spite of His many miracles. This proves its hatred to be irrational and willful. The world's hatred for Christ, while ultimately irrational, is being utilized by God in the accomplishment of His eternal purposes.

Jesus wants the disciples to know that they are not just left here to suffer, but to bear witness to Him. Under the leadership of the Holy Spirit they will be His witnesses to men. His motive for telling the disciples about the coming persecution is that He does not want them to be devastated when it actually comes. The persecution will assume various forms, from expulsion from the synagogue to execution. While many of the persecutors will suppose themselves to be acting in obedience to God, their ignorance of Him will be the real cause. Jesus reemphasizes that His disciples are going to endure persecution. He has delayed explaining this to them until now because He has been with them but is now going to leave them.

Application: Teaching and Preaching the Passage

Just as Jesus wants His disciples to know how much He loves them and how important it is to Him that they love one another, He must also tell them that the world hates them. He must explain to them and prepare them for this hatred. First and foremost, the world hates Jesus' disciples because it hates Jesus Himself. Second, the world hates Jesus' disciples because they are so utterly different. Third, the world hates both Christ and His disciples because it is altogether estranged from God. Fourth, the world hates both Christ and His disciples because they reveal its sin. Fifth, the world hates Christ and His disciples with what is, in the final analysis, a blind and illogical fury.

Jesus also wants His disciples to understand that there is a reason for their being left behind to endure the persecution of the world: they are to bear witness unto Christ. First, this ministry of witness will be under the guidance and control of the Holy Spirit (the Comforter). He will bear the primary responsibility for and guarantee the ultimate success of this mission. Second, the disciples will also have a personal involvement in and responsibility for this ministry of witness, yet their role will always be a subordinate and dependent one.

Finally, Jesus drives home the point that persecution is inevitable. His disciples are going to be persecuted and they must be prepared to accept the fact. There are certain facts about the persecution which Jesus wants His disciples to understand. First, the persecution will be of varying intensity. Not all Christians will undergo the same sufferings. Second, the persecution will often be carried on by those who claim to believe in God. Third, the persecutors will always be characterized by an ignorance of and lack of communion with the true God.

7. The Comforter (16:5-15)

Having explained to the disciples that they are going to face persecution, Jesus now goes on to tell them more of the ministry of the Comforter who will enable them to face, and even to triumph in, this persecution.

5 But now I go my way to him that sent me; and none of you asketh me, Whither goest thou?

At this point Jesus returns to the somewhat mysterious idea of His going away (see e.g. 7:33, 35; 8:14, 21; 13:33, 36; 14:2-4,12, 28). His statement that none of the disciples is asking Him where He is going creates something of a problem. Has Jesus forgotten the words of Peter in 13:36 and Thomas in 14:5? Should the sequence be readjusted so as to make this statement precede those of Peter and Thomas? Does the presence of these words at this point indicate an actual inconsistency and, therefore, an argument against the integrity and authenticity of the Fourth Gospel?

The truth seems both obvious and mundane. The questions of Peter and Thomas, just as the comments of the Jews in 7:35 and 36, grew out of a purely literal understanding of Christ's words about His going away. They did not understand, when they spoke, that Christ was talking about His return to Heaven. They were confused as to where (on earth) Christ was going when He went away on the trip He was planning. Likewise, the questions of Peter and Thomas were so misguided, and failed so completely to comprehend the true meaning of Jesus' words, that they did not deal with the real issue of Jesus' return to

Heaven at all. Therefore, when Jesus reproaches the disciples for their failure to inquire about His destination, He speaks quite seriously. They have now come to understand that Christ has been speaking of actually leaving this world, and yet they are still concerned only about the consequences of this event for themselves. They have not thought about what it may mean for Christ. Jesus is rebuking them for their self-centeredness and their lack of concern for Him.

6 But because I have said these things unto you, sorrow hath filled your heart.

A tone of rebuke still tinges Jesus' words as He continues. The disciples have focused exclusively upon the negative aspects of what Jesus has been saying to them: His leaving them, their persecution, etc. They have failed completely to focus on any of the positives: the coming of the Comforter, their own role as witnesses. Therefore, they experience only sorrow at Jesus' words. They are utterly saturated with sorrow, a sorrow so intense and pervasive as to obliterate every emotion but itself, a sorrow all the more destructive for being colored by self-pity.

7 Nevertheless I tell you the truth; It is expedient for you that I go away: for if I go not away, the Comforter will not come unto you; but if I depart, I will send him unto you.

In spite of the disciples' sorrow at His departure, Jesus tells them that His leaving will actually work to their advantage. Caiaphas has previously stated (11:50) that it would be "expedient" (Greek *sumphero*) for the Jewish leaders if Christ should die for the people (see comments). Now Jesus says to the disci-

ples that it is expedient (same Greek word) that He go away, because the Comforter will not come until He has done so. This fits very well with John's explanatory note in 7:39 to the effect that the Holy Spirit had not yet been given because Christ had not yet been glorified.

Jesus does not explain why the Comforter will not come until after He has gone away, simply that it is so. However, the reason seems to be that the Holy Spirit is to be given on the basis of the salvation that is to be wrought by Christ's death and, therefore, cannot be given until that salvation has been accomplished. Also it would seem that the inward and spiritual ministry of the Holy Spirit will actually be inherently superior to the ministry which Christ has carried on while present in the flesh.

8 And when he is come, he will reprove the world of sin, and of righteousness, and of judgment.

Having returned to the theme of the coming of the Holy Spirit, Jesus will now describe two of His distinct functions. He will convict the world (vv. 8-11) and guide the disciples into all truth (vv. 13-15).

Up to this point Christ has been explaining the work of the Holy Spirit in relation to the disciples. He will indwell them, teach them, empower them for witness, etc. Now He explains the nature of the Holy Spirit's work in relation to the world at large. Whereas He is to be an Advocate and Comforter to the disciples, He is to relate Himself to the world as an Accuser and Prosecutor. His role in regard to them will be to convict (Greek *elegcho*) them of their sin, righteousness, and judgment.

He will convict them in two senses. First, He will convict people in the sense of exposing their sin and proving them guilty before God's absolute justice. Second, He will convict them in the sense of convincing them of, and causing them to admit, their own error. An example of this conviction may be seen in Acts 2:37 where the Jews are "pricked in their heart" and ask Peter what they are to do in light of their terrible guilt for having killed the Christ.

9 Of sin, because they believe not on me.

The Holy Spirit will convict the world, first of all, in regard to its sin. There are various ways to understand the last part of the verse. It may be that Jesus is saying that, since the world does not believe in Him and, therefore, will not listen to Him, He cannot convince it of its sin and that, therefore, the Holy Spirit must accomplish this task. Or Jesus may mean that the world's most basic and characteristic sin is its refusal to believe on Him. Finally, Jesus may mean that the world's sin grows out of its refusal to believe on Him and that men's lack of belief causes them to remain in their sins and, thereby, to be in need of the Spirit's conviction. This last view is probably correct.

10 Of righteousness, because I go to my Father, and ye see me no more.

Not only does the Holy Spirit convict the world of sin but also of righteousness. What does Christ mean when He says that the Holy Spirit will convict the world of righteousness? The traditional interpretation is that Jesus is speaking of righteousness in the abstract and His own righteousness. The Holy Spirit will reveal to the world the true righteousness and demonstrate that Jesus really was a righteous man in spite of His having been crucified as a criminal (see e.g. Acts 2:32-36). He will cause the world to understand that Jesus was the personifi-

cation of, and man's only hope of attaining, righteousness. This interpretation requires that "convict" (carrying over from v. 8) be understood in the sense of "convince" rather than "convict" or "reprove."

D. A. Carson (141 ff.) feels that "convict" should be understood in the same sense (reprove, rebuke) with all three of the things mentioned (i.e. sin, righteousness, and judgment). He feels that Jesus means to say that the Holy Spirit will reprove the world's perverted and pretentious "righteousness." God says in Is. 64:6 that all man's righteousness is like filthy rags in His sight. The world, while it is actually desperately wicked, constantly prates about righteousness. Carson believes Jesus to be saying that the Holy Spirit will rebuke the world for the complacent and self-serving moralism which passes, in its own mind, as righteousness (see Rom. 10:3,4).

Jesus says in the last part of the verse that the Holy Spirit is going to assume the function of convicting the world of righteousness because He, Himself, is returning to Heaven and leaving the earthly scene. While He has performed this function to this point, it will now devolve upon the Holy Spirit.

11 Of judgment, because the prince of this world is judged.

As with v. 10, it must be determined whether "convict" should be understood as "convince" or "reprove." If it is taken in the sense of "convince," then Jesus is saying something to the effect that the world is pronouncing the ultimate judgment upon itself by identifying with Satan in His rejection and condemnation of Christ. This is so because, as Jesus has already explained in 12:31 (which see for comments), by attempting to judge Christ, Satan is actually bringing judgment upon himself. Therefore, those who join with Satan in his false judgment of Christ will actually share with him that judgment of God which his action will bring upon his own head.

If "convict" is taken in the sense of "reprove," then Jesus is rebuking the world for the falsity and injustice of its "judgment" (see Carson 145 ff.). The world is fundamentally wrong in its assessments of morality and ethics. It has an inherent, systemic aversion to real truth and justice. The false verdict that the world is about to pronounce on Jesus is not the only manifestation of this spirit, but it is an extreme and symbolic one. The world's condemnation of Jesus reveals how utterly wrong are the criteria of its judgment. Jesus is saying that the Holy Spirit will reprove and condemn the world for the wrongheaded and perverse standard by which it renders its judgments of what is true, right, and good.

12 I have yet many things to say unto you, but ye cannot bear them now.

There are many other things which Jesus would like to explain to the disciples, but He cannot do so because they are not presently able to properly understand and deal with them. Jesus does not explain just why this is the case, but there are at least three reasons why it may be so. First, Jesus has already told the disciples so much on this night that their minds have to be approaching the saturation point beyond which further data cannot be profitably assimilated. Second, much of what He has in mind to tell them is predicated upon events which have not yet occurred and which, therefore, the disciples cannot possibly comprehend as well now as they will be able to do after the fact. Third, the disciples are not yet indwelled by the Holy Spirit in the same way they will be later and are, therefore, far less spiritually perceptive than they will be later. For

whatever reason, Jesus says that He is not, at this point, telling the disciples all that He considers it appropriate for them to know and that certain things are to be withheld until a later time.

13 Howbeit when he, the Spirit of truth, is come, he will guide you into all truth: for he shall not speak of himself; but whatsoever he shall hear, *that* shall he speak: and he will shew you things to come.

Having described the Holy Spirit's function of convicting the world of sin, righteousness, and judgment, Jesus now proceeds to describe His function of guiding the disciples into all truth.

The later time at which the disciples will be told the things which Jesus is now withholding from them is when the Spirit of Truth (see comments 14:17), the Holy Spirit, is come. When He comes He will guide the disciples into all truth (see comments 14:26). By this Jesus means to say that the Holy Spirit will lead the disciples into a fuller and deeper comprehension of the ultimate truth of God which is bound up and epitomized in Jesus Christ. That truth into which the Holy Spirit will guide the disciples will merely continue and expand the truth given by Jesus. The reason this is so is that just as Jesus' message did not originate with Himself, but with the Father (see e.g. 3:11, 34; 7:16; 8:26, 28; 12:44; 14:10; 17:28), so shall the Holy Spirit speak only those things which He shall receive from God. When Jesus says that the Holy Spirit will reveal "things to come," He does not, apparently, mean to say that the Holy Spirit will predict the future, although He certainly could do so if He desired. Rather, He seems to be saying that the Holy Spirit will initiate the disciples into the mysteries of the new era which is about to dawn with Christ's own death, resurrection, and return to Heaven.

14 He shall glorify me: for he shall receive of mine, and shall shew *it* unto you.
15 All things that the Father hath are mine: therefore said I, that he shall take of mine, and shall shew *it* unto you.

One of the primary characteristics of the Holy Spirit's teaching will be that it glorifies Christ. Just as Jesus' purpose has been to glorify the Father (see 13:31; 14:13; 17:4), so the Holy Spirit's purpose will be to glorify the Son. His teaching will be thoroughly Christocentric, i.e. focusing primarily upon Christ. Any teaching or belief which conceives of the Holy Spirit as acting in such a way as to emphasize His own person or ministry rather than that of Christ is out of harmony with these words of Christ.

In v. 13 Jesus has said that the Holy Spirit, like Himself while upon earth, will speak only those things which He will receive from God. Now He develops that thought to say that those things which the Holy Spirit will receive will be "out of," i.e. "from among" the things of Christ. Jesus clearly means to say that the things the Holy Spirit will teach the disciples will be things concerning Himself (Christ). He seems also to imply that the Holy Spirit will be as dependent upon Him (Jesus) for His message as He was upon the Father for His own (see 7:16; 8:26,28; etc.), that He will bear to the Holy Spirit essentially the same relationship which the Father bore to Him during His own earthly ministry.

Jesus says that this is so because all things which the Father possesses are His as well. He surely means to say by this that there is no truth of which the Father has not given Him a complete understanding and which does not relate directly to Himself. He may also mean to say that God has given Him authority

over the communication of ultimate truth to men in a way similar to the way He has given Him authority over judgment and resurrection (5:22, 26, 27).

Summary
(16:5-15)

Jesus reintroduces the theme of His going away and rebukes His disciples for their self-centeredness and lack of concern for Him in the great trial which He faces. He also rebukes them for focusing only on the negative aspects of what He has been telling them, ignoring the positive aspects entirely and allowing themselves to be overcome by sorrow and self-pity. He tells them that, contrary to their expectations, His going away will actually work to their advantage since it will signal the coming of the Holy Spirit who, when He comes, will reprove the world of sin, righteousness, and judgment. He says that He has many other things which He would like to share with them, but that they are not yet able to understand them. He assures them, however, that the Holy Spirit will enable them to understand such matters when He comes. Since the Holy Spirit shares with Christ a complete harmony of understanding and purpose, He will glorify Christ even as He continues and expands His teaching ministry.

Application: Teaching and Preaching the Passage

The focus of this passage is clearly on the Holy Spirit, and it reveals four basic truths about Him. The first is that He will not come into the world until Christ has left it, Christ's leaving being the cue for His coming (v. 7). The second is that one great aspect of His mission will be to convict the world. He will convict the world of its sin, pretentious "righteousness," and false standard of justice by which it will presume to condemn the

Just One, Christ (vv. 8-11). The third is that another great aspect of His mission will be to guide Christians into all truth. He will lead Christians into a full understanding of the truth of God as it has been revealed in Christ. He will explain and enlarge upon Christ's revelation (vv. 12,13). The fourth is that the overall impact of His ministry will be to glorify and exalt Christ in the hearts and minds of Christians (vv. 14,15).

8. The Resurrection Predicted (16:16-22)

Jesus has been speaking of His "going away" as being a necessary condition for the coming of the Holy Spirit. Now He turns to speak more specifically of how His approaching crucifixion will affect His own personal relationship to the disciples. He speaks of how His "going away" will affect the disciples rather than of what His own experience of it shall be.

16 A little while, and ye shall not see me: and again, a little while, and ye shall see me, because I go to the Father.

In order to understand this verse (and the whole section which follows), one must determine just what Jesus means when He says that in a little while the disciples will not see Him, and then again a little while and they will see Him again. There are three possibilities of interpretation. (1) He may refer to His immediate return to the Father by way of the cross and His second coming at the end of the world. (2) He may refer to His going away and returning to the disciples in the person of the Holy Spirit. (3) Or He may refer to the fact that He will be gone from the disciples a short time (three days) and then return to them by way of His resurrection. While we should remember that the various as-

pects of Christ's "coming again" are not clearly differentiated in the Fourth Gospel and that there may be some intentional ambiguity in Jesus' words, it seems best to understand that here He is referring to His death and resurrection three days later.

D. A. Carson (158) gives several reasons for supposing such to be the case. First, Jesus' reference to "a little while" seems to suggest something like the three-day period during which He lay in the tomb, and the term "see" seems to describe the experience of the disciples with the post-resurrection Christ more accurately than it does the coming of the Holy Spirit at Pentecost. Second, the picture of the disciples weeping and mourning while the world rejoices (v. 20) describes the situation while Christ was in the tomb much more accurately than it does that which prevailed after His resurrection. After the resurrection, the disciples were filled with joy. Third, the analogy of the woman in labor fits best with a short period of intense pain such as the disciples experienced during the three days Jesus was in the tomb. Fourth, such an interpretation best fits the context of the Farewell Discourse in which Jesus has already referred to the other two aspects of His coming again (14:16-20) but has not mentioned His resurrection on the third day. It seems reasonable that He should do so now as He draws the discourse to a close.

17 Then said *some* of his disciples among themselves, What is this that he saith unto us, A little while, and ye shall not see me: and again, a little while, and ye shall see me: and, Because I go to the Father?
18 They said therefore, What is this that he saith, A little while? we cannot tell what he saith.

The disciples are puzzled by Jesus'

words and discuss their meaning among themselves. It is the term "a little while" (Greek, *mikron*) which throws them. In v. 10 Jesus has said that He was going away to His Father and that the disciples, therefore, would not see Him any more. Those words seemed to imply that Jesus was leaving them and returning to His Father permanently. Now He says that, while it is true that He is going to return to His Father, He is only going to be gone from them a little while. This is very confusing to the disciples. If He is going to return to His Father, how can He be gone only a little while?

19 Now Jesus knew that they were desirous to ask him, and said unto them, Do ye enquire among yourselves of that I said, A little while, and ye shall not see me: and again, a little while, and ye shall see me?
20 Verily, verily, I say unto you, That ye shall weep and lament, but the world shall rejoice: and ye shall be sorrowful, but your sorrow shall be turned into joy.

The disciples are perplexed and would like to ask Jesus to explain His meaning, but they refrain from doing so. Perhaps they feel they have revealed enough of their obtuseness for one night. Perhaps none of them wants to leave himself open to possible rebuke (see 13:38; 14:7,9). Jesus, perceiving the disciples' desire to question Him as well as their reluctance to do so, draws them out on the issue. He says, in effect, "You are confused about my statement that in a little while you will no longer see me and then, again a little while, and you will see me once more, aren't you?" Using the formula of solemnity, He goes on to tell the disciples that there is a difficult period just ahead for them, a period during which they will experience an extreme sorrow while the world (i.e. the unbelieving, Christ-rejecting world, particularly the Jewish authorities) is, in marked contrast, rejoicing. Jesus hastens to add, however, that this time of sorrow will not be permanent and that their sorrow will be transformed into joy. Jesus' point is not just that their sorrow will be replaced by joy, but that it will be *transformed* into joy. This is to say that the very event which provokes their great sorrow (Christ's crucifixion) will become the occasion of their subsequent rejoicing.

Christ's statement is obviously somewhat enigmatic. He does not suppose that the disciples will be able to deduce from it the details of His approaching death and resurrection. Rather He is giving them a general encouragement and basis for hope in the midst of the great sorrow which lies before them. He is giving them a broad outline of impending events so that when these actually occur, they will understand that Jesus knew what was about to happen and was not taken by surprise.

21 A woman when she is in travail hath sorrow, because her hour is come: but as soon as she is delivered of the child, she remembereth no more the anguish, for joy that a man is born into the world.

Jesus likens the disciples' approaching sorrow to the sorrow and travail of a woman in childbirth. The very event which is the occasion of extreme suffering and sorrow is transformed into the basis for rejoicing. During labor, the act of giving birth is characterized only by sorrow, but at the instant of birth the event is altogether transformed into one of the most joyous and exhilarating experiences that human beings can know, the realization that one has brought into existence a new life.

D. A. Carson sees another possible significance in Christ's figure of the woman in travail. The O.T. prophets (see e.g. Is. 26:16-19; 66:7-14; Hos. 13:13-15; Mic. 4:9,10) used the figure of the woman in travail to refer to Israel and the sorrow which she was to experience just prior to the coming of the Messiah. On the basis of such passages, the Jews sometimes spoke of "the travail pains of the Messiah." Jesus may have such Scriptures in mind and may mean to give a Messianic and eschatological significance to His statement. If so, that significance would seem to be that His approaching passion "is an eschatological event, in that it pronounces both ultimate judgment and ultimate justification; and so it is appropriate that the Messianic age inaugurated by this eschatological event likewise be prefaced by a period of sharp anguish" (Carson 162).

22 And ye now therefore have sorrow: but I will see you again, and your heart shall rejoice, and your joy no man taketh from you.

Just as the woman in the pangs of childbirth experiences suffering and sorrow, so do the disciples even now have sorrow. It should be noted that even though their sorrow will soon be greatly intensified, Jesus speaks of the disciples' sorrow as a present reality. They are already experiencing an overwhelming grief because of Christ's leaving them. Jesus hastens to add, however, that this is not the end, that He will see the disciples again and that their hearts will then be filled with joy, a permanent and indestructible joy. He does not mean that the disciples will never again experience any sorrow whatsoever, but that they will never again experience a sorrow so intense and oppressive as that which they are to know for the next few days.

These words very closely parallel Is. 66:14, "And when ye see this, your heart shall rejoice...." This similarity, in light of the fact that the figure of the woman in

travail is found in the same context, cannot reasonably be supposed to be coincidental. Jesus must be speaking with Is. 66:7-14 as a general background for His thoughts.

Summary
(16:16-22)

Having shown that His going away is a necessary condition to the coming of the Holy Spirit, Jesus now returns to His consideration of its implications for the disciples' own immediate future. He tells them that He is to be separated from them for a little while but that He will soon be with them again. The disciples are puzzled at His statement that He will soon be with them again. They have understood that His absence is to be permanent since He is returning to Heaven. Though they would very much like for Jesus to explain Himself, they refrain from asking Him to do so. Jesus, however, sensing their confusion, volunteers an explanation. He explains that they are to undergo a short period of intense sorrow, but that their sorrow will soon be transformed into joy. He likens their approaching experience to that of a woman in labor who suffers intensely just before her baby's birth but is filled with glorious joy as soon as he is born. Jesus reassures the disciples that their sorrow will soon be over, that He will soon be with them again, and that the joy which they experience then will be permanent.

Application: Teaching and
Preaching the Passage

In this section Jesus focuses upon His resurrection as a source of hope for the disciples during the trying time they are facing. First, He offers them words of comforting assurance (v. 16). Then, when those words create confusion in their minds, He demonstrates, secondly, a real sensitivity to their concerns. He anticipates their questions and hastens to assuage their doubts and calm their fears (vv. 17-19). Third, He reassures them that even though they are facing a period of intense sorrow, they will come through it to final victory. He states this, first, as an objective fact (v. 20). Then He illumines it by a revealing analogy (v. 21). Finally, He expresses it as a very personal and subjective promise (v. 22).

9. Special Encouragement for the Disciples (16:23-33)

23 And in that day ye shall ask me nothing. Verily, verily, I say unto you, Whatsoever ye shall ask the Father in my name, he will give it you.

Jesus' phrase "in that day" refers to both His resurrection and the coming of the Holy Spirit. He does not differentiate the two chronologically at this point (see comments on v. 16; 14:16,18,20,23, 26), allowing them to merge into one event.

The interpretation of this verse centers on the meaning of two different words for "ask." The word used in the first part of the sentence (Greek erotao) may mean either to ask a question or to make a request. The word used in the last part of the sentence (Greek aiteo) always means to make a request. The point in question is whether Jesus means to use the first "ask" in the sense of "ask a question" or "make a request." If He means "make a request," then the whole verse is talking about making requests and Jesus is saying something to the effect that after His resurrection and the coming of the Holy Spirit, the disciples will no longer request anything from Him, but will instead make their requests directly to the Father in Christ's name. If He means "ask a question," then there is a sort of play on the two words. Jesus is saying that after His res-

urrection and the coming of the Holy Spirit, the disciples will no longer need to ask such questions as they have been asking (see e.g. 13:6, 25, 36, 37; 14:8, 22) and are, even now, desirous of asking (vv. 17-19). Rather, they will then make requests to the Father in Christ's name. The first interpretation has in its favor the emphatic position of "me" where Jesus says, "You shall ask me nothing." The second has that it is just the kind of play on words and subtle shift of meaning which is so characteristic of John's Gospel.

Whichever interpretation is adopted, the point seems clearly to be that one of the great blessings that will come to the disciples through Jesus' going away and the Spirit's coming is that of answered prayer. Whatever they request of the Father in Christ's name will be granted them.

24 Hitherto have ye asked nothing in my name: ask, and ye shall receive, that your joy may be full.

Jesus has just promised the disciples that in the new dispensation which is about to dawn, the Father is going to grant them whatever they ask for in Christ's name. Now He goes on to say that this new privilege is to be more wonderful than they suspect. They have never made their requests to God in Jesus' name before. Previous to this they have prayed directly to the Father, or they have simply made their requests directly to Jesus. Now they are going to be able to pray in Christ's name: that is, on the basis of His completed atonement and their own spiritual unity with Him. Such prayer is going to be efficacious to a degree never before possible. Jesus encourages the disciples to exercise this glorious privilege when it becomes operative and, thereby, experience a wonderful new joy. In fact, He seems to imply that God's primary purpose for extending this new privilege to them is that their joy may be full.

25 These things have I spoken unto you in proverbs: but the time cometh, when I shall no more speak unto you in proverbs, but I shall shew you plainly of the Father.

Jesus says that all of His teaching has been couched in symbolic and enigmatic language (Greek *paroimia*, dark sayings, metaphors). But that a time is coming when this will no longer be the case and He will speak to them in plain, straightforward language. It should be noted that, contrary to the disciples' understanding (v. 29), this time has not yet arrived. It will come only after the resurrection has made so many of His previously obscure sayings completely perspicuous. Ultimately, it will come only after the Holy Spirit has come to indwell and instruct them. Jesus will instruct the disciples directly in the interim between His resurrection and ascension and through the Holy Spirit after the ascension.

26 At that day ye shall ask in my name: and I say not unto you, that I will pray the Father for you:
27 For the Father himself loveth you, because ye have loved me, and have believed that I came out from God.

At that day (i.e. after Christ's resurrection and the coming of the Holy Spirit) the disciples will begin to exercise their new privilege of making their requests to the Father in Christ's name. Jesus hastens to add that He does not mean by this that it will be necessary for Him to pray to the Father on their behalf but that they themselves will have direct access to the Father as they pray in Christ's name. This is because the

Father Himself loves them personally and is graciously inclined toward them. The Father's love for them is based upon their love for and acceptance of Christ (see 1:11,12). God loves them because they have received and believed upon His Son, because they have believed that He has come from Heaven.

28 I came forth from the Father, and am come into the world: again, I leave the world, and go to the Father.

Jesus repeats once again the truth which He has constantly affirmed and which ought not to be the least bit obscure to the disciples. He has come into the world from the Father (see 3:13; 4:34; 6:38; 7:29; 8:42; 9:4; 10:36), and He is shortly going to return to Him, His mission on earth being accomplished (see 7:33; 16:5, 10,16, 28).

29 His disciples said unto him, Lo, now speakest thou plainly, and speakest no proverb.
30 Now are we sure that thou knowest all things, and needest not that any man should ask thee: by this we believe that thou camest forth from God.

The disciples reply, with what they suppose to be great sagacity, that they get Jesus' point, that they understand that this saying is to be taken literally. Jesus has just explained to them very simply that the reason they are going to be able to have their prayers answered directly by the Father (without necessity that Christ act as their intercessor) is that the Father Himself loves them because they have believed that Jesus is the Son of God come down to them from Heaven. He certainly did not consider this statement to be in any way enigmatic or difficult. The disciples, however, suppose their comprehension of the obvious to be the first instance of the heightened insight which Christ has promised. They are like little children trying to speak on a par with adults. They take themselves far too seriously and suppose that they comprehend far more than they do. They suppose that the really significant thing in all that has just transpired between themselves and Jesus is that He is able to anticipate their questions (vv. 17-19). They suppose that this makes it absolutely certain that He is, indeed, the Son of God. While it is true that Christ's ability at this point is compatible with His identity, it is far from being the major point which He has been trying to put across. The disciples pick up on a relatively mundane point and then congratulate themselves on their perspicacity.

31 Jesus answered them, Do ye now believe?

Jesus replies with gentle sarcasm, "So now you believe, do you?" He knows that, while their faith is genuine, it is far from satisfactory. They have missed His point almost entirely and remain oblivious to the impact of His words even as they look knowingly at one another and relish what they suppose to be their esoteric insight. He does not even try to correct their misconception but simply goes on to show that neither their knowledge nor their faith is so great as they suppose.

32 Behold, the hour cometh, yea, is now come, that ye shall be scattered, every man to his own, and shall leave me alone: and yet I am not alone, because the Father is with me.

Jesus emphasizes the utter inadequacy of the disciples' understanding and faith by saying that they will all soon forsake Him. His words are very like those He spoke to Peter after His self-confident boast earlier (13:37, 38). The time of Christ's death is now so near that He speaks of it as a present reality. He is already experiencing the terrible loneliness of the cross by anticipation. The prospect of the disciples' abandonment obviously causes Him great pain. Yet, even though abandoned by them, He will not be truly alone. The Father will still be with Him and this intimate communion with the Father is the thing that is truly important to Him. These words bring into sharp focus the enormity of the agony which Jesus would express by saying "My God, my God, why hast thou forsaken me?" (Mt. 27:46).

33 These things I have spoken unto you, that in me ye might have peace. In the world ye shall have tribulation: but be of good cheer; I have overcome the world.

There is some doubt as to what Jesus means to refer by "these things." Some suppose Him to refer to His many difficult sayings throughout the whole evening; more likely He refers specifically to what He has just said in v. 32 about the disciples' deserting Him. While His statement here is similar to His words in 14:27, it has a special force in this context. Jesus is telling the disciples that, even though they are about to forsake Him and leave Him to die alone, He still loves them and offers to them the peace of God which He alone can give. Again, He tells them this ahead of time so that it will be an encouragement to them later (see e.g. v. 4).

Though the disciples are to have peace as they trust in Him, they will continue to experience tribulation as they are forced to live in the world (see 15:18-20). They are not to despair, however. The world will not persecute them long, for it and its master are about to be judged (16:11) and defeated by

Christ. It will still maintain the appearance of power and authority, but its destruction will have already begun. Jesus has overcome the world in the sense that He has triumphed over it personally and in the sense that He has defeated it once and for all for all men.

Summary
(16:23-33)

Jesus tells the disciples that in the future they will not ask Him such questions as they are now desirous of asking but will make requests directly to the Father. These requests, because they are made in Christ's name, are to be graciously granted. Heretofore, the disciples have experienced nothing like the wonderful efficacy of praying to the Father in Christ's name or the glorious joy of having their prayers so miraculously answered.

Jesus explains that all His previous teachings have been couched in enigmatic language but that the time when He will speak to them straightforwardly is very near. Another characteristic of the approaching time is that the disciples will begin to exercise their right to pray in Christ's name directly to the Father. Christ will not have to pray for them. Rather, they will pray directly to the Father. The Father extends to them this wonderful privilege because He loves them individually since they have accepted and believed upon His Son.

Jesus repeats what He has affirmed so often, that He has come into the world from His Father in Heaven and that He is soon to return there. The disciples mistakenly believe Jesus to be making the point that His ability to anticipate their questions proves Him to be the Christ. They assure Jesus that they have finally come to comprehend His admittedly rather difficult teachings. Jesus' reply conveys a sense of gentle irony. That they do not really understand

is obvious in the warning which follows. Jesus warns the disciples that they will all soon desert Him. Once more, however, He explains that His reason for telling them of approaching calamity is so that it will not overwhelm them when it comes. Then they will understand that all that will come about is a part of God's plan. Jesus assures the disciples that, though the world will persecute them, they must not despair for He is about to overcome even the world itself.

Application: Teaching and
Preaching the Passage

The theme of this passage is encouragement. As the arrest and crucifixion draw near, Christ wants to strengthen and encourage the disciples. He wants to prepare them for the terrible ordeal which He knows to lie immediately before them. There are at least four themes discernible in His words of encouragement to them. First, He encourages them concerning prayer. He informs them that very soon they will be able to pray with a wonderful new effect as they pray directly to the Father in Christ's name (vv. 23,24,26). Second, He encourages them concerning their future, expanded understanding: they will be able to comprehend exactly what Jesus is talking about rather than just getting the general idea by means of analogies and parables (v. 25). Third, He encourages them by assuring them that they are personally and especially loved by the Father. The reason the Father loves them deeply is that they have accepted and believed on His Son (v. 27; see also 1:12). Fourth, Jesus encourages the disciples by assuring them of ultimate victory. He tells them that, though things are going to seem rather hopeless for a while, they are not to despair. He assures them that, in choosing to cast their lot with Him, they have chosen the winning team (vv. 32,33).

10. Christ's Great High Priestly Prayer (17:1-26)

The time of His arrest and crucifixion being very near, Jesus now turns from simply encouraging His disciples to praying to the Father on their behalf. Yet, since He prays audibly in their hearing, He apparently intends even His prayer to be an encouragement to them.

1 These words spake Jesus, and lifted up his eyes to heaven, and said, Father, the hour is come; glorify thy Son, that thy Son also may glorify thee.

John relates Christ's prayer as he remembers it many years after the fact. No doubt he provides a summary rather than a verbatim account of Jesus' words. Yet He conveys very accurately both the substance and impact of Jesus' communication with the Father. He recalls that Jesus looked up to Heaven as he prayed. This was the normal practice of the day just as it is the custom today to bow one's head to pray (see Lk. 18:13).

Jesus first refers to the simple fact that His "hour" has fully arrived. He has already indicated this (12:23; 13:1; 16:32), but now, as He draws within hours of the cross, Jesus experiences it as an absolute and present reality. As He begins to experience the agony and ignominy of the cross, He pours out His soul to the Father.

He prays first that the Father may glorify Him so that He may, in turn, glorify the Father (see 13:31, 32). There is no inherent problem in this request. There is nothing inappropriate or immodest about Jesus' desiring that He should be glorified before men. This is a direct communication between the second and first persons of the Trinity. The Triune God fully recognizes that it is appropriate that He should be glorified

before and worshiped by His creatures. This is no less true of the second than of the first and third persons of the Trinity. (Jesus calls attention to the fact that He is praying specifically in His capacity as the "Son.")

During the time of His incarnation, Jesus has laid aside His own glory and has concentrated upon bringing glory to the Father (see e.g. 7:18; 8:50; 12:28), but that laying aside has been economic rather than essential all along and is now about to end. Jesus is soon to reassume His former glory, now enhanced by the additional glory of having become the only Redeemer of mankind. (It is this enhanced glory as "the Lamb" which will be in focus in John's Revelation of Jesus Christ.)

Jesus' whole purpose in coming to earth has been to bring glory to the Father. However, He has rendered to the Father all the glory that He can by emptying Himself. Now He is about to render to the Father that glory which He may render only as the exalted King of kings and Lord of lords. Now He takes His rightful place as the One before whom every knee must bow, the One whom every tongue must confess is Lord. There is, of course, the great irony that He is about to lay aside His humiliation and reassume His glory by one final and ultimate act of self-emptying, the cross (see 3:14).

2 As thou hast given him power over all flesh, that he should give eternal life to as many as thou hast given him.

"As" (Greek *kathos*), which could well be translated "just as," establishes a connection between the last clause of v. 1 and this verse. Jesus is saying that just as the Father has given Him power over all flesh so that He may give eternal life to those whom God has given Him (see 5:21-27), so He presently wants the Father to glorify Him so that He may, in turn, glorify the Father. In effect Jesus is saying, "Glorify Your Son now just as You have already glorified Him in the past by giving Him the authority to grant eternal life to lost men." It was just as much a glorification of Christ for the Father to grant unto Him the power to confer eternal life upon His disciples as it would now be for God to raise Him up to His heavenly glory. Jesus is asking the Father to follow through on the process of glorifying Him, the next step being to glorify Him openly before all men.

3 And this is life eternal, that they might know thee the only true God, and Jesus Christ, whom thou hast sent.

Jesus goes on to say that the connection between the request of v. 1b and that of v. 2 is more than just an analogy. The essence of eternal life is to know and experience the true God. Eternal life is not just to live forever, but to live in intimate communion and fellowship with God. God has facilitated this communion by revealing Himself through His Son. Therefore men come to know God by accepting and believing on His Son. Thus the glorification of the Son, which serves to convince men of His true identity, will cause them to truly believe in God and thereby experience eternal life.

4 I have glorified thee on the earth: I have finished the work which thou gavest me to do.

Jesus returns to His request that the Father glorify Him and offers an argument why such a course of action is appropriate. He says that His mission on earth, which has been to bring glory to the Father, has been accomplished. He has glorified the Father. He has revealed the glory of the Father to men. This has been the whole purpose of His life (see

1:14; 8:50). Jesus speaks as if His life were completed, as if the cross were already behind Him. Obviously it is not and, just as obviously, Jesus speaks by way of anticipation. His acceptance of the cross is so complete that He views it as having already occurred, as being already reality. Since these words transpire between omniscient persons of the Godhead, such an assumption is entirely appropriate.

5 And now, O Father, glorify thou me with thine own self with the glory which I had with thee before the world was.

Jesus' logic is that since He has fulfilled His purpose of bringing glory to the Father, it would now be appropriate for the Father to allow Him (Jesus) to share that glory with Him. This communication is on a very personal and intimate level. Jesus assumes His own essential equality with the Father. He says, "Father, I have completed my task. I have glorified You; now I ask You to glorify me. I ask You to return to me the glory which I shared with You from all eternity past [see 1:1; 8:58]. Allow me to share with You once again in that glory which I, by my life upon earth and my imminent death, have advanced." In a sense Jesus is reminding the Father of His own promise to Him (Jesus) in 12:28.

6 I have manifested thy name unto the men which thou gavest me out of the world: thine they were, and thou gavest them me; and they have kept thy word.

At this point the focus of Jesus' concern begins to shift from Himself to His disciples. He is fully aware of the terrible ordeal which they are about to endure and He asks the Father to strengthen and assist them in their time of trouble. However, there is no abrupt break in

238

Jesus' thought. He continues the thought of His glorifying the Father. One of the ways He has done so is by having manifested the Father's name unto the disciples. By manifesting God's name Jesus means that He has revealed the Father's character and being (see comments on "name," 1:12).

Jesus views His disciples as having been given to Him from out of the world by the Father in keeping with His eternal counsel and purpose. It is difficult to comprehend the exact nature of this action, but it seems, unavoidably, to imply some sort of sovereign act on the part of the Father. At the same time, however, the disciples have, in their own right, responded positively to Christ. Jesus perceives no logical contradiction in this. God's sovereignty and man's free will are perfectly compatible in His thinking.

7 Now they have known that all things whatsoever thou hast given me are of thee.
8 For I have given unto them the words which thou gavest me; and they have received *them*, and have known surely that I came out from thee, and they have believed that thou didst sent me.

When Jesus says that the disciples have come to understand that everything He has taught them has come from the Father, He means just that and no more. He has repeatedly emphasized that His teachings do not originate with Himself but come from the Father (see e.g. 8:28; 12:49, 50; 14:10). The disciples have finally come to understand that this is so (16:30). They do not fully comprehend all of Christ's teachings, but it has finally dawned on them that He speaks with the voice of God. Jesus has given them the Father's message. They have received it as being from God and have accepted Jesus as God's spokesman. They have believed the salient facts

about Jesus. They have believed that He has come from Heaven and has been sent by God into the world. This is not everything, but it is a great deal, and Jesus is very thankful for it.

9 I pray for them: I pray not for the world, but for them which thou hast given me; for they are thine.
10 And all mine are thine, and thine are mine; and I am glorified in them.

When Jesus says that He is not praying for the world but for those whom the Father has given Him, He does not mean to say that the world is beyond the area of His concern or that He is not at all interested in its fate. Rather His mind is, at present, focused upon His own disciples and this particular request is made on their behalf only. To suppose Jesus to be expressing a total indifference to the fate of the people of the world would be totally out of harmony with His whole purpose for coming into the world (3:16; 12:47) and with the clear implication of His request in v. 21b.

Jesus' logic in making this special request for His disciples is that they are, in the truest sense, not only His but the Father's as well and that the Father has as much interest in their welfare and success as does Christ Himself. They were the Father's originally and it is He who has given them to Christ. They continue to be not only Christ's but the Father's as well since the Father and the Son are in essential unity and share all things in common (see 5:17; 10:30). Anyone could truthfully say that all that he has is the Father's, but only Christ can say without qualification that all that the Father has is His. As already noted, the Father's whole purpose in sending Christ into the world was to glorify Christ so that He could, in turn, glorify the Father. Therefore Jesus urges Him to bless the disciples because they are an integral part of the process by which that dual glory is to be achieved, by which the eternal purpose of God is to be accomplished. Once again, Jesus urges upon the Father a logic derived from His complete comprehension of the Father's own thinking on the point at issue.

11 And now I am no more in the world, but these are in the world, and I come to thee. Holy Father, keep through thine own name those whom thou hast given me, that they may be one, as we *are*.

Jesus' work on earth is accomplished (see e.g. on v. 4) and He will soon be returning to Heaven, but His disciples are to remain behind on earth without Him. Therefore, He asks the Father to keep them in a state of unity analogous with that which exists between Himself and the Father (see 5:17; 10:30). Jesus speaks of this unity among His disciples as being already in existence and not as something which He desires should come to be (the verb "be" is in the present tense).

The state of unity which Jesus desires for His disciples is one which they already possess even as He prays. It is, therefore, a unity of purpose and spirit rather than of ecclesiastical organization. Christ's words are supposed by some to be the mandate for an "Ecumenical Movement" to unify the various denominations into one all-encompassing super-church. Clearly Christ has no such idea in mind. (He will return to the theme of unity in vv. 21-23.)

When Jesus asks the Father to keep the disciples by means of His own name, the name by which He has revealed Himself to Jesus, He is asking Him to keep them by means of His own character and being (see on v. 6 above). Christ's use of the term "Holy Father"

implies a recognition both of God's absolute and unbending holiness and of Christ's own personal relationship of loving intimacy with Him.

12 While I was with them in the world, I kept them in thy name: those that thou gavest me I have kept, and none of them is lost, but the son of perdition; that the scripture might be fulfilled.

During His earthly ministry Jesus has assumed the responsibility for keeping the disciples Himself. He has performed this mission successfully even as He has relied upon the power of the Father to enable Him to do so (i.e. He has done this in the Father's name, see v. 11). Those whom He has received from the Father, Jesus has kept safely. The implication seems clearly to be that the disciples have been kept not by their own faithfulness, but by the power of Christ. Yet at the same time, one of the twelve, Judas, the son of perdition, has been lost. Those who have been kept have been kept by Christ, while the one who has been lost has been lost by his own self-willed action. Yet even his apostasy is a fulfilment of prophecy and a part of the eternal purpose of God. Jesus' point is that all that He and the Father have jointly determined that He should accomplish has, in fact, been accomplished.

13 And now come I to thee; and these things I speak in the world, that they might have my joy fulfilled in themselves.

Jesus, still speaking of His approaching death as a present reality (see v. 4 etc.), says that He is praying for these things while He is still in the world so that the disciples will come to possess a joy like His own. Some believe Jesus' words to be intended primarily for the listening disciples' ears and to be, in essence, a restatement of 15:11. No doubt Jesus is aware that the disciples are listening and speaks with them in mind, but one need not suppose that His only concern is the impact of His words upon them. His prayer is very real and is, primarily, a conversation with the Father. Accordingly, Jesus is praying to the Father as He is so that the Father will act in such a way as to ensure that Christ's disciples will experience a joy like His own after He has left them. (For a discussion of the nature of Jesus' joy see comments 15:11.)

14 I have given them thy word; and the world hath hated them, because they are not of the world, even as I am not of the world.

Jesus continues to speak of His earthly ministry as already complete. When He says that He has given His disciples the Father's word He is saying essentially what He has already said in vv. 6 and 8, that He has revealed to men the Father's nature by revealing to them the Father's message. Jesus observes that the world hates His disciples, that the reason it hates them is because they have received and obeyed the Father's own message as Jesus has delivered it to them and as they have been radically transformed by it. Just as Jesus is not of this world (see 8:23), so His disciples, as they have received and been transformed by His message, are no longer of the world either (see 15:19).

15 I pray not that thou shouldest take them out of the world, but that thou shouldest keep them from the evil.
16 They are not of the world, even as I am not of the world.

Jesus is very specific about what He is asking the Father to do for His disci-

ples. He is not asking for them to be taken out of the world as He is about to be. Rather, He is asking for them to be protected from the evil one (masculine), Satan. Jesus realizes that it is Satan who energizes the hatred of the world against His disciples. He does not ask that they be exempted from the world's hatred and attacks but only that Satan's purpose in such attacks be frustrated, so that they will not be neutralized and overwhelmed. Verse 16 simply restates the truth of v. 14b for emphasis.

17 Sanctify them through thy truth: thy word is truth.

In the next three verses there is a play upon the word "sanctify" (Greek *hagiazo*) which means both to make holy and to set apart or consecrate. The sanctification which Jesus requests for the disciples includes both aspects of sanctification. He desires, first, that they may be purified from sin. This is undoubtedly connected with the thought of v. 15 that they should not be neutralized by being led into sin. Second, He desires that they may be set aside and consecrated to the task of world evangelization that has been assigned to them. The means by which this sanctification is to be accomplished is God's truth. By God's truth Jesus means specifically the Father's message which He has communicated to them (see v. 14, etc.), but His words are also applicable in principle to the Scripture. As their minds are bathed in the knowledge of God's truth (Scripture), men are gradually sanctified.

18 As thou hast sent me into the world, even so have I also sent them into the world.

Jesus expresses proleptically the same truth He will later state directly to the disciples in 20:21. He compares the mission which is to be assigned the disciples to His own mission in coming into the world. Just as the Father has sanctified Jesus for His mission, so Jesus asks Him (the Father) to sanctify the disciples for the mission which Jesus has assigned to them.

19 And for their sakes I sanctify myself, that they also might be sanctified through the truth.

Jesus goes on to say that the establishment of a group of disciples to continue His ministry is a very important part of His (and the Father's) purpose in His own sanctification of Himself to the task of bringing the Father's message to them in the first place. Jesus uses the word "sanctify" of Himself only in the sense of consecrating Himself to His death on the cross. The clear implication is that for the Father to fail now to sanctify the disciples for their mission will be to frustrate the original design of Christ's coming into the world. For a moment Jesus suspends viewing His work as finished and sees the cross as being still before Him. In effect He says to His father, "If You do not sanctify my disciples, the horrible death which I am about to undergo will be to no purpose."

20 Neither pray I for these alone, but for them also which shall believe on me through their word.

As Jesus prays for His disciples that the Father will, indeed, sanctify them to their ministry of carrying the truth which they have received from Christ on to others, His thoughts turn to those to whom they will carry it. He thinks of those who will come to know God's truth and possess eternal life through the ministry of this small band and He petitions the Father on their behalf. The present disciples are precious to Christ not only in that they themselves are very valuable, but also in that they represent

a glorious potential, a vast number who will become their fellows by means of their ministry. Jesus is totally aware of the full impact which His life and death are to have upon history. He is also aware that the glorious benefits which He brings to mankind will be extended far beyond the little company of His immediate disciples (see 10:16; 20:29).

21 That they all may be one; as thou, Father, *art* in me, and I in thee, that they also may be one in us: that the world may believe that thou hast sent me.

Just as He has asked unity for His present disciples, Jesus now requests that His future disciples may experience a unity analogous to that which exists between Himself and the Father. (See comments on v. 11 for a discussion of the nature of this unity.) He adds, however, that this unity is not only to be like the unity that exists between Himself and the Father, but also that it is to be experienced in, by means of, or through both the Father and the Son. Jesus' implication is that the only way that the disciples may remain in unity is by remaining in constant fellowship with God (see 15:5, 6). He adds also that His purpose in desiring the unity of His future disciples is that the world may be convinced of the genuineness of their unity and, thereby, of the complete efficacy of His redemptive work on their behalf.

22 And the glory which thou gavest me I have given them; that they may be one, even as we are one.

When Jesus says that He has shared with His disciples the glory which the Father has given to Him, there are at least four possible ways to interpret His statement. (1) He may refer to the glory which He shared with the Father from

242

eternity past (see v. 5). This does not seem reasonable, however, for the disciple can never really share in that glory. (2) He may refer to His own essential glory which has been so obvious to men during the days of His earthly mission (see e.g. 1:14). If so, Jesus is saying that He is giving to His disciples the ability to manifest to the world a glory which is, in some respects at least, analogous to His own. (3) He may refer to the "glory" of the cross (see e.g. 7:39; 12:23). Jesus' crucifixion is actually the means of His glorification. His greatest glory comes only through the most extreme humiliation. If so, it is that glory which comes only through self-humbling which He bequeaths to His disciples. (4) He may refer to that ultimate glory which will be His in the day of judgment. Clearly, it is the last of these glories which He has in mind in v. 24.

It is difficult to decide between these and determine the precise sense which Jesus intends "glory" to have. One may suppose that the second view is the correct one since He speaks of the glory as having already been given to the disciples. On the other hand, if He speaks proleptically, the third and fourth possibilities can be considered. Perhaps He means to include all of the ideas expressed above in one grand, undifferentiated concept (see 12:28).

An important key to understanding the meaning of "glory" is the fact that Jesus says that the reason He has given this glory to the disciples is so that they may be one even as He and the Father are one. From this perspective, the third view (above) seems best. The glory that is most apt to produce unity is the glory of self-abasement.

23 I in them, and thou in me, that they may be made perfect in one; and that the world may know that thou hast sent me, and hast loved them, as thou hast loved me.

Jesus continues the thought of the previous verse by describing the unity that He wishes to be produced in the hearts of His future disciples. He Himself will be in spiritual union with every disciple, the Father will be in essential union with Him, and, therefore, every disciple will be in perfect unity with every other disciple.

Jesus speaks of this unity as a "perfect" or "perfected" unity. What does He mean by this term? How is this "perfect unity" different from the unity spoken of previously? Apparently this "perfect unity" is not just an essential and ethical unity, but a unity of love and affection patterned after the relationship that exists among the persons of the Trinity.

In v. 21 Jesus expressed one purpose for the disciples' unity: "that the world may know that thou hast sent me." Now He adds another purpose: that the world may know that the Father has loved Christ's disciples even as He has loved Christ. The key attribute of this special unity which Jesus now seeks for His disciples is love. He has said before that what will finally convince the world that men are in fact His disciples is for them to truly love each other (13:35).

24 Father, I will that they also, whom thou hast given me, be with me where I am; that they may behold my glory, which thou hast given me: for thou lovedst me before the foundation of the world.

The final and most wonderful request that Jesus makes on behalf of His disciples is twofold. First, He desires that they may enjoy personal fellowship with Him throughout eternity (see 14:3 and Lk. 23:43). Jesus is totally aware of His own identity, His own awesome majesty. He recognizes fully that intimacy with Him is the highest pleasure and honor that could ever be afforded to man. His fondest wish for those whom He knows to truly love Him is that they will be privileged to experience eternal intimacy with Him.

Second, He desires that they may see Him in all His glorious splendor. He wishes for each of them to be present and observe when He steps forward, opens the book and claims the universe as His own (Rev. 5:5-10). He wants them to experience that moment for themselves. He wants them to be able to join the great shout of victory when He is crowned King of kings and Lord of lords. He wants them to share in all His glory. This is a glory in which they would have no part except on the basis of their unity with Him. He wants them to know fully and existentially the depth and the fullness of the love that exists between Himself and the Father.

25 O righteous Father, the world hath not known thee: but I have known thee, and these have known that thou hast sent me.
26 And I have declared unto them thy name, and will declare _it_: that the love wherewith thou hast loved me may be in them, and I in them.

In these last two verses Jesus offers a somewhat negative summary of His earthly ministry but goes on to express His complete assurance that He will not fail to accomplish God's eternal purpose for sending Him into the world.

He addresses God, "O righteous Father." This is similar to "Holy Father" in v. 11, but the emphasis here seems to be on God's justice rather than on His moral purity. Jesus commits His (outwardly unimpressive) ministry to the just evaluation of the Father. He is confident that His verdict will be quite different from the world's. The world has not known God and has, therefore, been

hostile to His truth as spoken by His Son (see 5:38). While the world has rejected His claims, Jesus is confident that He has spoken only the words of God and that the Father Himself will ultimately vindicate Him before all the universe (see e.g. 7:29; 8:26,55; 14:10).

Jesus is also thankful that there have been a small number who have believed Him and accepted Him as their Messiah, Savior, and Lord (see v. 8; 1:12). He refers once more to the fact that He has declared to these believers the Father's name, i.e. His character and being (see v. 6). Not only has Jesus declared it by His life of ministry and preaching, but He is about to declare it in the most forceful and dramatic manner conceivable: by His death, resurrection, and exaltation.

Christ now summarizes the whole purpose of His coming into the world of men. He has come so that those who believe on Him may experience the love that exists between the members of the Trinity. The means by which this is to be accomplished is by Christ's coming to live in the believer through the person of the Holy Spirit (see 14:16-20).

Summary
(17:1-26)

Realizing that the time of His suffering is at hand and that it is by this suffering that He is to be glorified, Jesus asks the Father to glorify Him so that He may, in turn, glorify the Father. Jesus asks the Father to glorify Him through the cross in a way analogous to the way in which He has already glorified Him by giving Him the power to grant eternal life to men. In fact, since eternal life is, in its essence, to truly know God and since the glorification of Christ will enable men to know God, the glorification of Christ will actually help to bring eternal life to men. Jesus offers as further justification for His being glorified by the Father that

He Himself has glorified the Father by His life and impending death. He now requests that He may once again share with the Father that glory which He has shared with Him from all eternity.

One of the ways Jesus has glorified the Father is by revealing Him to the disciples whom the Father has given Him. These have believed Jesus' teaching and have accepted that His message comes from God. Jesus prays particularly for them that the Father will keep them safe and preserve a spirit of unity among them. Jesus reminds the Father that since they share all things in common and since these belong to Him (Jesus), they belong to Him (the Father) as well.

While He has been in the world, Jesus has assumed responsibility for the disciples' keeping but, now that He is going away, He asks the Father to assume that responsibility for them. Jesus asks the Father to enable the disciples to experience a joy like Jesus' own. Jesus reminds the Father that the world hates this little band of disciples precisely because they have believed and obeyed the Father's message as Jesus has given it to them. He explains that He is not asking the Father to remove them out of the world but simply to keep Satan from overwhelming them. He asks the Father to sanctify the disciples, by means of the truth of His own Word, to the work which has been assigned them. He says that it is for the very purpose of so sanctifying them that He (Christ) has sanctified Himself to His own mission.

Not only does Jesus pray for His present disciples, He prays also for those who will become His disciples in the future as a result of their ministry. He prays that they all may share in the essential unity that characterizes the persons of the Godhead, the unity that grows out of perfect mutual love. Jesus prays that His disciples may enjoy personal fellowship with Him and share with Him His glory.

Jesus closes His prayer with the thought that, though the world at large has rejected Him, He has, indeed, been speaking the Father's own message and that this little group has accepted and believed on Him as He has done so. His declaration of the Father's message is not complete, however, since it will be by His crucifixion that He will declare it most fully. His purpose in this great declaration is that those who believe in Him may come to share in the wonderful love which characterizes His own relationship with the Father.

Application: Teaching and Preaching the Passage

There are several ways one may arrange the truths of this chapter. Perhaps the simplest is to follow the natural outline which Jesus seems to follow in His prayer: 1. Jesus prays for Himself (vv. 1-5). 2. Jesus prays for His present disciples (vv. 6-19). 3. Jesus prays for all those who will later become His disciples (vv. 20-26).

Jesus' request for Himself is straightforward. He asks the Father to glorify Him. He presents the following reasons for asking the Father to do so: 1. So that He may, in turn, glorify the Father (v. 1). 2. So that He may be able to grant to His disciples the fulness of eternal life (vv. 2,3). 3. Because He has already glorified the Father by successfully completing the mission assigned to Him (v. 4). 4. So that He may regain the glory that was originally and properly His in eternity past (v. 5).

In the second section, where Jesus prays for His present disciples, there are two elements: 1. statements about them and 2. requests concerning them.

The statements made about them are as follows: 1. They belong jointly to both the Father and the Son, belonging essentially to the Father, but having been specially given by Him to the Son from out of the world (vv. 6,10). 2. They have accepted Christ, believed that His message is from God, and have obeyed it (vv. 6-8). 3. They, unlike Christ, are to remain in the world and carry on His mission on His behalf (v. 11), yet, like Him, they too are essentially not of the world (vv. 14,16) and are hated by the world (v. 14).

The requests concerning them are as follows: 1. Christ prays that the Father may keep the disciples in His truth and in unity with one another (v. 11). 2. He prays that His disciples may come to possess a joy like His own (v. 12). 3. He prays that, while they are not to be removed from the world, they may be protected from the evil designs of Satan (v. 15). 4. He prays that they may be purified and consecrated to their task of evangelism (v. 17).

Jesus' requests for those who will later become His disciples are essentially three. 1. He prays that they may possess and manifest a true spirit of unity so that the world will be convinced that they are truly godly and that their master, Jesus, was truly God's Son (vv. 21, 23). 2. He prays that they may share with Him in His own great glory (vv. 22,24). 3. He prays that His disciples may come to share in the love that characterizes His own relationship with the Father (vv. 25, 26).

C. The Passion Narrative (18:1—19:42)

1. The Arrest and the Jewish Trial (18:1-27)

The last four chapters of the Gospel of John, which relate the death and resurrection of Jesus Christ, form the climax of the narrative. Jesus has antici-

pated His death, resurrection, and ascension all through the book and has referred to them (considered as one unified event) as His being "lifted up" (3:14; 12:32) and as His being "glorified" (7:39; 13:31; 14:13). Now John will describe that "glory" which, while always visible (1:14), becomes unmistakably obvious as Jesus lays down His life for His sheep (10:11,15).

1 When Jesus had spoken these words, he went forth with his disciples over the brook Cedron, where was a garden, into the which he entered, and his disciples.

Upon finishing "these words," i.e. the whole farewell discourse (13:31—17:26), but especially the prayer of chapter 17, Jesus goes forth with His disciples over the brook Kidron (Cedron). Some suppose this to mean that Jesus does not leave the upper room until this point. More likely, assuming that Jesus has already left the Upper Room at 13:31, He now leaves the city of Jerusalem, crosses the brook, and goes over onto the Mount of Olives just to the east of the city to a garden which the Synoptists call Gethsemane (Mt. 26:36).

The disciples go with Him. They are undoubtedly both disturbed and expectant. The climax Jesus has been speaking about must be near, but it does not seem likely that anything significant is apt to transpire in the middle of the night out in Gethsemane. The Synoptists' account of Christ's agony in the garden (Mt. 26:30,36-46), which John does not relate, should be placed here.

2 And Judas also, which betrayed him, knew the place: for Jesus ofttimes resorted thither with his disciples.

One is missing from among the

Twelve, Judas Iscariot. He has left early in the evening after having received the sop from Jesus (13:30). Again, John refers to him as "the betrayer" (6:71; 12:4). This time, however, the present active participle (in Greek) seems to call attention to the fact that Judas' betrayal is in progress at this very moment. This is very graphic. Judas is even now carrying out his act of betrayal. He has a very good idea where Jesus will be at this time. He knows that Jesus often resorts to this particular garden for solitude and sanctuary.

3 Judas then, having received a band *of men* and officers from the chief priests and Pharisees, cometh thither with lanterns and torches and weapons.

John expects his reader to read between the lines a little. Judas has gone to the Jewish authorities on the previous day (Wednesday) and begun the process of betrayal (Mt. 27:14-16). Jesus' words to him earlier in the evening indicate that He understood Judas' plans to be quite advanced (13:27b). Apparently Judas has been busy since he went out from the Upper Room. He has been working out the details and making the final arrangements for his insidious deed. Undoubtedly with the chief priests' assistance, he has been able to secure a large force to assist him.

This force is comprised of two elements. First, there is a "band" (Greek *speira*) of Roman soldiers. This is equivalent to the Roman cohort, comprised of from 600 to 1,000 men and commanded by a chiliarch (such as Claudius Lysias in Acts 22:24). John probably means to imply that only a detachment of soldiers, rather than the whole cohort, is present. The second element of Judas' force is a detachment of the Temple police. These are referred to as officers from the chief priests and Pharisees. The presence of the Roman soldiers adds a particularly ominous note to the occasion. Their presence indicates that the Jews consider that they are arresting Jesus on a capital offense. Only the Romans have the authority to execute a criminal. The force comes fully prepared for any eventuality. They have lanterns, torches, and weapons. They are prepared to track Jesus down if He attempts to flee and to overwhelm Him by force should He resist arrest.

4 Jesus therefore, knowing all things that should come upon him, went forth, and said unto them, Whom seek ye?

At this point it once again becomes apparent that John provides an eyewitness account of what he relates. John's account, while in no way incompatible with the Synoptists, presents his own personal perspective on Jesus' arrest. The thing that stands out to John is that it is Jesus who is in control of and dominates the situation. John marvels as he reflects upon Christ's quiet self-assurance, especially when it is remembered that He knew all that was about to transpire. Jesus does not cower in the darkness but goes boldly forth to confront His adversaries. He asks them whom they seek.

5 They answered him, Jesus of Nazareth. Jesus saith unto them, I am *he*. And Judas also, which betrayed him, stood with them.

When they reply that they seek Jesus of Nazareth (technically, Jesus the Nazorean), Jesus replies, "I am he." Some have observed that John means Christ's words to be understood on two levels. Jesus is saying on one level simply, "Yes, I am Jesus of Nazareth." On another level, He may intend to use the words "I am" (Greek *ego eimi*) as they are used to indicate God's own name, Jehovah, the I Am. While this point should not be pressed, it is very like John to subtly imply such a double meaning (see comments on "I am," 8:58).

At this point John recalls for his reader another of his personal impressions of that night. He distinctly remembers Judas as he stood there among those who came to arrest Christ. He cannot forget how one who had once been part of Christ's inner circle came to identify so completely with His worst enemies. John does not refer to Judas' kiss of betrayal (Mt. 26:48-50), but that act must transpire at about this point in John's narrative and certainly fits the situation as John describes it.

6 As soon then as he had said unto them, I am he, they went backward, and fell to the ground.

Jesus' reply that He is the one whom they seek causes those who have come to arrest Him to fall backward to the ground. That His personality has an overwhelmingly powerful effect upon them seems especially evident when one remembers that most of this band was comprised of professional soldiers and policemen. There is something awesome, something overwhelming about Jesus that a whole company of armed men cower before Him as they do. One must conclude that, for a moment at least, something of His inner majesty and glory shows through. These men seem to see something of that great glory of Christ which John is to encounter in all of its force on Patmos (Rev. 1:16, 17).

7 Then asked he them again, Whom seek ye? And they said, Jesus of Nazareth.
8 Jesus answered, I have told you that I am he: if therefore ye seek

me, let these go their way:
9 That the saying might be fulfilled, which he spake, Of them which thou gavest me have I lost none.

When Jesus asks once more whom they seek and is again told that they are seeking Jesus of Nazareth, He says to those who have come to arrest Him, "I am the one whom you seek; let these [i.e. the disciples] go." Jesus' solicitude for His disciples never wavers (compare 13:1). Even as He faces those who are to lead Him away to a cruel death, He thinks of His little band of disciples. John remembers Jesus' words in 17:12 that He has lost none of those whom the Father has given Him. John is deeply touched as He remembers those words and as He realizes how deeply Jesus meant them. He is not going to allow one of His disciples to be lost. Though He Himself is about to die, He is determined, to the very last, that He will allow no harm to come to His disciples. He is determined to remain the Good Shepherd who gives his life to save his sheep (see 10:11 and 15).

10 Then Simon Peter having a sword drew it, and smote the high priest's servant, and cut off his right ear. The servant's name was Malchus.

At some point, certain of the band step forward to arrest Jesus. When the disciples see what is happening, some of them ask Jesus if He wishes them to use the swords which they have brought at His direction to protect Him (see Lk. 22:36,38,49). Peter carries it one step further: he actually draws the sword He is carrying and strikes out at one of those attempting the arrest. The man attempts to dodge the blow, causing Peter to hit him a glancing blow on the right side of his head, cutting off his right ear. Only John reveals that it is Peter who strikes this blow and that his victim is Malchus, a servant of the High Priest. That he does so illustrates once more John's attention to detail. It may be that John knows Malchus' name because of his close association with the family of the High Priest (assuming that John is the disciple spoken of in v. 15).

11 Then said Jesus unto Peter, Put up thy sword into the sheath: the cup which my Father hath given me, shall I not drink it?

Luke reveals (22:51) that Jesus immediately touches Malchus' ear and heals the wound and tells Peter to sheathe his sword. He explains that those who take the sword will perish by the sword and that the Father would readily send an army of angels to deliver Him if He should ask for them (Mt. 26:52,53). He makes plain, however, that His Father wills for Him to submit to arrest and crucifixion. Since He has come into the world for the very purpose of fulfilling His Father's will and giving Himself to die for men, it would be illogical for Him to resist. Christ refers to His approaching agony as "the cup which [His] Father has given [Him]." This language is similar to that which the Synoptists indicate He has used in the prayer in Gethsemane (Mt. 26:39,42).

12 Then the band and the captain and officers of the Jews took Jesus, and bound him.

The original intention was probably for the Temple police to arrest Jesus themselves, and they apparently made an attempt to do so. But because of Peter's violent resistance, the Romans become directly involved. They formally arrest Jesus and bind Him, apparently the standard procedure in making an arrest. As noted above, this is probably a small contingent rather than a whole cohort, but the fact that the chiliarch himself is present indicates the importance he attaches to the action. The Synoptists state that the disciples all forsook Jesus and fled at this point (e.g. Mt. 26:56).

13 And led him away to Annas first; for he was father in law to Caiaphas, which was the high priest that same year.

According to the Synoptists, Jesus is taken before "Caiaphas the high priest" after His arrest. John, however, states that He is taken "first" to Annas. While some see a contradiction here, such a conclusion seems unnecessary. John simply gives more detail than the Synoptists. That Jesus is taken "first" to Annas presupposes that He will later be taken to someone else. Apparently John supposes that this appearance before Annas is less well-known than the later appearance. John is certainly aware of Christ's appearance before Caiaphas: see vv. 24, 28.

There are at least two ways to harmonize John with the Synoptists. The first is to understand John to mean that there are two stages in the examination of Christ by the "high priest." The first stage is before Annas and the second before Caiaphas, the transition coming at v. 24. The Synoptists do not so differentiate the two aspects and speak of the whole event as occurring before Caiaphas since it is before him that the most important part of the interview clearly transpires.

The other way is to suppose that John means to include Caiaphas from the very beginning. His mention of him in vv. 13,14 seems to imply that he is involved in some way in what John is describing. Perhaps Annas' sending Christ to Caiaphas (v. 24) merely marks a transition in the trial where Annas yields to Caiaphas as the prime interrogator. We should note that John does not say that Jesus is taken to Annas' house and then to Caiphas' house. Annas may simply have been at Caiaphas' house all along.

John's central point is that prior to the appearance before Caiaphas there was a preliminary interview with Annas of which he supposes his readers to be unaware and of which he wishes to inform them. Notice that John identifies Annas in terms of Caiaphas, whom he clearly supposes to be both better known to his readers and more important. (Annas was High Priest from A.D. 6-15. For many years after this, he remained the power behind the scenes as several of his relatives held the office of High Priest, among whom was Caiaphas, his son-in-law, who held it from A.D. 18-36.) John apparently draws upon his special knowledge of the high-priestly family to supplement the Synoptists at this point.

14 Now Caiaphas was he, which gave counsel to the Jews, that it was expedient that one man should die for the people.

John further identifies Caiaphas as the same High Priest previously mentioned as pronouncing that Christ was to die for the nation of Israel (11:49-52, which see for comments). It seems strange that John should speak so of Caiaphas if his account is focused only on Annas at this point, with Caiaphas coming into view only at v. 24.

15 And Simon Peter followed Jesus, and so *did* another disciple: that disciple was known unto the high priest, and went in with Jesus into the palace of the high priest.

As Jesus is led away, He is followed by two of His disciples. One of them is clearly identified as Peter. The other is referred to simply as "another disciple." It has commonly been accepted that this "other disciple" is the Apostle John and that this is another instance of his indirect reference to himself (see Introduction; also 1:35, 38; 13:23). Against this is argued that John could not possibly be acquainted with the High Priest and that the reference must be to some unknown but more highly placed disciple, perhaps Nicodemus or Joseph of Arimathea. It would seem, however, that since this "other disciple" is clearly present in the garden as Jesus is arrested (he is spoken of here as following the soldiers who have arrested Christ from the garden), he must be one of the eleven. That being the case, John seems to be the disciple indicated.

While it is *unlikely* that John would be well acquainted with the High Priest, one can certainly not say that it is *impossible*. Unlikely things are often true. Upon the assumption that John's mother, Salome, was the sister of Mary, mother of Jesus (compare 19:25; Mt. 27:56; Mk. 15:46), John would be kin to Elisabeth who was "of the daughters of Aaron." Therefore, it does not seem unreasonable that he could have ties with the priestly class. Zebedee may also have been of Aaronic descent: it would not be unusual for a daughter of Aaron to be married to one of the priestly tribe. He might even have been related to the family of Annas. While one cannot be dogmatic on the point, it seems very likely that John's "other disciple" here is himself. This other disciple, whoever he is, actually goes into the High Priest's palace as Jesus is taken there.

16 But Peter stood at the door without. Then went out that other disciple, which was known unto the high priest, and spake unto her that kept the door, and brought in Peter.

Peter is not admitted and must stand outside the door. The other disciple, however, speaks to the female servant who keeps the door and persuades her to admit Peter. Apparently this disciple is aware that Peter is outside and goes out for the specific purpose of securing his admission into the palace. This scenario seems much more likely to be true of John (who has, together with Peter, followed Jesus and His captors to the palace) than of either Nicodemus or Joseph of Arimathea. Whoever this "other disciple" is, he is well-known within the High Priest's household, for the servant girl clearly recognizes him and readily accedes to his request to admit Peter.

17 Then saith the damsel that kept the door unto Peter, Art not thou also *one* of this man's disciples? He saith, I am not.

Something about Peter arouses the servant girl's suspicion, so that she asks him if he is not one of Jesus' disciples. We do not know what prompts her challenge. Perhaps it is merely that Peter is a Galilean (Mk. 14:70). Some suppose that her use of the word "also" (Greek *kai*) implies that she knows the other disciple is a follower of Jesus and therefore wonders if Peter is one as well. This is not very likely, however, since there is no indication that the other disciple is under any suspicion and since the same word is used in the Synoptics with no such implication (Mt. 26:69).

The Greek form of the girl's question is open to a negative reply, as if she says, "You're not one of them too, are you?" She may even speak half jokingly. However that may be, Peter is not prepared for such a question. It catches him off guard. He responds almost reflexively, "I am not." He denies Jesus before He realizes what he is doing. Jesus has predicted that Peter will deny Him three times before the morning

(13:38). This is the first of those denials.

18 And the servants and officers stood there, who had made a fire of coals; for it was cold: and they warmed themselves: and Peter stood with them, and warmed himself.

The bitter, pre-dawn cold has prompted the servants and officers (i.e. those who have arrested Jesus and brought Him to the palace) to build a fire to warm themselves while they wait for their superiors to decide Jesus' fate. Peter, undoubtedly very much ill at ease, stands among them and warms himself at their fire. He is afraid that he will be recognized as one of those with Jesus in the garden—the one, in fact, who slashed off Malchus' ear. He can only hope that no one got a good look at him in the darkness. His firm denial of the servant girl's accusation seems to have deflected suspicion from him, at least for the moment.

19 The high priest then asked Jesus of his disciples, and of his doctrine.

Upon the assumption that there are two stages in Christ's examination before the "high priest," the first before Annas and the second before Caiaphas (see comments on v. 13), the "High Priest" referred to here is Annas. He apparently considers himself to be conducting an inquiry rather than a trial, for his approach is entirely inappropriate for a trial in which formal charges would be brought against the defendant and witnesses called to substantiate them. It may very well be that this preliminary appearance before Annas has no other purpose than to satisfy the curiosity of this extremely powerful and influential old man. Another possibility is that Annas hopes to trick Jesus into making incriminating statements.

Annas begins by asking Jesus about His disciples and His doctrines. When he asks about the disciples, he is probably trying to learn their number and identity. He may also want to know what is required of them and how Jesus exercises His authority over them. Annas may be trying to see how likely it is that Jesus' disciples will rise up to defend Jesus if the authorities move against Him, how effective that resistance may be, and whether the disciples might be able to rally the general populace to their cause.

The Synoptists make clear that one reason the authorities had not already moved against Jesus is that they feared the reaction of the people, with whom Jesus was very popular (Mt. 21:46). The question about Christ's doctrine was certainly not asked with the purpose of gaining a better understanding or appreciation of it but for the purpose of catching Jesus in some error or twisting His words so as to use them in formulating charges against Him.

20 Jesus answered him, I spake openly to the world; I ever taught in the synagogue, and in the temple, whither the Jews always resort; and in secret have I said nothing.
21 Why askest thou me? ask them which heard me, what I have said unto them: behold, they know what I said.

Jesus ignores Annas' question concerning His disciples. He is determined to protect them whatever the cost to Himself (see v. 8). Three times in these two verses He uses the emphatic form "I" (Greek ego). It seems obvious that His purpose is to draw attention to Himself and away from His disciples.

He is no more forthcoming regarding His teaching. He answers that His teach-

ing is a matter of public record, that there is no secret aspect of His teaching that in any way contradicts what He has said publicly. Therefore He need not repeat it. Jesus does not mean to say, of course, that He has never spoken privately, only that His public teaching accurately conveys the totality of His doctrine. Since His teaching has been completely public, there should be ample witnesses against Him if it has been, in any way, improper. Jesus' reply is actually a protest to the illegality of Annas' whole approach. If Annas has any witnesses against Jesus, he should produce them. If he does not, then he should not have had Jesus arrested in the first place. Jesus will not cooperate with Annas' fishing expedition by which he hopes to dredge up something to use against Him.

22 And when he had thus spoken, one of the officers which stood by struck Jesus with the palm of his hand, saying, Answerest thou the high priest so?
23 Jesus answered him, If I have spoken evil, bear witness of the evil: but if well, why smitest thou me?

Jesus' words provoke one of the Temple policemen to strike Him (almost certainly on the mouth) with the palm of his hand. His words, "Do you (dare to) answer the High Priest thus?" imply that Jesus has spoken disrespectfully to Annas. The rebuke implicit in Jesus' words has not been lost upon His hearers. In reply, Jesus states simply that if He has spoken disrespectfully or insultingly to the High Priest, then a formal charge to that effect should be laid against Him; but if He has not said anything to substantiate such a charge, then it is illegal and unjust for the Temple guard to strike Him. Jesus is again protesting the illegality of the whole proceeding.

252

24 Now Annas had sent him bound unto Caiaphas the high priest.

Annas has obviously found Jesus a more formidable adversary than he expected and has failed utterly in His attempt to entrap Him into some self-incriminating statement. At this point, then, he sends Jesus on to his son-in-law, Caiaphas, for the formal interrogation. The verb "sent" (in the Greek aorist tense, not in the past perfect as the KJV implies) cannot be used to argue that Annas had sent Jesus to Caiaphas at some point previous to this and that the preceding interview transpired between Jesus and Caiaphas rather than between Jesus and Annas.

25 And Simon Peter stood and warmed himself. They said therefore unto him, Art not thou also *one* of his disciples? He denied *it*, and said, I am not.
26 One of the servants of the high priest, being *his* kinsman whose ear Peter cut off, saith, Did not I see thee in the garden with him?
27 Peter then denied again: and immediately the cock crew.

At this point John picks up with the narrative of Peter's denial. Peter has been standing by the fire for "a little while" (Lk. 22:58). Again he is challenged, "You are not also one of His disciples, are you (still phrased negatively)?" Peter answers, (with an oath according to Mt. 26:72) and asserts forcefully that he is not. Then (about an hour later according to Lk. 22:59) a kinsman of Malchus (v. 10) who is also a servant of the High Priest says that he believes that he remembers seeing Peter with Jesus in the garden at the time of His arrest. Luke (22:59) says that this man confidently affirms that this is so; the

question here is phrased to suggest a positive answer. This accusation is clearly getting very near to the truth. Peter, realizing that the game is almost up, vehemently denies (with curses and swearing according to the Synoptics: Mt. 26:74) that this is so.

No sooner are these words out of Peter's mouth than the cock crows. While John does not describe Peter's devastation as do the Synoptists, he makes it clear that Jesus' prediction of Peter's denial of Him (13:38) has come true. It has been suggested that the three denials in John do not correspond directly to the three denials in the Synoptics. While this may be so, the evidence is far from conclusive. Even on such an assumption, however, there is no real problem. The point of Jesus' prediction of Peter's three-fold denial (13:38) was not that Peter was to deny Christ three times and three times only, but that He would deny Him repeatedly.

Summary
(18:1-27)

Finishing His farewell discourse, Jesus goes with His disciples out of the city of Jerusalem and across the brook Kidron to the Garden of Gethsemane. This place being known to him as one of Jesus' customary retreats, Judas leads a band of Roman soldiers and Temple police there to arrest his Master. Although He is fully aware of all that their coming portends for Him, Jesus, with quiet confidence, assumes the initiative and confronts those whom Judas has brought with the question, "For whom do you seek?" In reply to their statement that they seek Jesus of Nazareth, Jesus says that He is the one they are looking for. Something about His bearing is so overpowering as He speaks these words that His would-be captors cower before Him and fall backward upon the ground. Apparently allowing them a moment to compose themselves, Jesus again asks them whom they seek. When they reply again that they seek Jesus of Nazareth, Jesus once more identifies Himself and suggests that, since it is He they seek, they should allow His disciples to go free. To the very last, Jesus is determined to protect His disciples from harm. At this point, Peter strikes out with his sword at one of those who have come with Judas to arrest Jesus, Malchus by name. Jesus does not approve of Peter's action, however, explaining that He must accomplish that work for which He has come into the world.

Jesus is arrested, bound, and led off to the palace of the High Priest, Caiaphas (the one who suggested earlier that one man should die for the people). John supplements the Synoptics by informing his readers that Jesus appears before Annas, Caiaphas' father-in-law, just prior to His appearance before Caiaphas. John relates that one of Christ's disciples, apparently John himself, is sufficiently well-known within the High Priest's palace to secure admission for himself and Peter. As Peter warms himself at a fire in the courtyard, he is confronted with the accusation that he is a disciple of Jesus. Caught off guard, Peter denies that this is so.

Even as Peter denies Him, Jesus stands before Annas. Hoping to trick Him into incriminating Himself, Annas asks Jesus about His disciples and His teaching. Jesus ignores the question about His disciples and answers simply that since His teaching is a matter of public record, there is no need for Him to attempt to expound it all again. This answer provokes one of the officers to strike Jesus sharply. Jesus protests that such treatment is entirely unwarranted and illegal. Having failed to entrap Jesus, Annas sends Him on to Caiaphas for the main Jewish trial as recorded by the Synoptists.

Meanwhile, Peter is accused twice more of being Christ's disciple and, twice more, denies that this is so. As he denies Jesus the second time (for a total of three), the cock crows, signaling the fulfillment of Jesus' prophecy concerning him.

Application: Teaching and Preaching the Passage

This passage may well be comprehended under the title "Three Men on Trial." Obviously, Jesus is on trial, but there are two others who are on trial as well, Peter and Annas. The following topics may be considered for each of the three men on trial: (1) the nature of the defendant, (2) the nature of the court, (3) the nature of the trial, and (4) the nature of the verdict.

First to be considered is Jesus. He is the Messiah who has come into the world to reveal the character of the Father and to redeem mankind from sin. The court that tries Him is both illicit and prejudiced. The trial is a farce, its only object to trap Jesus into self-incrimination. The verdict and the sentence are both predetermined: He is guilty and the penalty is death. This verdict will be set aside by a higher court, however (see Acts 2:23, 24).

Second is Peter. He is the leader of Christ's disciples, the most fearless and courageous of them. He has proclaimed his determination to stand by his Master no matter the cost. He has taken bold, even if precipitate and hopeless, action on Christ's behalf. The court before which Peter is on trial is simply the mind of Jesus. No other court's verdict really matters. To Jesus he has boasted, and from Jesus he seeks acceptance. For a few moments Peter forgets the One before whom he is really on trial, supposing that he is on trial before the men who stand around the fire. But the crowing of the cock is to remind him that it is before Christ, and Him alone, that he is on trial. The trial is a simple test of loyalty. Is Peter ultimately loyal to his Master or to his own temporal safety and well-being? The verdict is self-evident. Peter pronounces himself guilty without extenuation and imposes upon himself a sentence of self-condemnation and misery.

Third is Annas, a pompous and presumptuous man. He supposes that his own empty prejudice embodies the pronouncement of God. Annas is actually on trial before his supposed defendant. He is being judged by Jesus. Jesus is observing how Annas conducts himself at what he supposes to be the trial of Jesus. In effect the Supreme Judge stands incognito in Annas' court to see if justice will be done. Annas does not bother to hide his prejudicial and unjust conduct from this final Judge of all mankind. He demonstrates His own guilt beyond all possible doubt. Christ pronounces His verdict upon Annas in a quiet and restrained manner, simply pointing out how Annas violates proper procedure. Someday, however, there is to be another trial when the roles of Annas and Christ will be reversed. Annas will be on trial and Jesus will be both judge and chief witness for the prosecution. The verdict of that court will also be self-evident. Because God is everywhere present, all sin is committed in His very presence, but this is especially so of Annas; the incarnate God observes his injustice firsthand.

2. The Trial Before Pilate
(18:28—19:16)

John presents the confrontation between Christ and Pilate as a tremendously significant and symbolic event. Pilate is the very embodiment of the earthly dominion raised up by Satan in rebellion against God, whereas Jesus is the incarnation of God's eternal kingdom of righteousness (compare 1 Cor. 2:7,8). It is apparent from the very first

that Jesus is much more than a Galilean peasant. He addresses Pilate with precise courtesy but with an undisguised assumption of His own superiority as well. There is clearly a tacit understanding and a great empathy between Christ and Pilate. Much more transpires during this conversation than is conveyed by the words which are exchanged.

28 Then led they Jesus from Caiaphas unto the hall of judgment: and it was early; and they themselves went not into the judgment hall, lest they should be defiled; but that they might eat the passover.

John omits any reference to the trial before Caiaphas. He says in v. 24 that Annas sent Christ to Caiaphas. Now he relates that Jesus is taken from Caiaphas to the Roman judgment hall, but as to what happens in the interim, he says nothing. Even so, his account apparently assumes the fact of the trial before Caiaphas as described in the Synoptics (Mt. 26:57-68). Logically, something of significance must transpire between Jesus' being sent to Caiaphas and His being taken from him. What more logical than the trial as described by the Synoptists? Indeed, as already noted, John's repeated references to Caiaphas (vv. 13,14,24) assume a more important role for him than he actually attributes to him. Evidently he assumes that his readers are familiar with the Synoptic account of the trial before Caiaphas and feels no need to give the details. (Apparently, there was also a second Jewish trial, involving the whole Sanhedrin, before Jesus was sent on to Pilate; see Mt. 27:1; Mk. 15:1.)

John includes, at this point, another of those incidental details characteristic of him: that it is "early." This is in keeping with the fact that just prior to the present moment the rooster has been crowing (v. 27). The time Jesus was sent to Pilate was probably between six and seven o'clock in the morning.

John states that the Jews who took Jesus to Pilate did not actually go into the judgment hall so that they would not be defiled and, thereby, precluded from eating the Passover. This statement, along with 13:1 and 19:14, seems to indicate that John is depicting Jesus as being crucified on the actual day of the Passover, whereas the Synoptics seem to indicate that He is crucified on the day following Passover, the day following His participation in the Passover meal with His disciples. The Synoptists leave no doubt that they consider the Last Supper to be a Passover meal (see Mt. 26:17-19; Mk. 14:12-16; Lk. 22:7-15). How is this apparent discrepancy to be resolved? Leon Morris deals with the problem in an excellent special section (774-786); he suggests five possible solutions:

1. The two accounts cannot be harmonized and John is to be preferred.

2. The two accounts cannot be harmonized and the Synoptists are to be preferred.

3. The Passover took place as the Synoptists suggest and John is not really in contradiction.

4. The Passover took place as John suggests and the Synoptists are not really in contradiction.

5. John and the Synoptists use different calendrical systems.

Most conservative scholars accept either solution 3 or solution 5. Solution 5 may be the correct one, and one certainly cannot be dogmatic on the matter. However, I tend to think that those who prefer solution 5 do so because of what they see as problems in solution 3, not because they really believe that solution 5 is all that convincing. I feel that there are no insurmountable objections to solution 3 and that it is, on balance, the best solution.

The question hinges on the meaning of the phrase "that they might eat the Passover" here in 18:28. This phrase may be understood not only as applying to the main paschal meal itself, but also in a somewhat generic sense to all of the various meals included in the Passover celebration. If this is the case, "eat the Passover" may be understood as meaning to eat one or more of the other ceremonial meals of the Passover celebration rather than the actual paschal meal. If this is the solution, the Jews have already eaten the paschal meal on the previous night and are now concerned about their eligibility to eat one of other ceremonial meals, called the *Chagigah*.

Edersheim points out (II:567,568) that their concern is intelligible only on the assumption that it focuses on the *Chagigah* rather than the main paschal meal. His reasoning is that such ceremonial defilement as the Jews would incur from entering into the judgment hall would last only for the rest of the day, being automatically nullified by nightfall. Therefore, the Jews' fear concerning their ability to eat the actual paschal meal would be misplaced because their defilement would be gone automatically at sundown and the paschal meal was not eaten until well into the night. On the other hand, entering the judgment hall would preclude them from the *Chagigah*, eaten during the day following the Passover when the ceremonial defilement would still be upon them, nightfall not yet having eliminated it.

Dr. Morris gives the impression that he very well might accept explanation three except for the fact that the term "the Passover" cannot be used to refer to any of the various meals of the Passover except the paschal meal itself. Morris' objection can be resolved upon the assumption that John here speaks by synecdoche, a figure of speech by which one may speak of a part as if it were the whole. In other words John is saying, "so that they might eat one of the ceremonial meals of Passover—the Chagigah, to be precise."

In summary, I believe that the Last Supper was a true Passover meal and that Jesus was crucified on the day after the Passover, i.e. Friday (see comments 19:31). (This is, essentially, the position adopted by D. A. Carson in his section on the order of events on the day of Christ's death in his commentary on Matthew in *The Expositor's Bible Commentary*.)

29 Pilate then went out unto them, and said, What accusation bring ye against this man?
30 They answered and said unto him, If he were not a malefactor, we would not have delivered him up unto thee.

John makes no attempt to introduce Pilate, assuming that his readers are familiar with him already. When Jesus was born (probably 6-4 B.C.) Judea was treated by the Romans as a "client-kingdom," with Herod the Great (37-4 B.C.) and his son Archelaus (4 B.C.—A.D. 6) ruling as "kings," subject to the Roman emperor's approval. But from A.D. 6-41, Judea was dealt with as a province, with a Roman governor ("procurator") appointed by the emperor. These governors lived in Caesarea (in a palace built by Herod the Great), but would reside temporarily in Jerusalem on such special occasions as Passover and the other major Jewish festivals. Pontius Pilate was procurator of Judea A.D. 26-36. He had only to please the emperor in order to keep his position. But that meant maintaining order and, to a certain extent, keeping his subjects happy with his administration.

Since the Jews are unwilling to come into his judgment hall, Pilate comes out to them. Apparently Pilate is used to accommodating himself to Jewish religious eccentricities. He is already aware that Jesus has been arrested, since the chiliarch certainly would not have involved himself in the arrest without Pilate's knowledge and approval. There has probably been further communication between the Jewish leaders and Pilate since the arrest, for the Jews seem somewhat taken aback when Pilate asks them the nature of the charges. They answer with what seems an indecorous if not dangerous lack of humility that they would not be bringing Him to Pilate for official condemnation if He were not guilty of some great crime. The Jews apparently suppose themselves to have an understanding with Pilate and expect only a perfunctory sanction of the death sentence which they have passed upon Jesus. They are angered and exasperated that Pilate proceeds to consider the merits of the case on his own.

31 Then said Pilate unto them, Take ye him, and judge him according to your law. The Jews therefore said unto him, It is not lawful for us to put any man to death.

Pilate, for whatever reason, refuses to proceed according to the tacit understanding the Jews suppose themselves to have with him. He tells them that if they do not wish him to hear the evidence and render a verdict, then they can simply try the case themselves. He is perfectly aware that the only reason for their bringing Jesus to him in the first place is for him to officially pronounce the death sentence which they have agreed upon but are impotent to pronounce or carry out. (The Jews' statement that they do not have the legal authority seems to be in harmony with Roman practice at the time and is logically inherent in the whole narrative.

They would not risk involving Pilate in the matter if it were not absolutely necessary.) He seems to enjoy tormenting and embarrassing the Jews. He forces them to offer evidence before him as any other complainant would have to do. He refuses to recognize that they have any special standing or privilege in his court. He refuses to respect their scruples and pretensions to sophistication. He forces them to admit that, for all their high-blown rhetoric, they are nothing but a lynch mob after Jesus' blood.

32 That the saying of Jesus might be fulfilled, which he spake, signifying what death he should die.

John draws attention to another of those little ironies which so often present themselves to his eye. He says that God is providentially superintending the whole process by which the Jews find it necessary to remand Jesus to the Romans for execution (by the characteristic Roman method, crucifixion) rather than execute Him themselves (by their own characteristic method, stoning). This consequently fulfills Christ's own prophecy (12:32) that the manner of His death would be by being "lifted up," that is, by crucifixion.

33 Then Pilate entered into the judgment hall again, and called Jesus, and said unto him, Art thou the King of the Jews?

At this point Pilate goes back into the judgment hall, has Jesus brought before him, and asks Him, "Are You (emphatic in the Greek order) the King of the Jews?" (The Synoptists put this same question with this same emphasis at just this point.) That he asks such a question seems to indicate that Pilate is somewhat surprised that a man such as he perceives Jesus to be should be the

cause of so much consternation among the Jews. He implies, in effect: "You certainly do not look like the type of fellow who could have stirred up such a commotion as this."

Clearly, Pilate has been given something of the details of the charges against Jesus, and his question indicates the nature of those charges. Simply put, Jesus has been accused of claiming to be the Messiah. This claim entails two basic aspects. It involves the seemingly blasphemous claim to be God: this is what provokes such extreme anger among the Jewish leaders. It also involves a claim to be the legitimate successor to David and, as such, the rightful King of Israel. This is the aspect of Jesus' claim that the Jews chose to emphasize to Pilate. They considered that this was most likely to produce a negative reaction since the Romans were quite sensitive to anything which involved the slightest possibility of rebellion against Roman authority. They painted the picture in the most garish colors possible (Lk. 23:2). Pilate does not seem to have been quite as incensed against this purported challenge to Roman hegemony as the Jews might have wished. He seems to have approached the whole matter with a great deal more objectivity and restraint than they hoped. Pilate, obviously, found the Jewish leaders' case somewhat less than overwhelmingly convincing.

34 Jesus answered him, Sayest thou this thing of thyself, or did others tell it thee of me?

Jesus answers Pilate with a question of His own. He asks Pilate if he is asking this question on his own initiative or at the suggestion of others (the Jews). Jesus does not ask this question just to be enigmatic or to gain rhetorical advantage over Pilate. He cannot truthfully answer Pilate's question until He clarifies just what is being asked. If Pilate is simply parroting the question which the Jews have suggested he should use to provoke a self-condemnatory statement from Jesus, then he is asking in essence, "Are you an aspiring politico who is conspiring to lead a rebellion against Rome?" A truthful answer to this question would be, "No." If, on the other hand, Pilate asks his question sincerely from his own curiosity, he may very well be asking, "Do You really claim to be the Messiah?" A truthful answer to this question would be, "Yes."

35 Pilate answered, Am I a Jew? Thine own nation and the chief priests have delivered thee unto me: what hast thou done?

Pilate replies somewhat testily, even contemptuously, saying in effect: "I am not a Jew, am I? (The Greek question expects a negative answer.) How can I be expected to understand one of your intramural Jewish squabbles? Your own authorities have brought the charges against you. One would suppose that they have not done so without any provocation whatever. What have you done to provoke the antagonism which they obviously bear toward you?" He is not willing to accept the Jewish charges at face value and summarily condemn Jesus without further ado. He senses that there is something amiss in this whole matter and would like to get to the bottom of it. Pilate considers that he is being remarkably patient with Jesus, bending over backward to be fair, but Jesus is beginning to try his patience. His sense of Roman justice had best not be stretched too far.

36 Jesus answered, My kingdom is not of this world: if my kingdom were of this world, then would my servants fight, that I should not be delivered to the Jews: but now is my kingdom not from hence.

On the basis of Pilate's response, Jesus is able to deduce his state of mind sufficiently well to proceed to deal with him. Therefore, He simply ignores Pilate's last question as to what He has done and answers, instead, his first question as to whether or not He is the King of the Jews. He does not specifically say that He is the King of the Jews, but His answer assumes that He is. Even so, He assures Pilate that His kingship is not the sort about which either he or Rome need be concerned. His kingdom is not of this world: it is spiritual rather than physical. He is the King of the Jews, but that fact has no implications as regards Roman authority in Judea. Jesus' concerns are only spiritual and religious.

Jesus offers as logical proof of the truth of this proposition that He would not have surrendered so meekly to His captors were His purpose to establish an earthly kingdom. He and His servants would have fought to prevent their dream of empire from being foreclosed. It is interesting to note that the word here translated "servants" (Greek *huperetes*) is the same word that is translated "officers" in vv. 3,12, 18, 22. Just as the priests have their "officers," so does Jesus have His.

37 Pilate therefore said unto him, Art thou a king then? Jesus answered, Thou sayest that I am a king. To this end was I born, and for this cause came I into the world, that I should bear witness unto the truth. Every one that is of the truth heareth my voice.

Pilate's next words are subject to different interpretations. He may speak sarcastically, but it is probably best to suppose that he simply intends to draw Jesus out on the matter, to elicit from Him a more forthcoming explanation of His "kingship." Jesus' reply, "Thou sayest," should be taken as an affirmation, although perhaps a reluctant one. Pilate has not phrased it precisely as Jesus would prefer, but his statement is, on balance, true. That "Thou sayest" does embody a positive response is obvious from the rest of Jesus' reply and from Christ's use of it in response to Caiaphas' question earlier (Mt. 26:64; Lk. 22:70). In his parallel to these verses (14:62), Mark has Jesus actually say "I am" (Greek *ego eimi*, as in Jn. 18:6, above). Furthermore, the response of the Jews on that occasion makes it unmistakably clear that the Jews understood Jesus' words to indicate a positive response to Caiaphas' question (Mt. 26:65; Mk. 14:63,64; Lk. 22:71).

Jesus' answer is, in essence, "Yes, I am, as you say it, a king. My only purpose in life, however, is to bear witness of the truth. It was for this purpose that I was born, that I came into the world. Everyone who comprehends and accepts the truth recognizes that I speak the truth and accepts what I have to say." These last words express essentially the same truth as His statements in 5:38; 8:42,47 (which see for comments).

38 Pilate saith unto him, What is truth? And when he had said this, he went out again unto the Jews, and saith unto them, I find in him no fault *at all*.

Pilate's cynical retort, "What is truth?" cuts Jesus short and terminates, for the moment at least, the interview. Pilate now knows that Jesus is no revolutionary and poses no threat to public order or Roman dominion in Judea. He seems, therefore, to determine that Jesus should be released. The Synoptists make it plain that Pilate understands the insincerity of the Jewish officials' charges against Jesus (Mt. 27:18).

At this point Pilate goes back out to the Jews and informs them that He does

not find Jesus guilty of any violation of the law. Pilate very well understands that these are not the words which the Jewish authorities are wanting or expecting to hear. He consciously places himself at odds with them. (It is at this point that Luke places Jesus' appearance before Herod, 23:4-12.)

39 But ye have a custom, that I should release unto you one at the passover: will ye therefore that I release unto you the King of the Jews?

Apparently sensing that the people at large are not nearly so intense in their hatred of Jesus as are the Jewish authorities, Pilate apparently attempts to go over the authorities' heads and appeal directly to the people. He reminds them that it is the Jewish custom for a prisoner to be released in connection with the Passover celebration and suggests that Jesus might very well be a fortunate choice as the one to be released this year.

This solution has something in it for everyone. It does not simply acquit Jesus and thereby dismiss the Jewish authorities' charges as groundless. It humors the general populace by recognizing and honoring a custom symbolic of their national identity even under Roman dominance. It allows Pilate to release a man whom he feels to be unjustly charged.

Matthew relates that Pilate expressed his suggestion that Jesus be the one released at this Passover in the form of a choice. He asked them if they would prefer to have Jesus or Barabbas released. He undoubtedly supposed that putting it this way would render their choice obvious since Barabbas was a notorious criminal: a murderer, bandit, and revolutionary (Mt. 27:16,17). Matthew also relates that Pilate received at approximately this point a message from his wife urging him to release Jesus (27:19).

40 Then cried they all again, saying, Not this man, but Barabbas. Now Barabbas was a robber.

Much to Pilate's surprise and dismay, the people cry out that they prefer to have Barabbas rather than Jesus released to them. The Synoptists reveal that the people made this choice at the urging of the Jewish authorities (Mt. 27:20; Mk. 15:11).

John tells his readers simply, but with a sad irony, that this Barabbas was, as he puts it, a robber. John finds it inconceivable that the Jews should prefer that mercy be extended to a robber rather than to Jesus. He cannot but remark on the extreme contrast between Barabbas the robber and Jesus the Savior. The Synoptists relate that when the Jews expressed their desire that Barabbas, rather than Jesus, should be released, Pilate asked them what they wished him to do with Jesus. They replied that He should be crucified (Lk. 23:21-23).

19:1 Then Pilate therefore took Jesus, and scourged *him*.

According to the Synoptists, Pilate's next act was to wash his hands of Jesus' blood and, after scourging Jesus, to deliver Him over to the Jews to be crucified (Mt. 27:24-26). Some have supposed that there is some conflict between John and the Synoptists at this point since John presents the trial before Pilate as continuing on for some little while subsequent to this. A closer examination, however, reveals that there is no inconsistency. The Synoptists summarize the conclusion of the trial by saying that Pilate delivers Jesus over to his soldiers to be put through the horrid process of scourging before delivering Him to be crucified. John, on the other hand, gives

a much more detailed picture of the remaining portion of the trial in which Pilate desperately tries to save Jesus.

According to John, Pilate's next act is to order Jesus to be scourged. This scourging is administered to the naked flesh of Jesus' back using a special whip consisting of several leather thongs with pieces of metal attached to them so as to dig into the flesh. Such a beating literally pulverizes the flesh and quite often kills its unfortunate victim.

There are at least two theories as to Pilate's motivation in scourging Jesus. Some believe that he did so because, while he did not view Jesus as guilty of any major crime, he saw Him as a zealot, a troublemaker who needed to be taught a lesson. Others believe that he supposed that seeing Jesus subjected to such barbarous cruelty would appease the mob's wrath somewhat and produce some natural human pity for Jesus, making it possible for Pilate to release Him. More than likely both motives were in Pilate's mind.

2 And the soldiers platted a crown of thorns, and put *it* on his head, and they put on him a purple robe,
3 And said, Hail, King of the Jews! and they smote him with their hands.

The soldiers who scourge Jesus mock Him. They seize upon the seemingly preposterous idea that He is the King of the Jews and fashion a crown out of thorns and put it upon His head. They place a purple robe upon Him (and according to Mt. 27:29 a reed in His hand, as a mock scepter). Then they bow before Him and sarcastically hail Him as "King of the Jews," all the while striking Him upon the face with their hands.

It is generally understood that the Synoptists present this mockery as coming after Pilate sentenced Jesus to death and just prior to His being led away to Golgotha (e.g. Mt. 27:30,31). This is not actually stated, however, and, assuming the scenario suggested above (see comments v. 1), the confrontation between Christ and Pilate continues on in the manner in which John indicates.

4 Pilate therefore went forth again, and saith unto them, Behold, I bring him forth to you, that ye may know that I find no fault in him.

Pilate has gone back into the judgment hall at some point subsequent to 18:38, apparently at v. 1 when he has Jesus beaten. Now, he goes back out to speak with the Jews once more. He tells them that he is going to bring Jesus out before them so that they may know that he finds no fault (i.e. no violation of Roman law) in Him.

The precise logic of Pilate's statement is not readily apparent. How will his bringing Jesus out before them convince the Jews that he finds no fault in Him? It seems obvious that his words presuppose and involve some reality implicit in the situation which is not specifically stated. That unspoken reality seems to be the horrifying appearance of Jesus after His scourging. That this is so may be deduced from the fact that Pilate urges the Jews (v. 5) to look at Jesus. Apparently he supposes that the sight of Jesus after His scourging will surely satiate their blood lust. Godet (p. 934) seems to have caught the essence of Pilate's logic. He paraphrases him thus, "Well, you must understand; there is enough of it now. I have consented to this [scourging] in the way of compliance with your request [although I actually consider the man to be innocent]; I will go no farther!"

5 Then came Jesus forth, wearing the crown of thorns, and the purple robe. And *Pilate* saith unto them, Behold the man!

Jesus, wearing the crown of thorns and the purple robe which the soldiers have placed upon Him in mockery of His being the King of the Jews, is now led forth before the people. Pilate commands the crowd to "behold the man." He means, by these words, simply to achieve the purpose mentioned above, to cause the mob to look upon the horrible effect which the scourging has had upon Jesus and be satisfied that He has suffered enough. However, John sees in Pilate's words a symbolic significance which far transcends Pilate's own understanding of them. He sees them as a challenge to the Jews to look carefully upon this man who stands before them, to consider carefully what their treatment of Him should be. He even sees Pilate's words as a challenge to all men everywhere to look thoughtfully and comprehendingly at Jesus the Messiah as He stands despised and rejected, a man of sorrows and acquainted with grief, as He is esteemed by none and as all hide their faces from Him (Is. 53:3,4). In effect John says, "Look at Him as He stands there before the Jews. Is not this truly the suffering servant described so graphically by the prophet Isaiah?"

6 When the chief priests therefore and officers saw him, they cried out, saying, Crucify *him*, crucify *him*. Pilate saith unto them, Take ye him, and crucify *him*: for I find no fault in him.

If Pilate supposes that the sight of Jesus' horrible state will move the crowd to pity Him, he is gravely mistaken. When the Jewish leaders catch sight of Jesus, rather than being moved with pity, they cry out for Him to be crucified. Though John mentions only the leaders, it seems reasonable that they are able to stir up the whole crowd to join them in their demand for Jesus' blood (see Mt. 27:20). While the Synoptists state that the Jews first cry out for Jesus to be crucified at the time (18:40) that they choose Barabbas over Christ (Mt. 27:22, 23), John does not mention crucifixion until this point. The cry which they raise is simply "Crucify," the "him" being added by the translators for clarification. One can easily imagine the mob taking up this one word slogan, "Crucify, crucify, crucify."

Pilate, apparently angered by the Jews' stubbornness, says sarcastically, "All right, you take Him and crucify Him, for I do not judge Him worthy of death." Pilate's emphasis on "you" and "I" is the key to understanding his meaning. He knows full well that the Jews do not have the authority to crucify Jesus, that only he has such authority. His words are, therefore, a taunt (see 18:31). In effect he says to them, "Look, you people cannot get your way in this matter apart from me. I am the one in control here. Just remember that." Pilate asserts his own absolute and unilateral authority in the matter.

7 The Jews answered him, We have a law, and by our law he ought to die, because he made himself the Son of God.

The Jews respond to Pilate's assertion by stating as forcefully as possible their case against Jesus. They answer, "We (emphatic) have a law, and by that law He ought to die." In effect they are saying, "He may not be guilty of any great wrong in terms of the Roman law, but according to our Jewish law, He is guilty of the great crime of blasphemy because He claims to be the Son of God" (see 5:18; 8:54; 10:33).

8 When Pilate therefore heard that saying, he was the more afraid;
9 And went again into the judgment hall, and saith unto Jesus, Whence art thou? But Jesus gave him no answer.

When Pilate hears that Jesus claims to be the Son of God, he becomes even more frightened than he is already (apparently having first become afraid in 18:36,37). Probably Pilate is a superstitious man, and the thought that Jesus may be divine is unsettling to him. Pilate has clearly been impressed by Jesus as he has questioned Him, his wife has informed him of a dream concerning Him, and now he hears that Jesus claims to be the Son of God. All of this together has an impact on Pilate's mind. So he goes back into the judgment hall to interrogate Jesus further. He asks Jesus where He comes from.

It is difficult to know precisely what Pilate meant by this question. Probably he was genuinely impressed with the idea that Jesus might be divine, and his question was the equivalent of, "Just who are You, anyway?" It is interesting that Jesus gave no answer. One cannot be sure as to why He did not. Perhaps it was because no simple answer would suffice. Perhaps He wished to draw Pilate out on the issue. More likely this refusal to answer was intended to produce just the effect that it did produce: that is, to provoke Pilate's haughty response. Jesus wished to communicate to Pilate the truth of v. 11, and therefore He had to provoke Pilate to ask the question of v. 10.

10 Then saith Pilate unto him, Speakest thou not unto me? knowest thou not that I have power to crucify thee, and have power to release thee?

Though Pilate is somewhat awed by

263

Christ, his haughty Roman spirit cannot long be subjugated. He speaks in his most imperious manner, "Are you not going to answer me? Do you not realize that it is within my authority to either crucify you or to release you? [This is your chance to defend yourself. I am even inclined to help you. The least you can do is show me the courtesy of answering my questions. You had best answer me if you know what's good for you.]" Even though he is intrigued by the possibility that Jesus may be in some sense divine, Pilate still supposes himself to be addressing his inferior.

11 Jesus answered, Thou couldest have no power *at all* against me, except it were given thee from above: therefore he that delivered me unto thee hath the greater sin.

Jesus does reply to Pilate, and His reply is absolutely devastating. He first informs Pilate that he could have no authority (Greek *exousia*) over Him at all if that authority were not delegated to him from God.

Jesus is clearly not impressed by the panoply of Roman power, nor by Pilate who wields it. He dismisses it all as of no real consequence. This is a terrible blow to Pilate. Here is a man who is neither impressed nor cowed by the awesome majesty of Rome. Here is one who speaks condescendingly, even disparagingly, of the very power by which Pilate is distinguished from all lesser mortals. These words reduce Pilate to the level of a mere man. Jesus assumes the role of the superior and addresses Pilate as distinctly subordinate to Himself. Then He adds that Pilate's role in the whole affair is an essentially peripheral one, anyway. The real initiative and, therefore, the real guilt lies not with Pilate, but with Caiaphas, who is merely using Pilate to accomplish his own designs.

These words are as destructive of Pilate's self-importance as are the former. A Roman procurator does not like to think of himself as merely peripheral to any matter. He is the personification of Roman authority, the very voice of Caesar. He holds the power of life and death, and his every word is, therefore, of the utmost significance. Now here is Jesus saying to him in effect, "This matter really does not concern you. You are obviously somewhat out of your element in trying to deal with it. Therefore, I really don't hold you primarily responsible for this inept travesty of justice." Pilate has never been addressed in such a manner. He is flabbergasted.

12 And from thenceforth Pilate sought to release him: but the Jews cried out, saying, If thou let this man go, thou art not Caesar's friend: whosoever maketh himself a king speaketh against Caesar.

From this point onward Pilate does his best to save Jesus. It would seem, therefore, that Pilate has been most powerfully impressed by this strange man who, though savagely beaten and comically attired, still manifests such an inherent majesty of spirit. Pilate is now convinced that Jesus is no mere Jewish peasant or aspiring religious charlatan. While he does not begin to comprehend His true identity, he knows that there is something supernatural, something Godlike about Him.

John does not relate the means by which Pilate communicates to the Jews this new determination to release Jesus. Regardless, the Jews cry out in response that if Pilate releases Jesus He will reveal that he is not Caesar's friend since anyone who proclaims himself to be a king (as this Jesus clearly has) is, by definition, speaking against Caesar. The Jews clearly perceive the change in

Pilate's attitude. They sense that he may very well release Jesus, so they adopt an entirely new approach. Heretofore they have sought respectfully to persuade Pilate to their position. Now they attempt to coerce him by means of a very thinly veiled threat. They make it plain that if Pilate releases Jesus, they will see to it that his action is represented to Caesar in the worst possible light.

13 When Pilate therefore heard that saying, he brought Jesus forth, and sat down in the judgment seat in a place that is called the Pavement, but in the Hebrew, Gabbatha.
14 And it was the preparation of the passover, and about the sixth hour: and he saith unto the Jews, Behold your King!

The force of this threat is not lost upon Pilate. He realizes full well how disastrously such an action could be presented to Caesar. While he likes to play the part of the incorruptible, fearless Roman, he is really just a petty bureaucrat intent upon not messing up his chances of promotion by offending his superiors. For the last time, therefore, he brings Jesus forth to the Jews. He takes his place upon the judgment seat so as to make what he will say entirely official. He realizes that the Jews have him trapped and that he has no choice but to crucify Jesus despite all his misgivings. Determined to express his contempt and anger, he speaks with bitter sarcasm, "Behold your King." Pilate clearly means to belittle the Jews by suggesting that this pitiable specimen is the King they deserve. While his anger is directed primarily against the Jews rather than Jesus, Pilate's words necessarily involve the idea of the absurdity of the idea that Christ is in any real sense a king. Pilate seems to have reached the decision to execute Christ and is now

hardening himself to that deed.

At this point John relates three of the incidental details which are so characteristic of him. He first informs his reader that the place where all this transpires was called the Pavement, or in the Aramaic, *Gabbatha*. Next, he mentions that these events transpired on "the preparation of Passover." Some understand this to mean the day on which the Passover lambs were killed and the feast prepared, i.e. Passover itself, 14 Nisan. According to this view, Christ would be crucified on Passover day and the Last Supper would not be a true Passover meal. Such a conclusion is not required, however. The term "preparation" (Greek, *paraskeue*) came to mean "preparation for the Sabbath" (or simply, "Friday") in Jewish Greek usage (see Morris 776, 800; Bruce 364). John is saying that these things happened on Friday of Passover Week.

Finally, John mentions that these events transpired at about the sixth hour, i.e. about noon (see comments 1:39,40). This creates something of a problem. John represents Jesus' trial as concluding at about the sixth hour while Mark (15:25) says that Jesus was crucified at the third hour. The answer seems to lie in the fact that in antiquity the reckoning of time was always approximate and imprecise. The "third hour" should be understood as "the middle of the morning" while the "sixth hour" should be understood as about noon. If Jesus was crucified at 10:30 a.m., both John and Mark can be understood as being correct in terms of their *approximate* reckoning of the time. Mark says that Jesus was crucified sometime just after mid-morning while John says that it was not long before noon.

15 But they cried out, Away with *him*, away with *him*, crucify him. Pilate saith unto them, Shall I crucify your King? The chief priests

answered, We have no king but Caesar.

The Jews are infuriated by Pilate's reference to Jesus as their King. They express their utter and unqualified rejection of the kingship of Jesus over them by screaming in unison, "Away with Him, away with Him, crucify Him." Pilate, from whatever motive, replies, "Your king [emphatic in the Greek order], you wish me to crucify your king?" Undoubtedly, Pilate's state of mind is essentially the same as in v. 14 (which see).

In response to this taunt, Caiaphas and his companions utter words that are at once absurd, blasphemous, and symbolic. They are absurd in that they suggest a complete satisfaction with and acceptance of the Roman occupation of the Jewish homeland. While this might be so for these high priestly Quislings, it certainly does not express the opinion of the great majority of the populace. They are blasphemous in that they utterly reject the theocratic nature of the Jewish nation. They reject entirely the idea that God alone is their king. They are symbolic in that they express reality far more accurately than those who speak them suppose. They have, indeed, rejected their Messiah, the one anointed by God to establish over them an eternal kingdom of righteousness and have chosen, instead, to live under the authority of Satan as it is exercised by the current manifestation of his earthly dominion, Rome. They speak the truth. Just as God is not their father (8:38-44), neither is He their king.

16 Then delivered he him therefore unto them to be crucified. And they took Jesus, and led *him* away.

Pilate realizes that he has lost. There is no way for him to save Jesus without running the chance of some negative consequence to himself. It galls him no end, but there is nothing else for it; Jesus must die. He therefore gives his official permission for the death sentence to be carried out. Jesus is led away to Golgotha. John's implication is that Pilate commits Jesus to the Jews for crucifixion. What John really means to convey is that, although the Romans carry out the literal act of crucifixion, the Jews are ultimately responsible for this awful crime. It is at their insistence that Jesus is to die.

Summary
(18:28—19:16)

Early on the morning following the night of His arrest, appearance before Annas, and trial before Caiaphas and the Sanhedrin, Jesus is taken to Pilate, the Roman governor. Since the Jews who bring Jesus refuse to enter Pilate's judgment hall for fear of ceremonial pollution, the governor comes forth to them and asks the nature of the charges against Jesus. Apparently supposing themselves to have an understanding with Pilate, the Jews are somewhat taken aback by this request and reply testily but weakly that they would not be bringing this man to Pilate if there were not sufficient cause for doing so. Pilate's response to their insolence is to sarcastically suggest that perhaps it would be best for them to deal with this sensitive matter themselves. The Jews must respond as Pilate intends by conceding that they cannot impose a death sentence without his sanction. John informs his reader that the ultimate reason for the Jews' coming to Pilate is so that Jesus' execution will be by the Roman method of crucifixion as He has, Himself, predicted.

At this point Pilate goes back into the judgment hall, has Jesus brought before him, and asks Him if He is the King of the Jews. Jesus responds with His own question, asking whether Pilate asks this of himself or at the suggestion of the Jewish leaders. Pilate's impatient response tacitly admits that the question has been suggested to him by the Jews. Not being a Jew, he obviously has no personal understanding of such Jewish esoterica. It is Jesus' own fellow countrymen who have brought the charges against Him. Jesus must have done something to provoke their action, and Pilate wants to know what it is. Jesus now responds to Pilate's first question, as to whether He claims to be the King of the Jews, by stating that His kingdom is of a spiritual rather than physical nature. He is therefore not in competition with Rome for temporal dominion. He offers as logical proof of this contention the complete lack of any resistance to His arrest. Surely one bent on establishing his own empire would not give up without a struggle. Apparently accepting Jesus' logic, Pilate asks Jesus to state clearly if there is any sense at all in which He claims to be a king. Jesus responds that in the sense He has just suggested He is, in fact, a king. It is for the very purpose of revealing this truth to men that He has come into the world, and everyone who has been enabled by God to do so will accept that all this is so. Pilate responds cynically, "Truth, what is that?"

At this point Pilate goes back out to the Jews and informs them that he has found no evidence of any wrongdoing on Jesus' part. He has a suggestion for them, however: since it is the custom for a prisoner to be released at the Passover, it might be a good idea for Jesus to be the one released this year. This would allow Pilate to avoid punishing one whom he supposes to be innocent without rejecting the Jews' charges as unfounded. The Jews reject this solution out of hand. If Pilate must release someone, they prefer Barabbas. Pilate's response to this reaction of the Jews is to have Jesus scourged, apparently supposing that this will appease the mob's wrath and stir up some natural sympathy for Jesus. In connection with this scourging, the Roman soldiers place upon Jesus a purple robe and a crown of thorns, strike Him with their hands, and mockingly hail Him as the King of the Jews.

After he has Jesus scourged, Pilate goes out to the Jews again and says that he is bringing Jesus out for them to behold so that they will understand that this is as far as he intends to go in punishing Him. As Jesus appears, the effects of the horrible scourging quite apparent, He still wears the purple robe and the crown of thorns. Pilate, with more significance than he suspects, calls upon the Jews to "Behold the man." They respond by crying out for Jesus to be crucified. Pilate, still angry and bitter, knowing full well the impossibility of what he suggests, says, "You take Him and you crucify Him, for I find no fault in Him." The Jews respond to this challenge by saying that, according to their law, Jesus is worthy of death because He has blasphemed in claiming to be the Son of God. The mention that Jesus claims to be the Son of God frightens Pilate, causing him to go in and try to find out from Jesus something more concerning His origin and identity. Jesus refuses to answer his questions, however, which angers Pilate and provokes him to remind Jesus that he has power either to crucify or release Him.

Jesus is neither impressed nor intimidated. He replies calmly that Pilate has no real authority in this matter except that which God has allowed him and that it is the Jewish authorities, rather than Pilate, who bear primary responsibility for the injustice being perpetrated upon Him. These words of Christ have a profound effect upon Pilate, who now becomes more determined than ever to release Him. The Jews, however, sense Pilate's intention and state ominously that he will be acting against Caesar if he releases Jesus, that anyone who claims to be a king is, *ipso facto*, speaking against Caesar.

The implication of these words is not lost on Pilate. He is fully aware of the damage such charges as these could do to his career. He realizes that he must bow to the Jews' wishes concerning Christ, but he cannot forbear one last insult even as he concedes defeat. He seats himself upon his judgment seat, has Jesus led forth once more, and proclaims to the Jews, "Behold your King!" The Jews respond to this taunt by screaming, "Away with Him, away with Him, crucify Him." Pilate again taunts them, "What, you want me to crucify your King?" It is the Jews who now speak with more significance than they suspect: "We have no king but Caesar." Pilate can resist them no longer. He delivers Jesus to them, and He is led away to be crucified.

Application: Teaching and Preaching the Passage

One cannot read this passage without noticing how Pilate keeps going in and out of the judgment hall. He comes out (18:29), goes back in (18:33), comes back out (18:38), goes back in (apparently 19:1), comes back out (19:4), goes back in (19:9), and comes back out for the last time (apparently 19:12). It seems entirely likely that John intends his readers to see in this constant going in and coming out a symbolic representation of Pilate's inner vacillation as to the verdict he will pronounce upon Christ. Be that as it may, Pilate's vacillation is clearly the theme of this passage. Pilate is confronted with the Son of God. He must make a decision on how he will respond to Him and what his verdict concerning Him will be. While the circumstances of

Pilate's dilemma and vacillation are especially acute and graphic, his position is not significantly different from that of all men who are confronted with Christ and must decide either for or against Him. His struggle is, therefore, both symbolic and instructive.

Pilate is characterized by a strange combination of pride, fear, nobility, and cruelty. His pride is apparent all through the passage and is manifested toward both the Jews (18:31; 19:14,15) and Christ (18:35,38; 19:10). His fear is manifested toward Christ (19:8) and men (19:12,13). Some semblance of nobility of character seems apparent (18:29,38; 19:12). His cruelty is apparent in the coldly calculating way in which he decides to scourge Jesus (19:1). These qualities all work together to produce failure in Pilate. He simply cannot find the courage to do what he knows is right and release Jesus. So it is with all men. They do not have within them the ability to do right. Apart from God's supernatural grace they will always do wrong. They will always choose against Christ.

Raymond Brown (865-872, 885-896) divides this passage into seven episodes as follows: (1) The Jewish authorities ask Pilate to condemn Jesus (18:28-32). (2) Pilate questions Jesus about kingship (18:33-38a). (3) Pilate seeks to release Jesus; "the Jews" prefer Barabbas (18:38b-40). (4) The Roman soldiers scourge and mock Jesus (19:1-3). (5) Pilate presents Jesus to His people; "the Jews" shout for crucifixion (19:4-8). (6) Pilate talks with Jesus about power (19:9-11). (7) Pilate yields to the Jewish demand for Jesus' crucifixion (19:12-16).

3. The Crucifixion and Burial (19:17-42)

17 And he bearing his cross went forth into a place called *the place of a skull*, which is called in the

Hebrew Golgotha.

John states that as Jesus goes forth from the judgment hall, He is bearing His own (Greek reflexive pronoun) cross, while the Synoptists (e.g. Mt. 27:32) relate that Simon the Cyrenian is compelled to bear Jesus' cross for Him. The traditional harmonization of these accounts is that Jesus bore the cross Himself as He left the judgment hall but that, weakened by the scourging, He soon collapsed beneath its weight. At that point Simon was compelled to bear it the rest of the way to Calvary. There is no good reason to reject this tradition. One cannot be certain as to whether Jesus bore the entire cross or just the horizontal portion of it.

The place to which Jesus was taken is called "the place of the skull." (The Hebrew or Aramaic name for this place is *Golgotha*, the Greek *Cranios Topos*, and the Latin *Calvaria*, all of which have essentially the same meaning.) There are various speculations as to why it is so named, none of which can be substantiated, but it seems to be a designated place of execution.

18 Where they crucified him, and two other with him, on either side one, and Jesus in the midst.

At the place of the skull the Roman soldiers (v. 23) subject Jesus to crucifixion, one of the most grisly and horrifying forms of execution ever devised by man. While John does not dwell on this gruesome procedure, it involves an extreme degree of agony and suffering. Still, the physical suffering of crucifixion constitutes only a small portion of Jesus' pain. Far more excruciating and devastating is the spiritual suffering imposed upon Him by the Father.

John, like the Synoptists, points out that two others are crucified with Jesus, one on either side and Jesus in the middle. Matthew and Mark (e.g. Mt. 27:38) call these men "thieves" (Greek *lestai*), the same word John uses of Barabbas (18:40). Some suppose that they are part of Barabbas' gang. If so, it seems that John means to emphasize the irony of Jesus dying, as it were, in Barabbas' place. Clearly, John seems to imply what Mark (15:28) specifically states, that Jesus' crucifixion between two criminals is a fulfillment of Is. 53:12. One may only speculate as to Pilate's motive for crucifying two thieves along with Jesus. Perhaps he means this action, in combination with the superscription (v. 19), to embarrass and humiliate the Jews.

**19 And Pilate wrote a title, and put *it* on the cross. And the writing was, JESUS OF NAZARETH THE KING OF THE JEWS.
20 This title then read many of the Jews: for the place where Jesus was crucified was nigh to the city: and it was written in Hebrew, *and* Greek, *and* Latin.**

Pilate follows the normal custom of posting the charge against a crucified criminal to his cross for passersby to see. The charge is written in Hebrew (Aramaic), Greek, and Latin so that all may read and understand: "Jesus of Nazareth the King of the Jews." As Pilate intends, many of the Jews read and are offended by this message since the place of the crucifixion is near to the city and apparently on a main road leading into it (Mt. 27:39). John sees in the posting of this superscription a tremendous symbolic significance and irony. John considers it astounding that God should cause the true reason for Jesus' death to be stated with such exact precision. Jesus is dying precisely because of His claim to be the Messiah, the king of the Jews, and that is exactly what Pilate's superscription indicates.

21 Then said the chief priests of the Jews to Pilate, Write not, The King of the Jews; but that he said, I am King of the Jews.
22 Pilate answered, What I have written I have written.

Caiaphas and others of the high-priestly family, apparently sensing something of the symbolic significance of Pilate's superscription, go to him and ask him to make a slight change in the wording. They want it to say that Jesus *claimed* to be the King of the Jews, rather than that He actually was. As one would expect, Pilate refuses their request outright and answers haughtily, "What I have written, I have written."

23 Then the soldiers, when they had crucified Jesus, took his garments, and made four parts, to every soldier a part; and also *his* coat: now the coat was without seam, woven from the top throughout.
24 They said therefore among themselves, Let us not rend it, but cast lots for it, whose it shall be: that the scripture might be fulfilled, which saith, They parted my raiment among them, and for my vesture they did cast lots. These things therefore the soldiers did.

It was customary among the Romans for those who carried out a crucifixion to receive the victim's clothing as compensation for their unpleasant task. The soldiers who crucify Jesus, therefore, are only following the usual custom as they divide His clothing into equal portions for each of the four of them. Among Jesus' garments is an under-garment, or tunic (Greek *chiton*) which is worn next to the skin. This garment is woven all in one piece and cannot, therefore, be divided without destroying

its value. The soldiers decide, therefore, to cast lots for it.

Upon later reflection, John perceived that by these actions the soldiers literally fulfilled one of the O.T. prophecies concerning the Messiah (Ps. 22:18). Some would insist that John either invented this episode or radically stylized it so as to make it conform with the prophecy. Such a suggestion serves no purpose but to emphasize the essential antisupernaturalism of those who make it. It is perfectly natural to suppose that the event transpired and was recalled precisely as John indicates. Of course, the soldiers did not intend to fulfill the prophecy. God simply managed the circumstances so as to ensure that they did so.

John concludes his description of this episode somewhat reflectively, even whimsically, "This is what the soldiers did." He is impressed that they should, for their own selfish, mundane reasons, have so literally and precisely fulfilled the ancient prophecy.

25 Now there stood by the cross of Jesus his mother, and his mother's sister, Mary the *wife* of Cleophas, and Mary Magdalene.

John informs his readers that four women are standing by the cross as (or shortly after) Jesus is crucified. The Synoptists also mention four such women, but describe them as standing "afar off." The apparent contradiction between "by" and "afar off" dissolves when it is noted that John makes reference to the women shortly after Christ is actually crucified whereas the Synoptists refer to them much later, after Jesus has died. They could well have changed their position for some reason in the interim.

A comparison with the Synoptics is also helpful in determining the identities of these women (Mt. 27:56; Mk. 15:40; and Lk. 23:49). The identities of Christ's mother and Mary Magdalene seem certain. The woman John identifies simply as Jesus' mother's sister is apparently his own mother, Salome (compare Mt. 27:56 and Mk. 15:40). This identification fits John's pattern of indirect and oblique reference to himself and his brother James (see the discussion of the identity of the Beloved Disciple in the Introduction) by extending it to his mother as well. If John's mother is, indeed, Jesus's mother's sister, then John and James are Jesus' first cousins. This could explain why Jesus would be inclined to entrust John with the care of His mother (vv. 26, 27; assuming, again, that John is the Beloved Disciple). Also such near kinship might help explain why the mother of James and John would suppose it reasonable that her sons receive special consideration and honor from Jesus (Mt. 20:20). The woman to whom John refers as "Mary the wife of Cleophas" is apparently the same woman whom Matthew and Mark call "the mother of James and Joses."

26 When Jesus therefore saw his mother, and the disciple standing by, whom he loved, he saith unto his mother, Woman, behold thy son!
27 Then saith he to the disciple, Behold thy mother! And from that hour that disciple took her unto his own *home*.

From the cross Jesus observes standing before Him His mother and the disciple whom He loves. It is significant that, even in the intensity of His suffering, He thinks not of Himself but of those whom He loves (compare 13:33; 14:1,18; etc.). He tells His mother that from this point forward she is to look upon the Beloved Disciple, i.e. John (see comments v. 25), as her son. He also tells John that he is to treat Mary as if she were his own mother. The reality underlying these

words is that Jesus Himself is departing this world and can no longer discharge this filial responsibility. John assumes this responsibility for Mary immediately. He takes her "to his own." The word for "his own" (Greek *idia*) is the same as in 1:11. There is no word "house," although providing a home for Mary will certainly be included in the responsibility which he assumes.

28 After this, Jesus knowing that all things were now accomplished, that the scripture might be fulfilled, saith, I thirst.
29 Now there was set a vessel full of vinegar: and they filled a spunge with vinegar, and put *it* upon hyssop, and put *it* to his mouth.

A short while after assigning responsibility for His mother to John, Jesus says, "I thirst." Again, as in 13:3 and 18:4 (which see for comments), John informs his readers that Jesus is fully aware of the significance of all that is transpiring. Specifically, He is aware that He has accomplished all that has been assigned to Him by the Father, that His redemptive work is complete. Only now can He accept any sort of anesthesia to dull His senses or ease His pain.

The "vinegar" which Jesus accepts at this point is apparently the same "wine mingled with myrrh" which, according to the Synoptists, He previously refused (Mt. 27:34; Mk. 15:23). Notice that there was a vessel of this vinegar set near the cross. This was an anesthesia specifically provided for use at crucifixions and not just some wine that a bystander happened to have with him. The soldiers fill a sponge with this vinegar and, placing it on a reed, hold it up to Jesus' mouth so that He may drink.

30 When Jesus therefore had received the vinegar, he said, It is

finished: and he bowed his head, and gave up the ghost.

After Jesus receives the vinegar, He says, "It is finished," bows His head, and dies.

The Synoptists (Mt. 27:50; Mk. 15:37; Lk. 23:46) relate that just before His death Jesus cried with a loud voice, although they do not reveal the content of that cry. It seems reasonable to assume that John provides the content of that cry. "It is finished" (Greek *tetelestai*) is a cry of victory. Jesus has achieved His purpose and accomplished His task. He has won. John relates that with this cry Jesus bowed His head and gave up the ghost. Luke (23:46b) attributes one last statement to Christ which, while John omits it, is in complete harmony with Christ's action as John describes it. Christ's last words, according to Luke, were, "Father, into Thy hands I commend my spirit." Jesus did not just die in the normal manner. He, by His own action, handed over His life to His Father. Jesus was in control of the situation up to and including the very end. His life was not taken from Him; He offered it willingly as a sacrifice for men (10:18). He simply bowed His head and died.

31 The Jews therefore, because it was the preparation, that the bodies should not remain upon the cross on the sabbath day, (for that sabbath day was an high day,) besought Pilate that their legs might be broken, and *that* they might be taken away.

The Jewish authorities do not think it fitting that Jesus and the two thieves should hang upon the cross during the Sabbath, especially since this is the Sabbath of Passover week, an extremely important one (KJV: "an high day"). Therefore, since it is Friday, they ask Pilate to break Jesus' and the two

thieves' legs so as to hasten their deaths and allow their bodies to be removed before the Sabbath arrives (at sundown).

The Romans had a standard procedure for hastening the death of one crucified. It was called *crurifragium* and consisted of breaking the victims' legs. This action hastened death in two ways. First, the shock and trauma of such an excruciatingly painful experience was often sufficient to produce death almost instantaneously. Second, when the victim was no longer able to support himself with his legs, the weight of his body pulling down on his arms so constricted his lungs that breathing became very difficult and the victim was soon asphyxiated.

John seems clearly to indicate that Jesus was crucified on Friday. As indicated earlier (see comments v. 14), "preparation" (Greek *paraskeue*) can mean simply "Friday." Mark (15:42) clearly equates this term with another one that definitely means "Friday" or "the day before the Sabbath" (Greek *prosabbaton*). The clear sequence which Luke presents of the crucifixion, burial, and the coming of the women to the tomb establishes beyond all reasonable doubt that Jesus was crucified on Friday. Luke says that the day was the preparation (Friday) and that the Sabbath "drew on" (23:54). After observing Christ's burial later that same evening, the women returned home and did not go to the tomb the next day because that day was the Sabbath, Saturday (23:56). As soon as the Sabbath was over and it was light enough for them to do so, however, they went to the tomb. Since it is specifically stated that the day they went to the tomb was the first day of the week, Sunday, it follows inescapably that the day preceding it, the day they rested, was the Sabbath following the Friday when Christ was crucified.

32 Then came the soldiers, and brake the legs of the first, and of the other which was crucified with him.
33 But when they came to Jesus, and saw that he was dead already, they brake not his legs:
34 But one of the soldiers with a spear pierced his side, and forthwith came there out blood and water.

Pilate clearly acquiesces to the Jews' request and issues instructions that the three men's legs be broken. The soldiers carry out this barbarous procedure upon the two thieves, but when they come to Jesus they see that He is already dead. They therefore do not break His legs.

Instead, one of them thrusts his spear into Jesus' side. The purpose of this action was apparently to make absolutely sure that Jesus was dead, as indicated by the absence of any reaction to the spear thrust. If not, the wound would undoubtedly kill Him. The soldier was probably following standard procedure in certifying the death of one crucified.

John informs his reader that the result of the soldier's thrust was an outpouring of blood and water. While there are many speculations as to the significance of the blood and water (both medical and symbolic), none of them can be substantiated, and it is probably best to ignore them. The point John seems concerned to make is simply that the blood and water proved conclusively that Jesus was dead. Later, when Pilate was surprised that Jesus had died so quickly, he asked the centurion in charge of the crucifixion if Christ was, in fact, dead. Apparently, on the basis of having observed this spear thrust and its result, the centurion could assure Pilate that He was.

35 And he that saw *it* bare record,
and his record is true: and he knoweth that he saith true, that ye might believe.**

John considers the spear thrust and the blood and water to be important. This is evident in the solemn manner with which he assures his readers that his statements are based on direct eyewitness testimony. Assuming that John refers to himself (see comments v. 25), he offers his readers his own personal assurance that he saw with his own eyes the blood and water pouring forth from the wound in Jesus' side. There is no doubt whatever that Jesus was already dead when the spear was thrust into His side.

36 For these things were done, that the scripture should be fulfilled, A bone of him shall not be broken.

John says that both the failure to break Christ's legs and the piercing of His side with a spear, while not intended by the soldiers to do so, actually fulfill the Scripture and accomplish God's purpose. First, he refers to a Scripture verse which he quotes thus, "A bone of him shall not be broken." There are two different verses that John may be quoting: Ps. 34:20 and Ex. 12:46.

If John has Ps. 34:20 in mind, then it seems that it means that God has protected Christ from having His bones broken. This would be rather odd, however, since in the original context, keeping the bones from being broken is a figurative representation of God's general protection of "the righteous." This seems rather out of place in the midst of a scene in which God has given His Son over into the hands of sinners to die and has turned His own back upon Him. The mere fact that none of Jesus' bones has been broken can hardly be seen as indicating God's protection in light of all the other horrors which have been perpetrated upon Him with the Father's acquiescence. In short, it seems unlikely that John would suggest that one detail of Christ's agonizing and lonely death would serve to call to the reader's attention a Scripture which emphasizes God's providential protection of the righteous.

The second possibility is Ex. 12:46 (see also Num. 9:12). This passage gives, as one of the requirements for the killing of the Passover lamb, that none of its bones were to be broken. This seems to tie in with the idea that Jesus is the antitype of the Passover lamb and that just as its bones were not broken, neither are those of Christ. This seems the more likely possibility. It is quite natural that John should point out an interesting and suggestive correspondence between the death of Christ and that of the Passover lamb.

37 And again another scripture saith, They shall look on him whom they pierced.

John's second quotation is clearly from Zech. 12:10. In this text the prophet said, of the future children of Israel, that they would look upon (the Messiah) whom they had pierced and be very much saddened that they had dealt with Him so cruelly. John clearly means to point out that the soldier's act of thrusting his spear into Jesus' side has literally and explicitly fulfilled this prediction of the "piercing" of the Messiah. He may also mean to suggest that even though a Roman hand held the spear, it acted at the behest of the Jews themselves, that it was the Jews who were primarily responsible for Christ's death, and that the Jews will someday come to regret their action, just as Zechariah predicted.

38 And after this Joseph of Arimathaea, being a disciple of Jesus, but secretly for fear of the Jews, besought Pilate that he might take away the body of Jesus: and Pilate gave *him* leave. He came therefore, and took the body of Jesus.

At some point after Jesus' death, Joseph of Arimathea goes to Pilate and asks permission to take custody of Jesus' body. His intention is to provide for Jesus' body an honorable burial. John describes Joseph as one of Jesus' secret disciples. Lest anyone miss the implication, John spells out that Joseph's refusal to publicly declare himself for Jesus grew out of his fear of the Jews.

In light of the fact that Joseph was very wealthy (Mt. 27:57) and influential, a member of the Sanhedrin, he had a great deal to lose (Mk. 15:43) and was, therefore, quite vulnerable to threats of censure and ostracism. All along, then, he has considered discretion the better part of valor. He has tried to use his influence to help Jesus, apparently even voting for His acquittal at the Jewish trial. It is no longer possible, however, to remain in the shadows. The barbarous death of his Master, rather than intimidating and silencing him, actually inspires him to bold and resolute action (Mk. 15:43). Pilate, probably because he is still disturbed about his role in condemning an innocent man, grants Joseph the permission he asks. John mentions only that Joseph takes possession of the body whereas the Synoptists reveal that he actually takes Jesus' body down from the cross (Mk. 15:46).

39 And there came also Nicodemus, which at the first came to Jesus by night, and brought a mixture of myrrh and aloes, about an hundred pound *weight*.
40 Then took they the body of Jesus, and wound it in linen clothes with the spices, as the

274

**manner of the Jews is to bury.
41 Now in the place where he was
crucified there was a garden; and
in the garden a new sepulchre,
wherein was never man yet laid.
42 There laid they Jesus therefore because of the Jews' preparation** *day;* **for the sepulchre was
nigh at hand.**

The Synoptists all mention the action
of Joseph of Arimathea in claiming
Christ's body, but only John mentions
the role of Nicodemus. In fact, there is
no mention of Nicodemus outside the
Fourth Gospel. John indicates that this
is the same Nicodemus who came to
Jesus by night (3:1 ff.) and who de-
fended Jesus to his fellow Sanhedrinists
(7:50,51). Nicodemus and Joseph, both
members of the Sanhedrin and secret
disciples of Christ, apparently act in concert as they take the body of Jesus and
wind it in linen wrappings. Into these are
packed the 75 pounds (100 Roman
pounds) of mixed myrrh and aloes
which Nicodemus has provided for the
embalming of Jesus' body according to
the Jewish custom.

These were the usual burial spices.
What is unusual is the extremely large
amount, an amount which would normally be used only for a king or some
great personage. Many suppose that Nicodemus and Joseph, having been afraid
to acknowledge Christ's kingship previously, are now making a point to give
Him a kingly burial. Joseph, in fact, do-
nates his own previously unused tomb
(see Mt. 27:60) for Jesus to be buried in.
They must work quickly because their
task must be completed by dark, when
the Sabbath begins. Their task is made
easier by the fact that the tomb is located near the place of execution.

Summary
(19:17-42)

Pilate finally having agreed to His
death, Jesus is led forth, bearing His
cross, to Golgotha where He is crucified
between two thieves. Pilate attaches to
His cross the charge against Him:
"Jesus of Nazareth the King of the
Jews." The chief priests ask him to
change it to read, "He said I Am the
King of the Jews," but Pilate refuses.
The soldiers who crucify Him divide His
clothing among them and cast lots upon
one garment which does not lend itself
to division, thus unknowingly fulfilling
Ps. 22:18.

Four women stand near Christ's
cross: His mother, His mother's sister,
Mary the wife of Cleophas, and Mary
Magdalene. Seeing His mother and
John, the disciple whom He loves,
standing before Him, Jesus commends
His mother to John's care, and John
treats her as his own mother from that
day forward.

Realizing that He has completed His
mission, Jesus asks for something to
drink and accepts the anesthetic potion
that is offered. Having done so, He says,
"It is finished," bows His head, and dies.
About this time, the Jewish leaders, because they do not want Jesus and the
thieves to be hanging on their crosses
on the Sabbath, ask Pilate to break the
legs of the crucified ones so as to expe-
dite their deaths. The legs of the two
thieves are, accordingly, broken, but
when the soldiers come to Jesus, they
discover that He is already dead. They
do not break His legs, therefore, but one
of them thrusts his spear into His side to
verify that He is dead. When he does so,
blood and water gush forth. These actions of the soldiers are said to fulfil two
O.T. prophecies, the first being that
none of Christ's bones will be broken,
and the second that He will be pierced.

After Jesus' death, Joseph of Arimathea, one who has kept quiet the fact
that he is Jesus' disciple because of his
fear of the Jewish authorities, goes to
Pilate seeking authorization to bury Je-

sus' body. With Pilate's permission, Joseph, in conjunction with Nicodemus, another secret disciple, prepares Jesus' body for burial and lays it in a tomb near the place of Jesus' execution.

Application: Teaching and Preaching the Passage

This passage naturally divides into three sections: Christ's crucifixion (vv. 17-27), His death (vv. 28-37), and His burial (vv. 38-42). Each of these may be further delineated as follows:

John's account of Christ's crucifixion involves the following aspects: (1) Attention is called to the barbarous procedure itself. While John is restrained, the very word "crucify" connotes an unspeakable horror to all who comprehend it. (It was a means of execution devised for no other purpose than to maximize and prolong its victim's suffering.) (2) There is mention of the two thieves who are Christ's companions in death. (3) The callousness of His executioners as they divide His clothes among themselves adds a mundane, if surrealistic, note to the account. (4) John focuses on the extremity of Christ's impoverishment and abasement, as even His clothing is taken from Him. (5) Yet, even in the midst of all His suffering, Jesus' thoughts are of others. John recalls His concern for the well-being of His mother. Luke mentions one of the thieves in this regard.

The account of Christ's death involves these aspects: (1) Christ does not die until His mission is accomplished. He enforces upon Himself such a discipline of will that He controls even His death. He will not let Himself die until "It is Finished." (2) When He does die, His death is a moment of victory rather than defeat. He dies with the cry of the victor upon His lips. (3) His death is no mere ephemeral, theoretical, or poetic event. It is a real, literal, actual death. The

thrust of the spear produces water and blood.

The account of Christ's burial suggests the following points: (1) Deserted by those closest to Him in life, Jesus is buried by those afraid to acknowledge Him previously. Joseph and Nicodemus are transformed by what they suppose to be Jesus' demise. (2) Jesus is buried in a style befitting "the King of the Jews." (3) That it is necessary to bury Him enforces irresistibly upon the minds of all those who love Him that He is, in the fullest and most tragic sense of the word, dead.

D. The Resurrection (20:1-31)

John's account of the resurrection is a totally independent one. He leaves out much that the Synoptists include and includes much which they leave out. This does not mean, of course, that his account is incompatible with theirs, only that it is different. The reader is referred to the various harmonies of the gospels and to Westcott's treatment (II:335,336) in his commentary.

1 The first *day* of the week cometh Mary Magdalene early, when it was yet dark, unto the sepulchre, and seeth the stone taken away from the sepulchre.

Very early on Sunday morning, before it is fully light, Mary Magdalene comes to Jesus' tomb and is surprised to find that the stone has been removed from its entrance. That John mentions only Mary, whereas the Synoptists mention four women, presents no real problem. Mary clearly plays the most prominent role in what will transpire, as indicated by the fact that she is mentioned first by all the Synoptists (Mt. 28:1; Mk. 16:1; Lk. 24:10). John, therefore, speaks only of her, although he is aware that she is not alone, indicated by the plural form "we know" (Greek *oidamen*) near the end of v. 2.

2 Then she runneth, and cometh to Simon Peter, and to the other disciple, whom Jesus loved, and saith unto them, They have taken away the Lord out of the sepulchre, and we know not where they have laid him.

Mary's instinctive reaction is to share her discovery with someone in authority, someone who will know what to do in light of this startling development, someone other than those who have come with her to the tomb. She instinctively thinks of Peter and John, the Beloved Disciple (see Introduction on identity of the Beloved Disciple), and runs to tell them of her discovery. While John does not specifically mention Mary's looking into the tomb and seeing that Jesus' body is gone, that either she or one of her companions did so is assumed by her statement to the apostles. She tells them that Jesus' body has been removed from the tomb to some unknown place by some unknown persons. One assumes that by "they" Mary refers imprecisely to the Jewish authorities. The half-formed thought in her mind seems to be that those responsible for Christ's death have now desecrated His grave. Certainly she does not suppose any of Christ's followers to be responsible.

3 Peter therefore went forth, and that other disciple, and came to the sepulchre.
4 So they ran both together: and the other disciple did outrun Peter, and came first to the sepulchre.
5 And he stooping down, *and looking in,* saw the linen clothes lying; yet went he not in.

Peter and John are clearly as sur-

prised and shocked by this news as Mary. If there is any plot by Christ's disciples to try to fake a resurrection, neither Peter, John, nor Mary Magdalene is in on it. The two apostles set off immediately, running toward the tomb to investigate the matter for themselves. John outruns Peter and arrives at the tomb first. He stoops down, looks into the tomb, and sees the linen graveclothes, which Jesus' body was wrapped in, lying there, but he does not go in. One can only speculate as to why he fails to do so. Given the circumstances, it does not seem unlikely that he is simply frightened.

6 Then cometh Simon Peter following him, and went into the sepulchre, and seeth the linen clothes lie,
7 And the napkin, that was about his head, not lying with the linen clothes, but wrapped together in a place by itself.

Whatever the reason for John's trepidation, it clearly does not affect Peter. Apparently he goes right into the tomb without any hesitation. There he sees not only the graveclothes, but also the separate cloth which covered Jesus' head lying by itself apart from the other graveclothes.

8 Then went in also that other disciple, which came first to the sepulchre, and he saw, and believed.
9 For as yet they knew not the scripture, that he must rise again from the dead.
10 Then the disciples went away again unto their own home.

Encouraged by Peter's example, John also steps inside Christ's tomb. As he stands inside the empty tomb and looks upon the graveclothes the truth dawns upon him for the first time. Christ has risen! He is alive!

John shares his experience of this intimately personal and supremely important moment with his readers. He reminds them that this insight is not so obvious as they might suppose, for it came at a time when there was not yet any general understanding of the teaching of the O.T. (e.g. Ps. 16:9,10; Is. 53:10-12) that Jesus was to rise from the dead. It seems that John did not voice his belief to Peter, and no mention is made of any similar insight by Peter. John says simply that they returned home. Surely the two apostles discussed the matter as they went, but John does not enlighten his readers as to the nature of their conversation.

11 But Mary stood without at the sepulchre weeping: and as she wept, she stooped down, *and looked* into the sepulchre,
12 And seeth two angels in white sitting, the one at the head, and the other at the feet, where the body of Jesus had lain.
13 And they say unto her, Woman, why weepest thou? She saith unto them, Because they have taken away my Lord, and I know not where they have laid him.

After Peter and John return home, Mary Magdalene, who has apparently returned to the tomb with the two apostles or at some point subsequent, remains weeping outside the tomb. After a while she bends down and looks into the sepulcher and sees two angels sitting on the stone slab where Jesus' body has been lying, one at the head, the other at the foot. The angels ask her why she is weeping. The fact that they address her as "woman" implies no disrespect or opprobrium. It is simply a standard form of polite speech.

In response to the angels' question,

Mary asserts that the cause of her grief is that Christ's body has been taken from its burial chamber and that she does not know where it has been taken. Certainly the main cause of Mary's grief is Jesus' death itself and not merely the fact that His body has been stolen. What Mary means is that, coming on top of all that has happened, the disappearance of Christ's body is just too much for her. That Mary still refers to Jesus as "Lord" shows that, though the facts are all against it, she has not given up the idea that Jesus is the Messiah.

14 And when she had thus said, she turned herself back, and saw Jesus standing, and knew not that it was Jesus.

Having expressed the reason for her sorrow, Mary turns round to find herself actually confronting Jesus. Strangely enough, she does not recognize Him. There are at least three explanations for Mary's failure to do so. One is that the thought of His resurrection was so foreign to her thinking that her mind did not even consider it possible that the person addressing her could be Jesus. Another is that her weeping so blinded and distracted her that she was unable to think rationally. Still another is that Jesus' appearance was somewhat altered as He stood before her in His glorified body. Perhaps her experience was like that of the two disciples on the way to Emmaus who, it seems, were supernaturally restrained from recognizing the risen Christ (Lk. 24:16, 31).

15 Jesus saith unto her, Woman, why weepest thou? whom seekest thou? She, supposing him to be the gardener, saith unto him, Sir, if thou have borne him hence, tell me where thou hast laid him, and I will take him away.
16 Jesus saith unto her, Mary.

She turned herself, and saith unto him, Rabboni; which is to say, Master.

Jesus addresses Mary by repeating the angels' question, "Woman, why are you weeping?" He adds a second question, however, "For whom do you seek?" Clearly Jesus wants Mary to recognize Him. She does not do so, however, and, mistakenly assuming that He is the gardener, addresses Him, "Sir, if you are the one who has removed my Master's body, tell me where you have laid Him and I will take His body away and deal with it properly." Mary apparently supposes that there has been some objection to Jesus' having been buried in this particular tomb and assures (the gardener) that she will assume the responsibility of finding another place to bury the body. Jesus speaks to her once more, calling her by Her name, "Mary." This time there is something about the tone of His voice or His manner which Mary recognizes and, turning to face Him, she says, "Rabboni," which means Master. This is apparently the term by which she has habitually addressed Jesus and, for some reason, John thinks it important that his readers know the very word she uses.

17 Jesus saith unto her, Touch me not; for I am not yet ascended to my Father: but go to my brethren, and say unto them, I ascend unto my Father, and your Father; and *to* my God, and your God.

On the basis of the KJV translation, some suppose that Jesus forbids Mary to touch Him since He has not yet ascended to His Father. They believe that right after this encounter with Mary, Jesus is going to ascend to Heaven for the purpose of ceremonially presenting His work of atonement to the Father and

that until this has been accomplished, it is inappropriate for anyone to touch Him. (Some even suppose that no one will be allowed to touch Jesus at any time prior to His final ascension.)

In order to properly interpret Christ's statement it must be understood that the verb which the KJV translates "touch" (Greek *hapto*) may also be translated "hold" or "cling to." And the Greek construction (a present tense prohibition) naturally means "stop clinging to me." By the same token, Christ's reference to His ascension can be understood in some sense other than that He is about to return to Heaven to officially present His atoning work to God. The correct interpretation of this episode seems to be that when Mary recognizes Jesus, she falls before Him, grasps His feet, and worships Him as do her companions when Christ appears to them (Mt. 28:9). After a moment Jesus says kindly and comfortingly words to this effect, "It's all right, Mary. You can turn me loose. I shall be with you yet awhile. I am not going to immediately ascend to my Father [i.e. return permanently to Heaven]." That Christ would forbid Mary to touch Him at all seems to be ruled out by the fact that He allows Mary's companions to hold Him by the feet and worship Him (Mt. 28:9). It seems strange that Christ would prohibit Mary from doing what He freely allowed her companions to do at a time not more than a few minutes removed.

It seems clear that there is an essential parallelism between Matthew's account of Christ's encounter with Mary's companions and John's account of His encounter with Mary. Jesus' first words to Mary's companions are "Be not afraid," followed by a command to convey a message to His "brothers." Jesus' words to Mary are essentially the same in their implication. He speaks to comfort and console Mary, not to rebuke her for or prohibit her from touching

Him. Just as in Matthew, His word of comfort is followed by the command to convey a message to His "brothers."

Another problem concerns the identity of Jesus' "brethren." Although Jesus has used this term previously to refer to His physical brothers (2:12; 7:3,5,10), it seems that He uses it here to refer to the disciples. Clearly Matthew considers such to be the case (Mt. 28:10,16). Jesus uses this term intentionally to speak of the relationship that now exists between the disciples and Himself. His death on their behalf has made them joint-heirs with Him of all the riches of the Father (Rom. 8:17). At the same time, the contrast between His Father and their Father, His God and their God, seems intended to differentiate between His sonship and theirs. While they, as well as He, may call God "Father," God is Christ's father in a different sense than He is theirs, and Christ is God's Son in a different sense than are they. Christ is God's *unique* Son (see e.g. 1:18). Jesus has comforted Mary with the fact that He is not going to immediately ascend to Heaven and leave His disciples behind, but now He makes it plain that He is in fact going to do so not far hence. His ascension will be the final stage of His "glorification" (see 3:14; 8:28; 12:32).

18 Mary Magdalene came and told the disciples that she had seen the Lord, and *that* he had spoken these things unto her.

That Mary understands "brothers" to refer to the disciples is apparent in that it is to them she conveys Christ's message. Mary apparently returns to Peter and John, who have been joined by others of the eleven, and proclaims to them excitedly, "I have seen the Lord."

According to Mark 16:10,11 the disciples did not believe her. In that case they probably did not pay much attention to the message which she said He

had given her for them. It seems that the disciples disbelieved Mary's report even though it was corroborated by the testimony of the other women who saw Jesus (Mt. 28:9,10). Certainly it cannot be said that they were unduly credulous or predisposed to think that Jesus would rise from the dead.

19 Then the same day at evening, being the first *day* of the week, when the doors were shut where the disciples were assembled for fear of the Jews, came Jesus and stood in the midst, and saith unto them, Peace *be* unto you.

As nightfall of this first Easter Sunday approaches, the disciples (ten of the apostles and a few others, Lk. 24:33) are gathered clandestinely together. They meet in secret behind closed (and apparently locked) doors because they are afraid of the Jewish authorities.

The exact reason for their fear is not specified. Perhaps the most natural explanation is that they are afraid that, having eliminated Jesus, the authorities' next step will be to eliminate His principle followers. They may also fear that any rumors of a supposed resurrection may provoke the authorities to move against them. The disciples meet behind locked doors because of their fear of the Jews, but John mentions it by way of preparation for what follows.

Suddenly, Jesus is present among them within the closed room. Clearly, John intends his reader to perceive this as a miraculous event. While no details of the miracle are given, Jesus' appearance is obviously supernatural. Something of the nature of His resurrection body can be deduced from the fact that He passes through walls or closed doors and yet is not just a spirit (v. 20).

Jesus greets the disciples with the standard Jewish greeting of the time (*Shalom*, i.e. "Peace"), but John clearly intends his reader to perceive that the greeting has a special significance in the context. Jesus had assured the disciples that they would have peace in spite of the catastrophic time through which they must pass (14:27; 16:33). Once again, this time alive from the dead, and the catastrophe past, Jesus wishes them His peace. How wonderfully calming and reassuring His words must have been.

20 And when he had so said, he shewed unto them *his* hands and his side. Then were the disciples glad, when they saw the Lord.

The disciples are quite shocked by Christ's sudden appearance in the midst of the locked room. In spite of His salutation they are filled with fear and doubt. As with Mary Magdalene (v. 14), the disciples do not seem to recognize Jesus. It seems almost incomprehensible that they do not, but this is indicated by the fact that Jesus attempts to convince them of His identity by showing them His hands and His side. He wants them to see that He is the very same individual who has been crucified and that He is truly alive from the dead. He may also wish to demonstrate to them that He is not just a spirit but that He has a real body.

When John states that the disciples were glad when they saw the LORD, he means, for one thing, that they rejoiced because they had become convinced that this truly was Jesus. He also means to imply that they realized in a fuller and more glorious way than ever before that Jesus truly was the Lord, that He was God.

21 Then said Jesus to them again, Peace *be* unto you: as *my* Father hath sent me, even so send I you.

At this point Jesus repeats His com-

forting greeting, "Peace be unto you." While He undoubtedly does this for emphasis, the question is why He wishes to emphasize it and why at this point. The answer seems to lie in the words that follow. In effect Jesus is saying, "I am able to speak peace to you because of the fact that I have fulfilled the task that my Father required of me (see e.g. 17:8,19). Now I am sending you out to others in a way analogous to the way in which the Father has sent me. You are to go at My Command as I came at His. You are to go in My name as I came in His. You are to bring the peace of God to others as I have brought it to you."

22 And when he had said this, he breathed on *them*, and saith unto them, Receive ye the Holy Ghost.

Having informed the disciples of the glorious ministry that lies before them, Jesus bequeaths to them the power of the Holy Spirit by which they will be enabled to carry out their task. As God breathed the breath of life into Adam (Gen. 2:7), so now Christ breathes upon the disciples the Holy Spirit.

That John represents Jesus as conferring the Holy Spirit upon the disciples on Easter night seems to conflict with Luke's statement that the Holy Spirit was not given until some 50 days later on the Day of Pentecost (Acts 2:2-4). There are various suggestions for dealing with this problem. Some suppose that the accounts cannot be harmonized and that they represent different traditions concerning the coming of the Holy Spirit (Barrett 475, for example). Others suppose that, while John and Luke refer to essentially the same event, they each, for their own theological and literary reasons, place it at a different point in their narratives. These suppose that John places the giving of the Holy Spirit at this point in his narrative for reasons of literary structure and impact rather than strict chronological precision (Brown 1038,1039, for example).

It is my opinion that the Holy Spirit's coming referred to here is not identical with that described in Acts 2. The Holy Spirit comes in an anticipatory and partial sense here, whereas He will come in all His fullness and power at Pentecost. Already in 14:17 Jesus has promised that the Holy Spirit will both "dwell with" the disciples and "be in" them. It may be that John refers to the reception of the Holy Spirit in a way that is analogous to His "dwelling *with*" the disciples, and that Luke refers to the reception of the Holy Spirit on Pentecost in a way analogous to His "being *in*" the disciples.

23 Whose soever sins ye remit, they are remitted unto them; *and* whose soever *sins* ye retain, they are retained.

This verse has been the occasion of great controversy. Some have interpreted it to mean that the apostles (and their successors) are granted an absolute authority to absolve sins. This idea must be rejected on the basis that the authority to forgive sins rests with God alone; see Mk. 2:7 which, while spoken by the scribes, is assumed accurate by Jesus. All sin is ultimately against God alone and can only be forgiven by Him (Ps. 51:4). This interpretation is also precluded by the fact that not all of those present are apostles (Lk. 24:33) and not all of the apostles are present (see v. 24). It follows, therefore, that the authority conferred is conferred upon those present as representatives of the Church at large rather than upon the apostles *per se*.

If Jesus does not mean to confer on the apostles an absolute authority to absolve sins, then what does He mean? It seems reasonable to interpret His words as a logical extension of what He has just said: that He is sending the disciples

into the world as He has been sent into the world by the Father (v. 21). He has conferred upon them the presence of the Holy Spirit to empower them for their task (v. 22). Now He assures them that they will certainly accomplish the task assigned them.

Jesus' logic is not essentially different from that in 14:12 and 13. He is speaking in the broadest possible terms. The net effect of the disciples' ministry will be that some will have their sins forgiven while others will not. While the salvation of lost men depends in an absolute way upon Jesus' obedience to the Father in coming into the world, it will depend in a lesser but analogous way upon the disciples' obedience to Christ in going into the world with His gospel. Their ministry will determine the destinies of souls. Christ's words are not to be understood as woodenly literal, but as a symbolic encapsulation of a great truth.

**24 But Thomas, one of the twelve, called Didymus, was not with them when Jesus came.
25 The other disciples therefore said unto him, We have seen the Lord. But he said unto them, Except I shall see in his hands the print of the nails, and put my finger into the print of the nails, and thrust my hand into his side, I will not believe.**

The implication is that Jesus' sudden appearance in the closed room convinces all those present of the reality of His resurrection. One apostle is missing, however: Thomas. He refuses to believe his fellow disciples when they tell him that the risen Jesus has appeared to them. He is not so much skeptical of their truthfulness as their accuracy. It is difficult to believe what seems inherently incredible even if it is attested by those one deems completely trustworthy. Thomas says that before he can believe, he must have clear, tangible evidence. He must see and touch the nailprints in Jesus' hands. He must thrust his hand into Christ's side.

Throughout the account John wishes to convey to his readers that the disciples confronted the reports of Christ's resurrection with a great deal of skepticism. They were not a group of romantic visionaries trying with all their might to believe in a myth which they knew to be intrinsically false.

26 And after eight days again his disciples were within, and Thomas with them: *then* came Jesus, the doors being shut, and stood in the midst, and said, Peace *be* unto you.
27 Then saith he to Thomas, Reach hither thy finger, and behold my hands; and reach hither thy hand, and thrust *it* into my side: and be not faithless, but believing.
28 And Thomas answered and said unto him, My Lord and my God.
29 Jesus saith unto him, Thomas, because thou hast seen me, thou hast believed: blessed *are* they that have not seen, and *yet* have believed.

Eight days later, that is, the following Sunday, the disciples are again gathered together. All things are essentially as they were on Easter night (see comments v. 19a) except that, this time, Thomas is present. Apparently, the disciples are still lying low for fear of the Jews. Suddenly, Jesus appears and greets them as before (see comments v. 19b). He then challenges Thomas to perform the very actions which he has previously enumerated as necessary to his acceptance of Christ's resurrection: to place his finger into one of the nailprints and to thrust his hand into His side. He

also challenges him to cease his unbelief and believe.

This doubling of the word "believe" is clearly intended to indicate that Christ places a very high value upon belief and that He is rebuking Thomas' unbelief. It follows, therefore, that faith is not just a reflexive response to evidence or the lack thereof, but that it is, at least to some degree, an act of the will for which one can be held accountable.

Thus confronted with the inescapable fact of Christ's being alive from the dead, Thomas expresses his belief by the words, "My Lord and my God." Thomas' attestation is entirely satisfactory in its content. Its only weakness is that it comes only after Thomas has confronted irrefutable evidence. Jesus unfavorably contrasts Thomas' reluctant and begrudging faith with that of those who will in the future believe without any such compelling necessity. One cannot escape that faith does involve a volitional aspect.

30 And many other signs truly did Jesus in the presence of his disciples, which are not written in this book:
31 But these are written, that ye might believe that Jesus is the Christ, the Son of God; and that believing ye might have life through his name.

John now concludes the main body of his Gospel by expressing his purpose for having written it. He has not written all that he knows about the life and ministry of Jesus but has chosen those acts and sayings of Christ which serve his own purpose. That purpose is to bring his readers to believe that Jesus is the Messiah and Son of God so that, by means of that belief, they may have eternal life.

When John says that all of Christ's many works were wrought in the presence of His disciples, he emphasizes the eyewitness aspect of the material he presents and very strongly suggests that he is, himself, one of those witnesses. (Verse 31 is treated extensively in the Introduction in the section, "Destination and Purpose.")

Summary
(20:1-31)

Very early on Sunday morning Mary Magdalene comes to Christ's tomb and finds the stone rolled away from the door. She runs and tells Peter and John that Christ's body has been removed from the tomb. Peter and John run to the tomb to investigate. Arriving first, John bends down and peers into the tomb and sees the linen burial clothes lying inside but does not go in. When he arrives, however, Peter enters the tomb and sees not only the linen grave clothes, but also the napkin that was used to wrap Christ's head, lying by itself. Following Peter into the tomb and looking on the place where Jesus has lain, John begins to believe that Christ has risen. The disciples are strangely blind to the fact that Jesus was going to rise from the dead. Having determined the tomb to be empty, they return home.

Mary Magdalene, however, remains by the tomb, weeping. After a while, stooping down and peering into the tomb, she sees two angels, one at either end of the slab upon which Jesus has lain. They ask her the cause of her weeping and are told that she weeps because of the disappearance of Christ's body. At that moment Mary turns to face the risen Christ, though she does not recognize Him and supposes Him to be the gardener. He also asks her why she weeps. She replies that if He knows where Jesus' body has been taken, she will appreciate knowing so that she can claim it. At this point Jesus addresses

Mary by name and she, instantly recognizing Him, replies, "Master." Jesus encourages Mary to turn Him loose and assures her that He is not going to ascend to Heaven right away. He also tells her to deliver a message from Him to the disciples that He is going to ascend to the Father soon. Mary obeys and carries His message to the disciples.

About sundown of the first Easter the disciples are gathered together in a room with the doors closed when Jesus suddenly and miraculously appears in the midst of them. He bids them peace and shows to them His hands and His side so as to convince them that He is really alive from the dead. He then informs them that, as He has been sent by the Father, so He is sending them into the world. Having symbolically breathed upon them, He exhorts them to receive the Holy Spirit who will empower them for their task. He assures them that their ministry will be successful and will produce results.

Thomas is not present at this first appearance of Jesus, and he refuses to believe his companions' assurances that Jesus has risen. He says that he will not believe unless he touches Jesus' wounds with his own hands. Eight days later Thomas is present with the rest of the disciples when Jesus appears again as before. He challenges Thomas to touch Him and verify that He is, indeed, alive. Utterly convinced, Thomas addresses Jesus as his Lord and his God. Jesus gently rebukes Thomas for his lack of faith by comparing him unfavorably with those who, in the future, will believe on the basis of much less evidence than he has required.

John closes the main body of his work by explaining that his purpose for writing and structuring his work as he has is that his readers may come to believe that Jesus really is the Messiah and, thereby, gain eternal life.

Application: Teaching and Preaching the Passage

This chapter may be understood as a presentation of evidence that Christ is alive. First, there is the circumstantial evidence of the empty tomb (vv. 1-10). This evidence is presented to Mary, Peter, and John. It is not, by any means, conclusive. Indeed, it seems to have no impact whatever on either Peter or Mary. Yet it is not altogether without force since John reveals that it was sufficient to kindle the first spark of belief in his own heart.

Second, there is the direct evidence of personal encounter with the risen Christ (vv. 11-28). The focus is first upon Mary Magdalene as she encounters Jesus just outside His empty tomb. She does not, at first, recognize Him and only does so when He addresses her by name. The scene then shifts to a group of Christ's disciples meeting clandestinely for fear of the Jewish authorities. Jesus appears miraculously in their midst and convinces them that He is alive. Finally, the focus is upon Thomas, doubting Thomas, who refuses to believe without personal verification of the truth for himself.

Third, there is the indirect evidence that comes to those far removed from the scene by both distance and time (vv. 29-31). Jesus speaks of these as if to encourage and commend them for believing on the basis of the witness of others. John assures them that, though the evidence is indirect, it is nonetheless reliable.

IV. EPILOGUE (21:1-25)

There is disagreement among critical scholars as to whether John 21 is an integral part of the Gospel as originally composed or a later addition. Some who hold it to be a later addition believe it to have been composed by the Apostle John, while others believe it to be the work of one of his disciples.

The reasons for believing chapter 21 to be a later addition are, first, that the last two verses of chapter 20 look very much like a conclusion; and, second, that chapter 21 provides clues as to its own origin. Thus some suppose that near the end of his life, John (or his disciple), realizing that many people wrongly supposed Jesus to have said that He would come again before John's death, and realizing, furthermore, that his own death could therefore be the cause of confusion, determined to set the matter straight (v. 23).

Those who hold that John 21 is an integral part of the Gospel point out that the style of this chapter is not discernibly distinct from that of the rest of the Gospel and that it is not necessary to believe that the last two verses of chapter 20 are intended as a conclusion. First John 5:13 looks very much like a conclusion (by this same logic), yet it clearly is not.

Furthermore, it does not seem inherently unlikely that a work which begins with a prologue should end with an epilogue, a perfectly acceptable literary device. While the epilogue might have been added as an afterthought some time after the completion of the main body of the Gospel, it is, by no means, necessary to believe this. If it was "added" to the main body of the Gospel, there is no reason to doubt that it was added by the Apostle John, himself, or that it was added very early. There is absolutely no documentary evidence that the Gospel ever existed without the epilogue.

1 After these things Jesus shewed himself again to the disciples at the sea of Tiberias; and on this wise shewed he *himself*.

At some point subsequent to the appearance to the disciples on the eighth day after His resurrection (20:26), Jesus once more manifests Himself to His disciples. The word "manifests" (Greek *phaneroo*) means to reveal something as it truly is. Jesus is doing more than simply convincing the disciples that He is alive from the dead. He is revealing Himself to them as He really is: the glorified, exalted Christ.

This incident takes place in Galilee near the Sea of Tiberias. The Synoptists relate that Jesus previously instructed the disciples to meet Him in Galilee following His resurrection (Mk. 14:28; 16:7; Mt. 28:7,10) and that they followed His instructions (Mt. 28:16). This episode seems to fit into this general context. Several of the disciples are together in Galilee. See comments on 6:1 concerning John's use of "Tiberias."

2 There were together Simon Peter, and Thomas called Didymus, and Nathanael of Cana in Galilee, and the *sons* of Zebedee, and two other of his disciples.

This group of seven disciples is comprised of Peter, Thomas, Nathanael, the sons of Zebedee, and two others who are not named. That they are not named may indicate that they are not among the Twelve. The fact that the Beloved Disciple is among this group (v. 7) suggests that John intends this chapter to be the clue to solving the "riddle" of the identity of the Beloved Disciple and that he himself is that disciple (see Introduction).

3 Simon Peter saith unto them, I go a fishing. They say unto him, We also go with thee. They went forth, and entered into a ship immediately: and that night they caught nothing.

Peter has not lost his natural initiative

and leadership qualities. He informs the others that he is going fishing. There is no reason to assume that Peter is renouncing his determination to follow Christ and returning to his former life as a fisherman. Christ's subsequent words to him do not imply this to be the case. It is more likely that he has become bored with inactivity and wishes to do something to occupy his mind. It may also be that financial concerns play a part in his action. At any rate, the rest of the group decide to go with him; together, they immediately embark upon a ship and sail out on the lake to fish. That they fish all night and catch nothing is really quite amazing since some of them, at least, are professional fishermen fishing waters they are completely familiar with.

4 But when the morning was now come, Jesus stood on the shore: but the disciples knew not that it was Jesus.
5 Then Jesus saith unto them, Children, have ye any meat? They answered him, No.

The coming of the dawn finds the disciples frustrated and exhausted. They have worked all night yet have nothing to show for their labors. At this point Jesus comes and stands upon the shore of the lake and calls to them across the approximately 100 yards (see v. 8) of water and says, "You haven't caught anything, have you?" (The Greek question is phrased to suggest the negative.) The answer is simple: they have caught nothing, as much as they hate to admit it.

It is not wise to make too much of the fact that the disciples did not realize that the Man on the shore was Jesus. They were at such a distance that it would be highly unlikely that they could recognize His voice. Certainly they need not be expected to recognize Him from such a distance in the gray light of dawn. They had no reason to suspect that it was Jesus who called to them. This scene has every appearance of realism. One can almost hear the voices echoing across the water.

6 And he said unto them, Cast the net on the right side of the ship, and ye shall find. They cast therefore, and now they were not able to draw it for the multitude of fishes.

Jesus calls to them again and tells them that they have their nets on the wrong side of the ship and that if they will cast them on the other side (the right side) then they will catch some fish. It is a mystery why these tired and disgruntled men accept this apparently foolish suggestion. What difference can the few feet of the boat's width possibly make? Perhaps they are just too tired to argue and, supposing that they can do no worse than they have already, they decide to give it a try. They pull in their nets (no small task) and cast them on the other side. As they start to draw in the net they discover it to be so full of fish that they are unable to draw it up into the ship.

7 Therefore that disciple whom Jesus loved saith unto Peter, It is the Lord. Now when Simon Peter heard that it was the Lord, he girt *his* fisher's coat *unto him*, (for he was naked,) and did cast himself into the sea.

Just as at the grave the sight of the graveclothes in the tomb moved John to believe, so now the miracle of the great catch of fish causes him to realize that the Man on the shore is Jesus, and he says as much to Peter. (For arguments identifying the Beloved Disciple as John, see Introduction.)

It may also be that the present episode instantly reminded John of an occasion some years earlier when Jesus miraculously guided them to a great catch of fish (Lk. 5:1-11). That episode is so similar to the present one that many suppose them to be different versions of the same event (see Brown 1089-1092). This conclusion does not seem necessary, however, in light of several differences of detail in the two accounts and their obviously different placement in the chronology of Christ's life. One is an aspect of the initiation of His earthly ministry and the other of its final culmination. Indeed, the reality of the earlier episode can easily be understood as contributing to John's immediate understanding of the present one.

Peter does not question John's statement at all. Perhaps, realizing the closeness between John and Christ, he accepts that John is probably correct. Or he may have independently arrived at the same conclusion. At any rate, Peter, realizing that he is not properly clothed and ashamed for Christ to see him so, hurriedly wraps his fisherman's coat about himself and jumps into the sea. It should not be supposed that Peter was completely naked. The word translated "naked" (Greek *gumnos*) does not always mean being wholly nude; it may mean simply that he had removed his outer garment and was wearing only his inner garment.

The exact motive for Peter's action is not clear. He has already encountered the risen Christ (20:19,26) and apparently has conversed privately with Him (Lk. 24:34), so it cannot be that he is shocked that Jesus is alive. His action is purely reflexive and seems to be related to his state of undress. He is naturally quite impulsive, and his embarrassment surely accentuates this tendency.

8 And the other disciples came in a little ship; (for they were not far

from land, but as it were two hundred cubits,) dragging the net with fishes.

None of the other disciples follow Peter's example. Rather they bring the ship to land, dragging the overfilled net behind them. John implies that the only reason they are able to drag the net to shore is that they are only about 200 cubits (100 yards) from land.

The word translated "little ship" (Greek *ploiarion*) is the diminutive form of the word translated "ship" in vv. 3 and 6 (Greek *ploion*). It should not be supposed, however, that John means to differentiate this "little ship" from the ship on which the disciples had already embarked. In other words, John does not mean to suggest that they came to shore by a small dinghy or rowboat, but simply that they brought the fishing boat to shore.

9 As soon then as they were come to land, they saw a fire of coals there, and fish laid thereon, and bread.
10 Jesus saith unto them, Bring of the fish which ye have now caught.

As soon as they reach land, the disciples see that Jesus has a fire going with some fish cooking and some bread. Everything is ready for a fisherman's breakfast, but Jesus asks the disciples to bring some of their miraculous catch. He may intend to cook these to supplement what He has provided. Be this as it may, Jesus clearly intends to focus the disciples' attention on the miracle which has just transpired.

11 Simon Peter went up, and drew the net to land full of great fishes, an hundred and fifty and three: and for all there were so many, yet was not the net broken.

Peter has somehow, whether by swimming or climbing back aboard the boat, gotten to land. Now, his moment of embarrassment behind him and being arguably the most skilled fisherman in the group, Peter assumes responsibility for drawing the overfilled net up on the shore. Upon counting them, the disciples discover that there are 153 large fish. There is no symbolic significance in this number. John states it merely for accuracy. The modern reader is not able to fully appreciate the impact of this number. It is clear however, that it was unusually large, so large, in fact, seems to suppose a second miracle to be the fact that the net did not break.

12 Jesus saith unto them, Come *and* dine. And none of the disciples durst ask him, Who art thou? knowing that it was the Lord.
13 Jesus then cometh, and taketh bread, and giveth them, and fish likewise.

The fish having been taken care of, Jesus invites the disciples to come and eat the breakfast which He has prepared and now proceeds to serve them.

John informs us that, as this transpired, the disciples were just dying to ask Jesus if He was really Himself but were embarrassed to do so since it was so obvious that He was. Apparently he means that they had mixed emotions. Jesus' appearance might not have rendered His identification *certain*, but His words and demeanor would be sufficient to convince the disciples that it was Jesus who was serving them breakfast. All of them shared with each other the common thought which none deemed it appropriate to express, "It is You, isn't it, Lord? We know it is You, but You certainly don't look like Yourself." (See commentary on 20:14, 20 for discussion of Jesus' post-resurrection appearance and the ability of the disciples to recognize Him.)

14 This is now the third time that Jesus shewed himself to his disciples, after that he was risen from the dead.

John pauses to inform his readers that this is the third of Jesus' post-resurrection appearances to the disciples. He seems clearly to refer to 20:19 and 26 as the first two appearances. If this is the case, then the sequence carries over from chapter 20 and tends to indicate a literary and logical continuity between it and the epilogue. This argues that the epilogue is an integral part of the Gospel rather than a later addition. The mention of the "third time" is similar to the device John uses in chapters one and two of a succession of "days" (1:29, 35, 43; 2:1). This similarity of literary structure seems also to indicate that the epilogue is an integral part of the Gospel. Evidently John is counting appearances to the disciples as a group, not those to individuals (like Mary, the two on the Emmaus Road, or Peter alone).

15 So when they had dined, Jesus saith to Simon Peter, Simon, *son* of Jonas, lovest thou me more than these? He saith unto him, Yea, Lord; thou knowest that I love thee. He saith unto him, Feed my lambs.

After they have all finished their breakfast, Jesus turns to Peter and addresses him in such a way as to convey great solemnity, "Simon, son of Jonas (John), do you love me more than these?" There are three different ways one might understand "these." Jesus may be asking Peter if he loves Him more than his fellow disciples love Him, if he loves Him more than he loves his fellow disciples, or if he loves Him more than he loves his boat and nets.

The second of these explanations does not seem likely. It seems inherently improbable that Peter is struggling with some tendency to love his fellow disciples more completely than he does Christ. The third explanation has in its favor that Peter has just spent the night in pursuance of his old occupation. It may be that Peter is discouraged and is considering returning to his old life.

On the whole, however, it does not seem that, after sticking with Jesus through thick and thin and even following Him into Caiaphas' palace, Peter would choose to desert Christ now that He is victoriously alive from the dead. The first explanation seems, therefore, to be the best one. Especially is this so in light of Peter's past statements that, although others might deny the Lord, he certainly would never do so (Mt. 26:33; Mk. 14:29; see also Jn. 13:37). Peter has boastfully suggested that he loves Christ more than the other disciples. Now Jesus asks him, "Do you still think that you love me more than the others, Peter?" The only thing against this view is the fact that it is the Synoptists, rather than John, who present Peter's earlier statement as implying a comparison between himself and the others.

Peter's answer is characteristically direct: "Lord, You know that I love You." (On differences between two verbs for *love* throughout this passage, see below.) To his great sorrow and shame, Peter cannot point to his actions as proof of his love for his Master. All he can do is refer to Christ's omniscient perception of the inner workings of his heart. He says in effect, "Lord, You can look right down inside me. You know every aspect of my being perfectly. On the basis of Your perception of my every thought, You know that, in spite of all the evidence to the contrary, I really do love You."

Jesus responds to Peter by giving him a command or commission, "Feed my lambs." (On the two words for lambs and sheep in the passage, and two for "feed," see below.) By this Jesus seems to be saying that if Peter loves Him, he will love what is dear to Him, those for whom He has died. Christ's meaning here does not seem appreciably different from Paul's in Acts 20:28. If (since) Peter truly loves Christ, the proper way to demonstrate the fact is by keeping His commandments (14:15; 15:14) and continuing His work by carrying His message to the world (15:16; 20:21), by involving himself wholeheartedly in the care of those whom Christ loves so dearly.

16 He saith to him again the second time, Simon, *son* of Jonas, lovest thou me? He saith unto him, Yea, Lord; thou knowest that I love thee. He saith unto him, Feed my sheep.
17 He saith unto him the third time, Simon, *son* of Jonas, lovest thou me? Peter was grieved because he said unto him the third time, Lovest thou me? And he said unto him, Lord, thou knowest all things; thou knowest that I love thee. Jesus saith unto him, Feed my sheep.

Jesus asks Peter the second time if he truly does love Him. This time Christ simply asks Peter if he loves Him, not if he loves Him more than the other disciples do. Again, Peter responds, "Yes, Lord, You know that I love You," to which Jesus again responds, "Feed my sheep." Jesus asks Peter yet a third time if he loves Him and is again assured that Peter does even though it grieves Peter very deeply that Jesus apparently has not fully accepted the first two assurances of his love. One last time Jesus exhorts Peter to feed His sheep.

Why does Jesus repeat His question three times? There seem to be two basic theories on this matter. The first is that

there are subtle differences of meaning to be observed in Christ's questions, Peter's answers and Christ's exhortations which build to a climax in the third exchange. The other is that Jesus asks Peter of his love three times because of Peter's having denied Him three times.

The idea that there are subtle differences of meaning in the conversation between Peter and Christ centers on the fact that there are three sets of synonyms which are used in each of the three exchanges. The first of these sets of synonyms is the two words for "love" (Greek *phileo* and *agapao*) in Christ's questions and Peter's answers. In Christ's first two questions, He uses the second of these verbs (*agapao*), while Peter answers with the first (*phileo*). The third time Jesus asks using Peter's word (*phileo*) and Peter answers with the same word. Many suppose that there is a distinction between the two types of love with the one in Christ's first two questions (*agapao*) signifying a deeper and more complete love than the one Peter answered with all three times (*phileo*). They suppose this distinction to indicate that there is a reluctance in Peter's love and that, while he is very fond of Jesus, he is not willing to express an unqualified love for Him. They also suppose that Jesus has to be satisfied with a lesser love from Peter than He would like to have and so sadly accepts Peter's word the third time He asks. Against this is the fact that many scholars reverse the relationship of the two Greek words, making *phileo* rather than *agapao* express the stronger emotion. It seems that no real distinction can be made between these two words and that John's use of them simply reflects his tendency to use a variety of synonyms in repetitive passages such as this one. No significance is to be seen in the shifts from one word to the other.

The second of these sets is the two words for sheep or lambs. Christ uses "lamb" (Greek *arnion*) in the first challenge and "sheep" (Greek *probaton*) in the second and third challenges. Some suppose that Jesus means to distinguish between sheep and lambs and to be assigning Peter separate responsibilities for each.

The third of the sets is the two words for "feeding" the sheep. One means to feed or tend (Greek *bosko*) and is used in the first and third exchanges. The other means to shepherd or care for (Greek *poimaino*) and is used in the middle exchange. Some suppose that Jesus distinguishes between two levels of pastoral care with shepherding (*poimaino*) superior to feeding or tending (*bosko*). Again, there is no basis for such a distinction. The differences between the two words are simply stylistic.

Against all of these supposed distinctions of nuance is the fact that all of them arise from Greek rather than the Aramaic in which Jesus and Peter originally spoke and which did not provide for such subtle distinctions. One cannot suppose Jesus and Peter to have communicated in Aramaic subtle nuances of meaning which inhere in the Greek words later used by John to translate their conversation. At best, one could say that John chooses the words to convey what he knows to be the connotation of the original conversation. All in all it seems best to believe that no subtle nuances of meaning are intended and that Jesus asks Peter of his love for Him three times because he denied Him three times. It is the repetition itself and not any subtle nuances of meaning which grieves Peter.

18 Verily, verily, I say unto thee, When thou wast young, thou girdedst thyself, and walkedst whither thou wouldest: but when thou shalt be old, thou shalt stretch forth thy hands, and another shall gird thee, and carry *thee* whither thou wouldest not.
19 This spake he, signifying by what death he should glorify God. And when he had spoken this, he saith unto him, Follow me.

Using the formula of solemnity (Greek *amen, amen*), Jesus makes what seems a very enigmatic prophecy concerning Peter. In his youth Peter has girded himself (i.e. dressed himself, cared for himself), but in his old age, he will stretch out his hands, be girded by others, and be carried where he does not wish to go.

While these words could, in themselves, be merely a picture of old age, John informs his readers otherwise. As he writes, long after Jesus said this to Peter, the import of Jesus' words has become perfectly clear. Peter himself has been crucified. It is this death of which Jesus prophetically spoke. Peter had said (13:37) that he was willing to lay down his life for Christ's sake. His words would be literally fulfilled. He would glorify God in death just as his Master had done. With all this in mind Jesus exhorted him, "Follow Me." (That Peter was to die by crucifixion seems inherent in this passage. That he actually did so is confirmed by Tertullian.)

20 Then Peter, turning about, seeth the disciple whom Jesus loved following; which also leaned on his breast at supper, and said, Lord, which is he that betrayeth thee?
21 Peter seeing him saith to Jesus, Lord, and what *shall* this man do?
22 Jesus saith unto him, If I will that he tarry till I come, what *is that* to thee? follow thou me.

At this point it becomes clear that Jesus and Peter have left the others and are walking as they talk, for Peter looks back and sees that John is following them. (For arguments identifying the Beloved Disciple as John, see the Introduction.) John presses the point of the identification of this Beloved Disciple by stressing that this is the same individual he has referred to in 13:23.

Seeing John, Peter asks Jesus what John's destiny is to be. One is tempted to see a bit of peevishness in Peter's words. He has just undergone a very painful challenge of his love for Christ and has been given a generally pessimistic prediction of the future course of his own life. He may be wondering if he is the only one who is going to have to suffer so, or if others—John for example—are going to suffer also. Misery loves company.

Most commentators are more generous with Peter, however. They suppose him to be quite happy and relieved to have received a new commission to feed Christ's sheep and to be genuinely solicitous of John's well-being. Jesus' answer seems to indicate that He understands Peter's question in the former sense, for He refuses to answer it and rebukes him for asking. He tells Peter that what happens to John is none of his affair, that if He wishes for John to live until the time of His second coming, that is none of Peter's business. It does not seem that Christ would deal with Peter so harshly for expressing a solicitous concern about the welfare of his friend.

23 Then went this saying abroad among the brethren, that that disciple should not die: yet Jesus said not unto him, He shall not die; but, If I will that he tarry till I come, what *is that* to thee?

John informs his readers that this saying of Jesus precipitated a false idea among the disciples that John was not to die but would remain alive until the parousia. He points out, however, that Jesus actually said no such thing and that the false idea derived from a mistaken inference by the disciples.

Jesus' words concerning John's remaining until the second coming are part of a conditional sentence in which the uncertainty of the future event is implied (the protasis of a third class conditional sentence). The fact that John feels it necessary to correct the false impression that he was not going to die seems to mean that he is still alive as these words are written, as would obviously be the case if John himself wrote them.

24 This is the disciple which testifieth of these things, and wrote these things: and we know that his testimony is true.

It is widely accepted that this verse constitutes the testimonial of an unidentified group of witnesses ("we") to the authenticity and accuracy of all that the writer of the Fourth Gospel has set forth. This interpretation hinges upon an unambiguous and straightforward understanding of the word "we" as referring to a group of people. This idea includes the assumption that since this group is differentiated from the writer, he is not part of the group.

I prefer to believe that John himself writes these words, that he includes himself in the group designated by "we," and that he uses this word as a literary device to refer to himself and his readers. In effect he takes his readers into his confidence and says something to the effect, "It is this Beloved Disciple who wrote all these things, and we know who that Beloved Disciple is, don't we? We know that he is telling the truth, don't we?" John continues to employ his device of esoteric and oblique reference to himself which he has used all through the Gospel to challenge his readers to believe the accuracy of all that he has told them. It is not at all unnatural for an author to use "we" in such a way as to include himself with his readers. (For the feasibility of such a use of "we" see comments on its usage in 1:14.)

25 And there are also many other things which Jesus did, the which, if they should be written every one, I suppose that even the world itself could not contain the books that should be written. Amen.

This verse expresses essentially the same truth as 20:30,31, which see for comments. John adds here the hyperbole that if one were to relate all that Jesus did while upon earth, it would take so many volumes that the world could not contain them. At the very least, this must be taken to mean that the author does not claim to have given a comprehensive, chronological account of Jesus' life.

Summary (21:1-25)

After the appearances to the disciples in Jerusalem, Jesus manifests Himself to seven of His disciples at the Sea of Galilee. The occasion of this appearance is a singularly unsuccessful all-night fishing excursion. Unrecognized, Jesus stands on the shore and calls out to ask the disciples if they have caught anything. Upon being told that they have not, He tells them to cast their net on the other side of the boat and they will. When they do so, the disciples find their net to be filled with more fish than they can hoist aboard.

At this point John perceives that the stranger on the shore is Jesus. Peter, who has stripped down to his inner garment, thereupon puts on his coat and casts himself into the water. The disciples drag the net to shore where Jesus

is waiting for them, having built a fire and cooked breakfast. He commands them to bring some of their catch which, when it is counted, they discover to consist of 153 large fish. As He serves the disciples breakfast, they are most anxious to ask Jesus if He is, in fact, Himself, but are afraid to do so.

The breakfast being over, Jesus addresses to Peter a three-fold challenge of that apostle's love for Him. Peter assures Jesus that he does, indeed, love Him and is commanded, therefore, to feed Christ's sheep. Jesus makes a prediction concerning Peter's future which John explains actually deals with the manner of Peter's death. Peter then asks what John's future is going to be and is told that it is none of his business. (A misunderstanding of Jesus' words developed to the effect that John would live until the second coming, but John informs his readers that this is not what Jesus said at all.)

In conclusion, John challenges his readers to believe that all he has told them has been accurate and refers once more to the fact that he has not been able to include all that he knows and could tell about Christ.

Application: Teaching and Preaching the Passage

The main focus of this chapter seems to be service, i.e. the care of Jesus' flock. John presents three aspects of this theme. The first is the futility of all service apart from Christ (vv. 1-14). This section seems an enactment of Christ's previous words, "Without me, ye can do nothing" (15:5). It does not seem unreasonable to suppose this fishing episode to have some connection with the work of preaching the gospel since Christ established an analogy between the two when the disciples were first called (Mt. 4:19; Mk. 1:17; Lk. 5:10). The disciples have fished all night and have caught nothing (vv. 1-3). When challenged by Jesus on the point, they must confess the utter futility of their own efforts (vv. 4, 5). Obedience to Christ's instruction brings immediate and overwhelming success (v. 6). Confrontation with Christ produces an overwhelming sense of their own wickedness (v. 7). Submission to Christ secures abundant provision (vv. 8-14).

The second aspect is that of love for Christ as the only sufficient motive for service (vv. 15-17). Real love is obedient love (14:15; 15:16). The only proof of love is obedience to Christ's command to carry His message to the world (15:16; 20:21). Therefore, Jesus tells Peter to feed His sheep if he truly loves Him.

The third aspect of service that John deals with is the cost involved with service—the cost of suffering (vv. 18-23). If one is to serve Christ truly, he must be prepared to follow Him, to follow Him if need be even unto death (vv. 18,19). One must not suppose that he will be exempted from suffering when Christ, Himself, was not (15:18-21). Each disciple's commitment is a personal matter between him and his Lord. He need not suppose that his circumstances will be the same as those of another. He must submit himself entirely to his Master's will for him (vv. 20-23).

BIBLIOGRAPHY: WORKS CITED IN THIS COMMENTARY

Barrett, C. K., *The Gospel According to St. John* (S. P. C. K., 1972)

Bernard, J. H., *The International Critical Commentary: John* (two volumes, T. & T. Clark, 1976)

Brown, Raymond E., *The Anchor Bible: The Gospel According to St. John* (vols. 29, 29A, Doubleday, 1970)

Bruce, F. F., *The Gospel of John* (Eerdmans, 1983)

Carson, D. A., *The Farewell Discourse and Final Prayer of Jesus* (Baker, 1980)

Edersheim, Alfred, *The Life and Times of Jesus the Messiah* (two volumes, Eerdmans, 1967)

Fredrikson, Roger L., *The Communicator's Commentary: John* (Word, 1985)

Godet, F. L., *Commentary on John's Gospel* (Kregel, Reprinted 1978)

Guthrie, Donald, *Jesus the Messiah* (Zondervan, 1972)

Guthrie, Donald, *New Testament Introduction* (Inter-Varsity, 1962)

Hendriksen, William, *New Testament Commentary: John* (two volumes, Baker, 1985)

Hunter, A. M., *The Cambridge Bible Commentary on the New English Bible: John* (Cambridge, 1965)

Morgan, G. Campbell, *The Gospel According to John* (Revell, n.d.)

Morris, Leon, *The New International Commentary: John* (Eerdmans, 1971)

Pentecost, J. Dwight, *The Words and Works of Jesus Christ* (Zondervan, 1981)

Plummer, Alfred, *Thornapple Commentaries: St. John* (Baker, 1982)

Robinson, J. A. T., *Redating the New Testament* (Westminster, 1976)

Robinson, J. A. T., *Twelve New Testament Studies* (SCM Press, 1962)

Smalley, Stephen S., *John: Evangelist and Interpreter* (Nelson, 1983)

Schnackenburg, Rudolf, *The Gospel According to John* (three volumes, Crossroad, 1982)

Tenney, Merrill C., *The Expositor's Bible Commentary: John* (Zondervan, 1981)

Westcott, B. F., *Thornapple Commentaries: St. John* (two volumes, Baker, 1980)

Yeager, Randolph O., *The Renaissance New Testament* (twelve volumes, Pelican, 1980)

Zahn, Theodor, *Introduction to the New Testament, Vol. III.* (Klock & Klock, 1977)